When Worlds Collide:

Another Look at the Lunar Nodes

Kathy Allan

First Edition
First Printing 2012

Cover Design by Mimi Alonso
Typesetting by Jera Publishing
Editing by Mark Springle

Parts of Chapters 1, 2, 3, 5, 15, and 18 were originally published by *The Mountain Astrologer*, Issue #143 Feb/Mar 2009, in the article: 'Re-Visioning the Lunar Nodes.'

A version of Chapter 24 was originally published by *The Mountain Astrologer* in Issue #153 Oct/Nov 2010, in the article: 'Funny Money and the Fed.'

Portions of Chapter 21 were originally published by *The Mountain Astrologer* in Issue #156 Apr/May 2011, in the article: 'Wikileaks and the Cardinal Cross.'

Portions of Chapters 1–3 were originally published in the *Geocosmic Journal*, Winter 2009, in the article: 'The Lunar Nodes as Timers.'

Published by:
Pollux Press
Fort Pierce, Florida
34981

ISBN: 978-0-9836866-2-0

You have got lost, and are trying to find your way back to your own true self.

- Lao Tzu

Acknowledgments

This book owes its life to the generous assistance and support of many. I am deeply indebted to my teachers and students who have made me a better astrologer. To the many inspiring authors I have read, my sincerest thanks for sharing your methods of chart interpretation and your understanding of astrology. To those living and dead whose charts I have delineated, I hope that my interpretation accurately reflects your thoughts and life experiences, and that your words and deeds are not taken out of context. I apologize in advance for any errors I have made.

In particular, I will be forever grateful to Mark Springle for his editorial insights, his attention to astrological and grammatical detail, and his instructive and entertaining commentary. He made this a better book. Many thanks to Scott Silverman for his encouragement, illuminating observations, and helpful discussions. Heartfelt thanks to Mimi Alonso, a talented artist, for the cover design. I am also grateful to Nan Geary from whom I learned much. A special thanks to Terri McCartney, an amazing astrologer who made it real. I would also like to thank Kimberly Martin and Stephanie Anderson at Jera Publishing for going the extra distance in typesetting the manuscript. I am sincerely thankful to Will, whose computing and technological expertise helped make this book happen. Also, many thanks to the members of the South Florida Astrological Association and the Florida Atlantic Chapter of NCGR for camaraderie and enlightened conversation over the years. I am also thankful to my parents for their interest and their enthusiasm. Finally, my eternal gratitude to Eugene 'Spiritweaver' Vidal who introduced me to the astonishing world of astrology.

Table of Contents

List of Figures xiii
List of Charts xiv

Introduction xvii

Chapter 1: History 1
  Jyotish Considerations 2
  Western Considerations 4

Chapter 2: Nodal Astronomy 11
  Declination and Latitude 14
  Eclipse Astrology 18
  Developing a Nodal Hypothesis 19
  Nodal Energy 20

Chapter 3: Nodal Delineation 23
  Four Nodal Points 25
  Chart Delineation 28
  Summary of Nodal Delineation 33

Chapter 4: Legalizing Astrology - Evangeline Adams 35
  Nativity 36
  Setting Up Shop 40
  Trial 42
  Marriage 44
  Death 46

Chapter 5: Dabbling in Spookery – Carl Jung 49
  Nativity 54
  Adolescent Trauma 58
  Father's Death 61
  Insane Asylum 63
  Marriage 66
  Fatherhood 68
  Gret Jung 70
  Collaboration With Freud 72
  Break-Up 75

Accidental Fall....78
Emma's Death....80
Jung's Death....82

Chapter 6: Alcoholics Anonymous - Bill Wilson....85
Nativity....86
Sobriety....90
Alcoholics Anonymous....92
Death....94

Chapter 7: A Poet and a Madman - Ezra Pound....97
Astrology....99

Chapter 8: A Visionary - Albert Einstein....103
Nativity....105
Mirabilis Annus....109
Gravitational Eclipse....111
Einstein's Eclipse....113
Nobel Laureate....115
Biggest Blunder....117
Death....119

Chapter 9: A Queen....121
Nativity....122
Inheriting A Crown....124
Death Of A King....126
The Great Fire....128
Death Of A Princess....130

Chapter 10: Some Fairy Tale - Princess Diana....133
Nativity....134
A Royal Proposal....138
The Wedding....140
An Heir....142
A Marriage Crumbling....144
Divorce....146
Accident....146
Death....152

Chapter 11: The Fall - Dominique Strauss-Kahn....155
Nativity....156
Alleged Rape....158

Chapter 12: The Oracle of Omaha - Warren Buffett 161
Nativity 162

Chapter 13: The Microsoft King - Bill Gates 165
Nativity 166
Taking Microsoft Public 169
Marriage 171
Stepping Down 173

Chapter 14: An Unlikely Corporate Superstar - Steve Jobs 175
Nativity 177
Pancreatic Cancer 180
Surgery 183
Transplant 185
Death 187

Chapter 15: An Unusual Scientist - Kary Mullis 189
Nativity 190
Polymerase Chain Reaction (PCR) 193
PCR Revolution Begins 196
Nobel Prize 199

Chapter 16: An Unusual Medical Doctor - Michael Crichton 201
Nativity 202
An Award Winning Novelist 206
A Dinosaur Romp 206
Death 210

Chapter 17: Master of Horror - Stephen King 213
Nativity 214
Carrie 217
Quitting Drinking 219
Car Accident 220

Chapter 18: A Super Hero - Christopher Reeve 225
Nativity 226
Love 229
The Accident 231
Death 233

Chapter 19: Hope and Change - Barack Obama 235
Nativity 236
State Senate 239

Congressional Loss 241
National Senate Win..... 243
Presidential Election..... 245
Election 2012 247

Chapter 20: 2012 Presidential Challenger - Mitt Romney..... 251
Nativity 251
Il Est Mort 255
Lost Senate Election 257
The Governor..... 259
Presidential Election 2012..... 260

Chapter 21: Hero or Villain - Julian Assange..... 265
Nativity 266
Wikileaks..... 269
Kenya Corruption Report..... 271
War..... 273
A Sex Scandal 275
Arrest 276

Chapter 22: U.S. Psyche 281
Nativity 282
A Defining Moment..... 285
The Effect..... 291

Chapter 23: Beating the Market..... 293
Nativity 294
The Great Depression..... 298
First Computer Instigated Crash..... 298
No Bank Bailout 300
Market Rally..... 302
Flash Crash 304
U.S. Downgrade..... 306

Chapter 24: Easy Money - The Federal Reserve..... 309
Nativity 311
U.S. Influence 316
No Bailout 317
Trillion Dollar Handout 319
First Audit 321

Chapter 25: Acts of God 325
Indonesian Tsunami..... 325

Indonesian Flood Impact 329
Hurricane Katrina 329
U.S. Storm Impact 332
Gulf Oil Spill 332
U.S. Spill Impact 336
Japanese Tsunami and Nuclear Meltdown 336
Japanese Flood Impact 340

Chapter 26: Conclusions 343
Nodal Energy 345
Nodal Myth 346

Notes and References 349
Natal Nodal Form 365
Event Nodal Form 366
Index 367

List of Figures

Figure 1. The Lunar Nodes and Axis 12
Figure 2. Taurus New Moon and Gemini Solar Eclipse 13
Figure 3: The Ecliptic and Celestial Equator 14
Figure 4. The Great Circles 15
Figure 5. Declination and the Tropics 16
Figure 6. Solar Declination and the Four Cardinal Points 17
Figure 7 Lunar Latitude and the Four Nodal Points 17

List of Charts

Chart 1: Evangeline Adams Nativity....37
Chart 2: Evangeline Starts Practice....41
Chart 3: Evangeline's Trial....43
Chart 4: Evangeline's Wedding....45
Chart 5: Evangeline's Death....47
Chart 6: Carl Jung Nativity....55
Chart 7: Jung's Adolescent Trauma....59
Chart 8: Jung's Father's Death....62
Chart 9: Jung Starts Work at Asylum....65
Chart 10: Jung's Marriage....67
Chart 11: Jung Becomes a Father....69
Chart 12: Jung's Daughter Gret Birth....71
Chart 13: Jung and Freud Meet....73
Chart 14: Jung's Split with Freud....77
Chart 15: Jung's accidental fall....79
Chart 16: Jung's Wife's Death....81
Chart 17: Jung's Death.....84
Chart 18: Bill Wilson's Nativity....87
Chart 19: Bill Wilson Sobriety....91
Chart 20: AA's First Meeting....93
Chart 21: Bill Wilson's Death....95
Chart 22: Ezra Pound Nativity....100
Chart 23: Albert Einstein Nativity....106
Chart 24: Einstein's Miraculous Year....110
Chart 25: Gravitational Eclipse....112
Chart 26: Einstein's Eclipse....114
Chart 27: Einstein's Nobel Prize....116
Chart 28: Einstein's Biggest Blunder....118
Chart 29: Einstein's Death....120
Chart 30: Queen Elizabeth II Nativity....123
Chart 31: Queen's Uncle Abdicates....125
Chart 32: Queen's Father's Death....127
Chart 33: Queen's Castle on Fire....129
Chart 34: Queen's daughter-in-law dies....131
Chart 35: Princess Diana Nativity....135
Chart 36: Princess Wedding Proposal....139

Chart 37: Princess Diana's Wedding 141
Chart 38: Princess Delivers an Heir 143
Chart 39: Princess Separates 145
Chart 40: Princess Divorce 147
Chart 41: Accident 150
Chart 42: Princess Death 153
Chart 43: Dominique Strauss-Kahn Nativity 157
Chart 44: DSK Alleged Rape 159
Chart 45: Warren Buffett Nativity 163
Chart 46: Bill Gates Nativity 167
Chart 47: Gates' Microsoft IPO 170
Chart 48: Gates' Wedding 172
Chart 49: Gates' Retirement 174
Chart 50: Steve Jobs Nativity 178
Chart 51: Jobs' Cancer Diagnosis 182
Chart 52: Jobs' Surgery 184
Chart 53: Jobs' Liver Transplant 186
Chart 54: Job's Death 188
Chart 55: Kary Mullis Nativity 191
Chart 56: Kary Mullis' PCR Insight 195
Chart 57: Mullis' PCR Revolution 198
Chart 58: Mullis' Nobel News 200
Chart 59: Michael Crichton Nativity 203
Chart 60: Crichton's Award Winning Novel 207
Chart 61: Crichton's *Jurassic Park* 209
Chart 62: Crichton's Death 211
Chart 63: Stephen King Nativity 215
Chart 64: King's *Carrie* 218
Chart 65: King Quits Drinking 221
Chart 66: King's Car Accident 223
Chart 67: Christopher Reeve Nativity 227
Chart 68: Reeve Meets Dana 230
Chart 69: Reeve's Accident 232
Chart 70: Reeve's Death 234
Chart 71: Barack Obama Nativity 237
Chart 72: Obama's State Senate Win 240
Chart 73: Obama's Congressional Loss 242
Chart 74: Obama's U.S. Senate Win 244
Chart 75: Obama's Presidential Victory 246
Chart 76: Obama and 2012 249

Chart 77: Mitt Romney Nativity 253
Chart 78: Romney's Car Accident 256
Chart 79: Romney's Lost Senate Election 258
Chart 80: Romney's Gubernatorial Win 261
Chart 81: Romney and 2012 263
Chart 82: Julian Assange Nativity 267
Chart 83: Assange and Wikileaks 270
Chart 84: Assange Kenya Corruption 272
Chart 85: Assange's War 274
Chart 86: Assange's Sex Scandal. 277
Chart 87: Assange's Arrest 279
Chart 88: U.S. Nativity 283
Chart 89: A Defining Event 288
Chart 90: U.S. Effect 292
Chart 91: New York Stock Exchange 295
Chart 92: Market Crash 1929 297
Chart 93: Market Crash 1987 299
Chart 94: No Bank Bailout 301
Chart 95: Market Rally 303
Chart 96: Flash Crash 305
Chart 97: U.S. Downgrade Effect 307
Chart 98: Federal Reserve Nativity 312
Chart 99: U.S. and Fed 315
Chart 100: Fed—No Bailout 318
Chart 101: Fed Handout 320
Chart 102: Fed Audit 322
Chart 103: Indonesian Tsunami Event. 326
Chart 104: Indonesian Flood Impact 328
Chart 105: Hurricane Katrina Event 331
Chart 106: Hurricane Katrina Impact U.S. 333
Chart 107: Gulf Oil Rig Blast Event 335
Chart 108: Gulf Oil Blast U.S. Impact. 337
Chart 109: Japanese Tsunami Event 339
Chart 110: Japanese Flood Impact 341

Astrology is a language. If you understand this language, the sky speaks to you.

—Dane Rudhyar

Introduction

For accurate chart interpretation, the astrological symbols need to be defined correctly, and express the way they are defined. This has not been the case with the lunar nodes (hereafter referred to as the nodes). They have acquired a multitude of contradictory meanings, none of which seem empirically precise. Currently, the popular nodal paradigm is that the North Node is good and helpful, and the South Node is evil and difficult. Planets benefit through contact with the North Node and are harmed through contact with the South Node. House position is of paramount importance: the North Node house indicates the area of life to embrace, while the South Node house shows activities to avoid. In practice, this delineation does not work consistently. Some people perform well in the house tenanted by their South Node, while for others neither nodal house is dominant. In addition, a planet conjunct the North Node is not always helpful, and a planet conjunct the South Node is not always ruinous. These observations, coupled with a desire to learn how the nodes reliably functioned in a chart, were the impetus for this research.

I began with a literature review, studying where the nodal meaning originated, how it evolved, and how it worked in practice. In the science of astrology, the actions of the symbols are verified through observation. Over time, the nodes taught me their meaning. We have been interpreting them inappropriately. The current delineation rests upon error, confusion, and omission. In the text, the misconceptions are outlined, solutions are offered, and a new method of delineation is proposed and tested in a multitude of charts. This is not a beginner's text, nor is it a cookbook, but rather a practical examination of how the nodes operate in the horoscope. It is a book primarily dedicated to natal delineation and *ex post facto* prediction, where the information given by the nodes is viewed in the context of the entire chart. International readers should be aware that the majority of charts pertain to U.S. public figures and U.S. news (writers must write what they know).

Some astrologers maintain that the nodes convey information regarding reincarnation and experiences in previous lives. With no way to prove or disprove this, I disregard it. I find that the whole chart is fated, with the nodes no more so than other points.

The text begins with a historical review of the nodes. In Chapter 1, I describe the Eastern (Jyotish) understanding of the lunar nodes, and the eclipse myth that explains the symbolism. Turning to the West where there is no traditional nodal myth, I trace the evolution of meaning over the past hundred years, with an emphasis on the contradictions and how they may be resolved.

Going back to basics, in Chapter 2, I outline the nodes, bendings, and eclipses astronomically. I look at the nodes in reference to both the lunar orbit and the seasons of the sun. I examine the differences in the energy fields of the 'North' and 'South.'

In Chapter 3, I offer a new method of natal delineation of the nodes and describe how to use the nodes in forecasting.

In Chapters 4–25, the method of delineation is applied to the charts of numerous personalities and mundane events (elections, natural disasters, and the stock market). The natal charts are delineated in depth, although the focus is on the expression of the nodal energy. I also examine prominent life events through the lens of the nodes and the most recent solar eclipse.

In Chapter 26, I summarize a Greek myth that does reflect the archetype of the nodes and illustrates the human predicament. When viewed from a perspective of the nodes, the cohesive theme of a chart becomes clear. The nodal energy animates a chart and describes a course of purposeful action that gives life meaning.

Trained as a scientist, I initially sought to critically examine the observable action of the nodes and disregard what could not be objectively verified. My intent was to keep the study scientific—but the nodes don't roll that way! The nodal literature is permeated with a spiritual connotation I wanted to ignore, but which proved impossible. Immersed in the nodes, the enchanted otherworld quickly appeared. This is not the sole purview of the nodes, but of astrology, where planetary events mimic human experiences in a correspondence that inspires wonder and amazement, and conjures the mystery and magic of the universe.

[Astrology] represents the basic nature of the forces at work in any given situation. The true art … is to translate these abstractions into concrete actualities.

— *W.M. Davidson*

Chapter 1
History

Initially in western astrology, the significance of the nodes was tied to eclipses, with which they are associated. At some point during the last hundred years, the nodes assumed meaning of their own. The North Node was compared to Jupiter and Venus, and said to bring benefits and success, while the South Node was compared to Mars and Saturn, bringing sorrow and harm. House position was important. Some astrologers thought the activities of the North Node house should be favored and the activities of the South Node house ignored, while others believed the opposite. Some made no distinction between the two nodes, and others thought we needed to work both. Some said the nodes were insignificant, while others thought they were the most important points in the chart.

Over time, the nodes became associated with fate and events over which we have no control. In horary, any point in the degree of the nodes was considered tragic or fatal, indicative of catastrophe or casualty. In the nativity, the nodes were seen as karmic indicators, providing information on previous lifetimes and serving as guideposts to spiritual evolution. They have been called an arrow, pointing the way to a productive future (North Node), away from the unhelpful clutches of a familiar, needy past (South Node).

Jyotish Considerations

The nodes have been used in Jyotish (Hindu) astrology for thousands of years. They are viewed as two parts of a beheaded beast or demon and behave accordingly. The North Node, known as Rahu, is the head of the dragon, while the South Node, known as Ketu, is the body or tail of the dragon. Both nodes are malefic and take the place of the three outer planets (Uranus, Neptune, and Pluto). They are considered the most powerful points in the Jyotish chart.

James Braha wrote in *Ancient Hindu Astrology* that the nodes were "animalistic and without intelligence," concerned only with "achieving all pleasure." Rahu represented insatiable worldly desire, but was also "capable of bringing power, fame, political success, money and beauty when beneficially placed." It was analogous to Saturn. Rahu, possessing the head, brain, and mouth, wanted to consume everything, but since he was unable to digest what he ate, he was always hungry and never satisfied. He didn't know when enough was enough. Ketu, who received the body without the brain, was like Mars. He was irrational, intense, compulsive, emotional, and capable of great rage and anger. Curiously, Ketu also carried the potential of spiritual understanding, enlightenment, and self-realization.

In practice, Braha noted, "… there is little discernible difference ... between the two. Both are responsible for all sorts of evils, such as incurable diseases, murder, theft, poison, snakes, fears, phobias, undiagnosable illnesses, imprisonment and on and on and on!" Jyotish astrologers believe the nodes "… are more like masses of energy than directed forces. Nor do they have the ability to cast aspects as other planets do. And although Rahu and Ketu are certainly malefics, it is often harder to know the exact injury they indicate in a horoscope."

According to Braha, "the most detrimental effects of the nodes occur when either one is closely conjunct another planet.… That planet behaves in a weird, compulsive, and unconscious or uncontrollable way," destroying both the planet and the house that it rules. Jyotish astrologers are undecided about the signs wherein the nodes have dignity, but since they are 'without intelligence,' they are better placed in Gemini and

Virgo, the signs of Mercury, which bestow reason and critical thinking. The nodes are more powerful if they are stationing or moving direct, when they are considered 'highly positive and energizing.' They are the enemies of the Sun and Moon, and are presumed to operate poorly in the signs of the luminaries (Leo and Cancer respectively).

In India, the myth *The Churning of the Ocean* explains the origins of eclipses and gives insight into the Jyotish meaning of the nodes. According to the story, many years ago there was a great battle between the demons and the gods. The demons had won the favor of Shiva, The World-Destroyer, and were winning the war. The gods were losing, growing weak and becoming mortal. The gods went to Vishnu, the Creator-Preserver, and asked for help. Vishnu told the gods that in order to become strong once more, they had to work with the demons to churn the ocean and extract the nectar of immortality. The demons also wanted the nectar and were happy to assist. To churn the ocean, a mountain was used as a churning stick, and the king of serpents became the churning rope and wrapped himself around the mountain. With the gods at one end of the snake and the demons at the other, the churning began. After much time, thirteen forms of power sequentially emerged from the ocean. The last was the physician of the gods, holding a cup of ambrosia, the nectar of immortality. Immediately the gods and demons began fighting over the cup. Again, the gods appealed to Vishnu who transformed himself into a seductive dancing maiden. As he engaged the rapt attention of the demons, the gods secretly shared the nectar amongst themselves.

The demon Rahu was not fooled. He saw through the deceit, disguised himself as a god, positioned himself between the Sun and Moon, and sipped from the cup. The luminaries noticed his treachery and raised the alarm. Vishnu drew his sword and beheaded him. However, having tasted the nectar, Rahu had gained immortality and could not be killed. For now and forever, the dismembered demon chases after his adversaries, the Sun and Moon. At times, Rahu is successful and swallows one or the other, giving rise to an eclipse. Because the head is dismembered, the luminaries pass through his severed throat, slipping out of reach, and the pursuit begins anew.

What does the myth mean? In myth, a demon or beast symbolizes the animal instincts of the ego gone awry. The gods represent the soul. The ocean is a symbol of the unconscious, and therein is found the elixir of immortality—the god within. As Pierre Teilhard de Chardin said, *We are not human beings having a spiritual experience.*

We are spiritual beings having a human experience. According to spiritual teaching, we are two in one: an ego and a soul, a physical body and eternal spirit, a beast and a god. The ego is concerned with the physical world and all it entails, whereas the soul is concerned with the spiritual world of the divine. While the ego acts in its own interests, the soul acts in the interest of the greater good, in willing service to a higher order.

The myth illustrates the battle between ego (demons) and soul (gods). When the story began, the ego was out of control and gaining strength, while the soul was growing weak. There was an appeal to a higher power for help and the appeal was answered. To become strong, the soul had to work with the ego to mine the unconscious and unearth the god within, thereby finding immortality. The myth explains the spiritual connotation of the South Node, the compulsive, egotistical striving of the North Node, the polarization between them, and the eternal longing for their fusion. The myth also implies that the crises associated with eclipses are encounters with the divine.

Western Considerations

Western astrology did not adopt the Jyotish meaning of the nodes. In the 17th century, William Lilly wrote that the North Node was fortunate and had the nature of Jupiter and Venus. When conjunct other planets, the North Node was good with good planets, and evil with evil planets. Conversely, the South Node was evil when conjunct good planets, and good when conjunct evil planets. Lilly wrote that while this was the long standing opinion of the ancients, it was not what he found in practice: the good North Node conjunct evil planets lessened the malevolence of the planets, and the South Node conjunct evil planets 'doubled or trebled' the malevolence. If a significator was conjunct the South Node and a horary question indicated a good outcome, there would be many problems, and many times the 'whole matter came to nothing.'

Zadkiel, his early publisher, added a footnote to an early publication of *Christian Astrology:* "These points are of no consequence in nativities, except as regards the Moon, who brings benefits when she reaches the Head in the zodiac by directional motion, and evil when she reaches the Tail."

In 1925, Charles Carter wrote that the North Node had the nature of Jupiter and gave 'honor and success,' while the South Node had the nature of Saturn and brought 'downfall and ruin.' He added that while "some deny or question their value, others attach much importance to them." He advised the beginning astrologer to ignore them.

Three years later, in *The Moon's Nodes* (1928), George White wrote the nodes were a "'disturber of the cause of the things' ... sometimes working with and often working against the tendencies otherwise shown in the horoscope." He found "the nodes in the main seem aligned toward material matters and mental processes, and the order or tendency of things toward what might be termed 'luck' ... the Head blessing our endeavors, and the Tail causing difficulties or miscarriages and frequently disgrace." He looked at the effect of the nodes when conjunct various planets, and found that planets were 'strengthened and improved' with the North Node, and lost virtue when with the South Node.

To determine the action of the nodes, he looked at their influence when placed near the Ascendant and Midheaven, or in aspect to these angles. At the Midheaven, the North Node brought all forms of success, while the 'evil influence' of the South Node there brought 'failure, dishonor, ignominy, and remorse.' He found people with the South Node in the 9th, 10th, or 11th house were advocates of 'unpopular sciences,' although 'such people do much service to the race, often largely reaping contumely [scorn] in return.' He wrote the North Node on the Ascendant gave height, and the South Node on the Ascendant took it away (common with dwarfs). The South Node on the Ascendant was also associated with gross deformities (such as missing vital organs, possibly the brain). While he was writing his book, a royal princess was born and he was horrified to see the South Node within one degree of her Ascendant. Expecting the worst, he refused to pass judgment on the chart. (We'll look at it later).

The founder of Uranian astrology, Alfred Witte, working up until 1941, made no distinction between the nodes. He considered the North and South Node to have the same meaning. Together they comprise one of six important points that unite the individual with the world, and symbolize 'connections' and interactions with others. Uranian astrologers consider aspects to the nodes to be significant, including the semisquare (45°), sesquisquare (135°) and semioctile (22.5°).

Carl Payne Tobey reported in his book, *Astrology of Inner Space*, that there was no difference between the North and South Node. He wrote, "… I have investigated the Hindu use of the nodes as beneficial for the ascending node and malefic for the descending node and found absolutely no evidence of the validity of the claim, and in twenty-five years of empirical testing I should have had some verification. I find that the ascending and descending nodes function exactly the same, but I also find the points ninety degrees away from the nodes have the same characteristics."

In the *Encyclopedia of Astrology*, Nicholas Devore wrote that the natal nodes point to the location of the prenatal eclipse. He thought a planet conjunct the North Node 'would bring honors and riches,' and a planet conjunct the South Node 'would bring poverty and afflictions.' He also wrote, "The nodes of themselves merely point to places where something may happen at such and such a time—which of itself is no small matter."

Dane Rudhyar was the first astrologer to equate the nodes with spiritual growth. In *The Astrology of Personality* (1936), he wrote, "**At the Moon's North Node we see Destiny at work; at the South Node human will** (emphasis mine)…. What is seen therefore through the Moon's nodes is the relationship between the 'human' will and the 'divine' will … The former [South Node] is largely the result of the individual's conditioning by heredity and environment; the latter is the true factor of Destiny [North Node]."

He found the nodal house placement more significant than the sign and suggested this was because the nodes, like the houses, form an axis. As an opposition, the axis divided the circle into a northern half and a southern half, whereby the north referred "to spiritual power while south represented intensity of biological experiences and emotional behavior. At least this is what these directions have meant for millennia in the northern hemisphere of the globe." He considered the nodal axis as "'a line of destiny' between the past and the future (the karma and dharma) of an individual."

According to Rudhyar, "The lines of nodes show us the direction of Destiny, the purpose of Destiny—and what is back of this purpose, in the past. More than anything else it tells the 'why' of individual life. Why the particular ego was projected out of the ocean of universal life—why we are born and what for …. At one end of this line we see the past (South Node), at the other, the future; what the personality emerged from, what it is meant to accomplish.... At the North Node, life is being absorbed, the substance of experience is being ingested ... and at the South Node we assimilate the contents of life, automatically, effortlessly, and eliminate the refuse."

Rudhyar also thought, "The South Node represents the work that has been done, the well-known accomplishment, the routine performance already gone through many times, perhaps—the easy way out. The South Node has been called the point of 'self undoing' because we have so often a way of following the line of least resistance." He believed the "North Node is the point of reception of spiritual power."

Ronald C. Davison was clearly influenced by Rudhyar, and in his 1964 book *Astrology*, tied the nodes to reincarnation. He called the North Node 'positive' and showed the 'native's special task,' while the South Node was 'negative' and showed 'previous tendencies.' Planets that were conjunct the North Node indicated qualities to be consciously developed during life, while planets conjunct the South Node showed those qualities that were "developed in past lives that were now habitual and therefore required little effort to bring into play." He was the first to look at the dispositors, which he thought showed the area of life (house of dispositor) where the qualities of the nodal sign were to be developed or expressed.

In the 1970s, three major books were published on the nodes. In *Karmic Astrology: The Moon's Nodes and Reincarnation*, Martin Schulman expanded Rudhyar and Davison's view. Schulman wrote the South Node was related to the sum of past lives and experiences and pointed to behavioral patterns that could trip up the personality. It was the weakest point in the horoscope, the 'Achilles heel' that could trap the ego in the past. However, if the personality had a solid base, the South Node could indicate the 'fruition of achievement.' He believed the North Node pointed the way to the future, but only after the allure and familiarity of the South Node were released. He thought there was spiritual aid at the North Node and experiences there were related to the growth and evolution of the soul.

In *The Node Book* (1973), Zipporah Pottenger Dobyns examined the planetary nodes, as well as the nodes of the Moon. She wrote, "Tradition states that the North Node symbolizes an area of intake, where matters flow with relative ease. The South Node, in contrast, is a point of release or outflow often with an accompanying sense of stress or tension or pressure." She believed the North Node was where we functioned with minimal strain and represented matters already learned. At the South Node we had to put forth effort to learn a lesson 'and then give to the world the fruits of our learning.' This view that the North Node represented familiarity and the South Node effort, was exactly opposite the view of Rudhyar, Davison, and Schulman, who said that effort was required at the North Node to shape the future, and that the South Node was familiar and effortless.

The source of the discrepancy was Rudhyar. After working with the nodes for forty years, he realized he had made a mistake. In *Person Centered Astrology* published in 1976, he offered a revised understanding of the nodes. Now he wrote, "**The North Node refers to whatever builds the personality ... and 'destiny' may be accomplished symbolically where the South Node is placed in one's birth chart. Something greater than the self may be fulfilled there or one's basic function in society or in the universe** (emphasis mine)."

His explanation for reversing the delineation was that, "In the past I accepted the statement the North Node hemisphere was constituted by the 180 degrees of the zodiac after the North Node following the natural order of the zodiac. However it occurred to me recently that this was not logical, for the nodes motion is retrograde." He went on to say that his previous delineation of the nodal axis (specifically in regards to the horoscope of Mussolini given in *The Astrology of Personality*) should be 'interpreted in a reverse manner.' Now, in a position identical to Zipporah Dobyns, he wrote, "the North Node, I repeat, is the point of *intake;* the South Node, the point of *release* or *evacuation.*" The South Node also refers to sacrifice and what the personality no longer needs, "is in a decaying or poisonous condition, or that is the positive and creative expression of the body-mind organism." He specifically indicated the South Node was not entirely negative and evil, though he warned of "the danger of using the negative traits of the sign."

Thus, Rudhyar initially said the North Node pertained to the soul and destiny, and the South Node to the ego or personality. He later reversed the meaning and said the North Node was related to building the personality. The North Node house showed where "the 'will' should find its field of most constructive action." The South Node possessed 'spiritual power' and the South Node house was related to 'destiny' but also loss (release or evacuation of what is no longer needed or necessary), sacrifice (surrender of ego-will to God or mankind) and fated action (fulfilling one's basic function in society or in the universe). He considered 'individuality' (North Node) and 'destiny' (South Node) to be "polar opposites, if by destiny is meant one's essential relation to what is greater than your personal self."

This mix-up of meaning has compromised nodal delineation for decades. It has had significant repercussions as to which node means what, which one should be given precedence, and for what purpose. Thirty-six years after Rudhyar's amendment, the original and inaccurate interpretation is still the prevalent delineation in the mainstream literature. However, his revised understanding, which appears to be correct, is gaining ground and appears in some modern texts.

In *Eclipses* (2006), Celeste Teal wrote that the North Node is a point of intake or gain, where benefits arrive more easily and without conscious effort, whereas the South Node is a point of loss or vulnerability, or where sacrifice is required. In *Lunar Nodes: Discover Your Soul's Karmic Mission*, she wrote, "the North Node is like a cup running over. Gifts from the higher powers are coming to us and good karma is rewarded. The South Node is an empty cup; we are expected to fill it up. We can provide a service that will contribute to another soul or to the growth and evolution of the planet."

In *The Lunar Nodes: Your Key to Excellent Chart Interpretation* (2009), Judith Hill described the nodes as "two ends of a great celestial pump, where energies favorably enter at the Head and exit or drain at the Tail." She sees the nodes akin to the tides; the tide comes in at the North Node and goes out at the South Node. She found planets conjunct the North Node to be lucky, and planets conjunct the South Node to be difficult and associated with hardship. She explains that the different perspectives of the nodes in the East and the West arise from cultural differences. In the East, the purpose of life is to gain spiritual enlightenment and toward this end, sacrifice, meditation, withdrawal, and submission are favored, and associated with the South Node. In the West, these activities have little value, and the ideal is to exert the ego in competition and acquire resources and money for power and domination, the arena of the North Node.

The two worlds, the divine and the human ... are actually one. The realm of the gods is a forgotten dimension of the world we know.

—Joseph Campbell

Chapter 2
Nodal Astronomy

To understand how the nodes operate astrologically, it behooves us to understand them astronomically. The word 'node' in Latin means 'knot.' In astronomy, the nodes are the points of intersection of two orbital planes. The orbit of the Moon defines the lunar plane, and the orbit of the Earth defines the ecliptic (the apparent path of the Sun). The two planes are tilted at an angle of 5°08' and intersect at the lunar nodes (Figure 1).

Latitude is the dimension North (above) or South (below) the ecliptic. As the Moon circles the Earth, it conjuncts a lunar node twice a month. When the transiting Moon is conjunct the North Node, it is coming up from below the plane of the ecliptic into the 'North.' The zenith of the lunar orbit has a maximum latitude of 5N08 and is called the North Bending. When the Moon is conjunct the South Node it is going down below the plane of the ecliptic into the 'South.' The nadir of the lunar orbit has a latitude is 5S08 and is called the South Bending.

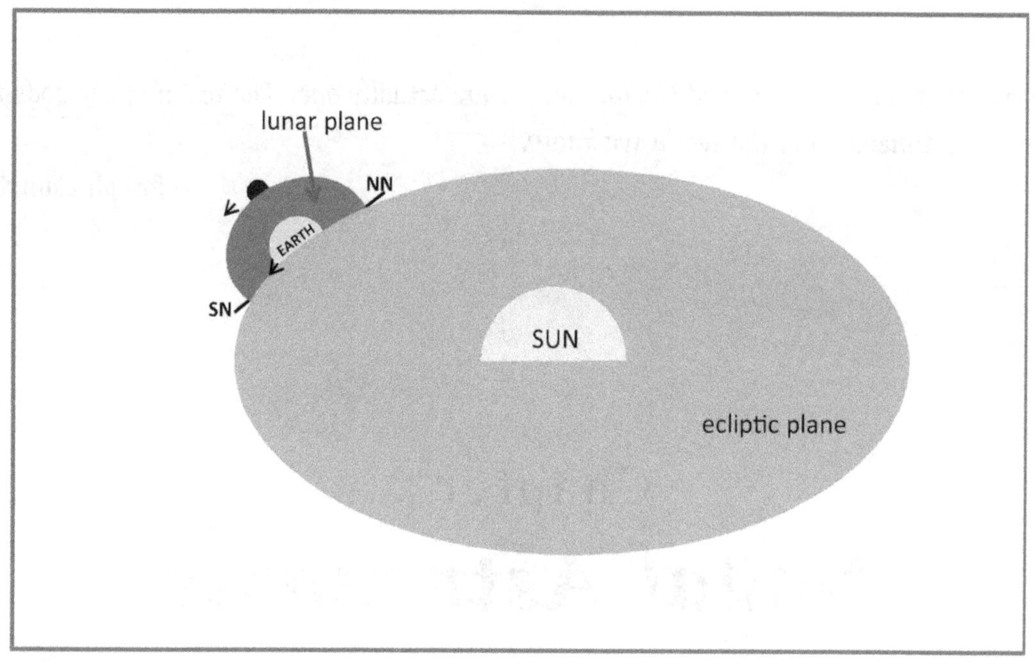

Figure 1.

The Lunar Nodes and Axis: NN = North Node; SN = South Node

As the Earth travels along the ecliptic, the Moon and nodes travel with it. The lunar nodes are always opposite each other (unlike the nodes of the other planets), and form an axis that moves slowly retrograde, traveling backwards approximately 3' a day, or 19° per year. The nodes traverse a sign in eighteen months, and the zodiac in eighteen-and-a-half-years. While their movement is called retrograde, the nodes are tied to the ecliptic and are not at liberty to move away from it. What does move is the lunar plate (shown in Figure 1 as a dark gray halo around the earth). The plate moves counter-clockwise like the planets. As the plate advances, it brings a lower degree of longitude to the node. For example, if the South Node in the diagram is at 17° Aries, when the plate advances it brings 16° Aries to the node, and then 15° etc.

The exact longitudinal positions of the nodes are imprecise. The degree of the North Node is given in the ephemeris as either the mean or true node. Both are estimates. The degree of the mean node is determined from average speed over time. The direction of the mean node is always retrograde. The degree of the true node is taken from the Moon's bimonthly conjunction with its node (an exact position) and extrapolated to give an approximate daily position. The true nodes wobble, primarily moving retrograde, but at times direct. Most of the written information about the nodes pertains to the mean nodes, but with the advent of computers, more astrologers have begun using the true nodes. The maximum distance between the mean and true node is 1°45'.

The speed the nodal axis moves varies over time. During the month of an eclipse, the nodes appear stationary, often remaining in the same degree for the entire month. During the preceding and proceeding month, the node will not move more than one degree. For the three months surrounding an eclipse, the node travels only 2°. A month after the eclipse, the nodes pick up speed, and for the next three months move an average of about 3°, for a total of about 9°, before slowing down as the next eclipse approaches.

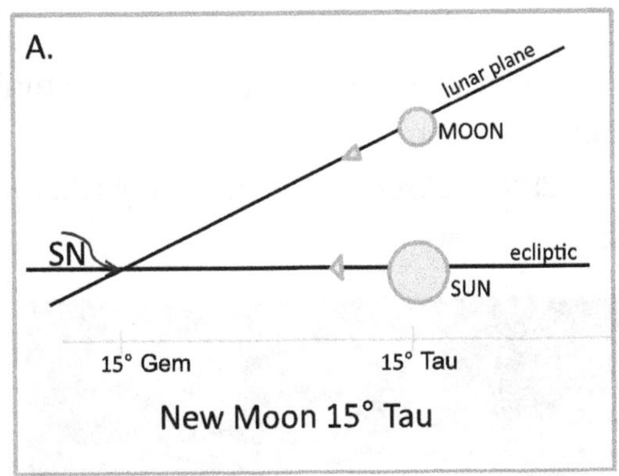

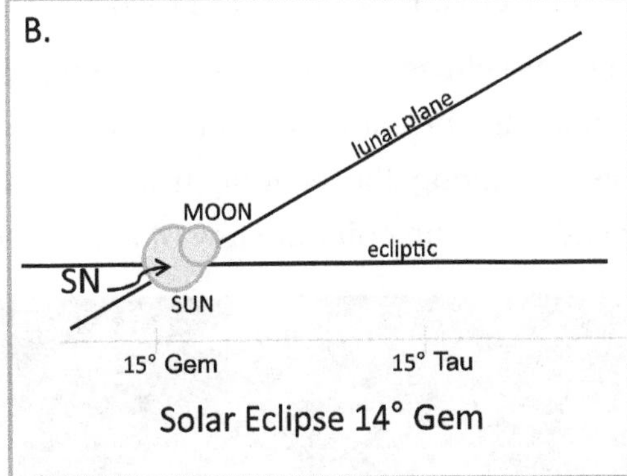

Figure 2.

Taurus New Moon and Gemini Solar Eclipse

Every month there is a New Moon (conjunction of Sun and Moon) and a Full Moon (opposition of Sun and Moon), and twice a month the Moon conjuncts its node. When these events happen at the same time, there is an eclipse (Figure 2). A solar eclipse occurs when the New Moon is near a node. At this time, the Moon moves in front of the Sun, blocking its light, and causing a darkening of the Sun. Two weeks later (or possibly two weeks earlier), when the Moon forms an opposition to the Sun near a node, there is a lunar eclipse. At this time, the Moon is darkened as it moves through the Earth's shadow. These events can only occur when the Moon is near its node, for only then is it on the ecliptic and aligned with both the Sun and Earth. Six months later, as the Sun nears the opposite node, there is another solar and lunar eclipse (for additional information see Bernadette Brady's *Predictive Astrology: The Eagle and the Lark*).

In general, every year, there are four eclipses: two lunar and two solar, occurring six months apart. As Judith Hill points out in *The Lunar Nodes*, there are four different types of eclipses with respect to the nodes. In a north nodal solar eclipse, the luminaries are conjunct the North Node. In a south nodal solar eclipse, the luminaries are conjunct the South Node. In a north nodal lunar eclipse, the Moon is conjunct the North Node and the Sun is conjunct the South Node. And, in a south nodal lunar eclipse, the Moon is conjunct the South Node and the Sun is conjunct the North Node.

Declination and Latitude

When an eclipse takes place, the Sun, Moon, and nodes are in aspect in longitude, declination, and latitude. Longitude is the coordinate astrologers typically use and is measured along the ecliptic from 0° Aries to 29°59' Pisces. The other coordinates depend upon the point of view of the observer.

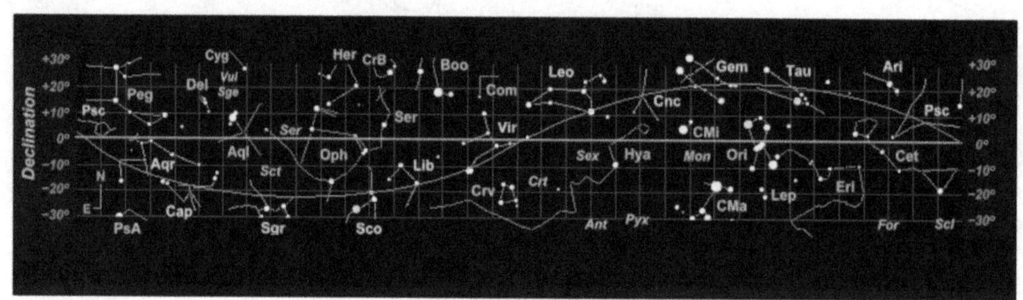

Figure 3:

The Ecliptic (sine wave) and Celestial Equator (straight line)

The ecliptic belt is approximately 16° wide with latitude measured above and below the center line, which is the ecliptic. The stars of the zodiac are found in this region, and planets for the most part are restricted to this region (Figure 3). Pluto, with its widely tilted orbit (angled to the ecliptic at around 17°) is often found outside the belt, along with Chiron. By definition, the Sun is always on the ecliptic, as are the Ascendant, Midheaven and the lunar nodes. Any celestial body on the ecliptic has a latitude of 0°. As noted, the Moon's maximum latitude is 5°08' above or below the ecliptic. Generally, Jupiter, Saturn, Uranus, and Neptune are found near 0°, but Mercury, Venus, and Mars are frequently off the ecliptic.

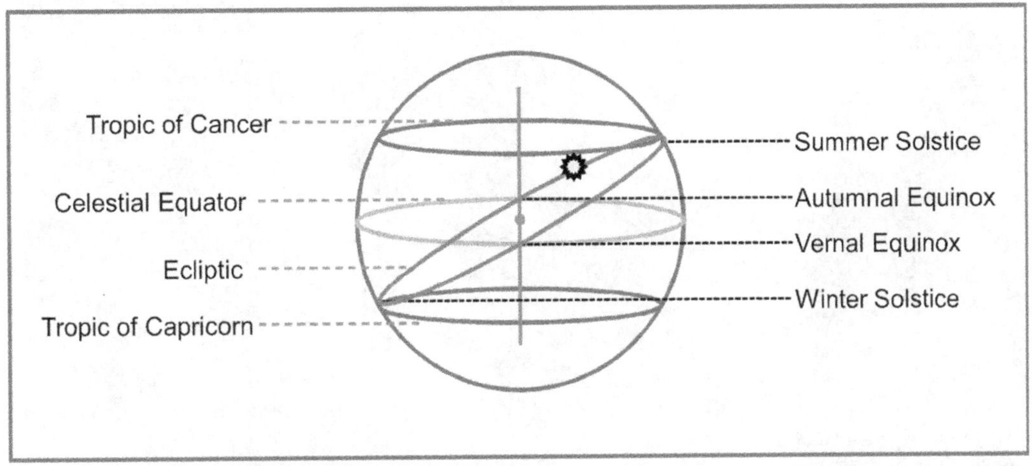

Figure 4.
The Great Circles

Declination is similar to latitude, only the reference point is the celestial equator, which is the Earth's equator projected into space. Declination is measured north or south of the equator (see Figure 3). The plane of the ecliptic and the earth's plane are tilted 23°26', and the points of intersection of the two great circles are 0° Aries (vernal equinox) and 0° Libra (autumnal equinox) (Figure 4). Only at these two points does the Sun have a declination of 0°. (In Figure 3 it appears these two points are in the constellations of Virgo and Pisces due to the precession of the equinoxes.) The Sun reaches a maximum north declination (23N26) on the Summer Solstice at a longitude of 0° Cancer at the Tropic of Cancer. The Sun is at a maximum south declination (23S26) at the Winter Solstice at a longitude of 0° Capricorn (Figure 5).

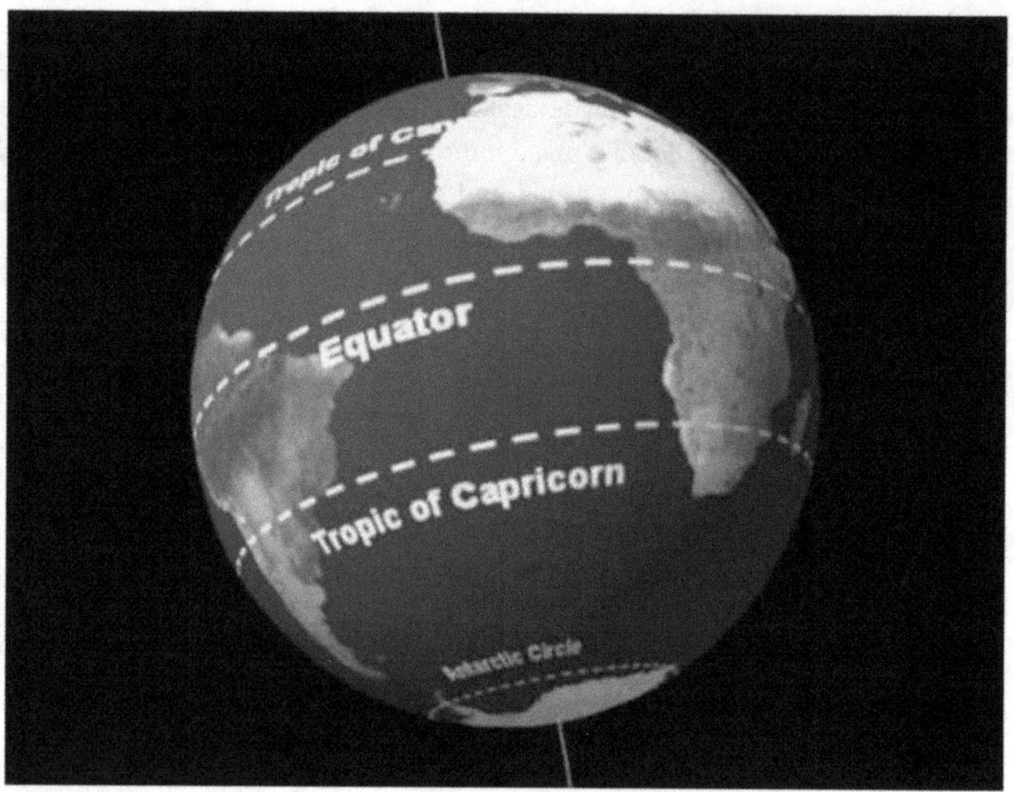

Figure 5.

Declination and the Tropics

In *Person Centered Astrology* (1976), Rudhyar suggested that the seasonal declination cycle of the Sun (Figure 6) was similar to the latitude cycle of the Moon (Figure 7). By definition, the lunar North Node is the place where the Moon has a latitude of 0° and is crossing the ecliptic into north latitude. This is analogous to the Sun at 0° Aries at the start of spring as the Sun begins its travels in north declination. The Moon reaches maximum latitude of 5N08 at the North Bending (square the nodes), equivalent to the Sun's maximum declination at the Tropic of Cancer at the onset of summer. At the South Node, the Moon is back on the ecliptic with a latitude of 0° and in a position similar to the Sun at 0° Libra and 0° declination at the start of fall. The Moon is square the nodes at a latitude of 5S08 at the South Bending, a point corresponding to the Sun at maximum south declination and 0° Capricorn at the start of winter.

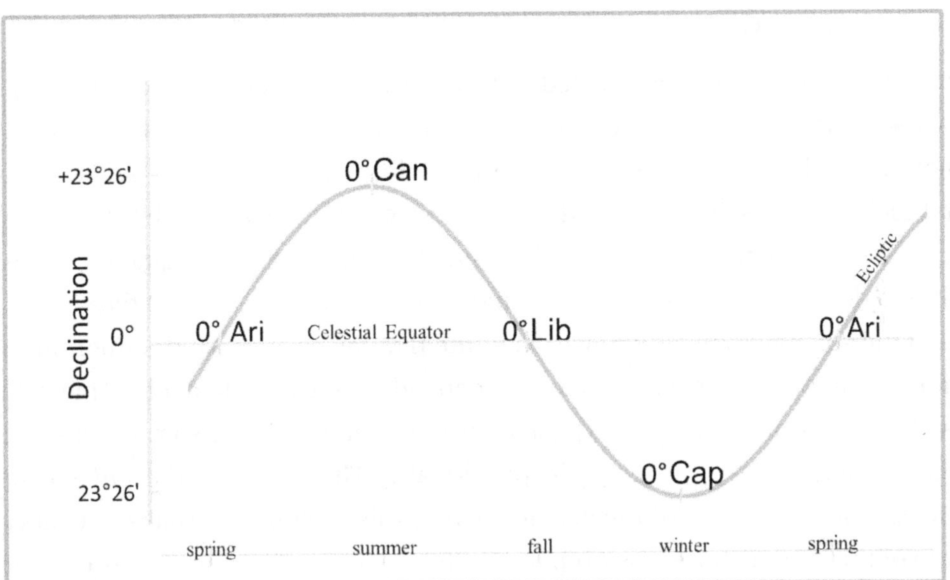

Figure 6.

Solar Declination and the Four Cardinal Points

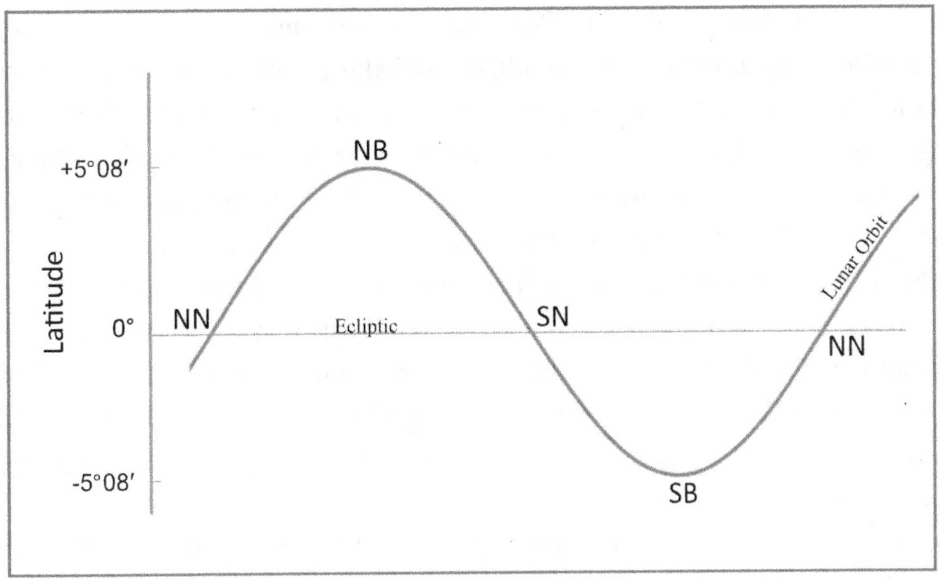

Figure 7

Lunar Latitude and the Four Nodal Points

Eclipse Astrology

Historically, eclipses were associated with crises. The exact degree of an eclipse remains a sensitized point in the chart for an extended length of time that lasts at least six months, and perhaps years. According to Robert Jansky, "the single most important fact to note is, in which of the 12 houses does the eclipse fall?" His key words for eclipses are 'emphasis' and 'crisis.' "It simply means you are required by events in your life to devote more time, attention and energy to some matter(s) than usual." The house of the solar eclipse shows an area of life that needs to expand "either physically, emotionally, mentally, or inspirationally, depending on the element." That is, if the eclipse falls in an earth sign, the expansion is physical; in a water sign, emotional; in an air sign, mentally; and a fire sign, inspirationally. The house of the lunar eclipse is usually opposite the house of the accompanying solar eclipse, and Jansky believed the purpose of the lunar eclipse was preparation for the upcoming solar eclipse: during the intervening six months it was time to get that house in order in advance of the coming solar eclipse.

With exception, the ruler of the sign of the eclipse is considered the lord of the eclipse. According to Celeste Teal, "That planet reveals much about how an eclipse is apt to manifest, the affairs it will spotlight, and the people whose interests will be brought into the limelight." The exception occurs when a planet is exactly conjunct (in the degree of) the eclipse, in which case that planet becomes the lord, as "that extra planet dominates the eclipse message … as if the eclipse, or in truth, the lunar portal, opens a doorway for this planet's domination."

Judith Hill found that when a North Node eclipse is conjunct a planet (within 3°), for that planet "a power surge occurs within one year, usually within three months. The power surge will relate to the planet, sign and house that is eclipsed." If a South Node eclipse is conjunct a planet (within 3°), then "a power outage occurs within one year, usually within three months. The power outage relates to the planet, house and sign that is eclipsed."

As Nicholas Devore noted, the natal nodes mark the location of nearby eclipses. Robert Jansky found the degree of the solar eclipse immediately before birth was as emphasized as if there were a planet in that place. He suggested marking the prenatal solar eclipse (PNSE) degree in the natal chart and watching it carefully. He considered the house of the PNSE to point to an area of life that needs to be expanded according to the element of the sign. It was "continually emphasized throughout the life of the individual, even though it might not contain natal planets or other astrological factors that would bring it into prominence." He found no similar effect of the prenatal lunar eclipse.

Developing a Nodal Hypothesis

Thus far we have seen: 1.The nodes are a point of intersection. 2. The nodes are important because they are related to eclipses, and in an eclipse, the Sun and Moon are in aspect by longitude, latitude and declination. The eclipse point remains active for months, possibly years. 3. Nonetheless, it is the lord of the eclipse, the planet ruling the sign of the eclipse, which determines how the eclipse will manifest. What does this mean in regards to the astrological interpretation of the nodes?

The points of intersection of the great circles form important points. The intersection of the celestial equator and the ecliptic is marked by the cardinal points of 0° Aries and 0° Libra (see Figure 4). In a natal chart, the Ascendant/Descendant axis is the intersection of the ecliptic with the earth's horizon. The Midheaven is the point of intersection of the ecliptic with the meridian (the highest overhead position reached by the Sun). Since the lunar nodes are also two points of intersection on the ecliptic, it would appear the nodes are similar to an angle.

The angles are amongst the most significant feature of any horoscope and denote places of incoming energy. According to Nicholas Devore, the angles are the "most powerful and important arcs in astrology. Planets therein become immensely potent, for good or for ill…." Celeste Teal considered the nodes as "portals through which cosmic energy flows." It would seem that if the nodal axis astronomically resembles an angle, behaves as an angle, it should not only be considered an angle, it is, in fact, an angle.

An angle has no inherent ability to act. It is not a physical body. It is an intersection that marks a point where energy flows. The energy of the angle is channeled by the ruler of the angle. In astrology, the prime importance of the ruler of the Ascendant and the ruler of the Midheaven is indisputable. This is also the case for the ruler of the eclipse: the lord determines how the energy of the eclipse will manifest. I suggest a similar case can be made for the nodes: **the planets ruling the nodes channel the energy of the nodes**. Thus, the significance of a node is not the point of intersection—the node itself—but the planet that rules the sign of the intersection. This directs attention away from the nodes themselves, and places the emphasis on their rulers.

Nonetheless, the nodes themselves are important—as are their houses—because when a planet is conjunct the node (natally or by transit), that planet is energized by the node and impacts the house where it is posited.

In addition, as we have seen, there are four different types of eclipses. If the PNSE was a north nodal eclipse, chances are it would share the same house as the North Node, which would be the house that would expand over the life. However, if the PNSE was a south nodal eclipse, then chances are it would share the same natal house as the South Node, and then it would be this house—the house of the South Node — that would expand. If this is so, it explains why the house influence of the nodes is inconsistent, and why some people are successful in the area described by the house of the South Node, and not as victorious in the house of the North Node. It is the house of the PNSE that develops and is important.

Nodal Energy

The four cardinal points of the ecliptic as described by the Sun's yearly journey in declination, define the turning points of the four seasons. In the North and South hemisphere, the seasons are well-defined, especially in regards to vegetative growth. In spring, after the death of winter, life begins anew, the earth warms up and a greening begins. In the summer, growth is at its peak and there is a burgeoning of color and life. In autumn, there is the harvest, followed by deterioration as growth stops and leaves fall. In winter, with solar energy at its weakest, there is hibernation and cold, and seeds lie dormant, awaiting the warmth of spring.

As mentioned, Rudhyar proposed that the declination cycle of the Sun resembled the latitude cycle of the Moon (see Figure 7). If this equivalence is valid, then the energy is similar between the North Node and Aries, the North Bending and Cancer, the South Node and Libra, and the South Bending and Capricorn. Four nodal points then, rather than two, have astrological significance.

The four nodal points serve as signposts. Similar to the four cardinal points, the nodal points are not inherently active, but identify four areas of potential activity. As Nicholas Devore wrote (although he was talking only about the nodes themselves), they "point to places where something may happen at such and such a time."

North Node energy, related to Aries, represents the push of the ego as it makes its mark in the world. It is selfish, self-centered, and reckless, but energetic, bold and confident. The energy is dynamic, bursting with life and serves to strengthen the ego. This agrees with Rudhyar's revised observation that the "North Node pertained to the building of the personality."

South Node energy, related to Libra, represents the ego in relationship with others, including a relationship with the inner self and the greater whole. There is a giving up of the ego, a sacrificing of the self for another, a giving oneself over in service for the better interests of the greater good. This agrees with Rudhyar's observation that "… the South Node indicated sacrifice and destiny, where something greater than the self may be fulfilled, where one may have to sacrifice the ego."

The latitude cycle also gives insight into the meaning of the positions square the nodes in longitude. The North Bending point is analogous to summer and corresponds with maximum productivity, abundant output, and the blossoming outward expression of the ego. The South Bending position equates to winter and corresponds to loss of physical vitality, weakness, death, but also spiritual renewal. Maurice Lavenant pointed out that Capricorn and the Winter Solstice correspond with the Yin force reaching its maximum, and is the time of rebirth of the solar gods and 'renewal of the relationship with the divine.' This point shows spiritual promise, as well as physical vulnerability.

In summary, a new delineation has been derived for the nodes that takes into consideration the revised meaning of the North and South Node, the relevance of the four nodal points, the importance of the PNSE, the significance of the nodal rulers, and the viewpoint that the nodes are similar to angles and act as channels with no inherent activity *per se*. The interpretation is outlined in detail in the following chapter.

The seat of the soul is there, where the outer and inner worlds meet.

— *Novalis*

Chapter 3
Nodal Delineation

The influence of the nodes is determined by examining how the nodal energy affects planets in a chart. The nodes are channels of astrological energy. In a natal chart, if there is no planet conjunct a node, then the node serves as a marker. The nodes identify the location of prenatal eclipses. Activities related to the house of the PNSE (which may contain either the North or South Node) expand during the lifetime.

The North Node channels the energy of the 'North,' which is related to the ego and the manifest world of physical reality. This is the territory of science—what is seen and measurable. 'North' energy is typically helpful in the outer world and lends success, maturity, wisdom, ease of expression, and manifestation. The energy supports the ego and enables advancement, recognition, acknowledgement, and personal glory. Since the energy is attuned to the manifest realm, it is helpful in boosting outward accomplishment.

The South Node channels the energy of the 'South,' which emanates from the otherworld, the spiritual world beyond earthly reality. The energy resembles the spiritual realm denoted by Neptune and Pisces, but these are of this world (as distinct from the otherworld). The energy of the 'South' is intuitive, spiritual, and willing to sacrifice and be of service. In the manifest world, a 'great work' may be released that serves others. However, the energy in the outer world is also related to physical loss, vulnerability, deficiency, scarcity, or absence.

A planet connected to a node receives the energy of the node. Planets are connected to a node through rulership or aspect. The North Node ruler is often emphasized so that the planet is overtly expressed, frequently for no evident astrological reason. The planet operates in an outwardly productive, mature, and experienced fashion. It seems blessed with inborn wisdom and practical know-how. The planet is often related to 'a calling'—a professional passion that gives life purpose. The physical world seems to support North Node planets and activities. North Node energy is like a gift from the gods. However, the energy can be excessive and spur a planet into overdrive, causing problems.

Planets sextile and trine the North Node ruler gain from its strength and benefit from the association. Planets in hard aspect to the North Node ruler also benefit from the connection, as the ruler will push its agenda to good effect. Planets quincunx the North Node ruler may experience more frustration than usual.

There is always some weakness or loss associated with the South Node ruler. The planet, infused with otherworld energy, is lacking in physical world know-how, and appears naïve, clueless, and inexperienced, causing problems and suffering. The South Node ruler may be weak, powerless, immature, clumsy, awkward, artless, and ignorant. It lacks practical understanding and common sense. While the South Node ruler may function well in non-material pursuits, it has no clue how to operate in the physical world, and no clue how the physical world works. However, with time and experience, the planet can eventually acquire an understanding of the physical world. When the planet acts on behalf of the greater good, and works selflessly to serve the greater whole, it can function well in the physical world. It can produce a 'great work.' When used selfishly for personal gain or glory, there is often a fall.

Planets in major aspect to the South Node ruler are negatively affected by the energy in regards to expression in the physical world. However, the planets may acquire spiritual insight from the association, in which case they can be used to good effect in the manifest realm. The sextiles and trines are more apt to express positively than the squares and oppositions. Planets quincunx the South Node ruler are often frustrated by conditions over which they have no control.

An interesting situation arises when the nodal rulers are in difficult aspect with each other (in longitude, latitude, or declination). The ease and wisdom typically associated with the North Node ruler is compromised by its connection to the South Node ruler. This is often expressed by a delay in positive output of the North Node ruler. However, the South Node ruler is helped by the refinement of the North Node ruler, and weakness is mitigated. Nonetheless, the hard aspect brings trouble for both planets, although this usually gets better over time. When the two rulers are in easy aspect and sextile/trine each other, the harm associated with the South Node energy is lessened, as is the egotistical thrust of the North Node energy, so that there is productivity, but also spiritual awareness. When the two nodal rulers are quincunx each other, there is frustration.

Four Nodal Points

There are four nodal points. A nodal point is active only when there is a planet present. Just as any planet at an angle has an outlet and is obvious in action, a planet conjunct a node gains expression—for good or for ill. A natal planet conjunct the North Node is imbued with the energy of the 'North' and is strengthened by the association. The planet functions intelligently in the outer world to good effect. The house(s) the planet rules also benefits from the energy. By transit, when a planet conjuncts the node (either a transiting planet to a natal node, or a transiting node to a natal planet), the planet receives an infusion of energy, and there is some form of manifestation in the physical realm related to the symbolism of the planet.

A natal planet conjunct the South Node acquires the energy of the 'South' and is physically weakened as a result, beset with difficulty, and hindered in expression. The house(s) the planet rules are undermined by the energy. However, the planet may function well in non-material (i.e. spiritual) pursuits. Over time, the planet can gain practical experience and learn how to be of service and apply spiritual energy productively in the physical realm. By transit, when a planet conjuncts the South Node (or the transiting South Node conjuncts a planet), typically something related to the planet is lost. Inwardly, it can be a time of great inspiration relating to spiritual clarity or awareness. It can also point to personal sacrifice, and is often seen at times of marriage, sickness, and surgery.

Planets that are square the nodes are at the North or South Bending. The South Bending is 90° clockwise from the North Node, and the North Bending is 90° counterclockwise from the North Node. Like the nodes themselves, the North and South Bendings mark degrees of potential energy. However, the energy is latent unless there is a planet at the bending. The unoccupied bending (or node) serves as a signpost: *watch out for rocks*. The ruler of the bending is not significant because the bending itself is not a point of intersection.

A planet at the North Bending is in a state of maximum tangible productivity. A natal planet here exhibits the traits of a planet conjunct the North Node, except the planet's expression is exaggerated. When a planet crosses the North Bending by transit (or a natal planet transiently occupies the North Bending of the transiting nodes), that planet acquires the energy of the bending, and there is an outward burst of activity, or a display of the ego in the physical realm.

A planet at the South Bending is at a place where otherworld energy is strong and physical energy is weak. Early on, planets here are powerless and express awkwardly in the physical world. They resemble a planet conjunct the South Node, only the effect is exaggerated and weakness is intensified. However, the planet is infused with strong psychic and spiritual energy, which with time and learning, can be employed in service and productive pursuits that benefit the whole rather than the self. When a planet transits the South Bending (or a natal planet transiently occupies the South Bending of the transiting nodes), there is often a loss or a letting go that occurs in the physical world. It can also be a time of heightened spiritual sensitivity or awareness, or when a great work that serves others is released.

Planets in aspect to the nodes receive the energy of the nodes. Natal planets sextile/trine the nodes receive a boost in power. Since they aspect both the South Node and North Node by easy aspect, the effect is usually beneficial. The nodes give the planet otherworld sensitivity, practical intelligence, and an outlet, resulting in astute expression. By transit, planets energized through a sextile/trine to the nodes do not precipitate events, but bring ease, added power, and/or emphasis to an event.

With a quincunx to the node, a planet acquires a boost of power that exacerbates the aggravation of the aspect. In my mind, the quincunx is a most under-rated aspect and should not be considered minor. (An inconjunct is a 150° aspect similar to the quincunx except one planet is in a fixed sign, which intensifies the irritation.) The quincunx requires an adjustment or a stretch out of the comfort zone. It is an aspect of frustration and helplessness: the planets involved 'want' something but have little ability to make it happen. This is in contrast to a square or opposition whose tension can be alleviated by action or a change in attitude. The quincunx is often related to health problems, which exemplifies the angst of the aspect: the situation requires acceptance. Nothing can be done to right what is wrong. A yod formed by two quincunxes and a sextile is only all the more aggravating: the situation is still nearly impossible, only the sextile offers hope, often false, giving rise to high frustration. When an inconjunct is involved in the yod, the aggravation is increased further as the fixed planet is unyielding.

Aspects formed with the nodes in declination are also active. A planet parallel the node is considered to act similar to a longitude conjunction. A planet parallel the North Node acquires energy useful to the ego in the outer world. A planet parallel the South Node acquires an otherworld influence helpful for spiritual/psychic work and service. The energy is not helpful in selfishly serving the ego. In latitude, where the nodes are always on the ecliptic, a planet near 0° latitude forms a parallel not only with both nodes, but with the Sun and angles as well, giving the planet a powerful means of expression.

In forecasting, using eclipses in concert with the nodes provides a potent predictive tool. While the house of the transiting eclipse typically indicates the area of life that is emphasized and thrown into crisis, the lord of the eclipse assumes high focus and becomes a planet to watch closely. The archetype is stimulated, so that the natal, progressed, and transiting planet are often active at the time of an event. When the transiting North Node forms a conjunction to a planet or is square a natal planet at the transient North Bending, there is some observable manifestation related to the symbolism of the planet. If it is the South Node making the connection, there is some kind of difficulty, loss, or sacrifice in the manifest realm. However, there can also be gain in the inner world that may not be evident to outsiders.

There is little difference between a transiting node making an aspect with a natal planet, or a transiting planet making an aspect with a node: energy is transmitted and events related to the symbolism of the planet transpire.

Chart Delineation

All this theory is speculation unless it is shown to be empirically valid—not in some cases, but in every case. In the following chapters, I delineate a number of charts with a focus on the nodal planetary energy. A sample Natal Nodal Worksheet and Event Worksheet are provided in the appendix (and can be freely copied). In the text, I look at the degree and house of the PNSE. In instances where a solar eclipse occurs within three weeks after birth, I use the degree of this eclipse. Although Jansky was silent on the matter, my research indicated that when a person was born a short time before a solar eclipse (up to three weeks), it was this solar eclipse that was active. In looking at event charts, it became apparent that an upcoming solar eclipse that occurred within three weeks of a notable event was more relevant than the solar eclipse that occurred nearly six months previously. I arbitrarily adapted this three-week window (it might be longer). In instances where there are two PNSEs before birth, the houses containing the degree of both eclipses are activated. An eclipse degree remains sensitive for at least six months, and when two solar eclipses occur near an event, both eclipse degrees and eclipse lords have heightened significance.

I use Placidus houses, but consider the house cusps to be flexible with the exception of the angles. I consider a planet 3–4° degrees before a house cusp to be active in the following house. The variable house systems in use by different astrologers (leading to different interior house cusps), is another factor which has contributed to the inconsistency of expression of the house of the natal nodes. For example, in one house system a node may be in the 8th house, in another system the 9th, and another the 7th. There is currently no solution to this problem.

In the nativity and event transits, I use tight orbs, usually no more than 3–4°, except in the case of a running aspect (where a third planet bridges two planets in wide aspect). In some instances, a wide aspect seems to be active, in which case it cannot be ignored. In progressions I use an orb of about 1°, except in the case of the fast moving Moon, which gets an orb of about 3°.

I use the position of the true nodes, not because their position is more accurate than the mean nodes, but because the true nodes move forward and retrograde and thus give direction. When looking for aspects, I check the position of both, and consider an aspect is valid if it is within 3–4° of either the mean or true node. As always, a closer aspect is more active.

To locate the bendings, I start at the North Node and go clockwise 90° to the South Bending, continue 90° to the South Node, and continue 90° more to the North Bending. In the nativity, I look for planets at these four positions. I check to see if the Moon is near maximum latitude. If so, the Moon is at a bending even if it is not square its nodes in longitude. This is not the case with the other planets. In transits, I look at the four nodal positions related to the transiting nodes. Because the transiting nodes move, the transiting bendings also move and briefly align with natal planets.

In declination, I note planets that are parallel the nodes. (Here there are no contraparallels because a planet contraparallel one node is parallel the other node.) In *Declination in Astrology*, Paul Newman found qualitative differences between planets in north and south declination. In this study, I ignore this information and simply note the presence of the aspect.

Planets in wide aspect in longitude can be in close aspect in declination or latitude (which explains why the wide aspect in longitude is active). In declination, two planets may be conjunct and parallel, or opposite and contraparallel. Both formations create an occultation, which is similar to an eclipse. The repeated aspect adds to the impact of the planets' expression.

I watch planets that are out-of-bounds in declination. These planets are traveling outside the ecliptic belt and are beyond the influence and control of the Sun. According to Kt Boehrer, "Out-of-bounds planets are so consistently involved in unexpected, uncommon matters and conditions, their key phrase is 'beyond normal expectations.' It pays to watch them closely." The keywords used by Newman for out-of-bound planets are: unrestrained, extreme, independent, wild, awkward, vulnerable, privileged, and magnified.

In declination I use a variable orb because, as Newman writes, the 'degrees are more stretched out near the equator' where the Sun moves faster. This is in contrast to the Sun at maximum declination, where the Sun appears to reach a standstill. I use an orb of about 1° (60') at a declination of 1–10°; about 45' at a declination of 10–20°; and about 25' above a declination of 20°.

In latitude, I will mention only those planets near the center line of the zodiac and on (or approaching) the ecliptic where the Sun, angles, and nodes are found. Here my orb is less than 0°10'. This is a small orb and will exclude most aspects, but the ones that are used are quite potent.

In chart delineation, I always look at the three big players, the Sun, Moon, and chart ruler. In this study, my focus will be on the planets stimulated by the nodal energy, which are those planets that rule or aspect the nodes in longitude, declination, and latitude. This typically not only gives enough information to understand the chart accurately, it highlights the planets that define a life. In general, if I want to know what the native is good at, I look at the North Node ruler. There is flowering and abundant output of a planet at the North Bending. It is obvious in action. If I want to know what planet will be weak and cause trouble, I look at the South Node ruler. When a planet comes to the South Node, it is releasing all physical accouterments and entering the non-physical realm of the spiritual otherworld. A planet at the South Bending is mired in the otherworld, and as far away from the physical world as it can be.

In reading a chart, I don't use cookbook explanations, but rather interpret aspects the way they are actually being expressed in any given context. Because the symbolism for each planet is extensive, I will not list every possible mode of expression, but instead confine myself to pertinent descriptions. I give the position of Chiron in the chart, but generally ignore it unless it is prominent (angular or casting a close aspect). I delineate the asteroid simply: the energy is either wounding or healing.

In forecasting, I use secondary progressions, transits, and solar eclipses as they impact the natal chart. These are shown as a triwheel, with the natal chart on the inner wheel, secondary progressions on the middle wheel, and transits on the outer wheel. In general, planetary transits activate the natal chart, bringing about an event promised by the nativity. If an indication is not present in the natal chart, no transit can bring it about. An exception to this is planets transiting the angles, which acquire energy and precipitate events in accordance with the nature of the planet and the angle. In secondary progressions (hereafter abbreviated progressions), planets which are not in natal aspect, can come together temporarily (or longer if the outer planets are involved), and introduce new energy into the chart. For the eclipses, I note the lord and watch that planet's activity natally, progressed, and by transit at the time of an event. I pay extra attention to planets at the cardinal (Aries) points, which have an outlet to the world at large, and reach an audience typically broader than expected or usual.

I won't enumerate every aspect, but rather those that seem related to an event. Often at one time many things are transpiring in a person's life as reflected by transits and secondary progressions, but not all are relevant to the discussion. For the most part, I've limited myself to three or four notable events for any given personality. Not to be morbid, if there is a death chart, I'll look at it (an 8th house Sun can't help it).

Due to the non-tangible nature of south nodal energy, the observable influence from an outside perspective is frequently that of loss. The internal inner world is personal, and enlightened experiences are usually private (with the exception of Carl Jung). While the delineation of the South Node energy may seem to emphasize loss and weakness, there may be wondrous inner experiences that are not outwardly evident and go unremarked.

For rulership, I use the new generational planets: Uranus, Neptune, and Pluto. Although traditional astrologers would disagree (vehemently) with this, the new rulers work. In this study, I looked at both the old rulers and the new, and the new were at least as accurate as the old. In the text, for simplicity, I only describe the activity of the new rulers (in practice, I use both).

My rationale for using modern rulership is that any science evolves as new information is acquired, and to ignore new information because the ancients did not have it or use it, seems to me to deny progress. The recent seven year long mutual reception of Uranus (explosions, revolutions, computer technology, innovation, freedom) and Neptune (expansion, collective consciousness, sharing without boundaries or borders, music, movies, and graphics) coincided with the explosive expansion of the World Wide Web and a sharing of information on a global scale that neither planet on its own could accurately describe. With these two planets in each other's signs, they synergistically helped each other to exponential effect.

In addition, while it is true the outer planets move slowly, Uranus is hardly a generational planet (it spends 7 years in a sign). Jupiter (1 year/ sign) moves at a speed two-and-a-half times that of Saturn (2 ½ years/sign); Saturn moves at a speed of two-

and-a-half times Uranus (7 years/ sign); Uranus moves at a speed double that of Neptune (14 years/sign) and triple that of Pluto (21 years/sign); making their relative speeds equivalent. Thus, an outer planet may move slower, but not disproportionately so. Finally, while the Table of Dignities may be thousands of years old, in the sixties, Ivy Goldstein-Jacobson modified it to include the outer planets. I do not go that far, and in horary still use the traditional rulerships and Ptolemy's Table of Dignities.

I pay attention to dispositors. Any planet is mentored by its dispositor, and looks to it for guidance on how to behave and which interests to pursue. Dispositors add richness and detail to a planet's expression. As Carl Payne Tobey pointed out, there are twelve different possible Aries Suns, depending on the sign of Mars, the dispositor of the Sun. The same is true for the nodes. When the North Node is in Gemini, there are twelve different ways the nodal energy can be expressed, as shown by the sign of Mercury. The nodal energy of Gemini is expressed differently when Mercury is in Aries as opposed to when Mercury is in Pisces, or any other sign.

For ease of communication, I write as if the planets are bringing things about, but this is not the case. As I see it, the archetypal energy is stepped-down and expressed through various layers of reality. The energy assumes different physical form, but all of these forms reflect the energy of the underlying original. For example, an archetype may express as a Greek god, planet, rock, gem, country, plant, animal, and related emotions, activities, desires, drives, etc. When the archetype is stimulated, all of its multiple forms are simultaneously expressed. In this manner, a planetary aspect and an event may simultaneously occur, but one does not cause the other.

Finally, I envision the nodes as passageways, between the manifest and the unmanifest, the physical world and the otherworld, the mortal and the immortal, the mundane and the miraculous. They mark the points of intersection where the 'North' and 'South' worlds collide—and real magic happens.

Summary of Nodal Delineation

The energy of a node is channeled through its ruler, and planets that conjunct the node or the bendings.

North Node energy is related to: ego development, manifestation, output, production, achievement, accomplishment, ease of expression, maturity, wisdom, power, knowingness and innate understanding of the physical world.

The North Node ruler is a driver of the chart and directs the energy of the North Node into practical expression in the physical world. A planet conjunct the North Node has power that translates into output and manifestation in the physical world. A planet at the North Bending is similar only its expression is exaggerated.

South Node energy is: physically weak, naïve, uncivilized, vulnerable, inexperienced, immature, awkward, ignorant, clumsy and artless. There may also be deficiency, shortage, or absence. There is a lack of understanding of how the physical world works. However, the energy is also intuitive, spiritual, enlightened, and willing to sacrifice and be of service. It can be used inwardly for self-growth, and outwardly to assist others, or to produce a 'great work.'

The South Node Ruler is initially associated with loss or weakness. It channels otherworld energy that is useful spiritually and can be expressed in service in the physical world. A planet conjunct the South Node is weakened and can cause problems in the manifest world, but has spiritual power and is best used for the greater good. A planet at the South Bending is similar only its expression is exaggerated.

A planet sextile, trine, or parallel (in either declination or latitude) the nodes or nodal rulers, receives a boost in energy that excites the planet. Planets quincunx the nodes acquire energy that can exacerbate a situation that has no resolution.

Knowledge of what you love somehow comes to you; you don't have to read nor analyze nor study. If you love a thing enough, knowledge of it seeps into you …

—Jessamyn West

Chapter 4

Legalizing Astrology

Evangeline Adams

Working at the turn of the 20th century when astrology was considered fortune-telling, Evangeline Adams elevated the practice of astrology to a science. Her family, distantly related to two presidents (John Adams and John Quincy Adams), was against astrology, believing it to be heathenism. According to her, "Sometimes, as I look back, I smile to think how much easier it was to overcome the persecution of the law than the persecution of my own family. Naturally, I regarded the legalization of astrology as the finest thing an Adams had done since the signing of the Declaration of Independence. But the Adamses didn't think so! In fact, from the very beginning, they opposed my connection with astrology by every means within their power."

Nonetheless, after studying for ten years and recognizing auspicious progressions, Evangeline moved to New York and started her practice. On the day she moved, she gave a reading for her new landlord and predicted calamity. The next day his hotel burned to the ground and she made headlines.

During the course of her career, she counseled over one hundred thousand clients, collaborated with Aleister Crowley, and read for Edgar Cayce, Joseph Campbell, and J.P. Morgan. She predicted the future of countries, monarchies, economies, and presidential elections. In forecasting she used horary, progressions, and transits to the natal chart (without the insight of Pluto, which had not been discovered). She was arrested for doing astrology and went to trial. She admitted using palmistry in astrology readings, but claimed she stayed true to her 'science' and read the indications of the planets, "never claiming to know the future nor inform with certitude what would or would not come to pass." She was exonerated and brought legitimacy to the practice of astrology in the U.S.

While many today consider her clairvoyant and psychic, Evangeline believed she adhered to strict astrological rules. In a brochure she sold for ten cents she wrote, "The lesson of astrology is to teach you nature's intention as indicated by the planets; to deviate from it tends to failure, to know it gives power, to pursue it success." She strove to send her clients off with hope, and to never leave them "depressed or discouraged ... for inspiration to others is, in my philosophy, the soul of astrology."

It was her whole life, and according to Aleister Crowley, "She talks astrology day and night. She dreams of it. She sets a horoscope for her vast family of cats and dogs, and is scared out of her life when some planet threatens her horoscope." When she died at the age of sixty-four, she had studied astrology for nearly forty-five years and had been a professional astrologer for thirty-five years.

Nativity

Evangeline has a 12th house Aquarian Sun, Pisces rising, and a Pisces stellium consisting of Mercury (in detriment), Jupiter (dignified former ruler), and Venus (exalted and conjunct the Ascendant and Chiron) (Chart 1). She was born three hours after a lunar eclipse at 18°57' Leo. The Sun is in the sign of astrology and rules the 6th house of daily work, which for her was astrology. Placed in the 12th, she had psychic ability, which she must have used in her readings whether she knew it or not (the 12th house of what is hidden from us). The Sun is opposite the Moon, which gives difficulty in reconciling the ego's drive with emotional needs. With the Moon in Leo, there is a desire for the limelight. While the Sun in the 12th prefers to remain behind the scene, the Moon in Leo

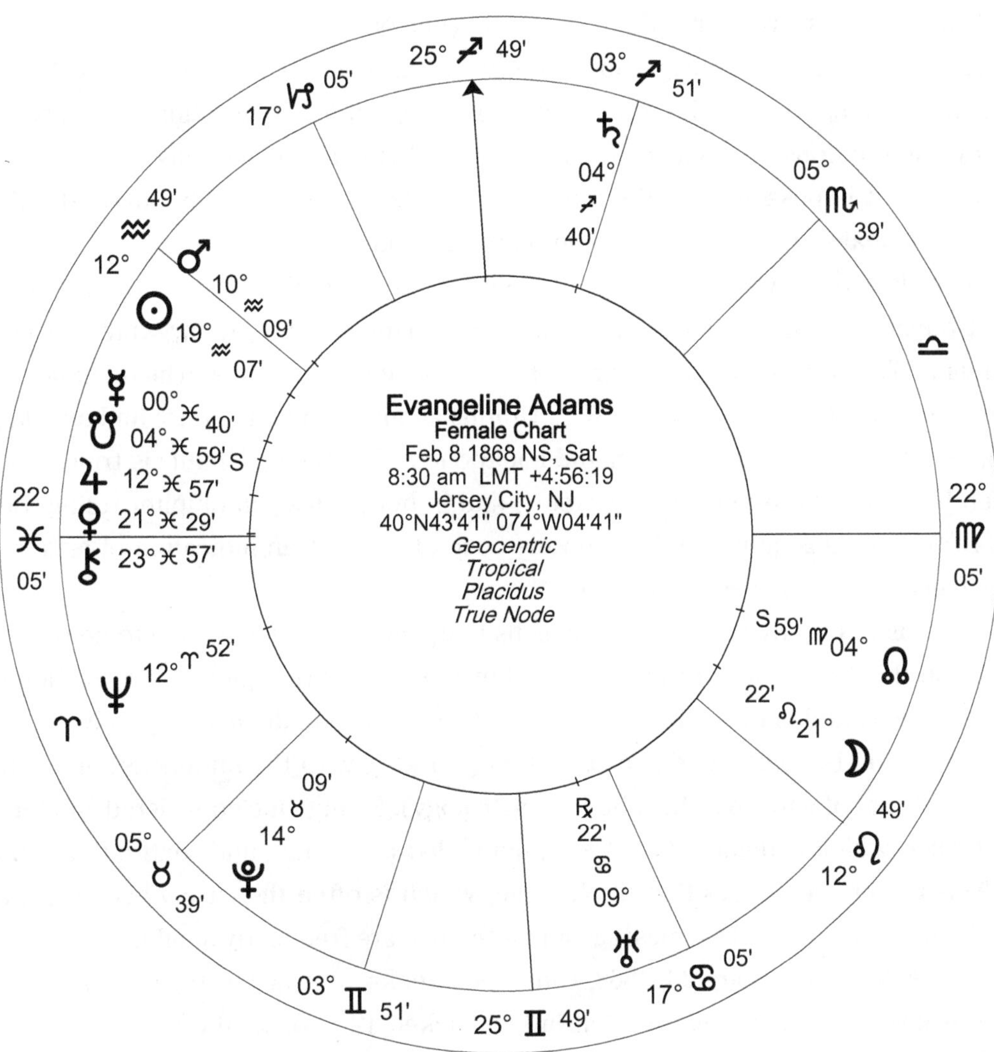

Chart 1:

Evangeline Adams Nativity

needs appreciation. With the Moon in the 6th (her practice) trine the Midheaven, she found the exposure and recognition she craved through her profession. The Moon is quincunx Venus, which rules the 2nd and intercepted 7th, suggesting difficulty with money and relationships. Since she made a good living and eventually married (albeit late in life), it is possible that the money she made and the man she married did not bring emotional satisfaction or meet her expectations.

There is a three-way relationship through dispositorship between the luminaries and Uranus: Uranus disposits the Sun, which disposits the Moon, which disposits Uranus … The remaining planets are in turn disposited by Uranus, which explains the dominance of astrology in her life. With Uranus angular in the 4th house and angular by sign, astrology was the foundation and backbone of her being. Uranus is trine Jupiter, which brought luck, especially in lawsuits and in her profession (Jupiter ruling the 9th and 10th). Uranus is quincunx Mars on the cusp of the 12th, an indication of aggressive hidden enemies she never saw coming.

Pisces is rising, giving compassion, sensitivity, and a genuine desire to help others. Venus on the Ascendant brought charm, but not beauty (conjunct Chiron). Neptune rules the chart and is in the 1st in Aries, which suggests she did act on psychic impressions. Neptune is sextile its dispositor Mars (working with the numinous) and square Uranus (denial of using psychic ability in astrology). Evangeline considered Jupiter her chart ruler, which is dignified in Pisces, domiciled in the 12th, and sextile Pluto in the 2nd. This placement echoes that of Neptune, which is often the case when comparing the old and new rulers: their message and influence are frequently similar.

The PNSE on February 23, 1868, came two weeks after her birth, and was a south nodal eclipse at 4°17' Pisces that fell in her packed 12th house, the house that would undergo expansion. The eclipse was conjunct her natal South Node (channel of non-ordinary otherworld energy), activating it for a lifetime. She had stationary nodes, which would turn direct in twenty-one hours. As mentioned, the speed of the nodal axis slows as an eclipse approaches. People born near an eclipse have near stationary nodes that progress little over a lifetime. In Evangeline's case, her nodes stayed in the same degree for most of her life.

The South Node is ruled by Neptune, which is also the chart ruler. Through its association with south nodal energy, there is loss related to Neptune. She was born into an established family who neither approved of nor accepted the psychic realm. As a result, numinous reality was lost to her early in life. Astrologically, Neptune is weak by sign (in the sign adjacent its own) and trapped through interception (hampering expression despite angularity). Neptune's outlet is through its ruler, Mars in Aquarius, and she eventually used Neptune in service, inspiring clients through astrology.

The North Node is ruled by Mercury, suggesting a gain through Mercury and Mercury's houses (3rd, 4th, and 7th). She had many clients (one hundred thousand, seriously?) and she was an effective communicator. She wrote compelling astrology books and gave popular radio broadcasts. She knew how to promote herself and made much of her successes and downplayed her failures. She became famous because she was frequently in the news.

However, Mercury is harmed by its association (wide conjunction) with the South Node. In addition, Mercury in Pisces is debilitated, both in detriment and fall (in her case, the North Node ruler is in worse condition than the South Node ruler). She had open enemies (7th house) who fought against her in court (Mercury square Saturn on the cusp of the 9th). She was careless in chart erection, which she did by hand, sketching out the chart as the client sat across from her and waited. She had difficulty at home (4th house) in her family of origin due to her spiritual inclinations. She also used palmistry in her readings (using the hand to channel information from the other side). Conjunct the South Node, Mercury easily received information from the otherworld, which as the ruler of the North Node, was expressed outwardly. According to Karen Christino in *What Evangeline Adams Knew*, with Mercury so weak, Evangeline was confident she would triumph over her enemies.

Saturn in Sagittarius on the cusp of the 9th is concerned with higher education, law, and being recognized as a learned authority. Saturn's placement is mixed. Saturn is without dignity, makes no close major planetary aspects, is in a cadent house, and rules a cadent house. Yet, it is the most elevated planet in the chart, in its own hemisphere, and the handle of a bucket, all of which increase its potential to act. However, Saturn, the planet of business, is at the North Bending, and in a position to elicit maximum output in the manifest realm. She was a savvy and spectacular businesswoman, adept at professional self-promotion. She also proved her business was legitimate in the eyes of the law.

Setting Up Shop

Evangeline was thirty-one when she moved to New York and opened her practice. There were two north nodal solar eclipses prior to her move. The first was on December 13, 1898, at 21°32' Sagittarius, with Jupiter (long distance move) serving as lord 1; and the second was on January 11, 1899, at 21°33' Capricorn, with Saturn (career) as lord 2.

She moved during a mundane opposition between Saturn and Neptune (a coming out of the numinous into physical reality) that fell across her MC/IC axis and made the aspect personal (Chart 2). When she moved, transiting Saturn (lord 2) was conjunct the Midheaven and the 1st solar eclipse point, and transiting Neptune was conjunct the IC (answering a professional calling despite family opposition). With the progressed Sun conjunct progressed Jupiter (lord 1) and natal Venus at the natal Ascendant, she recognized luck (Venus–Jupiter) when she saw it and struck out on her own to fulfill her life purpose (Sun). However, with the transiting Saturn–Neptune opposition forming a t-square with progressed Sun–Jupiter and natal Venus, there was resistance and it would not be easy going.

Transiting Mars was opposite the 2nd solar eclipse point, conjunct the progressed IC, and trine progressed Sun, Jupiter (lord 1) and natal Venus–Ascendant, when she simultaneously moved and correctly predicted a fire at her new residence/office, which brought much helpful publicity at the start of her new career. Transiting Jupiter (lord 1) was trine natal Uranus, repeating the natal trine, signaling that the move and her astrology business would ultimately prove successful.

There was a double-whammy —a situation when an aspect is repeated, which serves to double its power, and indicates a manifest event. Transiting Uranus was at the North Bending of the natal nodes (conjunct progressed Saturn), while the transiting South Node was widely conjunct progressed Uranus. The symbolism expressed as an astrology practice and astrology given in service. The transiting South Node was also parallel natal Uranus, forming a triple-whammy, and reinforcing the emphasis on Uranus. In addition, progressed Mars was in partile conjunction with the progressed South Node, describing personal action that serves others. She moved at a time of intense south nodal activity, which suggests she either ignored the nodes or did not view the South Node as malefic.

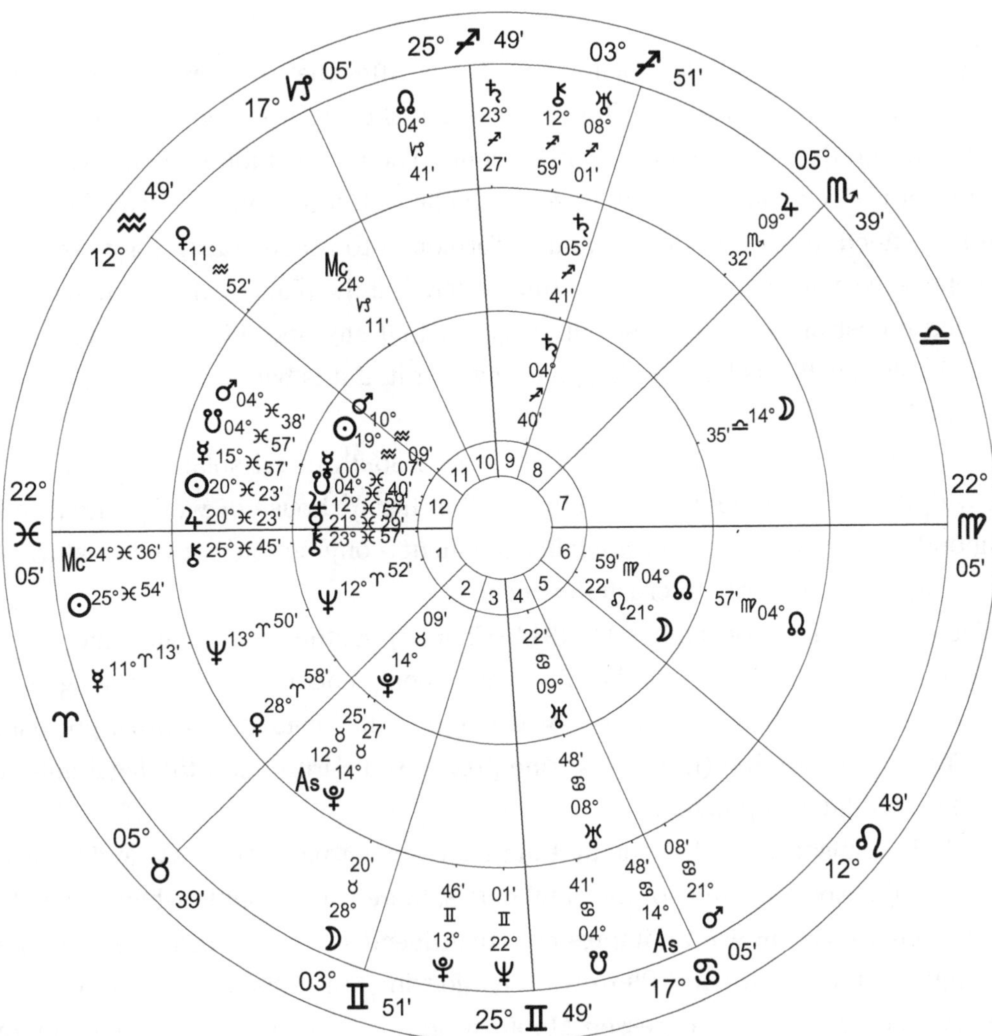

Chart 2:

Evangeline Starts Practice, March 16, 1899, New York, NY, noon

Trial

Evangeline was arrested twice for fortune-telling. After the first arrest on January 12, 1911, the charges were dropped. Three years later, she was arrested again in an undercover sting and this time the case went to court. The prosecution had one witness, an undercover policewoman who had posed as a client. If found guilty, Evangeline could have been fined, thrown in prison, and/or forbidden to practice astrology ever again. Her defense was that she was not a fortune-teller, that the planets didn't tell the future, and "that no astrologer can conscientiously say that any one thing will happen … In fact, I simply say, this is likely to be, guard against it, if it is bad, if it is good, make the most of it."

In the summer before her arrest, there was a south nodal solar eclipse at 27°35' Leo, with the Sun as the lord. The eclipse fell in her 6th house of work (threat to her livelihood), and was sextile an applying mundane conjunction between Saturn and Pluto (attempt of authority to crush the occult).

The trial began on December 11, 1914 (Chart 3). At the time, Evangeline had just finished a nodal reversal, a period of life when people encounter life-changing events. She went to court. Transiting Jupiter was conjunct her natal Sun (lord), portending luck. The progressed Sun (lord) was trine progressed Saturn, and the legal authority (judge) looked kindly upon her.

With the transiting North Node in Aquarius conjunct natal Mercury, and transiting Mercury at the North Bending of the natal nodes, there was a double-whammy; and the widely publicized event was an impressive advertisement for her business. The transiting conjunction of Saturn and Pluto was sextile/trine the transiting nodes, trine natal Mercury, and sextile the progressed Moon, which bode well for a positive outcome both for astrology and her practice. Transiting Uranus was conjunct the progressed Midheaven and natal Mars, and she was fighting for astrology and the right to practice her profession, and she won. In the eyes of the law she differentiated astrology from fortune-telling. The trial legitimized astrology and heightened her standing as an astrologer. The judge was impressed and said, "Adams raises astrology to the dignity of an exact science."

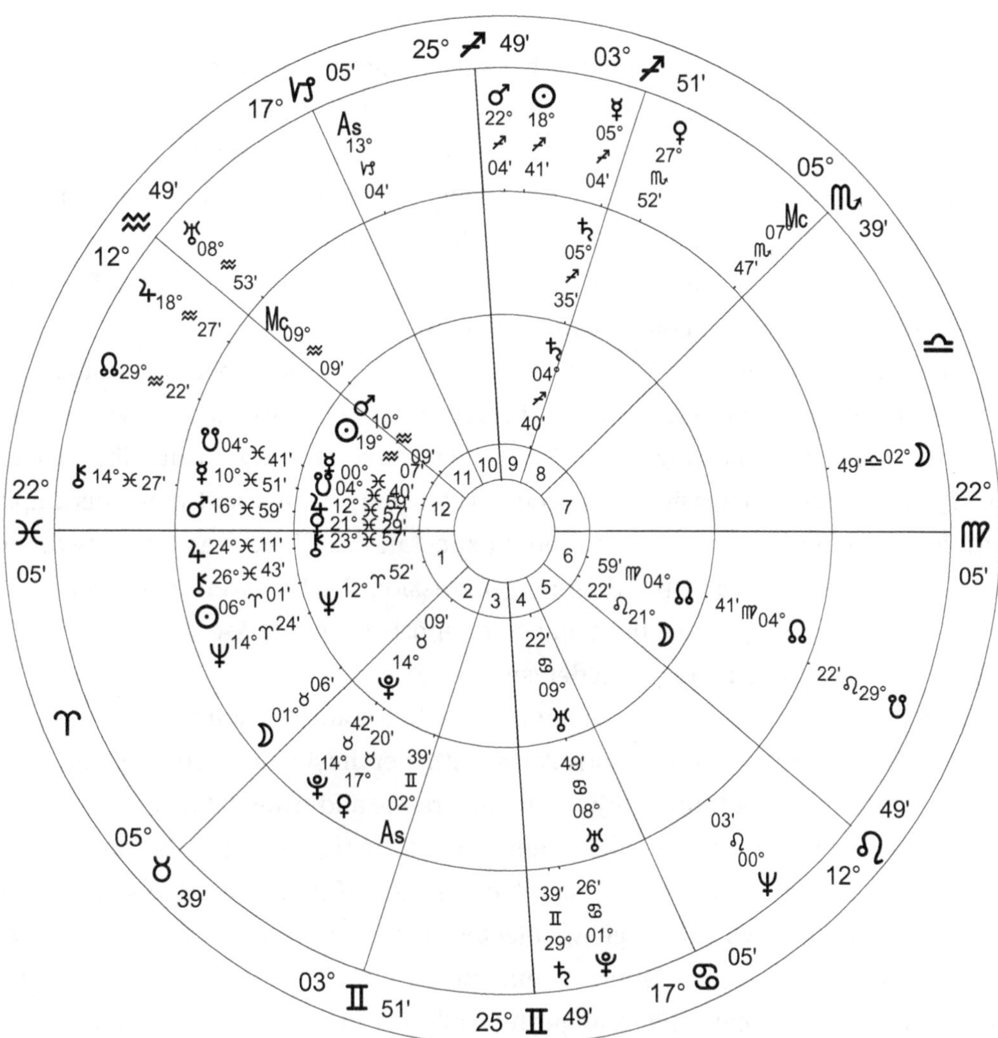

Chart 3:

Evangeline's Trial, Dec. 11, 1914, New York, NY, 9:00 a.m. EST

Marriage

Evangeline was fifty-two when she met her husband-to-be. According to Karen Christino, he was a 'disagreeable man' but helpful in business. With his aid, Evangeline turned her practice into a 'vast astrological enterprise,' reaching many through books and radio broadcasts. The south nodal solar eclipse before the wedding was on March 17, 1923, at 25°54' Pisces, making Neptune (delusions or dreams coming true) the lord. The eclipse fell in her 1st house conjunct progressed Jupiter, the planet Evangeline considered the strongest and most beneficial in her chart.

At the time of her marriage (Chart 4), the transiting South Node was conjunct the natal Ascendant and Venus (giving herself up for love). Progressed Mars was conjunct natal Chiron and the transiting South Node, suggestive of loss or wounding from the man. By secondary progression, the Moon was square Venus and quincunx Jupiter, describing a relationship that fails to meet expectations. There was a triple-whammy between Neptune (lord) and the Sun: by progression the two were conjunct, and by transit, Neptune was opposite the natal Sun, and trine progressed Sun–Neptune, an indication of heightened fantasy and delusion.

Transiting Jupiter was opposite natal Pluto, while transiting Saturn was inconjunct natal Pluto, suggestive of power struggles with her husband regarding her career. However, with transiting Pluto conjunct natal Uranus and trine natal Jupiter, the marriage was beneficial to her practice. She seemed to marry with this in mind. (For an excellent discussion on the wedding election, see Karen Christino's book *What Evangeline Adams Knew.*) Evangeline elected to marry on a day when there was a transiting conjunction of the Moon, Venus, and Uranus. These were conjunct natal Jupiter and trine transiting Jupiter, auguring well for astrology, home life and finances. However, the transiting Moon was in an applying yod, and quincunx transiting Saturn and inconjunct transiting Neptune, suggesting frustration at work and dreams that don't meet expectations. Transiting Mars was conjunct progressed Venus, describing a coming together of the opposites, but this aspect was separating, and separating from a sextile with progressed Jupiter, and a square from the progressed Moon, suggestive of unheeded last minute doubts. Transiting Saturn was moving through her 7th house of marriage, and opposite progressed Sun–Neptune and transiting Chiron, suggestive of a wound, and friends (Saturn ruling the 11th) against the marriage.

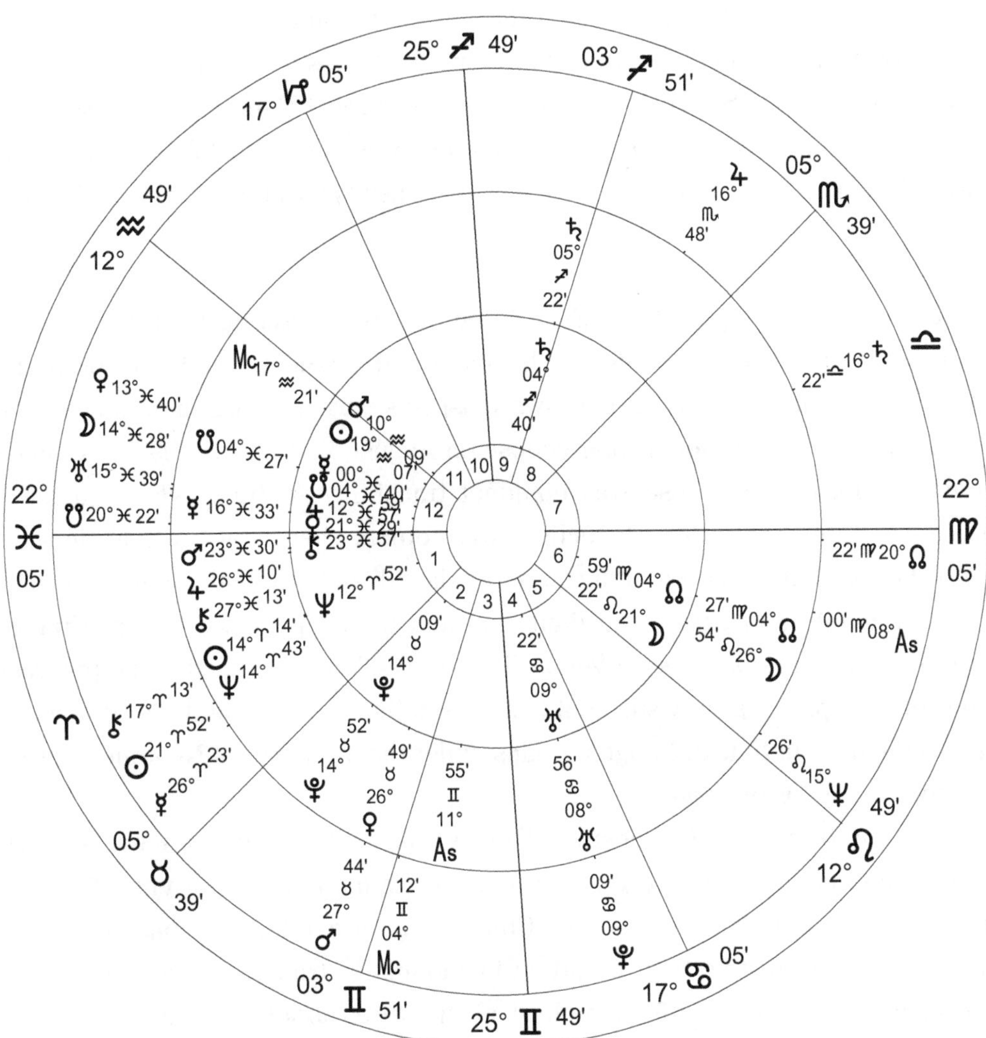

Chart 4:

Evangeline's Wedding, April 12, 1923, New York, NY, 2.45 p.m. EST

In declination, transiting Saturn and the transiting South Node were contraparallel (sacrifice for the profession). The transiting North Node was parallel natal Neptune (delusion), and the transiting South Node was parallel progressed Mars (either a weak man, or one who would serve her work). Transiting Venus was parallel natal Jupiter, an aspect that would be fixed by the marriage, indicative of monetary success through business.

Death

Five days after suffering a stroke, Evangeline died of a cerebral hemorrhage on November 10, 1932 (Chart 5). While her husband and a student said she foretold her death, others maintain she saw no untoward aspects during the last autumn of her life. There was a south nodal (loss) solar eclipse on August 31, 1932 at 8°09' Virgo, making Mercury the lord. The eclipse was conjunct transiting Neptune, which carries the significance of the chart ruler. The eclipse was conjunct her natal North Node and fell in her 6th house of illness, portending a crisis in health and physical vitality. The eclipse was square natal Saturn (physical limitation and hardship), sextile natal Uranus (a sudden event), square progressed Venus (loss of well-being), and trine the progressed Moon (hope misplaced). How she could have seen these aspects and not been worried stretches the imagination, although perhaps under the influence of Neptune, there was denial and a hope for the best.

On the day of her death, transiting Uranus was sextile/trine the natal Sun–Moon opposition and conjunct the progressed Sun, suggesting a sudden event affecting the heart. There was a progressed Mercury, Chiron, Jupiter conjunction that formed a yod with a sextile to transiting Saturn and an inconjunct to transiting Mars, describing a major blood-related wound affecting physical structures about which nothing could be done. The transiting South Node was conjunct transiting Jupiter, and opposite natal Jupiter–transiting North Node, forming a double-whammy, which in this instance was related to a loss of health (transiting Jupiter in the 6th), hospitalization (activation of natal Jupiter in the 12th), and the manifestation of a long journey (ruled by Jupiter, which also rules the 9th).

Soon-to-be discovered transiting Pluto (ruling the 8th) was trine the natal Ascendant, square the progressed Sun, and widely inconjunct the natal Sun. In addition, the

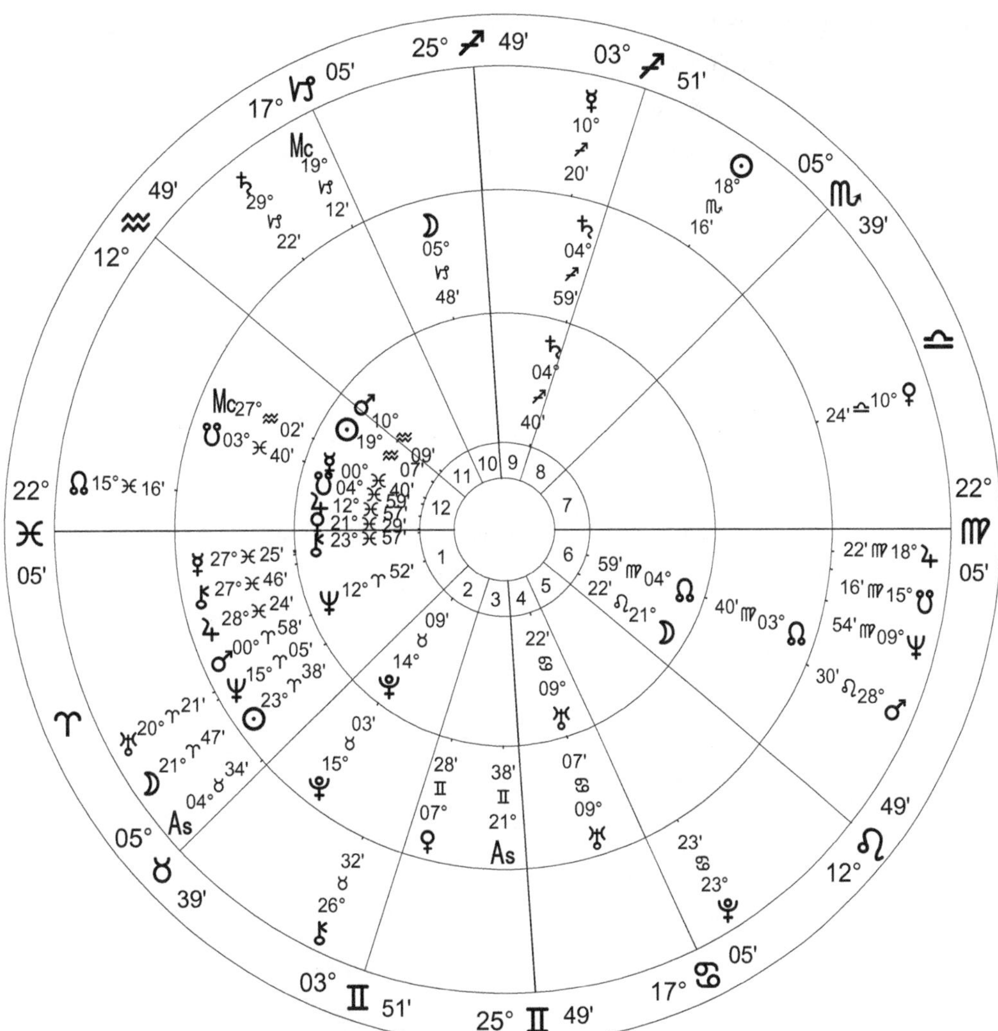

Chart 5:

Evangeline's Death, November 10, 1932, New York, NY, 4:00 p.m. EST

transiting Sun was opposite progressed Pluto, forming a triple-whammy, giving multiple indications of death (which she would not have seen). The trigger for the event was transiting Mercury (lord) square the eclipse point and transiting Neptune, symbolizing dissolution and the grave (Mercury ruling the 4th and the end of the matter).

We're in trouble because we don't recognize that the god's energies are our own energies. We don't understand that the energies personified in the god are the very energies of our own lives. We don't realize that the gods are not out there somewhere. They live in us all. They are the energies of life itself.

—Joseph Campbell

Chapter 5
Dabbling in Spookery
Carl Jung

C.G. (pronounced Say-Gay) Jung was a medical doctor, psychiatrist, and depth psychologist. The son of a poor pastor and a fey housewife, he grew up in the countryside close to nature, and had a rich and vivid imagination. He said he was born as if knowing that dreams were important. As a boy he was aware that he had two personalities whom he named Number 1 and Number 2. He wrote in his autobiography *Memories, Dreams, Reflections* that "No. 1 was the son of my parents who went to school and was less intelligent, attentive, hard-working, decent and clean than many other boys. The other (No. 2) was grownup – old, in fact – skeptical, mistrustful, remote from the world of [people], but close to nature, the earth, the sun, the moon, the weather, all living creatures, and above all close to the night, to dreams, and to whatever 'God' worked directly in him.... In my life No. 2 has been of prime importance, and I have always tried to make room for anything that wanted to come to me from within."

Jung recalled a dream where he was in dense fog, cupping a candle, and being pursued by a 'gigantic black figure.' He knew whatever happened, he had to keep the candle lit. When he awoke, he realized "that this little light was my consciousness, the only light I have. My own understanding is the sole treasure I possess, and the greatest. Though infinitely small and fragile in comparison with the powers of darkness, it is still a light, my only light." The dream told him "that No. 1 was the bearer of light and ... in the role of No.1 [he] had to go forward—into study, moneymaking, responsibilities, entanglements, confusions, errors, submissions, defeats...."

He went to medical school, became besotted with Emma (an heiress he later married) and began working at an asylum, studying the new field of the unconscious. He conducted word association experiments in order to compare the responses between normal people and neurotics. His initial idea was to conduct statistical tests, but he was averse to math and quickly became interested in individual responses as he tried to 'catch the intruder in the mind' and prove the validity of the unconscious.

Freud was the leader in the field, and the two met in 1907 and began to collaborate. Freud believed that sex was the ultimate motivation of behavior and the cause of mental neurosis, but he was reluctant to present his views openly in public, and wanted Jung to do it for him. From the beginning Jung did not accept Freud's view of the supremacy of sexual motivation: "Above all, Freud's attitude toward the spirit seemed ... highly questionable... [Any] expression of spirituality [he saw as] repressed sexuality."

By 1911, Jung had discovered astrology and was using it for insight into the dementia of his patients. In a letter to Freud he wrote, "My evenings are taken up very largely with astrology. I make horoscopic calculations in order to find a clue to the core of psychological truth. Some remarkable things have turned up which will certainly appear incredible to you. For instance, it appears that the signs of the zodiac are character pictures, in other words libido symbols which depict the typical qualities of the libido at a given moment."

In another letter, he wrote, "I am looking into astrology, which seems indispensable for a proper understanding of mythology. There are strange and wondrous things in these lands of darkness. Please don't worry about my wanderings in these infinitudes. I shall return laden with rich booty for our knowledge of the human psyche. For a while longer I must intoxicate myself on magic perfumes in order to fathom the secrets that lie hidden in the abysses of the unconscious."

Freud was not impressed with Jung's 'dabbling in spookery,' and despite Emma's efforts to smooth out their differences, the two men were growing ever more estranged. They split at the onset of World War 1. As Jung wrote in his autobiography, "After the break with Freud, all my friends and acquaintances dropped away. My book was declared to be rubbish; I was a mystic and that settled the matter… I had known that everything was at stake and that I had to take a stand for my conviction. I realized that the chapter 'The Sacrifice' meant my own sacrifice."

Jung was sidelined and black-balled by the psychological community. He had opened a private practice in his home and was seeing patients, but by the autumn of 1913, he was 'menaced by psychosis,' besieged by visions and dreams he could not understand. In the *Tao of Jung*, David Rose wrote, "Jung courageously began to live what was to become the core of his psychology; death of the false self and birth of the true self." According to Jung, "he felt as if he had fallen into an immense hole … and the single most important achievement in his life was that he saved [himself] from that hole and didn't drown in it."

Although Jung became suicidal, he considered those years as the "most important time of [his] life—everything else can be derived from it. My whole life consisted of reappraising what had broken free of the unconscious back then and flooded me like a mysterious stream and threatened to destroy me."

Jung began treating himself as if he were his own patient, observing himself, noting his meditations, and keeping a detailed daily diary. He had many visions, conducted numerous inner dialogues, and spent hours in the garden conversing with an imaginary old man of 'simply superior knowledge' who was teaching him and 'almost seemed real.' This old man was No. 2, who "represented a force which was not myself … I held conversations with him, and he said things which I had not consciously thought… He said I treated thoughts as if I generated them myself, but in his view thoughts were like animals in the forest, or people in a room … If you should see people in a room, you would not think that you had made those people, or that you were responsible for them. It was he who taught me psychic objectivity, the reality of the psyche."

In the midst of the break-up with Freud, Emma gave birth to their fifth child. Two weeks later, Jung began his affair with a former patient, twenty-six year old Toni Wolfe. Explaining his adultery, he says, "back then I was in the midst of the anima problem. What could you expect from me? – the anima bit me on the forehead and would not let go."

The marriage became strained. Toni became Jung's professional assistant and Emma was sidelined. Although three times she threatened to end the marriage, Jung always fell sick and she could not leave. Jung was dependent on her money, and although Swiss law would give him the children, Emma did not want to lose them.

When Jung came out of seclusion in 1917, his private practice grew to the point where appointments had to be made a year in advance. He lectured, traveled, and was the only psychoanalyst to rival Freud. Jung founded the Psychological Club in Zurich, which hosted guest speakers and enabled analysts to keep up with current theory. Over the years he met many influential people: Albert Einstein, Hugh Walpole, H.G. Wells, F. Scott Fitzgerald, and James Joyce. He treated Herman Hesse and James Joyce's psychotic daughter.

In 1929, after reading Richard Wilhelm's alchemical text, Jung developed an interest in alchemy, which to him symbolized the evolution of inner growth. In 1931, Jung treated a patient for alcoholism. He saw drinking as a disease of the spirit, and gave the later-formed Alcoholics Anonymous organization, their major key to recovery.

World War II came. Jung turned the front yard of his house into a garden to grow food. He was forced to work as a physician. During this time he was accused of being a Nazi sympathizer, although he said he was on their hit list. After the war he returned to counseling, writing, and traveling.

In 1948, the Jung Institute opened in Zurich, where Jung, Emma, and Toni taught and trained other analysts. By 1950, Jung was cementing his ideas of synchronicity that had interested him for twenty years. He renewed his former interest in astrology, which he considered to work through synchronicity: "Acausal orderedness occurs in an ongoing way in nature, but synchronistic events are acts of creation at specific moments in time." He realized he needed astrological help from people who knew more astrology than he had time to learn, and he recruited four volunteers, one of whom was his daughter Gret.

For three years Jung conducted astrological research. He published the results in *Mysterium Conjunctionis*, even though he knew he would be criticized for the astrology, "which American readers would never take seriously." He considered the book to be "nothing less than a restoration of the original state of the cosmos and the divine unconsciousness of the world …" It was an alchemical text, which outlined three stages of individuation. The first stage entailed becoming conscious of the Shadow: 'the darkness gives birth to light.' In the second stage, the opposites (the male—the highest heaven; and the female—the lowest earth) were united. This led to the third stage, and the connection of the ego to the self, which he called actualization, and was equivalent to spiritual wholeness.

The goal of Jungian analysis is to increase consciousness by becoming aware of the unconscious. To Jung, the psyche was comprised of the conscious and the unconscious. The ego stood at the center of consciousness, while the self stood at the center of the psyche. He thought the unconscious had two parts, which he termed the 'personal' and the 'collective.' The personal unconscious (the Shadow) contained the unwanted and unrecognized parts of the personality that were rejected, and either buried or projected. Part of his therapy involved learning to accept the discarded pieces, so that they were less likely to be acted out inappropriately or projected onto others.

He viewed the collective unconscious as the archetypal realm that was represented in myths and dreams, which could not be understood with reason, but through feelings and symbols. It was also the domain of spirit, of 'God,' but since 'God' was too unscientific a term, Jung called it the collective unconscious. To him, they were one and the same.

Jung's model of the psyche is that of psychological astrologers. The Sun is the ego, the center of consciousness; Pluto is the Shadow, the personal unconscious; Neptune is the collective unconscious; and Uranus is the urge to be true to the inner higher self. The astrological chart as a whole represents the psyche, with the higher self at the center.

In late 1957 at the age of eighty-two, in an effort to describe his inner world, Jung began writing his autobiography. Of the outer world, he thought only two things had happened of great importance: a trip to India and a heart attack. At the end he wrote, "I am satisfied with the course my life has taken… Much might have been different if I myself had been different. But it was as it had to be; for all came about because I am as I am."

Nativity

Jung has a Leo Sun on the 7th house cusp that rules the 7th (Chart 6). He (ego) was interested in partnerships and closely involved with others (wife, clients, and lovers) in one-to-one relationships. The Sun is powerful in Leo but weakened by a square to Neptune (the pair form a duet and make no other aspects). Throughout his life he was swamped by the contents of his unconscious—this was the threat to his light, 'his only light.' He dealt with his unconscious by communicating with it (Neptune on the cusp of the 3rd) and objectifying it to the extent that it became real (Neptune in Taurus). This enabled him to have a relationship with it and ultimately learn from it. Jung was a man whose primary relationship was with himself.

Jung has an exalted 3rd house Moon in Taurus ruling the 6th. The Moon represents the inner world of the emotions, and his work entailed 'talk therapy' as a means to process emotions, bringing them out of the ether and down to earth where they could be examined. With the Moon square Uranus, he experienced many unexpected and earth-shattering personal upsets. His emotional center was frequently thrown off balance to the extent that he became suicidal. Eventually he learned to heal his emotions through verbal communication with his personal unconscious (Moon sextile Mercury ruling the 8th house of the personal unconscious) and through art (Moon in mutual reception with Venus ruling the intercepted 8th). Daily work with the unconscious ultimately brought him peace and well-being (the goal of a Taurus Moon).

Uranus rules the chart, and is sextile/trine the nodes, acquiring an added boost of power. He was an intelligent, innovative thinker who understood and studied astrology—atypical for a scientist. However, given a choice to learn astrology or alchemy, he chose alchemy because he thought it would be less objectionable to mainstream science (conservative Saturn in Aquarius in the 1st). To Jung, the purpose

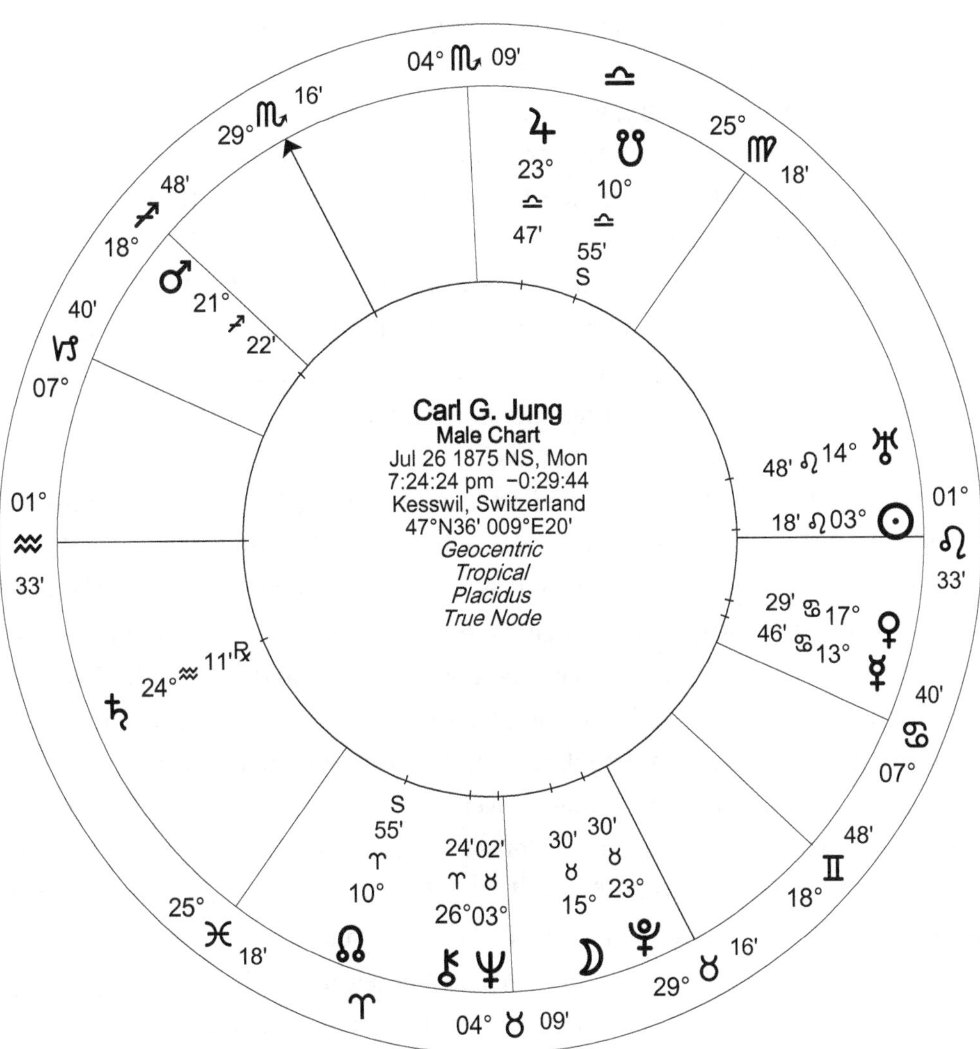

Chart 6:

Carl Jung Nativity

of life was individuation (Uranus in Leo); the work to expose and to integrate unconscious contents in order 'to become what I myself am.' The process is similar to the 'churning of the ocean' in the Hindu eclipse myth, only in Jungian terms, the ocean is the unconscious. Through working with the unconscious, different forms of power are discovered, including the immortal nectar of life—the spiritual awareness that God is within. This is Neptune, the experience of the numinous, distinct from Uranus, the awareness of universal intelligence.

The prenatal north nodal solar eclipse was at 16°03' Aries, and fell in his 2nd house, an arena which would expand during Jung's life. Growing up in poverty, he had a driving need for money, which fueled his enrollment in medical school, and perhaps his enchantment with an heiress. Although his wealth magnified astronomically, money remained a concern over the course of his life.

Jung had stationary nodes that turned retrograde the day before he was born. The North Node (and the PNSE) is ruled by Mars in Sagittarius, and placed in the 11th house of goals, groups, and friends. This was an active and accomplished Mars, and Jung was a medical doctor, professor, university lecturer, scientific publisher, and worldwide traveler. He forged a new paradigm of psychiatry and started the Psychology Club in Zurich, which morphed into Jung Institutes scattered throughout the world. Professionally, he found fame and adulation, and was a renowned psychoanalyst with a lucrative practice. However, Mars was in over-drive sexually and he had a bad reputation as a womanizer, which caused problems in both his marriage and his profession. In declination, Mars was way out-of-bounds (27S53) and beyond the confines of the ecliptic, adding to its extreme and uncontrolled expression.

The South Node is in Libra, ruled by Venus in Cancer in the 6th. Venus is peregrine and without dignity. This weakness is exacerbated since Venus is the South Node ruler. Early on, Venus was related to the loss of robust health (6th house influence), money (signification of Venus), emotional equilibrium (unable to feel happy with himself), and women (he had no 'adventures' before he was married). Eventually, his service was to help others heal troubling emotions through talk therapy (Venus rules the 3rd and intercepted 8th).

At first glance, Mercury's importance is not obvious. It is in a cadent house and casts only two aspects (although one is a sextile to a luminary). Mercury is not angular and it does not rule or aspect an angle. Yet, Mercury and the 8th house of the unconscious that it rules, defined Jung's life. Mercury is dominant because it is at the North Bending of the nodes, in a position of maximum outer productivity. Jung was a prolific writer and psychotherapist. He spent his days discussing feelings (Mercury in Cancer) and unearthing repressed contents for processing.

With Venus the ruler of the South Node, conjunct Mercury at the North Bending, Jung explicitly communicated the personal, private details of his inner world. He not only wrote them down, but he developed a technique of healing based on his otherworld journeys. Venus is also sextile the Moon, and initially he suffered emotionally (untoward influence of the South Node energy). Yet, his participation in the otherworld brought about emotional healing, which he gave away in service to others.

Any aspect involving the North Node ruler is generally expressed outwardly in an obvious and dynamic manner. Here, Mars the North Node ruler is involved in a four-planet configuration, which was a driving force of Jung's life. Mars is sextile Saturn and Jupiter, which trine each other; Mars forms a yod with a sextile to Jupiter and quincunx to Pluto; with Pluto square Saturn. The configuration is related to his psychotic experiences and the healing of his psyche that resulted in individuation. As we will see, this four-planet complex was always highly activated during critical times of his life.

Taking the aspects one at a time, the sextile between Mars and Jupiter in Libra in the 8th reflects a doctor of the unconscious specializing in healing the psyche through one-to-one interactions. With Mars in the sign of Jupiter and sextile it, there were expansive travels, both inward and outward, which were successful and transformative. Jupiter however is in the sign of Mars' detriment, and the help (through the sextile) Mars gave Jupiter was compromised, as Jung's womanizing caused professional problems and harmed his reputation.

Jupiter is trine Saturn, a combination that suggests professional ambition, discipline, and success. Saturn is rising in the 1st house, a testament to his destitute start in life, seriousness, capacity for hard work and professional ambition. In Aquarius, a sign of its dignity, Saturn is forward seeking, but only within the conservative limits of mainstream acceptability. With the ruler of the 12th in the 1st, the unconscious gained expression through him; at first nearly crippling him, and then working with him as he sought to map its landscape and understand the energy of the archetypes. Mars is sextile Saturn, and he was willing to work hard and his hard work paid off. He developed analytical techniques to bring unconscious contents (Saturn rules the 12th) out into the open where they could be processed and integrated into the personality.

Pluto is in Taurus in the 3rd, and rules the 9th house of higher education and study, and the 10th house of the career. He became famous through his study of the unconscious and the methods he developed to communicate with it. In declination, Pluto is parallel the North Node, and acquires additional power through the contact. Jung was confronted by his own neurosis, but when he figured out how to deal with his demons, he was able to help others deal with theirs. Saturn square Pluto is an aspect of destruction. Since Saturn symbolizes structures (the world you build for yourself), the square with Pluto indicates a world that can come crashing down. His own neurosis threatened his survival. With Pluto representing obsession and desire for power, and Saturn representing authority, the square shows power struggles. Jung had to be the boss, to answer to and serve no one but himself. Pluto square Saturn also suggests the long-term trouble he had getting his work on the unconscious accepted by scientific authorities. Yet, Saturn square Pluto also shows determination—he would never give up or give in. He also had powerful hidden enemies (Saturn ruling the 12th) who were working against him and trying to discredit him, exacerbating his psychosis (Freud after their split).

Adolescent Trauma

Jung experienced his first psychosis when he was twelve. After being bullied by a classmate, he fell and banged his head, losing consciousness. When he recovered and was forced to return to school, he had fainting spells. The bullying made him physically ill and prevented him from returning to school. The episode lasted six months, until he overheard his father bemoaning the financial burden of a sick child. Jung recognized he had 'asked' for the neurosis and realized he could think himself well. He did so and returned to school determined to work hard. He never fainted again.

Although the exact date is uncertain, Jung states in his autobiography that the incident happened during early summer, and the transits and progressions are set for July 1, 1887 (Chart 7). Because there is no precise date, the positions of the fast

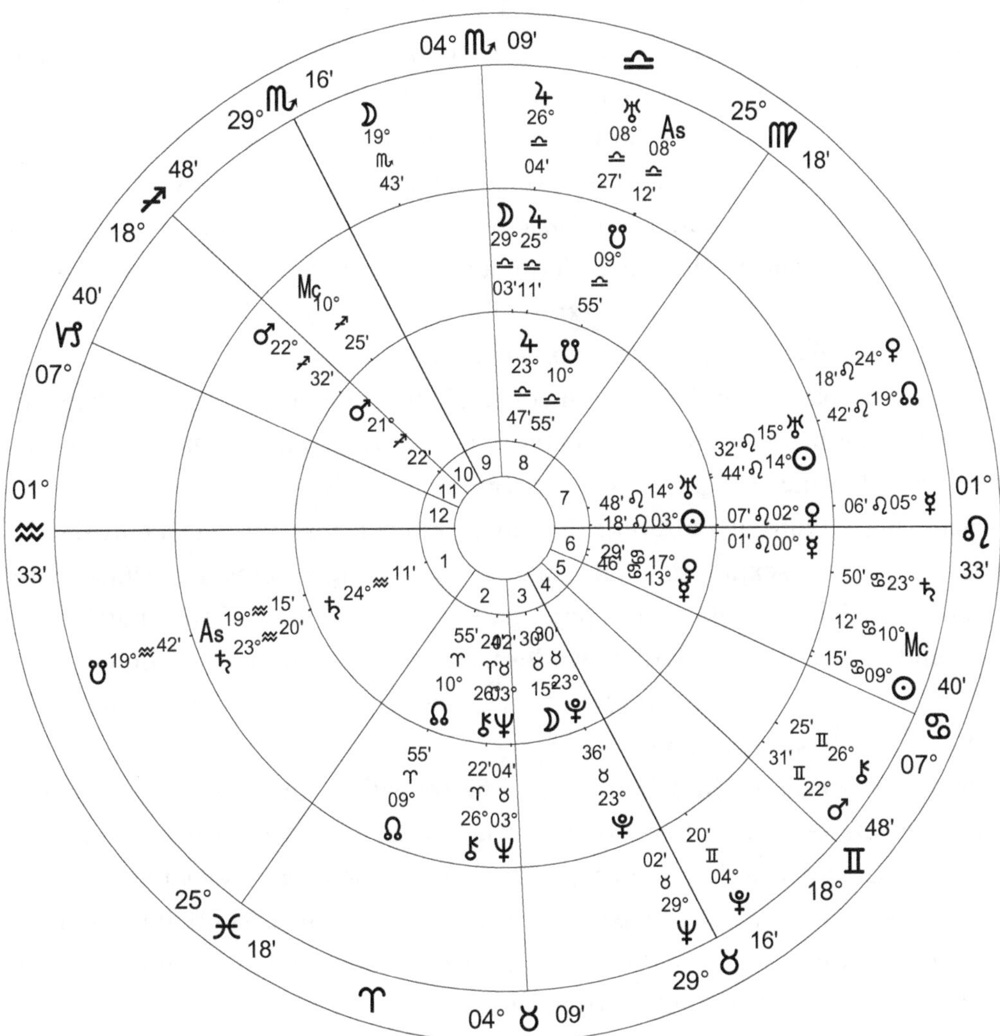

Chart 7:

Jung's Adolescent Trauma: July 1, 1887, Kesswil, Switzerland, noon

moving planets (Sun to Mars) will be ignored. On February 8, 1887, there was a north nodal solar eclipse at 19°22' Leo, with the Sun serving as the lord. The eclipse marked a period of crisis for the ego (consciousness). There was a sudden, upsetting attack involving an open enemy (eclipse in the 7th conjunct the progressed Descendant and widely conjunct progressed Uranus). The transiting North Node coming to the eclipse point likely triggered the event. The eclipse activated a progressed Sun–Uranus conjunction that was square to the natal Moon, and what previously may have been an internal, emotional response, became externalized. According to Jung, "when an inner situation is not made conscious, it appears outside as fate."

The natal four-planet configuration involving Mars, Jupiter, Saturn, and Pluto was activated by numerous factors, an indication this configuration was involved in both generating and healing the eruption of unconscious contents. The transiting nodes were square natal Pluto at the South Bending, bringing loss through neurosis. The transiting nodes were sextile/trine natal Mars, empowering a bully. Transiting Saturn was square natal Jupiter (failure of hope), and formed a double yod with natal Saturn and Mars, and natal Mars and Pluto; powerlessness and a frustrating situation he could do nothing about. Jung responded by becoming mentally ill. He checked out, stayed home, and stopped going to school.

It was a low period for Jung personally. The transiting South Node was conjunct the progressed Ascendant and separating from a conjunction with natal/progressed Saturn, symbolizing defeat for the personality through the loss of social standing. He was humiliated and ashamed. Transiting Uranus was conjunct the natal/progressed South Node, and there was a sudden fall. He was literally suddenly and shockingly pushed down, and he had difficulty getting back up.

In declination, the transiting South Node was parallel natal and progressed Saturn and the progressed Ascendant, indicative of Jung's depression and withdrawal: attending school was too great a burden to bear. The aspect was repeated in latitude, where transiting Saturn was near the ecliptic and contraparallel natal Venus, crushing happiness.

Transiting Neptune was conjunct the IC, and in the inner world, spiritual energy was flowing, giving Jung glimpses of non-ordinary reality on the earth-bound plane. During his six months hiatus from school, he grew close to nature (transiting nodes coming to square the Taurus Moon at the South Bending putting him emotionally in touch with the earth). He had a passion for being alone, delighting in solitude. "Nature seemed to me full of wonders, and I wanted to steep myself in them. Every stone, every plant, every single thing seemed alive and indescribably marvelous." In latitude, the progressed Moon was conjunct Neptune and he saw numinous energy in every day things.

He also came to realize, "that I myself had arranged this whole disgraceful situation. That was why I had never been seriously angry with the schoolmate who pushed me over. I knew that he had been put up to it, so to speak, and that the whole affair was a diabolical plot on my part." This was an extraordinary insight into the power and influence of the personal unconscious (transiting Pluto sextile natal Sun–progressed Venus).

Father's Death

Jung lived at home while attending the University of Basil. Driven by a need for financial security rather than a love of the profession, he enrolled in a program leading to medical school. He was twenty, in his second year of university, when his father got seriously ill and died. This nearly ended Jung's medical career for he was expected to work and support his mother and younger sister as there were no family savings, no pension, and no money for schooling. Fortunately, at Jung's request, a wealthy uncle helped him financially and Jung stayed in school.

Jung's father died on January 28, 1896 (Chart 8). There was a north nodal solar eclipse two weeks later at 24°30' Aquarius that was conjunct natal Saturn (father). The lord of the eclipse was Uranus, which was square the eclipse degree, natal Saturn, and transiting Mercury (ruler 8) on the day of the death.

The transiting North Node was conjunct the progressed Ascendant (the two also parallel in declination) and 'at the time, a bit of manliness and freedom awoke in [him] (empowerment of the projected self).' The transiting nodes were sextile/trine natal Neptune, and soon after his father died, Jung had two similar dreams in which his father had recovered and was coming home. The dreams were so real, Jung woke up feeling guilty for thinking his father had died. For the first time, Jung began thinking about the afterlife.

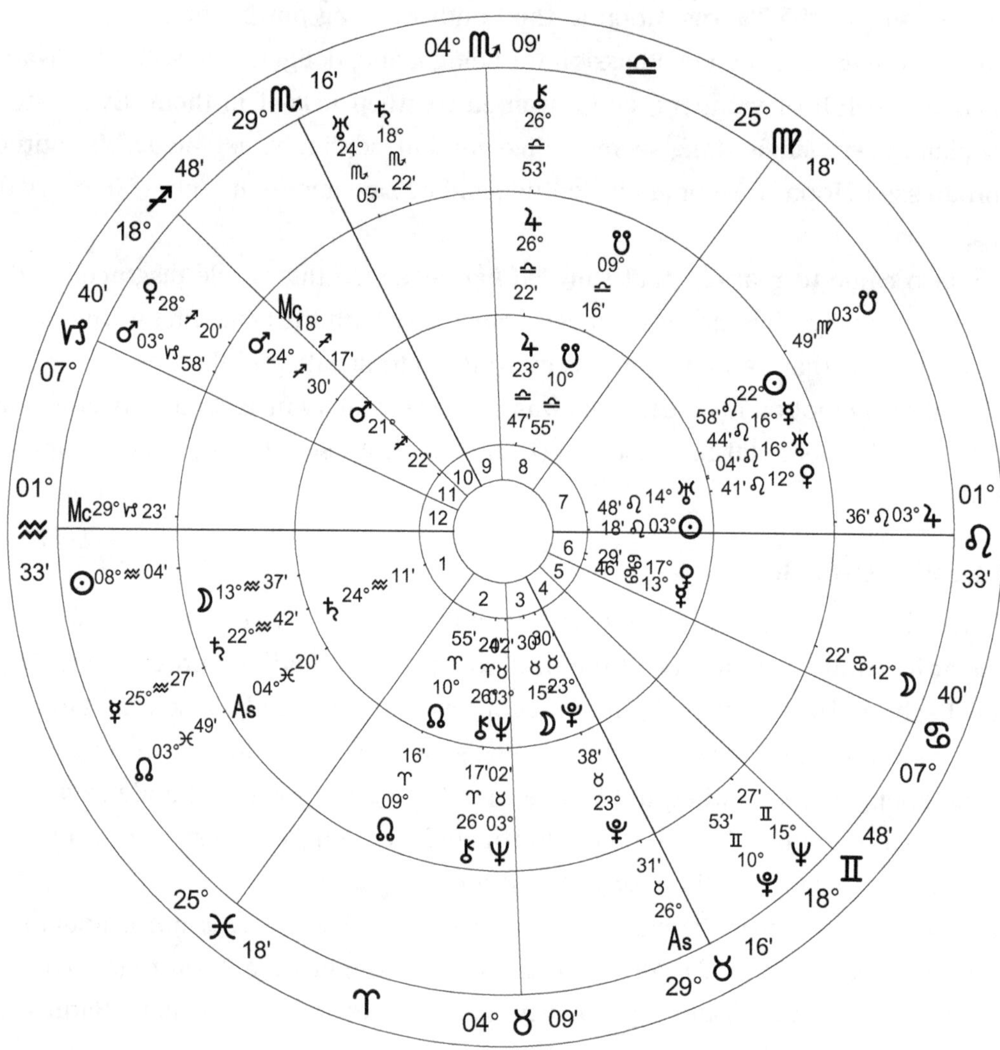

Chart 8:

Jung's Father's Death, January 28, 1896, Kesswil, Switzerland, noon

The progressed Moon was opposite natal Uranus and progressed Venus, which rules the 4th house (the father) and money in general; pointing to trouble with money and a separation for the mother (Moon). Two grand crosses had formed, a signal of how stuck Jung must have felt at the sudden death that brought financial limitation and the burden of responsibility. The progressed Sun was square transiting Uranus, opposite progressed Saturn, and square natal Pluto; and transiting Saturn was square progressed Mercury and Uranus, opposite the natal Moon and widely square the progressed Moon. The Moon and Mercury in the second grand cross represents the mother and younger sister whom Jung was now obliged to support. However, a paternal uncle (Jupiter) loaned Jung money, which enabled him to continue his education (transiting Jupiter conjunct the Descendant and natal Sun).

Insane Asylum

Before and during college, through his mother's side of the family, Jung became involved with the occult and attended séances. The title of his medical dissertation was: *On the Psychology and Pathology of the So-Called Occult Phenomena.* When Jung finished medical school, he met Emma and was smitten with her, but his affections were not reciprocated. She moved to France, while he, to the dismay of many, moved to Zurich and began an internship at the Burgholzli Mental Hospital, specializing in psychiatry, 'the most despicable branch of medicine.' He was twenty-five. Of his early experiences there, he wrote, "… life took on an undivided reality—all intention, consciousness, duty, and responsibility. It was an entry into the monastery of the world, a submission to the vow to believe only in what was probable, average, commonplace, barren of meaning, to renounce everything strange and significant, and reduce anything extraordinary to the banal. Henceforth there were only surfaces that had nothing, only beginnings without continuations, accidents without coherence, knowledge that shrank to ever smaller circles, failures that claimed to be problems, oppressively narrow horizons, and the unending desert of routine."

For six months Jung lived like a recluse, never leaving the hospital. He had no money for entertainment or clothes, and was overworked by the hospital director. In the early days, "he was 'deeply humiliated' to see how Bleuler [the director] and his only other assistant doctor moved so confidently about their duties, while he was all the time 'more and more' baffled and plagued by such 'feelings of inferiority that [he could] not bear to go out of the hospital.'" Jung was sending his whole salary to his mother and had no money to socialize. During this period, he resented his parents "intensely for their poverty and the resulting shame he felt about his lack of experience in life."

Jung began work at the hospital on December 10, 1900 (Chart 9). The previous north nodal solar eclipse on November 22, 1900, at 29°33' Scorpio, was conjunct his natal Midheaven (career, professional visibility). The lord of the eclipse was Pluto, and the six-month activation of the planet would coincide with his growing interest in the personal unconscious—the 'intruder in the mind'. The eclipse was square his progressed Sun, highlighting his insecurity. However, he was undergoing a number of beneficial progressions. The progressed Sun and Mercury were conjunct and sextile progressed Jupiter, describing a time of luck, opportunity, and increased learning. The progressed Moon was trine progressed Uranus, indicating a move, freedom, and independence. The progressed Moon was in a grand trine with natal Mars and progressed Venus, denoting high passion and desire for Emma. But the progressed Moon was square natal Venus, and she didn't want him back. In addition, Jung had money troubles.

When he started work, the transiting North Node was conjunct the natal Midheaven (also parallel in declination, strengthening the interaction) at the solar eclipse point, timing the start of his employment. The nodes were sextile/trine the natal Sun, giving his ego a boost, despite his insecurity regarding his professional competence. Transiting Jupiter was conjunct the progressed Midheaven and natal Mars, activating the natal four-planet configuration related to Jung's work on the personal unconscious.

Transiting Neptune (hospitals, delusions, irrationality) was opposite natal Mars (and transiting Chiron) and in a grand trine with progressed Jupiter and natal Saturn, describing life in an asylum where he was studying mental illness. Transiting Pluto was sextile the progressed Moon and sextile progressed Uranus and Venus, and opposite transiting Uranus, Sun, Jupiter and natal Mars, further activating the natal four-planet configuration, only now with the additional influence of Uranus (insight and scientific

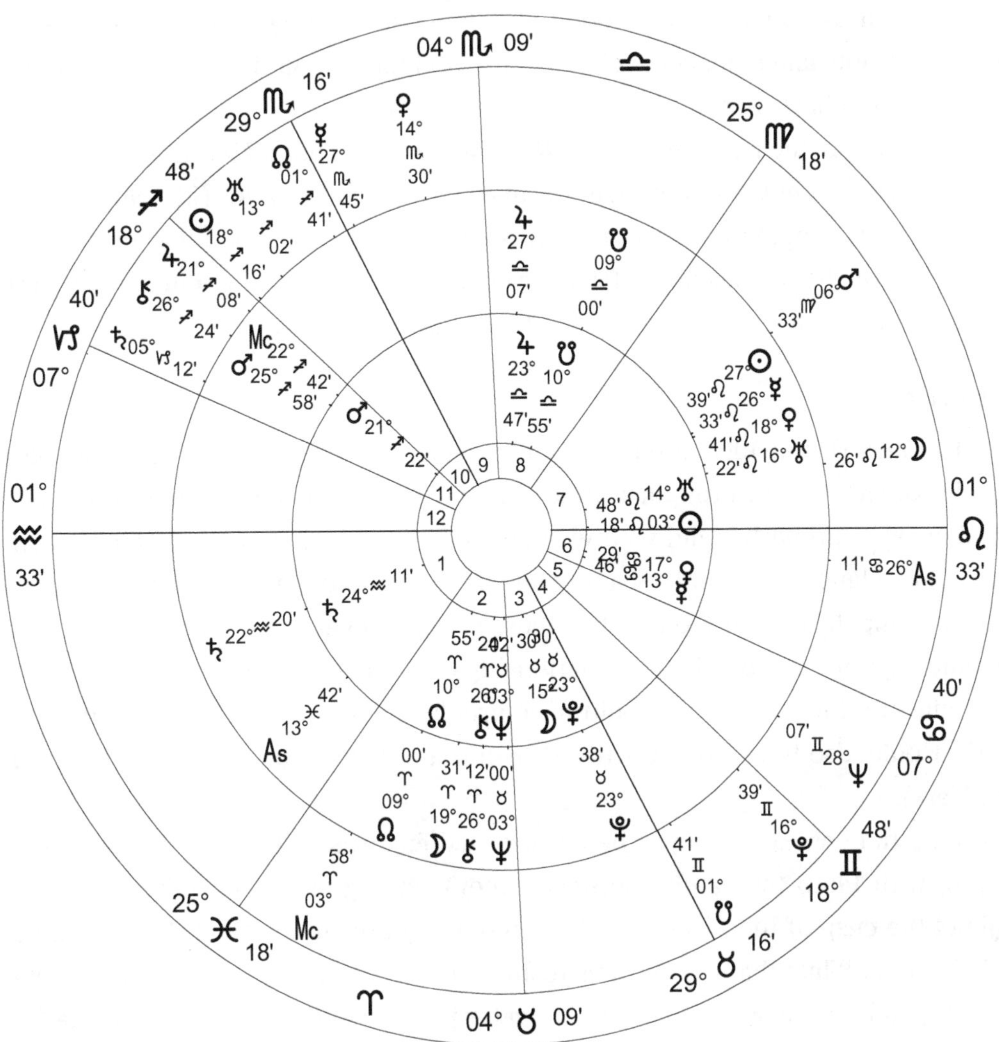

Chart 9:

Jung Starts Work at Asylum: December 10, 1900, Zurich, Switzerland, noon

study), as well as Venus and the Moon (a fondness and feeling for the work). He would grow into his job, and quickly developed a method for pinpointing specific experiences that caused psychic traumas.

In declination, the transiting South Node was parallel natal Mercury, describing his mental inferiority, but also his inspired insights into the psyche (Mercury ruling the 8th). In latitude, progressed Mercury and Neptune were contraparallel, representative of his study of the unconscious. Progressed Moon, Venus, and Jupiter were parallel, symbolizing his feelings for Emma, who was far away.

Marriage

On Valentine's Day in 1903, after a long courtship and an initial refusal, Jung married his heiress. Her wealth brought a practical end to his financial difficulties. Up until then, Jung was 'properly timid with women, he had not had an adventure before, so to speak.' As he later told Freud, as a boy he was 'a victim of sexual assault by a man he once worshipped,' and his feelings had hampered him ever since (natal yod with Pluto, Mars and Jupiter). He found close relationships with men 'downright disgusting' (natal Mars quincunx Pluto), and he would have problems with male friends throughout his life. He would also have trouble with women (natal Moon square Uranus; Venus quincunx Mars).

The north nodal solar eclipse before the wedding was on October 31, 1902, at 6°58' Scorpio, with Pluto (sex and inherited money) serving as the lord. The eclipse was conjunct the cusp of the 9th house of ceremony, square Jung's natal Sun and opposite natal Neptune. While the Sun pertains to Jung (ego), as ruler of the 7th it also symbolizes Emma, and the square to Neptune indicates problems for each. It is possible Emma was not marrying the man of her dreams, and Jung may have been worried about marrying into her upper class family.

On their wedding day (Chart 10), natal Venus was at the South Bending of the transiting nodes. This is often seen during times of marriage and can be interpreted as a sacrifice of self for another out of love. The transiting North Node was conjunct transiting Mars, trine transiting Pluto (finally some 'adventure'), and square the South Bending natal Venus (love). There was a partile trine between progressed Venus and natal Mars, describing the union.

Chart 10:

Jung's Marriage, February 14, 1903, Zurich, Switzerland, noon

In declination, transiting Mars was parallel the progressed South Node, a statement opposite to that of the transiting Mars–North Node conjunction. For Jung there was loss pertaining to Mars; perhaps marriage and a spouse brought reduced autonomy and will-power. Her riches would also be a prison, beholding him to her.

Transiting Mercury was stationing direct at the time of the marriage, an indication that any second thoughts were behind him. Transiting Mercury was conjunct transiting Saturn and the natal Ascendant, and opposite the natal Sun; a heavy transit suggestive of a new start, the assumption of new responsibility, but also fear and worry about not measuring up. Transiting Saturn and Mercury were also square Neptune on the cusp of the 3rd, suggesting problems or misunderstandings in communication; or the need, but not the ability, to discuss practical issues.

Theirs would be a troubled marriage, and the activation of the natal four-planet configuration at its inception guaranteed that the partnership would activate Jung's Shadow and an outpouring of his personal unconscious. Transiting Pluto was opposite natal Mars and transiting Uranus (wide), suggestive of sudden and explosive anger (also sexual liberty). Progressed Venus was opposite natal Saturn and square natal Pluto and the progressed Moon; a reference to his multiple affairs and mistresses, which harmed the marital pact and brought upset and loss of love.

Fatherhood

During the first year of his marriage, Jung was hard at work at the asylum, acting as 'director, senior physician, and first assistant,' and losing fourteen pounds in the process. But he was happy, "For what satisfies us in life more than real work?" Emma helped him at the hospital until she became pregnant.

Agathe, the first of Jung's five children, was born on December 26, 1904 (Chart 11). The previous solar eclipse was on September 9, 1904, at 16°42' Virgo, with Mercury (ruling the 5th house of children) as the lord. The eclipse was sextile natal Venus and Mercury (birth of a girl).

The progressed Moon was conjunct the 5th house cusp. Transiting Pluto (birth and transformation) had just entered the 5th and was activating the four-planet configuration and in opposition to natal Mars, and in a grand trine with natal Jupiter

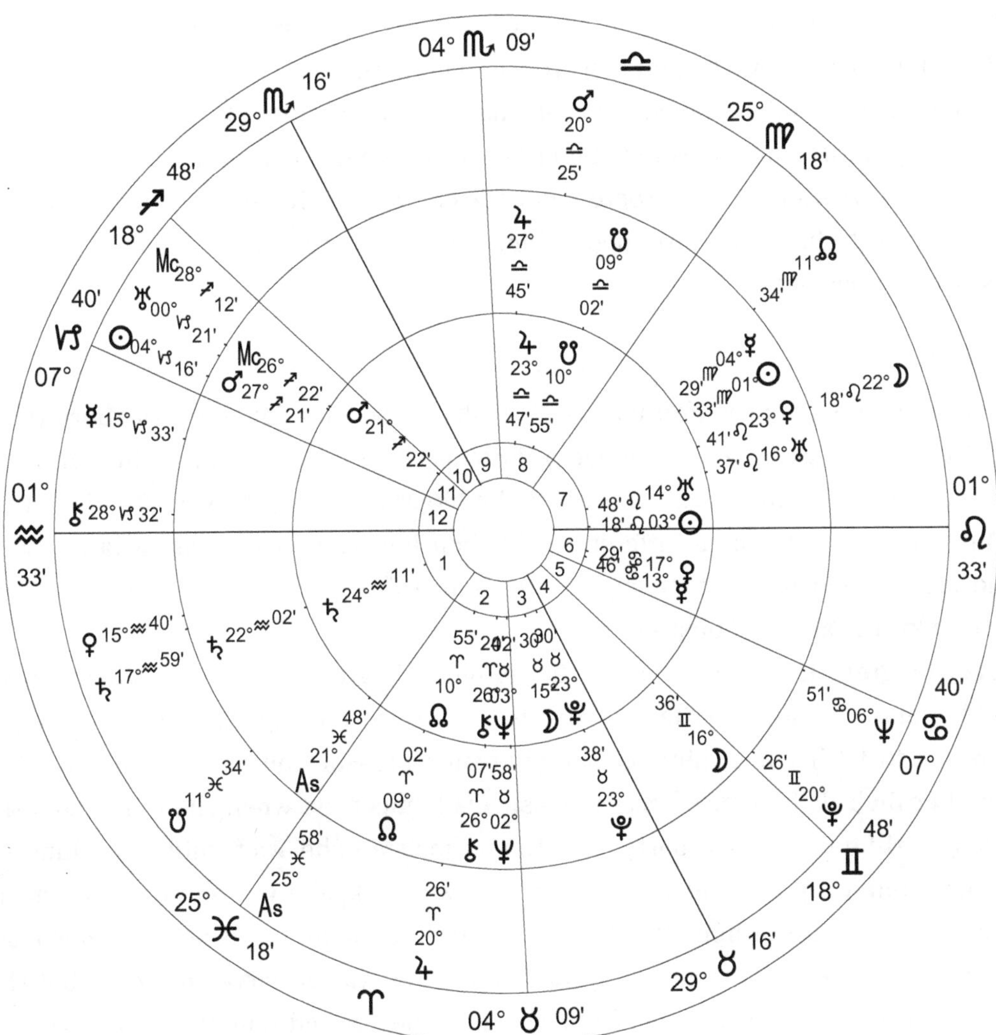

Chart 11:

Jung Becomes a Father: Dec. 26, 1904, Zurich, Switzerland, noon

and Saturn. Having a child may have been a distraction from work, but served his studies of the psyche and helped him grow and mature.

The transiting nodes were sextile/trine natal Mercury, ruler of the 5th, while transiting Mercury (lord) was opposite natal Mercury and Venus, triggering the event. Transiting Neptune was square the progressed nodes at the North Bending; an aspect which seems related to his work with mental illness since Neptune is on the cusp of the 6th house of employment.

Gret Jung

Fourteen months later, on February 8, 1906, Jung's second daughter was born (Chart 12). Gret was an astrologer. Jung had a difficult relationship with her throughout his life. According to Deirdre Bair who wrote the biography *Jung*, he was afraid Gret was 'slightly unwell.' She was a different child than her sister who was "a large, sunny blond child, independent, outgoing, and easy to raise; [whereas] Gret was dark and thin, cranky, irritable and obstreperous."

As Gret grew up, the tension with her father only grew worse. "The truculent Gret was 'the family problem.' [She] exasperated [Jung] so terribly that he would beg the others not to let her near him, as 'she puts such pressure on one' that he could not sleep after their daily battles." She was especially incensed when she found an 'astrologically fortuitous day' to marry, and Emma insisted she wait until after Jung had returned from a trip to Africa. Later, when he was sick, she wanted to move into the house and take care of him, but "because of the lifelong tension between her father and herself, she was the least likely candidate. Gret was a marvelous cook, but their relationship was so quarrelsome that each time she cooked one of her superb meals for him, he claimed she ruined his digestion."

On the day of her birth, there was a Venus, Sun, South Node conjunction that was conjunct his progressed Saturn. Her birth was likely depressing to him. The South Node–Saturn connection suggests personal loss—he had another daughter and wanted a son. The transiting nodal axis was square natal Pluto at the South Bending, a further indication the birth was equated with loss. Transiting Neptune was square the nodes at the North Bending, constellating the irrationality of Neptune. Jupiter was conjunct Pluto, activating the four-planet configuration and his neurosis.

Chart 12:

Jung's Daughter Gret born: Feb. 8, 1906, Zurich, Switzerland, noon

Because the event chart is her birth chart, it shows their synastry. Throughout her life, Gret brought out her father's Shadow; she effortlessly pushed his buttons (his Pluto at the South Bending of her nodes, and her Jupiter conjunct his Pluto). Her natal North Node was trine his natal Mars, and she made him mad. He acted out around her, once throwing a lit firecracker at her that exploded and permanently impaired her hearing. Her Uranus and Saturn formed a yod with his Sun, which explains his frustration, expressed as animosity in what became a constant battleground (her Pluto opposite his Mars). But her Pluto also formed a grand trine with his Jupiter and Saturn, and they were stuck in an endless loop with no way out.

In declination, she had a Pluto–North Node parallel, as did he. Her North Node–Pluto was contraparallel her Sun (representing the father); and she was as at odds with him as he was with her. Her North Node–Pluto was also contraparallel Jung's Saturn; and she (her Shadow) was a depressing burden to him that he could never get past. The great 'mind doctor' never learned how to manage his unconscious response to his daughter.

Collaboration With Freud

Jung read Freud's *Interpretation of Dreams* when it was first published in 1900, but he did not grasp its significance until 1903. "What chiefly interested me was the application to dreams of the concept of the repression mechanism …. I had frequently encountered repression in my experiments with word association; in response to certain stimulus words the patient either had no associative answer or was unduly slow … such a disturbance occurred each time the stimulus word had touched on a psychic lesion or conflict … the repressive mechanism was at work here."

In 1906, Jung published *Diagnostic Studies* and sent a copy to Freud who promptly responded with praise for the book. According to Jung, before their first meeting "there was a 'knowledge' inside him … that 'something unconsciously fateful' ... was bound to happen. It belonged somewhere in his future, and he already knew about it 'without knowing about it.'"

On March 3, 1907, Freud invited Jung to Vienna. They met at one o'clock and talked for thirteen hours. Immediately Freud anointed Jung as his scientific 'son and

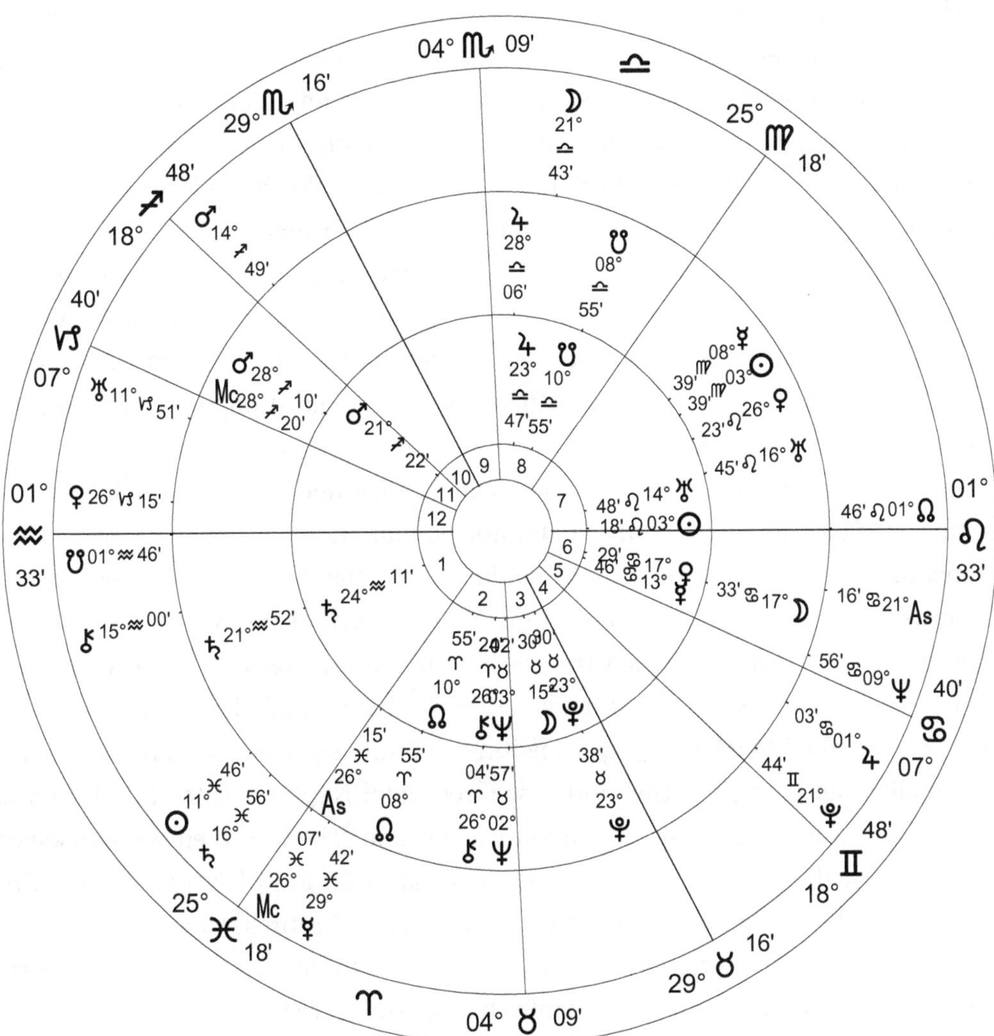

Chart 13:

Jung and Freud Meet, March 3, 1907, Vienna, Austria, 1.00 pm CET

heir.' The most recent solar eclipse was on January 14, 1907, at 22°55' Capricorn, with Saturn (profession) serving as the lord. The south nodal eclipse fell in Jung's 12th house of the unconscious, and was square natal Jupiter and trine natal Pluto, activating Jung's four-planet configuration related to his work on the personal unconscious.

On the day of the meeting (Chart 13), the transiting North Node was at 1°46' Leo conjunct Jung's Descendant and natal Sun. There was a manifestation of a business partner and a father figure whom Jung did not see clearly (natal Sun–Neptune square), and with whom he disagreed on spiritual issues. The transiting South Node was conjunct Jung's natal Ascendant, and the young scientist was subservient to the Vienna master. His role was to support Freud's theories without question, not to compete with him or to offer theories of his own.

There was a mundane opposition between Uranus and Neptune (insight into the unconscious) that was square Jung's natal nodes, making the mundane aspect personal. Transiting Uranus was at the South Bending of the natal nodes and Jung was channeling inspired otherworld ideas. Transiting Neptune was at the North Bending of the natal nodes, marking a time when the secrets of the unconscious were brought out into the open for discussion (transiting Neptune conjunct natal Mercury).

There was a double-whammy, as transiting Neptune squared the natal nodes at the North Bending, and the transiting nodes squared natal Neptune at the South Bending, signifying both a loss and a manifestation of Neptune. The two men were discussing the influence of dreams and the unconscious (manifestation of Neptune). Yet Freud devalued all things spiritual, calling them the effect of repressed sexuality (loss of Neptune). Two visible Neptune events occurred while the men were in Freud's office. Jung described an experience with a knife that shattered for no reason and Freud did not believe him (a South Bending Neptune response). Soon after, without cause, a loud noise from a nearby glass bookshelf made them jump. Jung called it a 'catalytic exteriorization phenomenon,' which Freud called 'nonsense.' Jung said there would be another noise, and there was. "Freud looked at me with horror then," Jung remembered. "This raised a distrust of me in him, for you see, something like that isn't possible, something like that doesn't exist in his world view." In any event, they changed the topic of conversation and moved on.

The appearance of a benefactor who would help Jung professionally was shown by progressed Mars conjunct the progressed Midheaven and sextile progressed Jupiter. The progressed Sun was trine progressed Neptune, illuminating the planet of invisibility and the world that is unconscious and unseen. The aspect was a repeat of the natal square, and while some astrologers believe the nature of the natal aspect always takes precedent over the progressed aspect, I don't agree. A beneficial progressed aspect brings insight and enlightenment, and illustrates how the difficult natal aspect can work well. As a boy, Jung was overwhelmed by his unconscious, but now as an adult, he was studying it scientifically. On the day he and Freud met, this aspect was repeated a third time (a triple-whammy), with the transiting Sun trine transiting Neptune (and natal Mercury), as they discussed neurosis and became more conscious of the unconscious.

The natal four-planet configuration was still activated by transiting Pluto (which had moved only a degree since Gret's birth) and was opposite natal Mars, and in a grand trine with natal Jupiter and Saturn, reflecting the initial grand excitement, and presaging the upcoming philosophical rift.

The timer of the event was the transiting Moon coming to square the January solar eclipse point and trine natal Saturn (lord). Transiting Saturn was also trine the progressed Moon and natal Venus, and he had found a like-minded soul who shared his professional interest in psychotherapy and who understood the powerful influence of the unconscious.

In declination, the transiting North Node was parallel Jung's natal Sun, Moon, Mercury, Ascendant, and Midheaven, giving a positive boost to the ego, the inner emotional self, the rational mind, and the profession. According to Bair, "*[E]verything!* about the day was such an incredible, stimulating experience that Jung believed he had finally found what he had been looking for... Now here was Freud, offering so much collegiality that Jung was willing, indeed eager, to suspend his disbelief ... Freud wanted to be the kind of father Jung had always wanted, so why not become his 'son and heir' and enjoy the opening of the professional doors that such a relationship would bring."

Break-Up

Five years later, in the autumn of 1912, their relationship was disintegrating. They had reached a stalemate that culminated with Jung's publication of *The Psychology of the*

Unconscious (later retitled *Symbols of Transformation)* in which he used myths to explain psychology. Freud refused to recognize the validity of the collective unconscious and considered the book "nothing more or less than the record of Jung's own fantasy life, recklessly projected onto ancient symbols and myths."

Their association ended in January 1913, when Freud wrote to Jung: "I propose that we abandon our personal relations entirely. I shall lose nothing by it, for my only emotional tie with you has long been a thin thread—the lingering effect of past disappointments... Take your full freedom and spare me your suppressed tokens of friendship." Jung received the letter on January 6th and replied, "he would never 'thrust' his friendship on anyone, and 'the rest is silence.'"

Four months before the final split there was a south nodal solar eclipse at 16°52' Libra, with Venus (relationships) as the lord. The eclipse fell in Jung's 8th house, signaling a crisis related to the personal unconscious. Natally, Venus rules the 3rd, 4th, and intercepted 8th houses. The eclipse was square natal Mercury and Venus and quincunx the Moon, alluding to emotional and mental upset, and loss of equilibrium that shook his personal foundation. At the time, Jung was thirty-seven and undergoing a nodal return. This is a period when a new cycle is starting and a new direction is forged. The transiting node has completed the circuit and arrives home to the natal position after the long journey with a new understanding that necessitates an update in life direction. It is often a time of drastic change.

On the day Jung wrote his reply (Chart 14), the progressed Midheaven was at the South Bending of the transiting nodes, indicating professional loss. Freud would not only split with Jung, he would do everything he could to discredit and undermine him. However, the transiting North Node was conjunct the progressed Ascendant and the progressed North Node, pointing to strength in the projected personality. Jung would go on alone. Since the progressed South Node was conjunct the progressed Descendant, Freud was the more vulnerable of the two. The progressed Moon was conjunct the progressed South Node–Descendant, suggesting that Jung's heart was with Freud, and that Jung felt the loss deeply. According to Bair, Jung "was racked by feelings of loss, trepidation over the magnitude of what had transpired, and fear for his immediate professional future: 'After all, I knew nothing beyond Freud, and yet, I dared to take

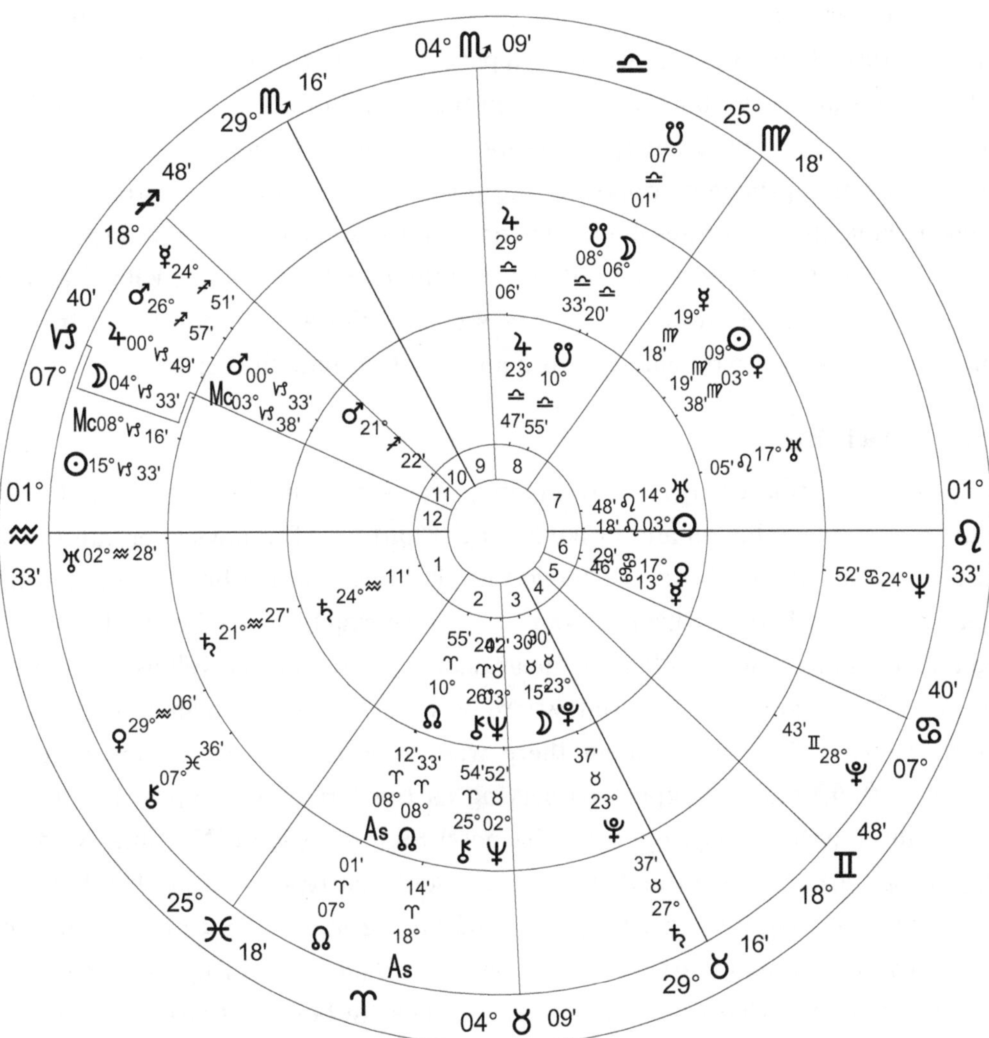

Chart 14:
Jung's Split with Freud, Jan. 6, 1913, Kusnacht, Switzerland, noon

the step into darkness." Later, Jung described it as 'falling out into that which is not known.' He thought he was 'experiencing a psychological disorder.'

Progressed Mercury and transiting Neptune were both impacting the natal four-planet configuration, constellating the eruption of the personal unconscious. Transiting Pluto was in approaching opposition to progressed Mars and the progressed Midheaven, an indication of professional tension and disagreement. Transiting Saturn was conjunct the natal IC, the cusp of endings, and the end of the matter with Freud (Saturn) felt like death. The transiting Sun was square the eclipse point, and transiting Venus (Lord) was square transiting Saturn and the IC, timing the crisis.

Accidental Fall

Twenty-seven years later, in 1944, when Jung was sixty-nine, he was taking his daily afternoon walk when he fell and broke his leg (Chart 15). Ten days later, after emboli from the fracture broke loose and lodged in his lungs and his heart, he had a heart attack. He remained hospitalized for four months. During this time he was treated with oxygen and camphor, which elicited a near-death experience, as well as sensations of being at the "'outermost border,' somewhere between 'a dream and an ecstasy.'"

Two weeks before the accident there was a south nodal solar eclipse at 4°32' Aquarius, with Uranus (unexpected) serving as the lord. The eclipse fell in the 1st house of the physical body, opposite the natal Sun and square Neptune (weakened vitality, hospitalization). On the day of the accident that resulted in broken bones and surgery, the transiting Sun was conjunct natal and progressed Saturn (bones), opposite progressed Uranus (chart ruler, lord, and mundane ruler of upset), sextile natal Mars (surgery), and trine transiting Saturn (successful bone-setting). Transiting Uranus was sextile the natal Sun, and formed a grand trine with the Ascendant and transiting Neptune, which expressed as sudden bodily mishap and unavoidable hospitalization.

Progressed Mercury and Jupiter were at the North Bending of the transiting nodes, symbolizing doctors, medical staff, and thoughts of death. The transiting nodes were square natal Neptune at the South Bending, indicating hospitalization, but also other-world experiences under the influence of drugs. He was having what he considered

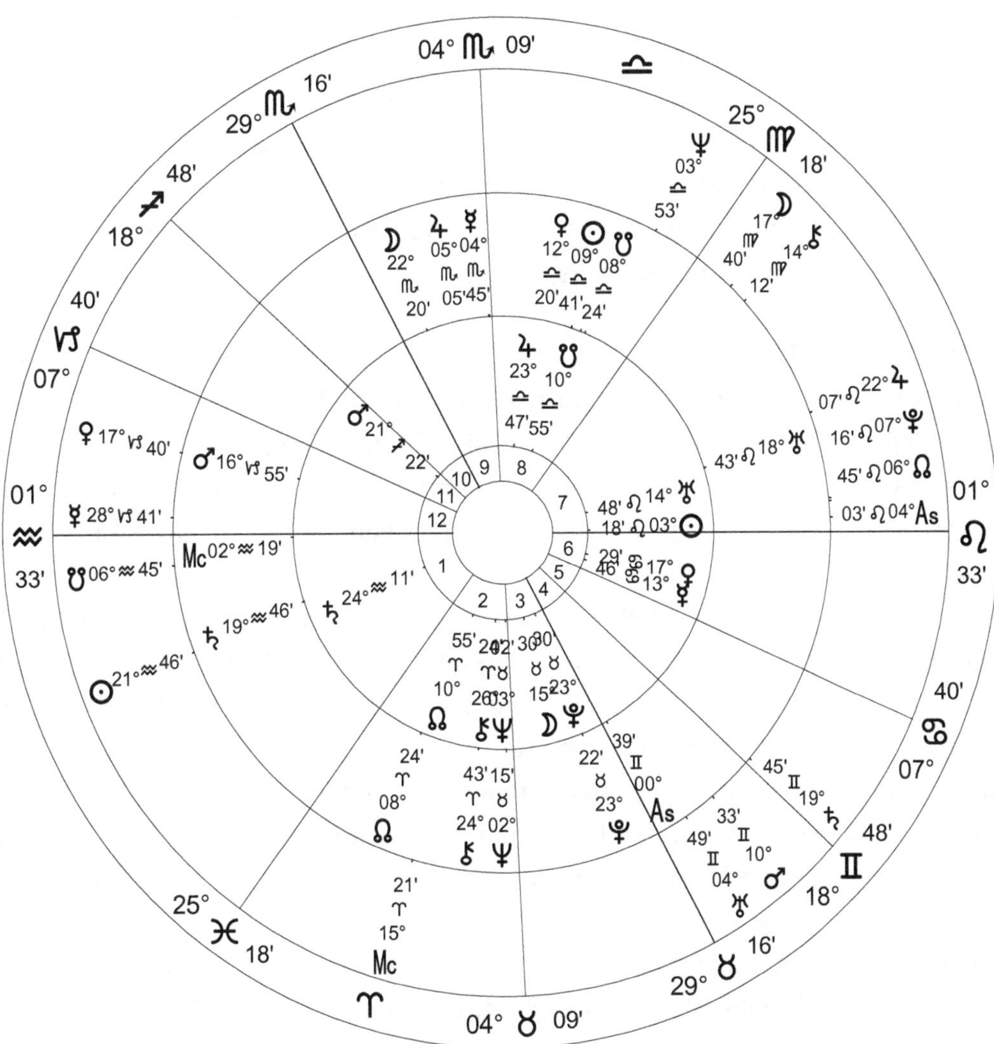

Chart 15:

Jung's accidental fall: Feb.11, 1944, Kusnacht, Switzerland, 4:00 pm

fantastic visions. The transiting North Node was conjunct the natal Sun and transiting Pluto, and he had a near-death experience. "But there have been protests against my leaving and I must return." He became depressed and it took him three weeks to will 'himself to live again' (transiting Saturn opposite natal Mars; transiting Pluto conjunct natal Sun square Neptune). By progression, the Sun, Venus, and South Node were parallel, and there was physical loss of vitality, but also joyous otherworld experiences. He begrudgingly recovered and was released from the hospital in late June 1944.

Emma's Death

The Jungs celebrated their 50th wedding anniversary on Valentine's Day in 1953. The following month, Toni Wolfe, a long-time chain smoker, died in her sleep at age sixty-five. By this time, she had made amends with Emma and was more comfortable in her company than in Jung's. He was too emotional to attend her funeral and Emma went in his place.

But Emma was also not well. She had stomach cancer. Her symptoms first appeared in late 1952, but she ignored them and did not see a doctor for almost a year. By then, she had developed a back ache that made it difficult to walk. In 1954, she had surgery, chemotherapy, and radiation. Her adult children were told she had back trouble! In the summer of 1955, Jung publicly celebrated his eightieth birthday and Emma was well enough to attend. By November, she was bed-ridden. The cancer had spread to her spine and brain, and her kidneys were failing. She died November 27, 1955.

There was a north nodal solar eclipse three weeks after her death at 21°30' Sagittarius, conjunct Jung's natal Mars. In his chart, Mars rules the intercepted 2nd, which is Emma's 8th (taking her 1st house as his 7th in the turned chart). Jupiter was the lord of the eclipse.

On the day Emma died (Chart 16), transiting Uranus was conjunct the natal Descendant (spouse) and the natal Sun, and Jung was shocked by her death. Two days earlier he had been hoping she had months to live (denial shown by Sun square Neptune). The transiting North Node was conjunct and parallel the progressed Descendant (external event for his partner), while the transiting South Node was

Chart 16:

Jung's Wife's Death, Nov. 27, 1955, Kusnacht, Switzerland, noon

conjunct and parallel the progressed Ascendant (loss for Jung) The transiting nodes were sextile/trine his progressed Saturn–Uranus opposition, signifying an unexpected separation.

Transiting Venus was sextile a triple conjunction of progressed Venus, transiting Mars, and transiting Neptune, sextile natal Saturn, and trine transiting Pluto, suggesting that for Emma (Venus), death was a relief. Transiting Saturn was square transiting Pluto, repeating Jung's natal square and forming a grand cross with it. He was boxed in with devastation and despair. Transiting Jupiter (lord) had just entered Virgo and was square the Midheaven–IC and transiting Mercury (his 8th house ruler), timing the event. According to Bair, "he turned inward and was mostly silent, it was 'touch and go whether he would ever come back.'"

Jung's Death

Emma had managed the money throughout the marriage and after she died, Jung was left to deal with the finances. Though Emma had great wealth, she left Jung only that which was required by law. The rest she gave to her children. Though far from poor, Jung began to worry about money. Afraid he would lose his house, he had an architect draw up designs for apartments he could rent out. He minimized the household help and chastised those who remained for leaving on lights and turning up the heat. He started hiding money. He fell into a depression that lasted five months. He retired to his home in Bollingen and started carving stones. He wondered why he had survived and what purpose he had to fulfill before he could die. At eighty-two, he began writing his autobiography.

In the last years of his life, his health was failing. In the spring of 1961, a number of heart attacks and a stroke left him unable to speak. He died on June 6, 1961 (Chart 17). The transits and progressions are mixed, an indication of the trauma experienced by the physical body, but also the liberation of the soul. In regards to his mother's death, Jung wrote in his autobiography, "I had a feeling of great grief, but in my heart of hearts I could not be mournful, and this for a strange reason: during the entire journey I continually heard dance music, laughter, and jollity, as though a wedding were being celebrated. … This paradox can be explained if we suppose that at one moment death was being represented from the point of view of the ego, and at the next from that of the psyche. In the first case it appeared as a catastrophe; that is how it so often strikes us, as if wicked and pitiless powers had put an end to a human life.... From another point of view, however, death appears as a joyful event. In the light of eternity, it is a wedding, a *mysterium coniunctionis*. The soul attains, as it were, its missing half, it achieves wholeness."

The south nodal solar eclipse before his death was at 26°25' Aquarius, with Uranus (natal chart ruler) serving as the lord. The eclipse fell in the 1st house of the physical body conjunct natal Saturn (Grim Reaper). Transiting Saturn was conjunct the natal Ascendant and progressed Mars, and square the progressed Sun; an indication of low vitality. Transiting Uranus was conjunct the progressed IC and progressed Uranus, and square natal Pluto; death and sudden liberation.

The transiting nodes were square the IC at the South Bending, suggesting physical loss and otherworld gain at the end of the matter. Transiting Mercury, ruler of the 8th was at the North Bending of the progressed nodes, which expressed outwardly as physical death. Transiting Mercury was also in a grand trine with progressed Jupiter–transiting Neptune, and transiting Chiron, suggesting joy. The progressed Moon was at the North Bending of the natal nodes conjunct natal Mercury, merging the 6th and 8th houses of illness and death. The transiting North Node was trine natal Neptune–transiting Venus, and sextile progressed Venus, an indication of an easy, unresisting passing.

From the point of view of the ego, there was stress. Transiting Jupiter was opposite the natal Sun and square natal Neptune, while transiting Neptune was conjunct progressed Jupiter and square transiting Jupiter. These difficult aspects show strain, dissolution, and far away travel. In declination, the transiting North Node was parallel natal Neptune as "Jung's sleep [gave] way to a quiet death … after a long slow sunset and gradually fading light."

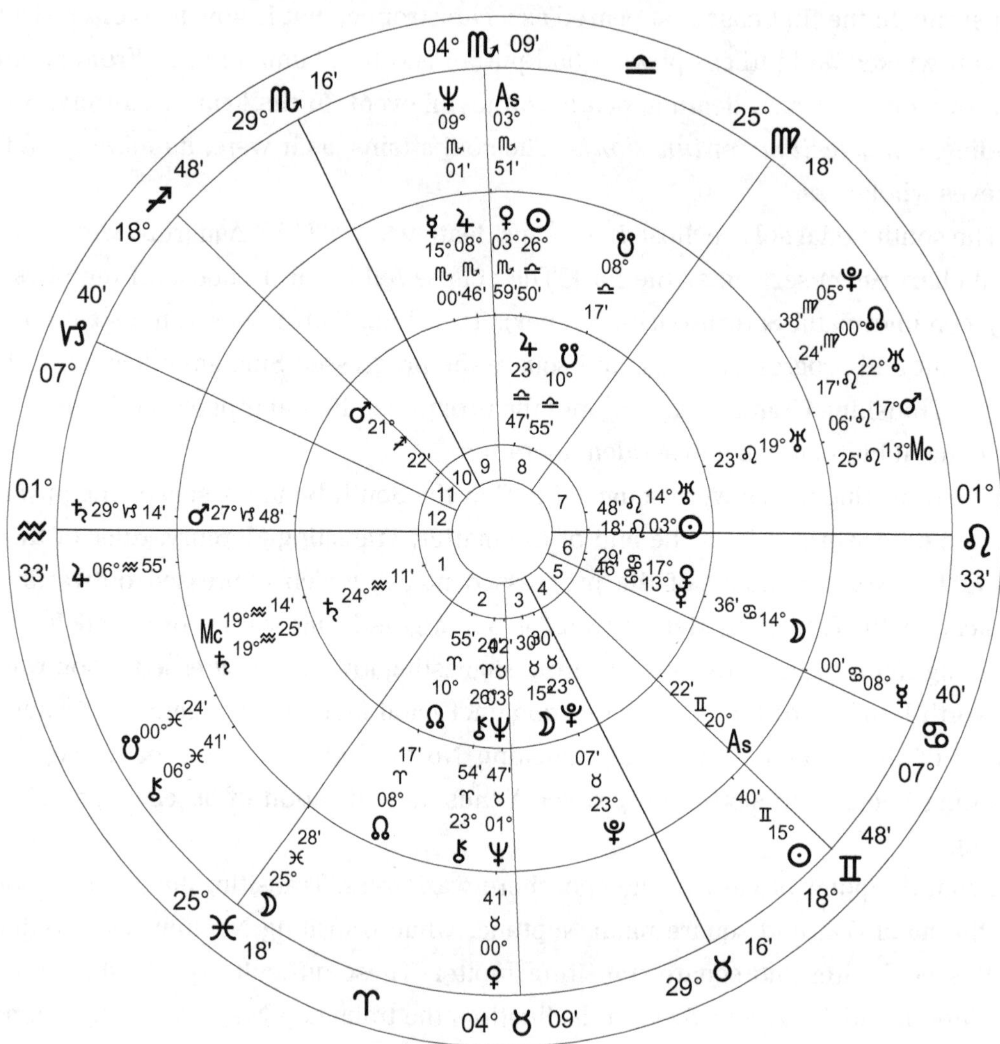

Chart 17:

Jung's Death, June 6, 1961, Kusnacht, Switzerland, 4.30 p.m.

That's the thing with magic. You've got to know it's still here, all around us, or it just stays invisible for you.

— Charles de Lint

Chapter 6
Alcoholics Anonymous
Bill Wilson

For instructions on how to use South Node energy, one need look no further than *The Twelve Steps and the Twelve Traditions* of Alcoholics Anonymous (AA). Written by co-founder Bill Wilson, the text describes how to align the self in service to a higher power for the greater good.

Growing up in Vermont, Bill W. was raised by his grandparents after being abandoned by his parents who split up and went their separate ways. He was sickly, shy, and prone to depression. He took his first drink at twenty-two and soon after declared, 'I have found the elixir of life.' He went on to drink for seventeen years, nearly killing himself. He worked as a stockbroker, but lost any money he made while binging. He acquired a bad professional reputation as a result of his drinking. He was thirty-nine, lying in bed after being hospitalized for the fourth time for alcohol rehabilitation, when he cried out for help for his addiction: "I'll do anything. Anything at all. If there be a

God let him show himself." He immediately saw a bright blinding light, felt ecstasy, and knew he was having a spiritual experience. He never drank again.

His formulation of the AA principles emerged from the teachings of the Oxford Group, an evangelical Lutheran offshoot of Christianity that preached surrender to God and adherence to the divine guidance of the Holy Spirit. Believers were to sit quietly every morning with pen and paper and await instructions from God—a practice similar to spiritual channeling. Long interested in the occult, Bill W. sought daily advice from God. When writing *The Twelve Steps and the Twelve Traditions*, he believed he had help from 'both over here and over there.'

Newly sober, Bill W. was in Akron on a business trip and found himself craving a drink. Through the local Oxford Group he met Dr. Bob, an active alcoholic. They talked for hours. The day of their first meeting is considered by AA to be the birth of the fellowship. Dr. Bob soon quit drinking and the two men began to share their program of recovery with other alcoholics.

They were the first to call alcoholism a physical disease, rather than a moral failing as it was viewed at the time. Carl Jung's insight was that alcoholism was a disease of the spirit that could be cured by a spiritual awakening, which the twelve steps bring about. The steps include an admission of powerlessness, surrender to God, taking a moral inventory, forgiving others, dedication to serving others, and the daily practice of seeking higher guidance.

Nativity

Bill W.'s chart is a fascinating mixture of darkness and light (Chart 18). He has a Sagittarius Sun, and he was moral and religious. The Sun in mutual reception with Jupiter repeats the message: he needed something to believe in and his beliefs guided his life. The Sun is unaspected and rules the 11th house of groups. He poured his heart into the AA fellowship, a program where recovering alcoholics help each other. The Sun is in the 2nd house and he made money working as a stockbroker. He also came to the realization that the greatest value a person has is their own true self.

The Moon is in Pisces, giving both a spiritual bend and a desire to escape the burden of physical existence. He understood that alcoholics used alcohol to escape from

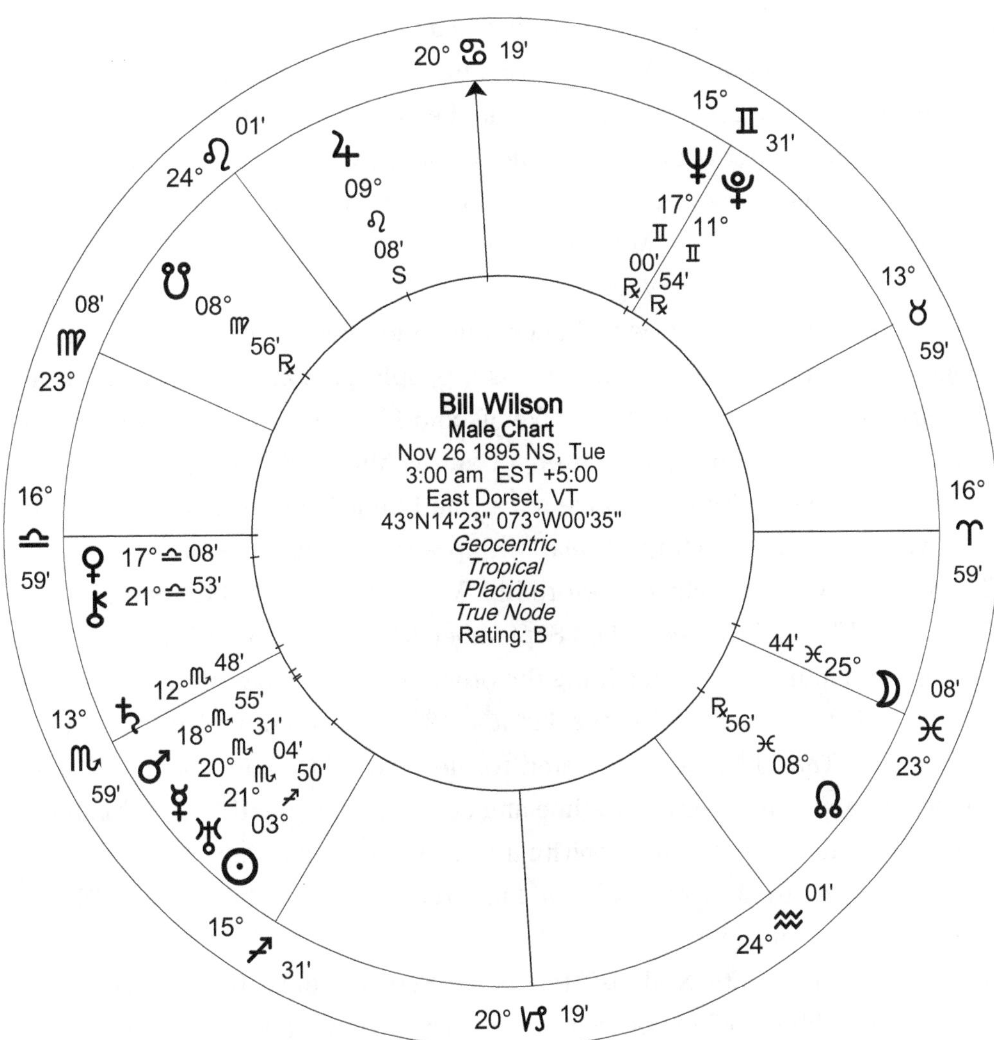

Chart 18:
Bill Wilson's Nativity

their emotions—from themselves—and that healing required alcoholics to learn how to handle troubling emotions. With the Moon in the 6th house of illness, daily work and routine, his program of recovery of emotional health requires taking a daily inventory, immediately righting any wrongs with others, and praying daily to improve conscious contact with a higher power. In this way, an emotional center is maintained that precludes a need for alcohol. The Moon rules the 10th house and Bill W. achieved recognition for his program of recovery.

Libra is on the Ascendant, with Venus, the chart ruler, rising and dignified in her own sign. With a prominent Venus, he was a people person, with charm, likeability, and intellect. Given the prominence of Venus and Libra, he was not averse to finding an easy way out. Relationships were important to him, and during his drinking days these were with other drinkers. Once sober, he bonded with others in recovery. He also showed addicts how to forge a relationship with their higher self.

There were two solar eclipses before Bill W. was born, with the first on August 20, 1895, at 27°13' Leo, and the second on September 18, 1895, at 25°40' Virgo. Both PNSEs were near the South Node, highlighting the otherworld and suggesting difficulty in the physical world. The PNSEs fell in the 11th and 12th houses, both of which were standouts in his life. The 11th house is related to the fellowship, and 'friends of Bill' who expanded exponentially over his lifetime and continue to expand. The 12th is related to alcoholism, self-undoing, but also spiritual awareness. The South Node is in the 11th, the house activated by the first PNSE; and in Virgo, the sign of the second PNSE, tying the South Node to both eclipses.

The ruler of the South Node is Mercury in Scorpio, initially a source weakness, loss, and vulnerability. While outwardly the world may have seen the lightness of Venus rising and the optimism of a Sagittarius Sun, Bill W. was depressed and lived in the darkness of Scorpio, which he termed 'stinkin' thinkin'. Mercury in mutual reception with Pluto only added to the compulsion and emotional intensity. Astrologically, Mercury is weak and its association with South Node energy exacerbated the trouble. Mercury is without dignity, conjunct Mars, and overruled by it. According to Vedic astrologers, in a close conjunction, the planet at the lower position in longitude has more power than the planet at the higher position, and 'wins the war.' Mars is strong in his sign of dignity, at the lower degree, and thus the dominating player and over-rules the weak Mercury. Also conjunct Uranus, Mercury is hemmed in by the lesser malefic and the planet of upset. These three are parallel in declination and form an occultation (similar to an eclipse except planets rather than luminaries are involved), giving the three added strength and influence.

A major component of the behavior associated with alcoholism is resentment and rage, which can consume and take over the personality. With Mercury, Mars, and Uranus in Scorpio, Bill W. was no stranger to destructive emotions that poison the mind. Sober, he considered these emotions to be character defects that had to be corrected. For recovery, the manner of thinking needs to be reformatted and transformed. This transformation is achieved through facing the self, recognizing imperfections and powerlessness, and accepting outside assistance (both in this world and the otherworld). For Bill W., this meant taming Mars. When he achieved this, he used Mars to empower Mercury (ruling the 12th house of God and the 9th of mainstream religion) to forge a new belief system.

The ruler of the North Node is Neptune in Gemini in the 9th. He believed in God and the ability to talk to God came easily to him. He also drank enough to drown himself. In recovery, he published books describing the steps to take to achieve sobriety and a spiritual awakening.

The ruler of the South Node disposits the ruler of the North Node, tying the two nodes together through dispositorship. Mercury and Neptune are also inconjunct and form a tense, frustrating and intractable 150° aspect. The difficult combination of the two nodal rulers suggests a mighty struggle between the inner and outer realms. The battle led to the lowest of lows and the highest of highs, which ultimately brought inner and outer transformation. If the darkness of Mercury in Scorpio was the problem, then the illumination of God through Neptune was the answer that brought recovery.

Pluto, the ruler of Scorpio and the planet of obsession and compulsion, is in Gemini at the North Bending of the natal nodes, ensuring all things pertaining to Pluto would manifest. Bill W. nearly destroyed his life, health, profession, and marriage. Fortunately, he found the way out, and escaped from hell through transformative beliefs that empowered the personality (Jupiter sextile Pluto).

Natal indications of Bill W.'s inclination to drink include Venus trine Neptune (seeking easy escape), and Jupiter square Saturn sextile Pluto (warding off despair through inebriation). In declination, the Sun and Neptune are contraparallel (fortifying the ego with alcohol and God); and in latitude, the Moon and Neptune are contraparallel (drowning emotions with alcohol, and relying on God to heal emotions). His ability to transform his life is shown by Pluto at the North Bending, as well as the triple occultation of Mars, Mercury, and Uranus, which enabled him to reinvent his thought processes.

The *Serenity Prayer* adopted by AA shows the distinction between south nodal and north nodal energy: *Grant me the serenity to accept the things I cannot change (South Node); courage to change the things I can (North Node); and the wisdom to know the difference.*

Sobriety

Near death, in the hospital, Bill W. had a spiritual awakening that enabled him to stop drinking. There was a south nodal solar eclipse on August 10, 1934, at 17°01' Leo, with the Sun serving as the lord (crisis of consciousness and threat to physical life). The eclipse was square natal Mars, Mercury, and Uranus (crisis of will and personal might) and a progressed conjunction of Saturn and the Ascendant (encounter with death). The eclipse was sextile natal Neptune, the planet of alcohol and spirituality.

On the day he quit drinking (Chart 19), transiting Mercury was at the South Bending of the natal nodes, marking a time when he had reached his bottom mentally. The progressed North Node was square the natal Sun at the South Bending indicating a low point for the ego. With the progressed Moon widely conjunct the progressed South Node, he was also at a low point emotionally. However, with the Sun, Moon, and Mercury under the influence of south nodal energy, he was most susceptible to otherworld influences. Under these conditions, he experienced a spiritual awakening—a direct encounter with God.

The transiting North Node was sextile the natal Sun (empowering the ego) and quincunx the progressed Moon (an emotional stretch required to seek new answers). The progressed Moon (which had recently ingressed into Virgo, the sign of health) was

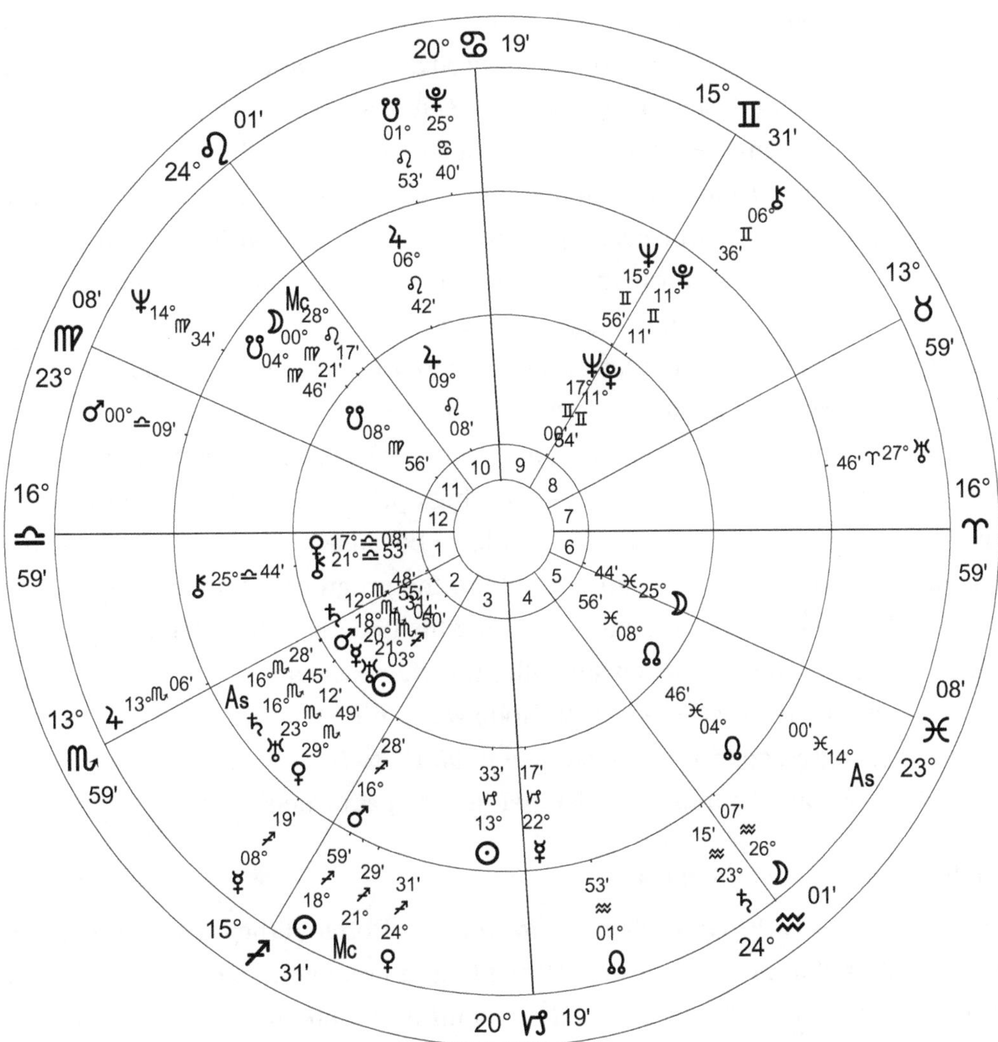

Chart 19:

Bill Wilson Sobriety, Dec. 11, 1934, New York, NY, noon

separating from a square to progressed Venus in late Scorpio. It was time to face practical reality and the consequences to health brought on by addiction. Progressed Mars was opposite progressed Neptune (battle between alcohol and willpower) and formed a t-square with transiting Neptune (God was called upon to resolve the conflict).

Transiting Uranus (unexpected inspiration) and transiting Pluto (transformation) were square each other, with transiting Pluto in a grand trine with the natal Moon and progressed Uranus, which brought inner spiritual understanding (Moon in Pisces), change, and freedom from addiction. Progressed Mercury was sextile progressed Uranus and opposite transiting Pluto, enabling modified thought patterns. Often, when people become free from addiction, Uranus is involved.

Transiting Jupiter was conjunct natal Saturn, activating the natal Jupiter–Saturn square, delivering new beliefs that came at a high price. He realized his problems did not make him drink, but rather he had problems because he drank. Transiting Jupiter and natal Saturn formed a yod with a sextile to the progressed Sun and a quincunx to progressed Neptune and natal Pluto, reflecting his understanding that he needed outside help. The ego could not heal itself without higher assistance.

In declination, the progressed North Node was parallel natal Chiron (physical healing), and the progressed Moon was parallel natal Pluto (emotional transformation). In latitude, the Moon and Uranus were parallel (emotional turn-around).

Alcoholics Anonymous

AA was born six months later when Bill W. met Dr. Bob and they realized that two or more alcoholics sharing their stories, strength, and hope with each other would help heal the secretive, brooding angst of the resentful and emotionally closed alcoholic. There was a south nodal solar eclipse three weeks after their meeting at 8°04' Cancer with the Moon serving as the lord. The eclipse fell in the 9th house of beliefs.

On the day the two men met (Chart 20), a grand trine had formed between the natal Moon (emotions), progressed Uranus (freedom and fellowship) and transiting Pluto (transformation). Transiting Jupiter was conjunct a progressed Saturn–Ascendant conjunction, and Dr. Bob (Jupiter) materialized. The transiting North Node was conjunct progressed Mercury and opposite a transiting conjunction of Pluto and the South

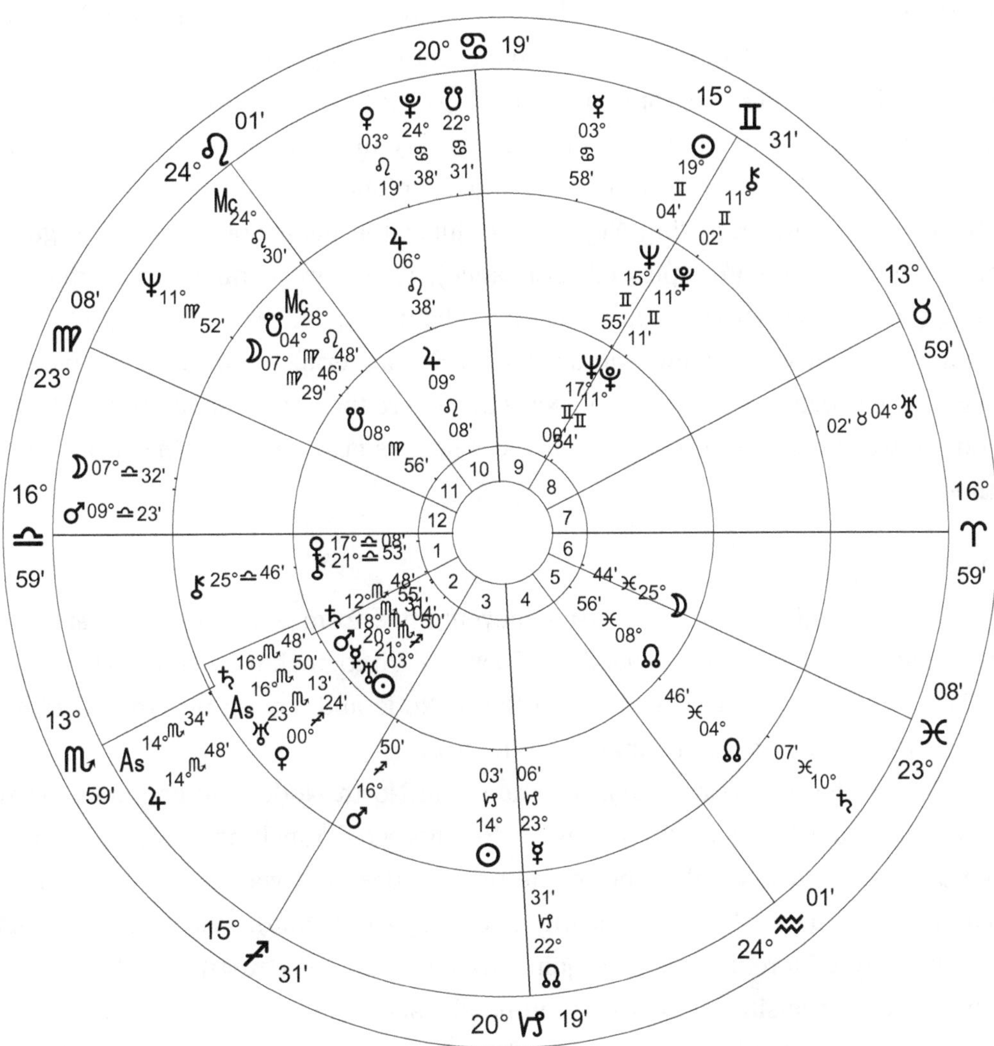

Chart 20:

AA's First Meeting, June 10, 1935, Akron, OH, 5.00 p.m.

Node: the two men had a long, deep discussion about alcohol addiction and the need to face dark feelings. There was a mundane Saturn–Neptune opposition in Pisces–Virgo, describing the AA program: practical steps leading to a spiritual awakening and a direct experience of God, empowering every day life. The opposition aligned with Bill W.'s natal nodal axis, with transiting Saturn conjunct the natal North Node (taking practical action), and transiting Neptune conjunct the natal South Node–progressed Moon (emotionally helpful spiritual assistance), all square natal Pluto at the North Bending (outward transformation). With this alignment, Bill W. personally channeled the mundane opposition, which actualized in the material realm as his program of recovery. The progressed North Node was still square the natal Sun at the South Bending, but he was no longer at the bottom. Now he was giving himself in service to help another.

Death

A long-time smoker, Bill W. died at age seventy-five from emphysema. There was a south nodal solar eclipse on August 31, 1970 at 8°4' Virgo, making Mercury (breath) the lord. The eclipse was conjunct his natal South Node and square progressed Pluto at the natal North Bending (manifestation of death).

On the day he died (Chart 21), the transiting North Node was conjunct the progressed Sun, indicating an outward event for the ego. Transiting Mercury (lord) acquired a boost from a sextile/trine to the natal nodes, and was conjunct progressed Venus (ruler of the 8th house of death) and progressed Mars (the malefic bringing harm). Transiting Mercury was also quincunx natal Jupiter (frustration that time has run out), square transiting Uranus at the natal Ascendant (the end coming suddenly and too soon), and sextile natal Saturn (ruler of the 4th and the grave). The progressed nodal axis was square a transiting conjunction of Mars, Jupiter, and Neptune, all conjunct the natal Sun at the South Bending, an indication of futile bargaining with God, surrender and acceptance of the inevitable. Progressed Mercury was square natal Mars and progressed Saturn, indicating physical hardship. Progressed Mercury was also in a grand trine with natal Neptune, natal Venus, and the Ascendant, suggesting enlightenment and close contact with God.

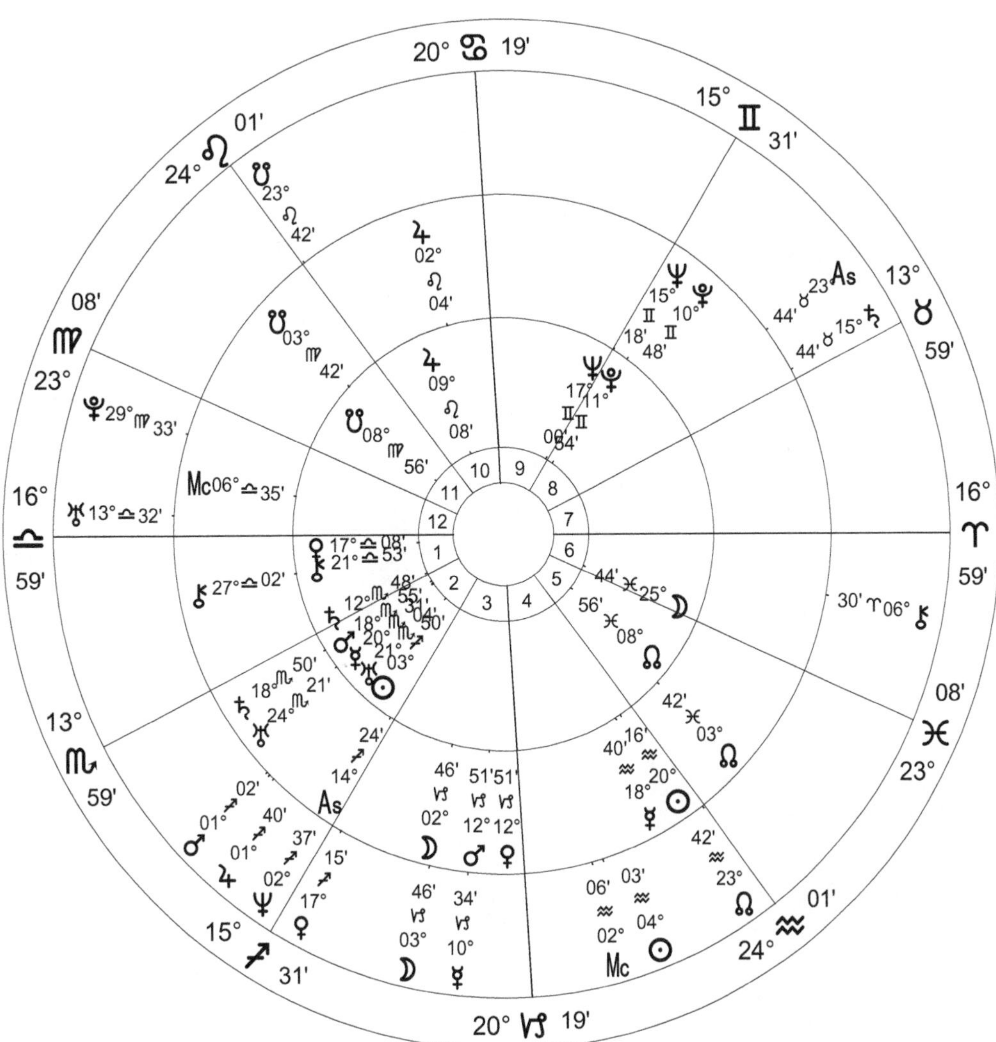

Chart 21:

Bill Wilson's Death, Jan. 24, 1971, Manhattan, NY, noon

I have known no man of genius who had not to pay, in some affliction or defect either physical or spiritual, for what the gods had given him.

— Max Beerbohm

Chapter 7
A Poet and a Madman
Ezra Pound

Ezra Pound was a writer who knew all his life that he wanted to be a poet. He vowed to know everything there was to know about poetry before he turned thirty, and to this end he learned nine languages. He was born in Idaho, traveled to Europe at thirteen, and started university at fifteen. Upon graduation, he taught romantic languages at a conservative college in a conservative town. He was not happy and called it 'the sixth circle of hell.' He was deliberately provocative and left the college after a scandal with women.

He moved to England and worked in London as a foreign editor for American literary magazines. There he met, influenced, and promoted the work of T.S. Eliot, James Joyce, Butler Yeats, and Ernest Hemmingway, all of whom won the Nobel Prize for literature after Pound edited their work.

He was flamboyant. In the biography, *Ezra Pound: Poet,* by Anthony David Moody, Pound was described as "approaching (with) the step of a dancer, making passes with a cane at an imaginary opponent. He would wear trousers made of green billiard cloth, a pink coat, a blue shirt, a tie hand-painted by a Japanese friend, an immense sombrero, a flaming beard cut to a point, and a single large blue earring." According to Hemingway, "He defends [his friends] when they are attacked, he gets them into magazines and out of jail. He loans them money ... He writes articles about them. He introduces them to wealthy women. He gets publishers to take their books. He sits up all night with them when they claim to be dying ... he advances them hospital expenses and dissuades them from suicide."

Pound believed his ability to write poetry was connected to his ability to seduce women. He was married, but he ran around with other women and his wife preferred not to notice. He had two children, one with his wife and one with a long-time lover. The two children grew up separately with opposite lifestyles. An illegitimate daughter was raised by a peasant foster-mother, while the legitimate son was raised in privilege with the affection of a mother and grandmother.

During World War I, Pound was disgusted by the loss of life and blamed the war on 'finance capitalism' and usury (lending money at high interest). He moved to Italy and supported Mussolini and Hitler. He lived there during World War II and had a radio show where he denounced America, Jews, and F. D. Roosevelt. On one show he said, "Understanding of usury is central to understanding of history. Until you know who has lent what to whom, you know nothing whatever of politics, you know nothing whatever of history, and you know nothing whatever of international wrangles." He also said, "There is no freedom without economic freedom. Freedom that doesn't include freedom from debt is plain bunkum. It is fetid and foul logomachy [dispute over words] to call such servitude freedom."

In 1945, he was arrested for treason and extradited to the U.S. The only defense that could spare his life was mental illness and his lawyer argued that he had suffered a mental breakdown and was unfit for trial. The judge agreed and sent him to an asylum. There he wrote poetry, causing his detractors to question the diagnosis of mental instability. He was incarcerated twelve years and released after famous friends campaigned for his freedom. He returned to Italy and lived out the rest of his life depressed, stricken with insomnia, and terrified of microbes and of catching an infectious disease. He died of intestinal blockage in 1972.

His life and his horoscope illustrate how north nodal energy can go awry. While energy is flowing in at the North Node that can be useful in the manifest realm, left uncontrolled and undisciplined, the energy can be excessive and bring harm. Pound was born with Jupiter conjunct the North Node trine Neptune.

Astrology

Ezra had a Scorpio Sun, giving intensity, depth, and an interest in sex, power, and big money (Chart 22). His Sun was in the 7th house and relationships were primary in his life. The Sun rules the 6th, describing his job editing and improving the work of aspiring authors. With the Sun trine Saturn (ruling the 10th and 11th), he took his relationships seriously, achieved professional success, and enjoyed meaningful professional friendships. The Sun was square the Moon, an indication that his actions and feelings were often at odds. The Moon is in Leo, ruling the 5th and he was creative, pouring emotion into his poetry. Though he had two children, he was an absent father in every respect (Moon in the 5th square the Sun).

If the time of birth is correct, then the Aries Point is rising, bringing the personality to the attention of the world (or a bigger audience than would otherwise be typically expected). He was a fighter, and with Mars in Leo in the 6th, he worked to bring the literary efforts of others to light. Mars was trine Venus, describing his fondness for women and his crusade to expose corrupt money practices (that are still in effect today). With Mars square Neptune, he was fighting for utopia, especially in regards to economic policy (Neptune in Taurus in the 2nd).

The north nodal solar eclipse before birth was at 16°18' Virgo that fell in his 6th house of work, highlighting the house that would expand over his lifetime. His nodes were stationary and had turned direct five hours before he was born. The North Node is ruled by Mercury, indicating ease, output, and innate knowingness of the planet of communication, which expressed outwardly in writing, teaching, editing, and broadcasting. With Mercury in Scorpio, in the 8th in mutual reception with Pluto, he was significantly interested in what is hidden and corrupt. He was repulsed by the uselessness of war and disgusted by usury. When he realized how war benefited profiteers, he spoke out vehemently against capitalism. He used his radio shows (Mercury ruling the

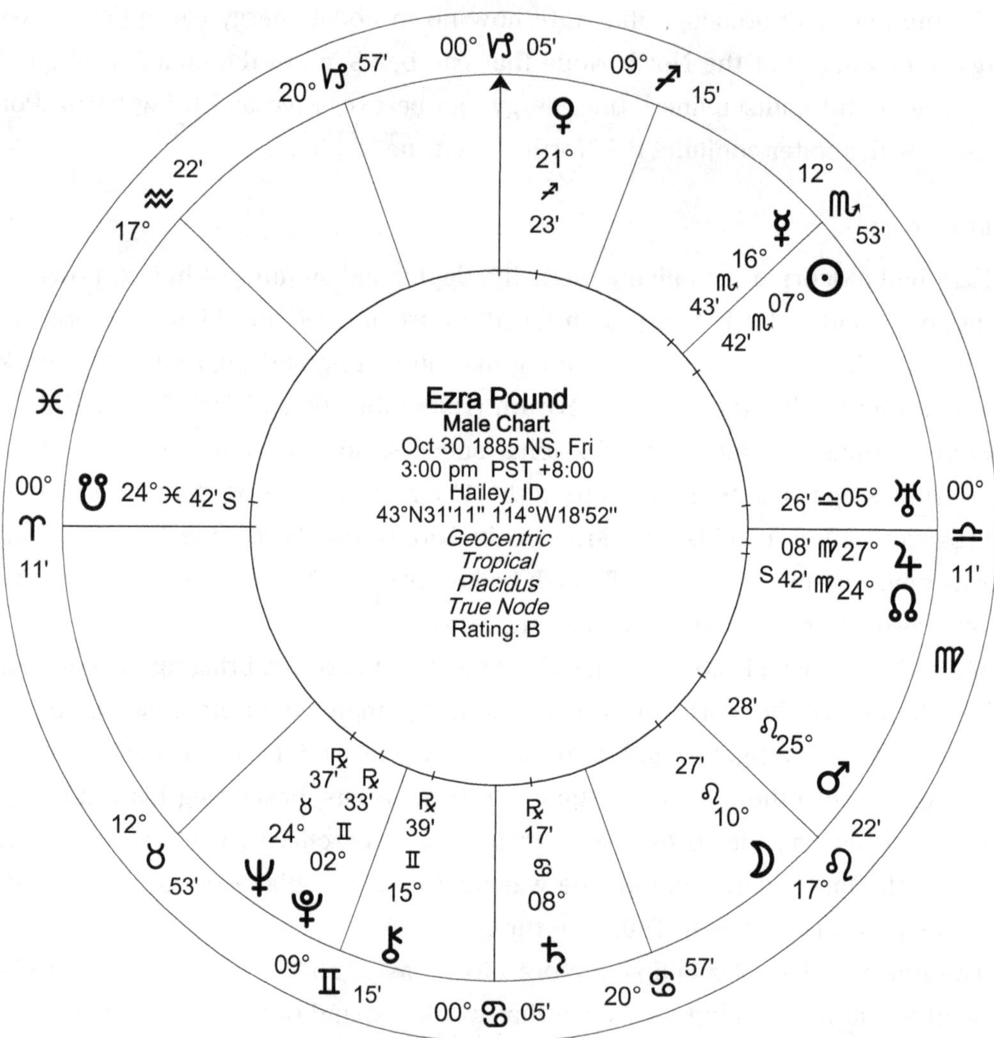

Chart 22:

Ezra Pound Nativity

3rd) to educate his listeners about economics. He decried banks that earned interest on money they created out of thin air.

The South Node is ruled by Neptune in the 2nd. He was not a spiritual, otherworld type person, and this may be the loss related to Neptune. However, he served the artistic efforts of others and tried to raise consciousness about the harm wreaked by a flawed economic policy. Declared mentally unfit, he lost his reputation through alleged insanity (Neptune). He languished in an Italian prison cage and an American asylum (loss to the Pisces house intercepted in the 12th house of confinement). By calling him insane, the government was able to discredit his economic opinions, which were neither unreasonable nor unjustified.

Jupiter in Virgo is conjunct (and parallel) the North Node, and therefore stimulated by a sustained rush of incoming energy available for work in the manifest world. Jupiter rules long distance travel, publishing, higher thought, philosophy, and all things foreign. The 9th house has a similar meaning, as does Sagittarius, and here Sagittarius is on the 9th house cusp ruled by Jupiter. Ezra was an expatriate, he spoke nine languages, he helped authors polish their manuscripts, and he promoted a philosophy of fair economic policy. This was an over-reaching Jupiter, and a productive one, but he went too far. Jupiter in Virgo is in fall, and he had trouble as a lecturer at university, and he created serious trouble for himself with his radio broadcasts. His overarching compulsion to speak his truth at any cost brought his downfall.

Venus in Sagittarius is at the North Bending of the nodes, a position that fosters maximum output. Ruling the 2nd house, Venus was less concerned about making money and more concerned about promoting an equitable monetary policy (Venus ruling the 2nd). Aside from money, the North Bending Venus also manifested many women and artists (Venus ruling the 7th).

The true mystery of the world is the visible, not the invisible.

— *Oscar Wilde*

Chapter 8
A Visionary
Albert Einstein

Einstein revolutionized Newtonian physics and gave science a new understanding of energy at both the subatomic and cosmological level. He did not start talking until he was three and did not speak fluently until he was nine. He was four when his father showed him a compass and Einstein realized there had to be something invisible that made the needle move. By ten, he was reading Kant and Euclid, and showed a talent for mathematics and physics. At twelve, his study of science led him to reject the stories of the Bible and mistrust authority, believing the 'youth [were being] intentionally deceived by the state through lies.' He thought in pictures, not in words, thinking visually rather than verbally. Although Jewish, his parents were unobservant and he attended a Christian school. He loved music and played the violin.

After graduating from university, he searched in vain for two years for a college-level teaching post. He finally settled for a job in a patent office examining new technologies related to electromagnetism. He had a daughter (revealed thirty years after his death) who may have been given up for adoption or who died in infancy. After her birth, Einstein married her mother, a woman he had met at university. They had two sons, the oldest became an engineer, and the youngest was schizophrenic.

In 1905, while working in the patent office, Einstein had four papers published that transformed the field of physics. After an earlier dissertation was rejected, he earned his doctorate that year. Three years later he quit his job to become a Professor of Physics at the University of Zurich. He was absent-minded, unkempt, and a rambling and unpopular lecturer. He was a prolific writer and during his lifetime he published over three hundred scientific papers and more than a hundred and fifty articles.

In 1919, he divorced and remarried. That same year he proved his theory that gravity bent starlight. This was shown during an eclipse when the position of stars near the eclipse appeared to change position due to the proximity of the Sun.

Einstein won the Nobel Prize in Physics in 1921 for explaining the photoelectric effect (incoming light causing the ejection of electrons). Although he had been working on relativity, it was considered too controversial for the prize.

In 1933, as the Nazis rose in power, Einstein moved to the U.S. and accepted a post at Princeton. Afraid Germany was working on a nuclear bomb, he pushed President F. D. Roosevelt to do the same—pressure he later regretted.

His goal in physics was to combine the four grand forces (nuclear, electron, radioactive, and gravitational) in a model of the universe that united space, time, mass, energy, motion and light. Although his calculations showed the universe was expanding, he believed it to be static and introduced a fudge factor in his equations to support his beliefs. He later called this 'cosmological constant' his greatest blunder. During the last twenty years of his life, he had a falling out with modern physicists over his rejection of probability in quantum mechanics, believing 'god didn't play dice with the universe.'

He was agnostic, 'a deeply religious nonbeliever.' He said, "If something is in me which can be called religious then it is the unbounded admiration for the structure of the world so far as our science can reveal it." For Einstein, "God appears as the physical world itself ... an orderly system obeying rules which could be discovered by those who had the courage, imagination, and persistence to go on searching for them."

In his credo, he wrote, "…I do not believe in free will… Man can do what he wants, but he cannot will what he wills." By this, Einstein meant that thinking followed the laws of nature and therefore humans did not get to 'choose' their thoughts and thus their actions. He said, "This awareness of the lack of free will keeps me from taking myself and my fellow men too seriously as acting and deciding individuals, and from losing my temper … (Nonetheless) I am compelled to act as if free will existed, because if I wish to live in a civilized society I must act responsibly. I know that philosophically a murderer is not responsible for his crime, but I prefer not to take tea with him."

After his death in 1955, Einstein's brain was preserved for later study. In 2009, published papers indicated that his brain was anatomically different from ordinary brains. It was smaller than average and missing a structure in both frontal lobes. In a normal brain this region contains Boca's area, a structure important for speech. In compensation for the missing part, the inferior parietal lobe, the part of the brain responsible for powerful visualization, mathematical processing, and collating information from multiple brain regions, was fifteen percent wider than usual. In this region there was a truncated groove, and as a result of this missing fissure, neurons that would otherwise be separated were brought closer together. In the inferior parietal area of the left hemisphere (related to logic and linear thought), there was an increase in glial cells, which support neurons (brain cells). High brain cell activity in this region may have caused the increase in glial cells. Alternatively, an increase in glial cells in the region may have fostered higher brain cell activity.

Nativity

Before we begin, I would like to clarify my understanding of the astrological significations related to science and astronomy. Rex Bills gives science in general to the 9th house (universities, philosophy, beliefs); Jupiter (higher thought, grand theories), Uranus (brilliance, innovative cutting-edge thinking, breakthroughs), and Aquarius (scientists, humanitarian advances and endeavors); also possibly, Mercury (linear thinking and processing), Virgo (critical, numerically prone,) Gemini (collecting information) and Saturn (practical application of scientific theories and the status quo). To this I would add Libra, which is mathematically inclined. While Pisces symbolizes oceans, it also represents the oceans of outer space and therefore the cosmos. Bills

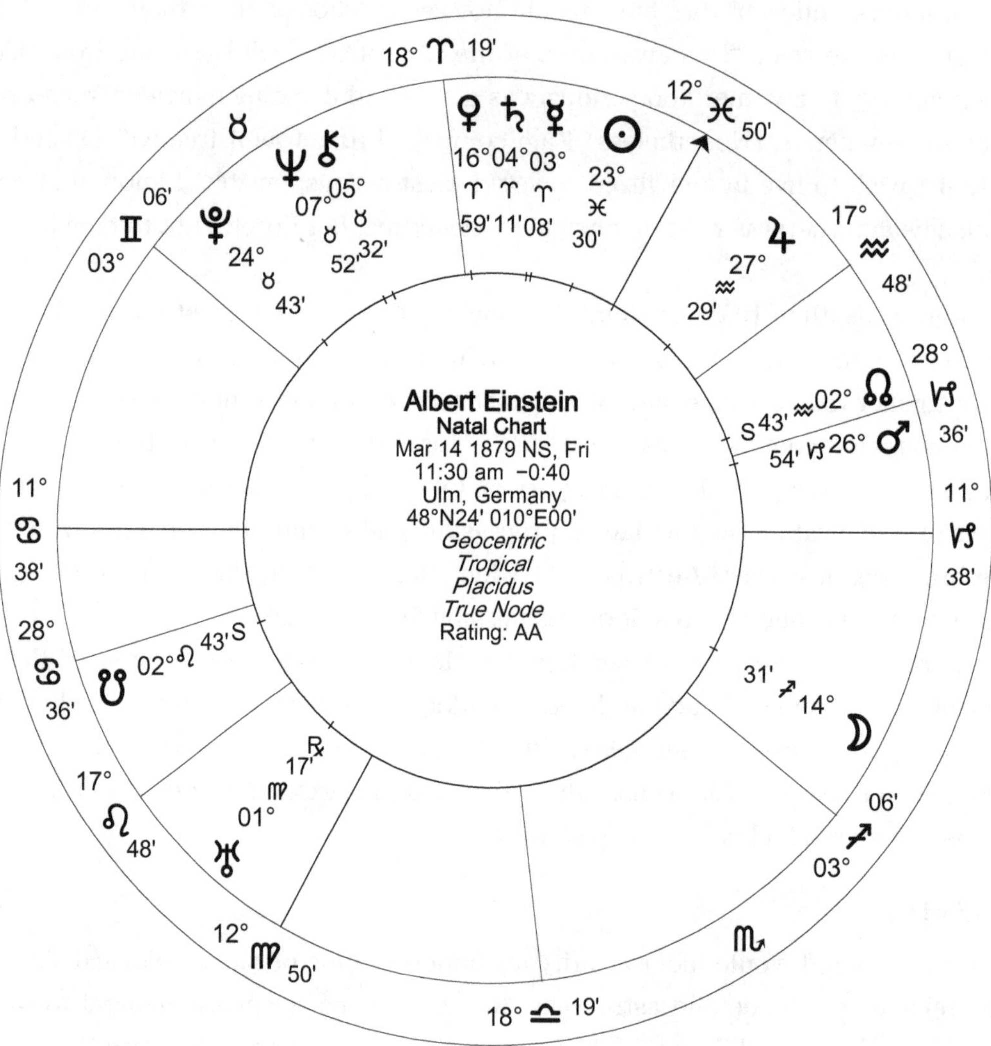

Chart 23:

Albert Einstein Nativity

gives rulership of both oceans and outer space to Neptune; scientific research to Scorpio and Uranus; nuclear and atomic science to Pluto and Scorpio; and scientific publications and institutes to the 9th house, Sagittarius, and Jupiter.

In brief summary, Einstein has an Aries stellium, and a mutual reception between Mars and Saturn, which together are the final dispositors of the chart (Chart 23). He has a stunning lack of dignified planets. The Sun, Mercury, and Jupiter are peregrine. Venus is in detriment. Saturn is in fall. The Moon has weak dignity by face, and Mars, with the strongest dignity, is exalted. In declination, the Moon (26S21) is out-of-bounds (unrestrained by convention).

He has a Pisces Sun, which gives imagination, an ability to visualize, attunement to non-ordinary reality, and a desire for unification. He sought a unified model of the universe and said, "There is no logical path to these laws, only intuition." The Sun rules the 3rd house of rational thinking, and he thought in pictures (Pisces). The Sun is in the 10th house of the career and public recognition, giving ambition, high purpose, and professional visibility.

The Sun rules the South Node, an indication of loss in regards to the luminary. He had a hard time gaining employment, he was a bad lecturer, and he was a questionable father (what happened to his daughter?) As a boy, his Sun shone dimly, and some thought him mentally challenged. He was slow to speak (Sun ruling the 3rd), and yet had precocious insight into invisible forces of energy. As he aged, he gave away his Sun (himself) in service. He did not work for personal or professional glory, but to understand the mysteries of the universe. He was absent-minded. There is a story that he met an acquaintance at lunchtime one day, and after they had conversed a few moments he asked his friend if he had been heading towards the university or towards home. When told the former, he said that was good for it meant he had already eaten lunch and was on his way back to work (lack of awareness of self).

The Moon is in the 6th house in Sagittarius and rules the Ascendant. His life was his work and he worked hard, up until the day he died. His desire was to understand the physical and non-physical (energetic) worlds. He wanted to know the truth. He also did much traveling, lived in foreign countries, and worked at a university. The Moon is trine Venus and he enjoyed his work.

The north nodal PNSE was at 2°08' Aquarius and fell in his 8th, the house that expanded during his life. He was interested in the mysterious forces of the physical world. He did not think of himself as smart, but rather as curious, "To sense that behind anything that can be experienced there is a something that our minds cannot grasp … To me it suffices to wonder at these secrets …"

The natal nodes are stationary and turned direct within the day. The North Node is in the degree of the PNSE and ruled by Uranus, which acquires wisdom, maturity, and knowingness through the association. In Virgo, in the 3rd house of the mind, Uranus was a driver of his life: he desired to know "the mind of God…. I want to know his thoughts…. What I am really interested in is knowing whether God could have created the world in a different way." With Uranus, the planet of cutting-edge science, ruling the 9th house (philosophy, higher education) from the 3rd, his unique way of thinking inspired grand theories of how the universe works.

Chiron cannot be ignored as it is at the North Bending of the nodes. Einstein's *opus magnum* healed a distorted perception of physical reality (Chiron in Taurus). Chiron is conjunct Neptune, the planet of the cosmos, which links Neptune to the North Bending. Neptune manifest outwardly. Einstein studied space. He had great insight and used his imagination and intuition to study the forces of nature—the non-ordinary intangible reality of the physical plane. Both the career (Neptune ruling the 10th) and the Sun (in Pisces) were empowered by the north nodal influence of Neptune.

Two configurations explain his attention to physics (first configuration) and his scientific drive and talent (second configuration). In the first, the Sun, Mars, and Pluto form an easy isosceles triangle, which describe his (Sun) interest in the forces of energy that underlie physical reality (Mars trine Pluto in earth signs). The easy aspects are prodded to action by a Jupiter–Pluto square, driving him to explore the 'mind of God.'

Jupiter ties the first configuration with the second. This is a boomerang (a yod with an opposition) that has Uranus (science) at the apex inconjunct the North Node, quincunx Mercury–Saturn (mental determination and perseverance), and opposite Jupiter (grand theories). The inconjunct of Uranus to the node, adds further strength to the planet, but introduces frustration. While the configuration was associated with his scientific ability, it also alluded to his professional difficulties. He had a hard time getting a university job. He alienated scientists who didn't agree with his theories. His first Ph.D. thesis was rejected. Minor research won him the Nobel Prize. He modified an equation to give him the result he desired—twisting the facts to fit his theory.

Mirabilis Annus

At twenty-six, after working three years as a patent clerk, Einstein published his papers on time, space, and matter. Since I am looking at a period of productivity rather than a certain date, the focus will be on the progressions and outer planetary transits set for his twenty-sixth birthday (Chart 24). There was a solar eclipse a week before his birthday at 14°57' Pisces, with Neptune (unification) as the lord. The eclipse fell on his 10th house cusp and marked the turning point of his career.

Progressed Mercury was at the North Bending of the progressed nodes, indicating a period of impressive intellectual expression. The progressed Ascendant was conjunct the progressed and natal South Node at a time of heightened otherworld insight. The transiting nodes had just crossed the MC/IC and were sextile/trine natal Neptune, denoting empowerment of the imagination and receptivity to non-ordinary otherworld reality.

The square between natal Jupiter (higher study) and Pluto (subatomic energy) was activated by transiting Saturn (conjunct natal Jupiter), and during this time he earned his Ph.D. and became a respected scientific authority in physics.

There was a mundane Uranus–Neptune opposition (scientific study of outer space) that activated the natal boomerang, denoting a time of applied, inspired, and cutting-edge scientific research. The transiting Uranus–Neptune opposition formed a t-square with natal Mercury and Saturn, describing his thought experiments. Outside a university setting and without the backing of its resources, the lowly patent clerk with a failed dissertation used his imagination (Neptune) to advance the frontiers of science (Uranus).

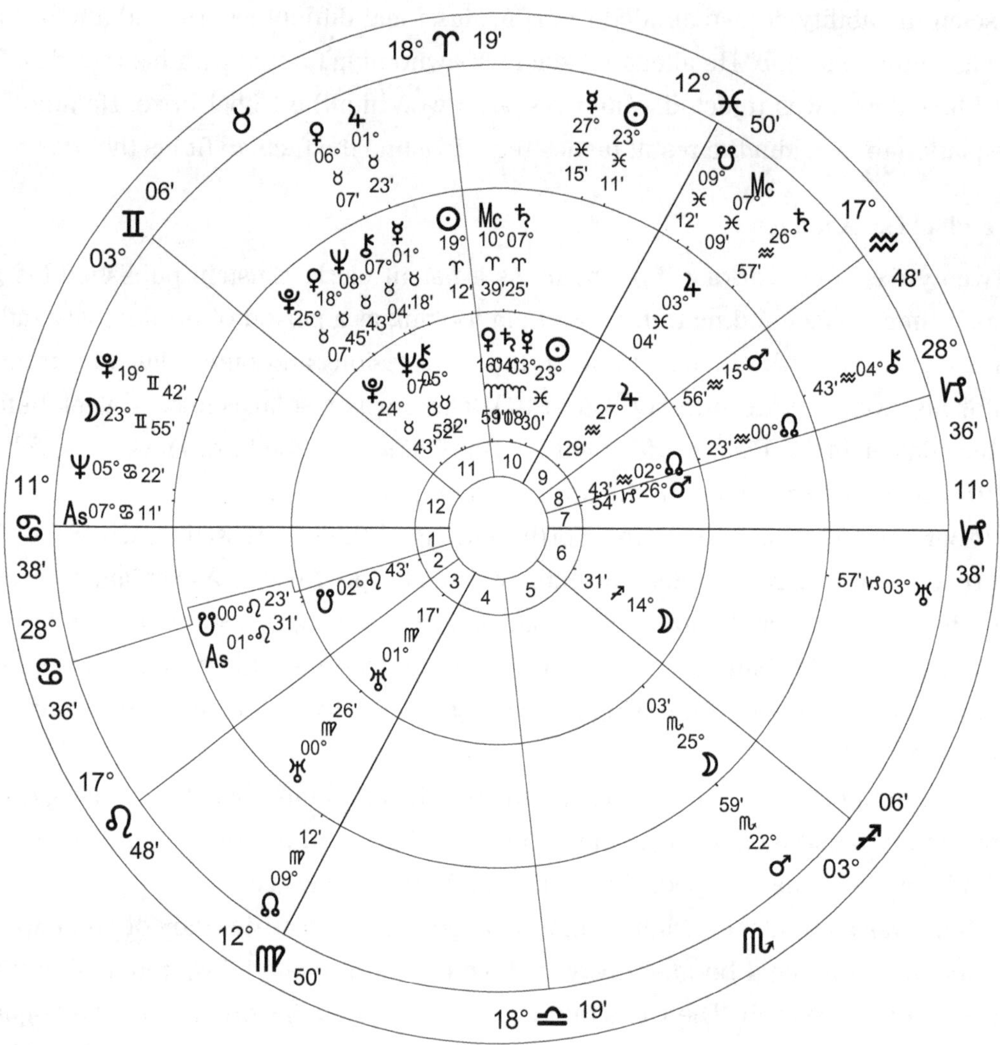

Chart 24:

Einstein's Miraculous Year, Mar 14, 1905, Ulm, Germany, 11:30 a.m. CET

Gravitational Eclipse

Einstein employed the May 29, 1919, solar eclipse to test his hypothesis that gravity could warp space and time. The eclipse reached totality at 1:11:34 pm over the West African island of Principe. In the minutes leading up to the eclipse, the sky was overcast, but as the Moon began to conjunct the Sun, the sky cleared and darkened, enabling the eclipse and the nearby stars to be photographed.

The eclipse occurred in the constellation of Taurus at a sidereal position of 13°29'. The locations of the four brightest stars in the Hyades cluster were measured. These stars form the V of the bull, along with the brightest star Aldebaran, which is much closer to Earth and not a part of the star cluster, but in line with it. The same sector of the sky was photographed six months later when the Sun was far away in Scorpio. When the positions of the stars in the two photographs were compared, they differed by the distance approximately predicted by general relativity. Einstein had proved the gravitational field of the sun warped space and bent the light of stars. According to headlines, 'men of science were agog.'

In the stand-alone eclipse chart (Chart 25), the degree of the lunation is 7°06' Gemini. (While the eclipse occurred in the constellation of Taurus in the sky, in the tropical chart where longitude positions are measured from 0° Aries, the eclipse was in Gemini due to the precession of the equinoxes). Mercury (fact gathering) is the lord, and was square Saturn (clouds and delay of results). Uranus at 1° Pisces was square the stationary lunar nodes at the North Bending, coinciding with a revelatory (North Bending) scientific discovery (Uranus) about the cosmos (Pisces). Neptune in Leo was sextile/trine the nodes and the Gemini solar eclipse, as illuminating information about outer space was acquired.

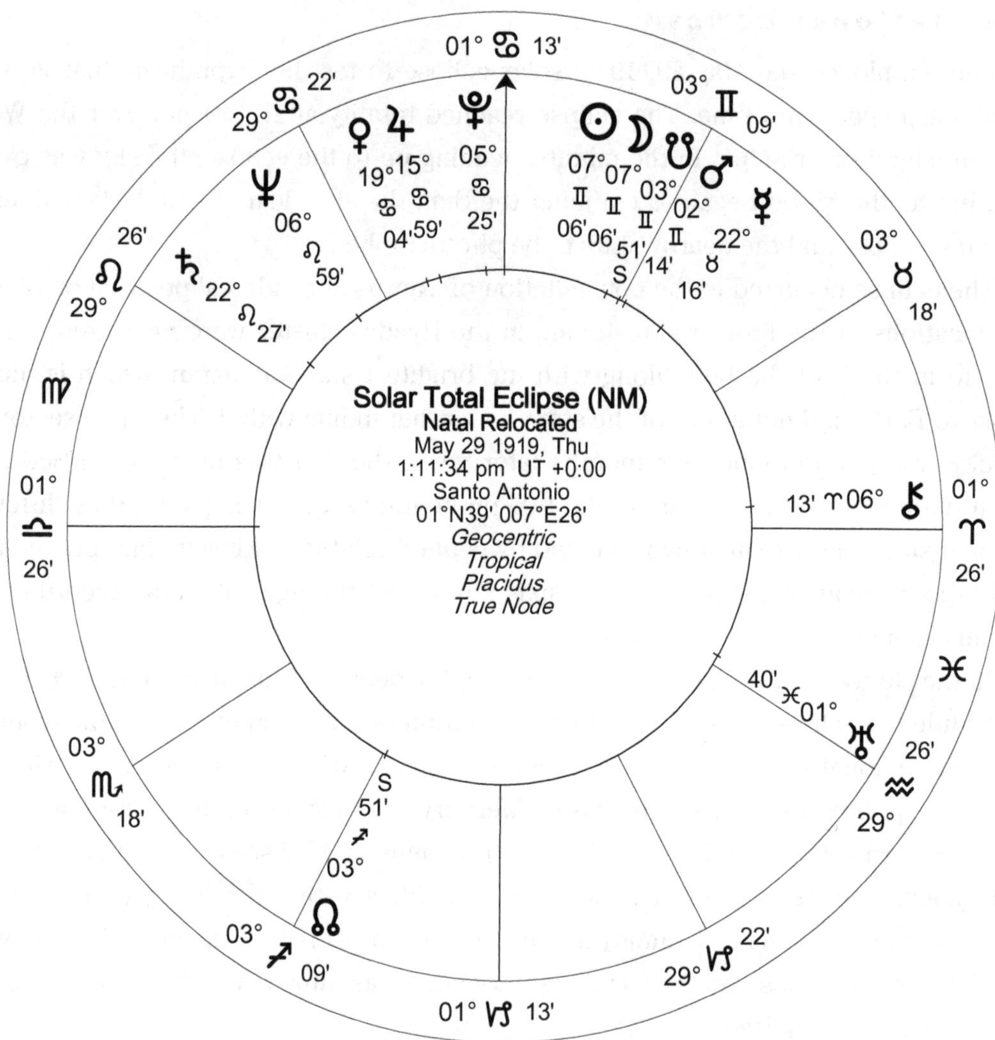

Chart 25:

Eclipse Gravitational Experiment

Einstein's Eclipse

At the time of the eclipse (Chart 26), Einstein was forty years old and undergoing his Uranus opposition and Neptune square. He was in a mid-life crisis, on the brink of a divorce and remarriage, and some aspects are in reference to this. The eclipse fell in his 12th house of the unknown.

Transiting Uranus was at the North Bending of the transiting nodes, while natal Uranus was at the South Bending, forming a double-whammy that activated the natal boomerang and described innovative scientific research. The progressed Sun was at the North Bending of the natal nodes, marking a period of recognition and ego-achievement. Transiting Mars was conjunct the transiting South Node and both were conjunct progressed Venus, and formed a t-square with natal Uranus and progressed Jupiter, alluding to the experiment and the scientific hopes on which the results rested. Progressed Jupiter was at the North Bending of the transiting nodes as the experiment was conducted. The progressed Moon was conjunct progressed Pluto and in a t-square with transiting Saturn, progressed Mars, and natal Jupiter. This activated the triangular configuration with the Sun, Mars, and Pluto related to his work on the mysterious forces of nature. Transiting Neptune was square itself and trine natal Mercury–Saturn, while transiting Pluto was square natal Mercury–Saturn, reflective of the experiment and the last minute problems (clouds) that nearly prevented it.

In declination, the transiting luminaries, South Node and Mars were parallel the progressed South Node, and Einstein channeled the energy of the eclipse into his work. Transiting Pluto was parallel the natal South Node, and he gained insight into the intangible forces of nature. In latitude, transiting Neptune was at the 0° line of the ecliptic, contraparallel progressed Mercury, as he collected information from the cosmos.

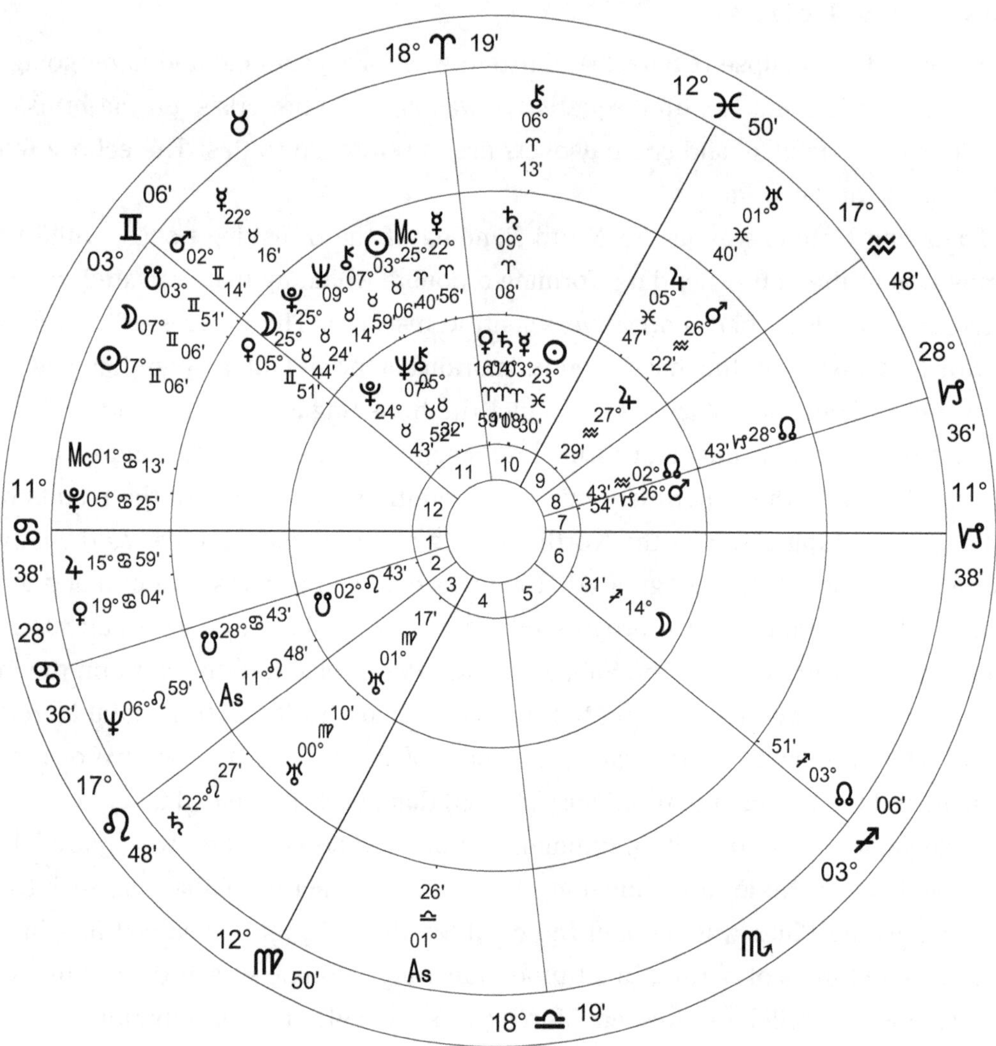

Chart 26:

Einstein's Eclipse, May 29, 1919, Santo Antonio, 1:11: 34 p.m. UT

Nobel Laureate

In 1922, Einstein was awarded the 1921 Nobel Prize "for his services to Theoretical Physics and especially for his discovery of the laws of the photoelectric effect." He received the award on December 10, 1922 (Chart 27). Two months before the ceremony on September 21, 1922, there was a north nodal solar eclipse at 27°24' Virgo, opposite his natal Sun. The lord of the eclipse was Mercury (news).

On the night of the event, the progressed Midheaven was at the North Bending of the progressed nodes, signifying a time of outward professional culmination. The progressed Sun was conjunct natal Neptune (ruler 10) and sextile progressed Jupiter, signifying high professional honors. There was also a progressed Venus–Saturn sextile, repeating the message of professional acknowledgement and achievement. The transiting South Node was conjunct the natal Sun, and he was recognized for his 'services' to physics. Transiting Neptune formed a grand trine with progressed Mercury (lord), natal Venus, and transiting Sun–Mercury, indicating joy, news, and dreams coming true. Transiting Pluto was conjunct the natal Ascendant and progressed Moon, sextile progressed Neptune, and in a grand trine with progressed Jupiter and transiting Jupiter, denoting long distance travel, a ceremony, and personal empowerment.

There was a mundane transiting trine between Uranus and Pluto, and a transiting sextile between Saturn and Neptune, which aligned with the angles of Einstein's chart. On a night he won recognition for his research on light energy and the effect of excitable electrons, transiting Uranus was conjunct his natal Midheaven, and transiting Pluto was conjunct his natal Ascendant and progressed Moon. Transiting Neptune was conjunct his progressed Ascendant, indicating widespread personal recognition.

However, not all was rosy. Transiting Saturn was opposite natal Venus and progressed Mercury, and though he had developed a model of the universe, he was not recognized for it. Transiting Mars was conjunct progressed Mars and natal Jupiter, and square progressed Pluto, suggestive of angst that his grand theory won no prize.

In declination, the transiting South Node was parallel natal Sun and contraparallel progressed Saturn, a simple statement of personal recognition for service.

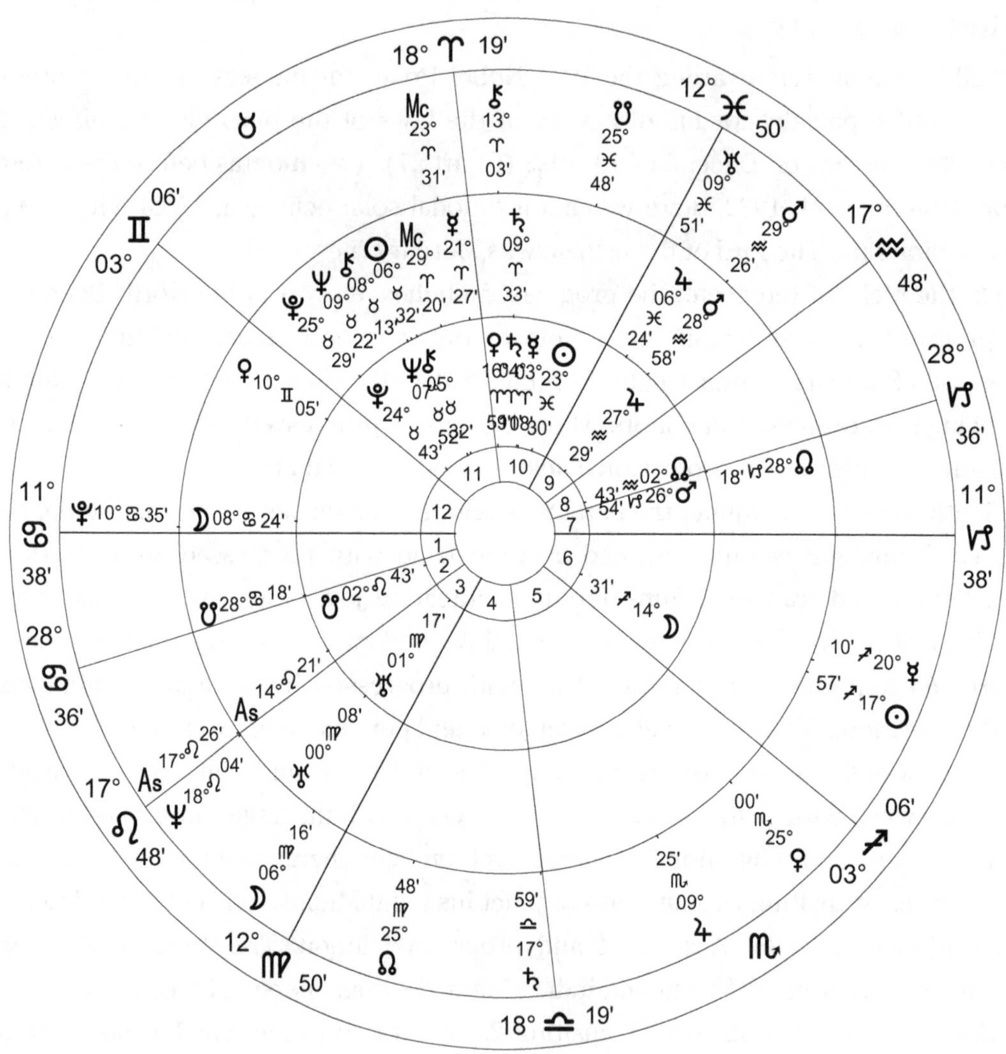

Chart 27:

Einstein's Nobel Prize, Dec. 10, 1922, Stockholm, Sweden, 8:00 p.m. CET

Biggest Blunder

Up until 1929, the prevailing scientific view of the universe was that it was static (fixed in size). Although Einstein's mathematical equations showed it was expanding (into what, exactly, is an interesting question), he introduced a cosmological constant to keep it static. Then, in March 1929, Edwin Hubble published a paper proving that galaxies were receding and the universe was, in fact, expanding.

Because the date of the journal's publication is not known, I will ignore the faster moving planets and look at the outer planets and progressions in mid-March (Chart 28). The solar eclipse before the Hubble paper was published occurred on November 12, 1928, at 19°46' Scorpio. It was a south nodal eclipse (loss) with Pluto (death) serving as the lord. The eclipse was square the progressed Ascendant–Descendant, marking a crisis for him personally, as well as a crisis with partners—collaborators and fellow scientists.

The progressed Moon was sextile/trine the natal nodes, emphasizing an emotional reaction, which in this instance was devastation. The progressed Moon was quincunx progressed Mars (no action could amend his error) and opposite natal Saturn–Mercury (reeling from a public mistake). Progressed Chiron was conjunct progressed Neptune, reflecting his incorrect (wounded) model of the universe. Transiting Neptune formed a t-square and was conjunct natal Uranus, square natal Pluto and opposite natal Jupiter, denoting faulty intuition and a confused model of the cosmos. Transiting Saturn was at the Capricorn Aries Point square natal Mercury–Saturn, transiting Uranus (widely) and trine transiting Neptune–natal Uranus, reflecting his error that came to the attention of the world. The transiting North Node was conjunct natal Pluto (lord) signifying literal death—of his model.

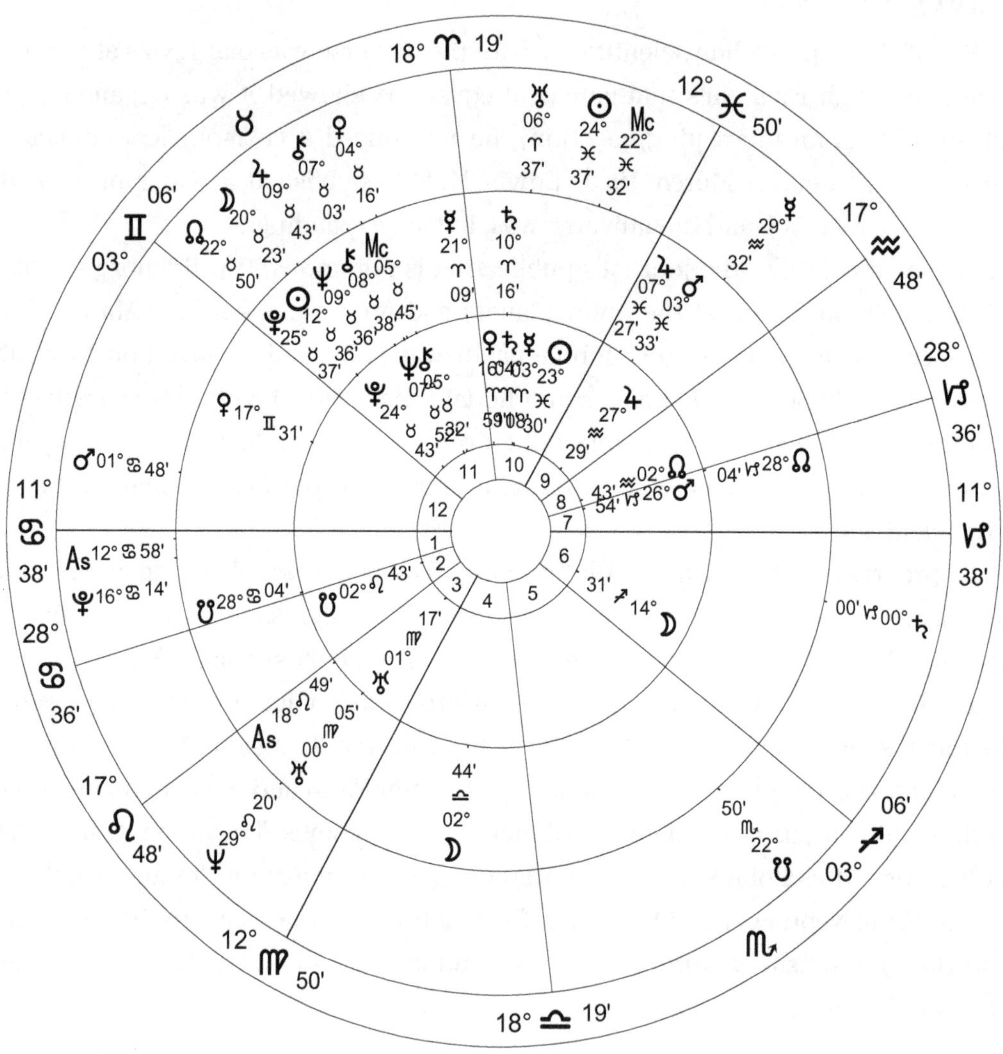

Chart 28:

Einstein's Biggest Blunder, March 15, 1929, Princeton, NJ, noon

Death

At seventy-six, a blood vessel ruptured suddenly in Einstein's abdomen and he was rushed to the hospital. He took notes for an impending TV interview, but he ended up refusing the surgery that would have repaired the vessel. "I want to go when I want. It is tasteless to prolong life artificially. I have done my share, it is time to go. I will do it elegantly." He died at 1.15 a.m. on April 18, 1955 (Chart 29).

The solar eclipse before his death was on Christmas Day at 2°59' Capricorn. It was a north nodal eclipse (outer event) that fell in his 6th house of illness. While Saturn was the ruler of the sign of the eclipse, transiting Mercury at 2°52' Capricorn, was in the degree of the eclipse, making it the lord. Natally the two planets are conjunct and the eclipse was square the conjunction.

On the day of his death, in a double-whammy, progressed Mars (blood) was conjunct the natal Sun, and transiting Mars was conjunct the progressed Sun (square the progressed Ascendant). He refused surgery and his will prevailed. A transiting cardinal t-square had formed between the Sun, Jupiter–Uranus and Neptune, that formed a grand cross with his natal Mars and the progressed North Node, reflecting a sudden life-threatening blood related event and his refusal of surgery. Transiting Jupiter–Uranus were in the 1st house conjunct the progressed South Node, signaling a huge and sudden loss for the physical body. Transiting Neptune was at the South Bending of the progressed nodes, bringing acceptance. He had no desire to fight death.

The timer for the event was transiting Mercury, lord of the eclipse and ruler of the 4th house of the end of the matter, coming to quincunx transiting Saturn (ruler of the eclipse and the 9th house of death). Transiting Mercury at the North Bending of the progressed nodes brought an outer event, which in this case was the end of life.

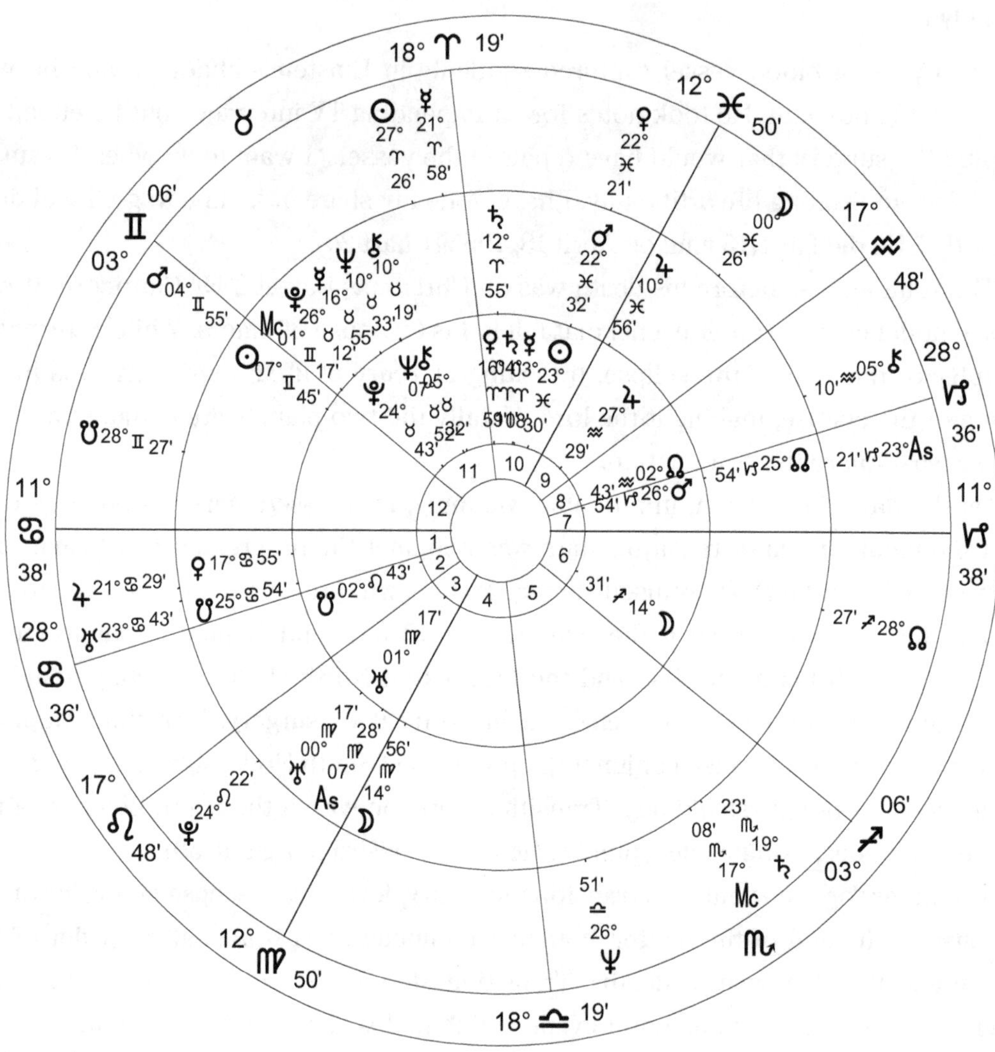

Chart 29:

Einstein's Death, April 18, 1955, Princeton, NJ, 1.15 a.m. EST

The spiritual path—is simply the journey of living our lives. Everyone is on a spiritual path; most people just don't know it.

— Marianne Williamson

Chapter 9
A Queen

The un-named royal princess born in 1926 as George White was finishing his book on the lunar nodes was the Queen of England. White had a pessimistic view of the South Node and considered it to bring grave harm. "When a child is born with the nodes in either pair of angles, do not immediately commence delineating, for with these positions you at times get the most extreme forms of abnormality without any horoscopic indications to point them out.... The child may be born with half the head missing, or any of the vital organs missing or deformed; or it may be a microcephalic idiot, though the horoscope shows a philosopher or an astute man of business." Since the nodes were not understood by most astrological writers of the time, he was worried the royal chart would be misinterpreted and the injury of the nodes would be overlooked.

Elizabeth Windsor was the first-born daughter of Prince Albert, who was first in line to the British throne after his brother. When she was ten, her uncle abdicated and Elizabeth became heir to the crown. Currently eighty-five, she has been a popular monarch and has served as the Queen of England for sixty years.

Nativity

The PNSE was on January 14, 1926, at 23°46' Capricorn, with Saturn serving as the lord. The eclipse fell on her Ascendant, and the first house (that contains the South Node) would expand during her lifetime.

The Queen (Chart 30) has a Taurus Sun, and she is practical and down to earth. In the 3rd house, she is a communicator. The Sun makes no planetary aspects but is conjunct Chiron, indicative of a wound to her ego or, alternatively, she has a capacity to heal others. The Sun rules the intercepted 7th, reflecting the importance of one-to-one relationships in her life.

The Moon is in Leo and she is, after all, a queen. The Moon is in the 7th house and rules the 6th and 7th, alluding to a day job that involves emotionally connecting with her millions of subjects. The Moon rules the North Node and without effort on her part, she inherited a throne and became queen. Her Leo Moon knows how to be regal and behave in a manner befitting the monarchy (a quality lost on her children and their spouses).

Capricorn is rising and from childhood she was known for her responsible attitude. Saturn rules the chart and is conjunct the 10th house cusp, a position signaling a rise in station—an elevation of the personality to great heights. Saturn also rules the South Node, and the associated loss was her personal life, sacrificed for the kingdom. Saturn is in Scorpio and she has a tenacious hold on her crown. She came unexpectedly (Saturn trine Uranus) to power through a sex scandal and once on the throne, has been loath to give it up. With Saturn in Scorpio, she may resort to underhanded and manipulative measures to consolidate power. Saturn is sextile/trine the nodes acquiring a boost of energy. She is a powerful authority, not merely a figurehead. Saturn is also sextile/trine the Ascendant and Descendant, giving Saturn an outlet personally, and she projects professionalism, hard work, and austerity. In relationships, she is dutiful, responsible, and accountable. Conjunct the 10th cusp, she is seen as a world authority.

Saturn is at the apex of a difficult planetary t-square, squaring both a first house conjunction of Mars and Jupiter in Aquarius, and a 7th house Neptune. With Neptune related to glamour, the square to Saturn reflects a queen who appears to be a royal

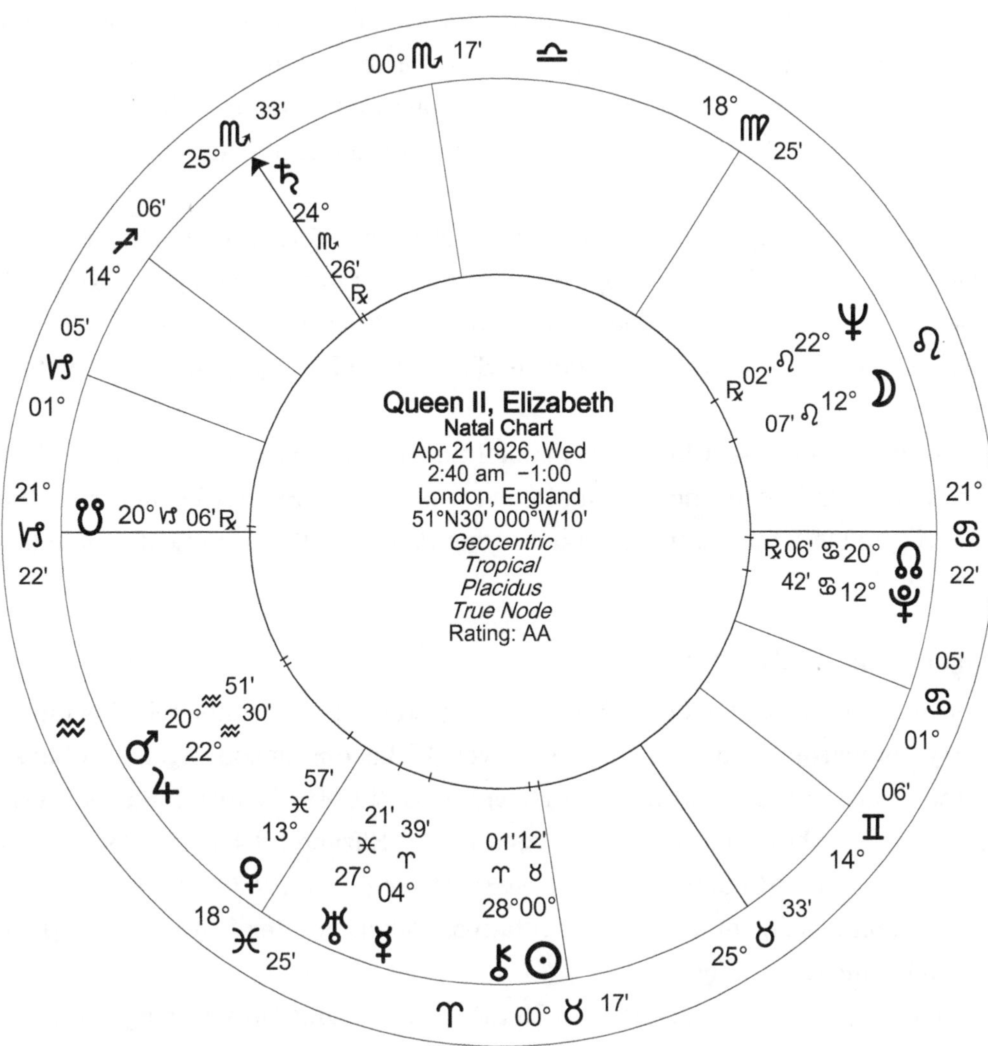

Chart 30:
Queen Elizabeth II Nativity

figurehead, but who actually wields political power. The Mars–Jupiter conjunction in the 1st in Aquarius points to a personal desire for independence, which is inhibited through duty (Saturn) and the royal expectations of her many subjects (Neptune). Despite calls for modernization, she has remained rigid in maintaining the monarchy as it has been for centuries.

In declination, Jupiter is contraparallel Neptune, forming an occultation and strengthening the divide of the opposition, and the almost mythological expectations that people have of her. Mars and Jupiter are inconjunct the North Node, alluding to frustration from the loss of independence. She has paid a high personal price for her position.

In latitude, Venus and Chiron are parallel the Sun, angles and nodes at the 0° mark on the ecliptic. As queen, she inherited great wealth and property (Venus rules the 4th and intercepted 8th). In longitude, Venus is trine Pluto, another significator of immense wealth.

Inheriting A Crown

On December 10, 1936, the Queen's uncle, King Edward VIII, announced his intention to marry his married and once-divorced lover, Wallace Simpson. Against a backlash from the Church of England and the government, the King chose Simpson over his royal duties and abdicated the throne. As a result, Elizabeth's father, Albert, became King. There was a north nodal solar eclipse on December 13, 1936, three days after the abdication announcement, at 21°48' Sagittarius, making Jupiter (royal events) the lord for the following six months.

On the day of the announcement (Chart 31), transiting Mars was square the progressed nodes at the North Bending, reflecting a weak monarch (Mars in detriment), renouncing royal duty in the name of love (Libra). The transiting North Node was conjunct the progressed Moon and square progressed Venus and progressed Uranus at the North Bending, bringing unexpected fortune and upset. In latitude, transiting Jupiter was parallel natal Venus, promising a regal title and great wealth.

There was a mundane opposition of Saturn and Neptune in the sky, aptly symbolizing the confusion in the royal authority. The opposition was sextile/trine Elizabeth's

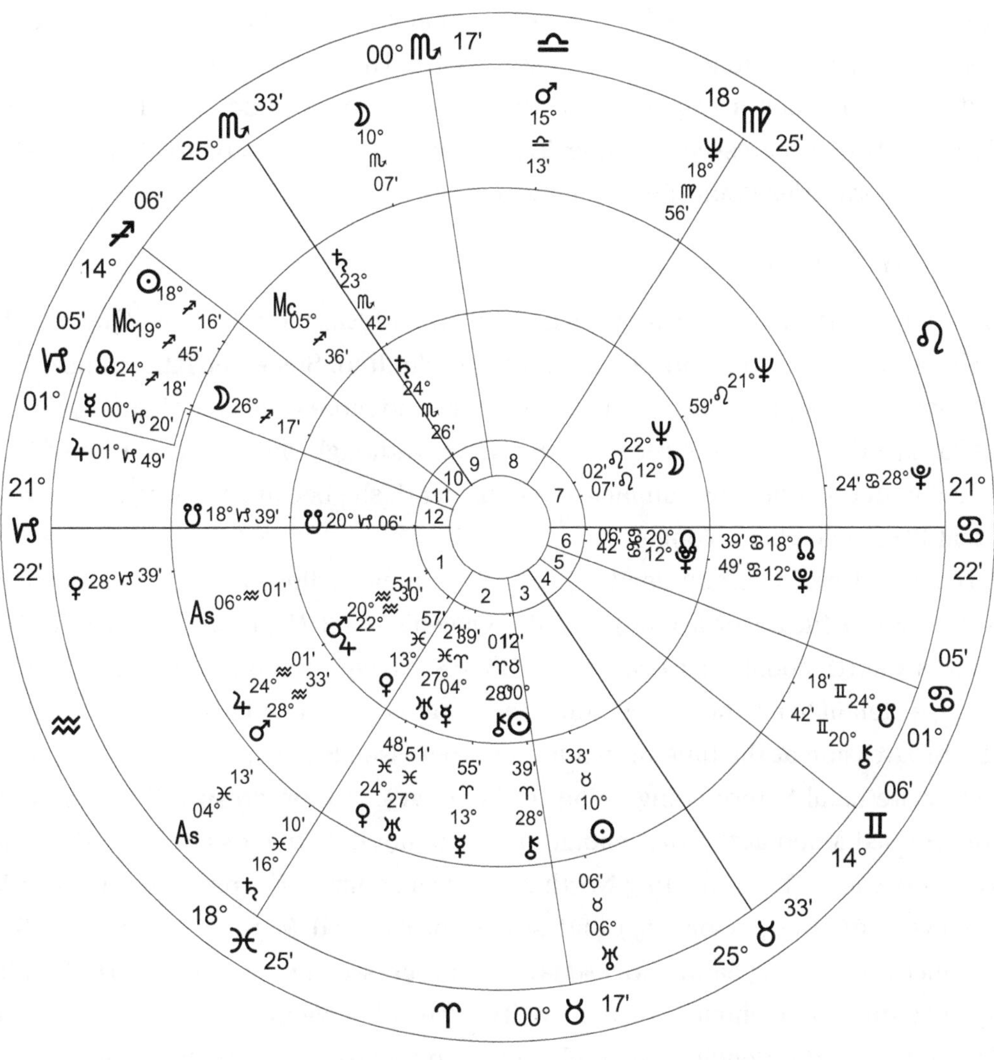

Chart 31:

Queen's Uncle Abdicates, Dec. 10, 1936, London, England, noon

progressed nodes, thereby affecting her personally. Her life changed irrevocably (transiting Uranus conjunct the progressed Sun). The trigger for the event was the transiting Sun making a t-square with the mundane opposition, sextile natal Mars–Jupiter, and trine progressed Neptune. Transiting Mercury was conjunct Jupiter (lord) at the Capricorn Aries Point (far-reaching news).

Death Of A King

On February 6, 1952, ailing King George VI died and Elizabeth became Queen (Chart 32). She was twenty-five, married, and had two children. Since her father's health had been poor for some time, she had assumed more and more of his royal duties. She was on safari in Kenya when she received the news. Although she would not be officially crowned until the following summer, upon his death she became the reigning monarch of Great Britain and her colonies.

Six days after the King's death, there was a lunar eclipse at 21°13' Leo conjunct transiting Pluto (death of a king) and the Queen's natal Neptune. Two weeks later, there was a north nodal solar eclipse at 5°43' Pisces, with Neptune serving as the lord. The eclipse fell in her 1st house, conjunct the progressed Ascendant.

By progression at the time of death, the progressed Sun was conjunct the natal IC and opposite natal Saturn (King going to the grave). The progressed Sun was sextile the progressed Moon at the Descendant, marking not only the loss of her father, but a move to the castle. The transiting North Node was conjunct the progressed Ascendant (outer event for the personality) and sextile progressed Mercury (ruling the 8th of inheritance). Transiting Saturn was square the progressed nodes at the North Bending, signaling a time of heightened responsibility. Transiting Neptune was square the natal nodes at the North Bending, symbolizing an outward event in the collective consciousness, and an acquisition of astounding wealth (Neptune ruling the 2nd). Transiting Uranus was conjunct natal Pluto and square transiting Jupiter and progressed Venus (sudden death bringing upset and change).

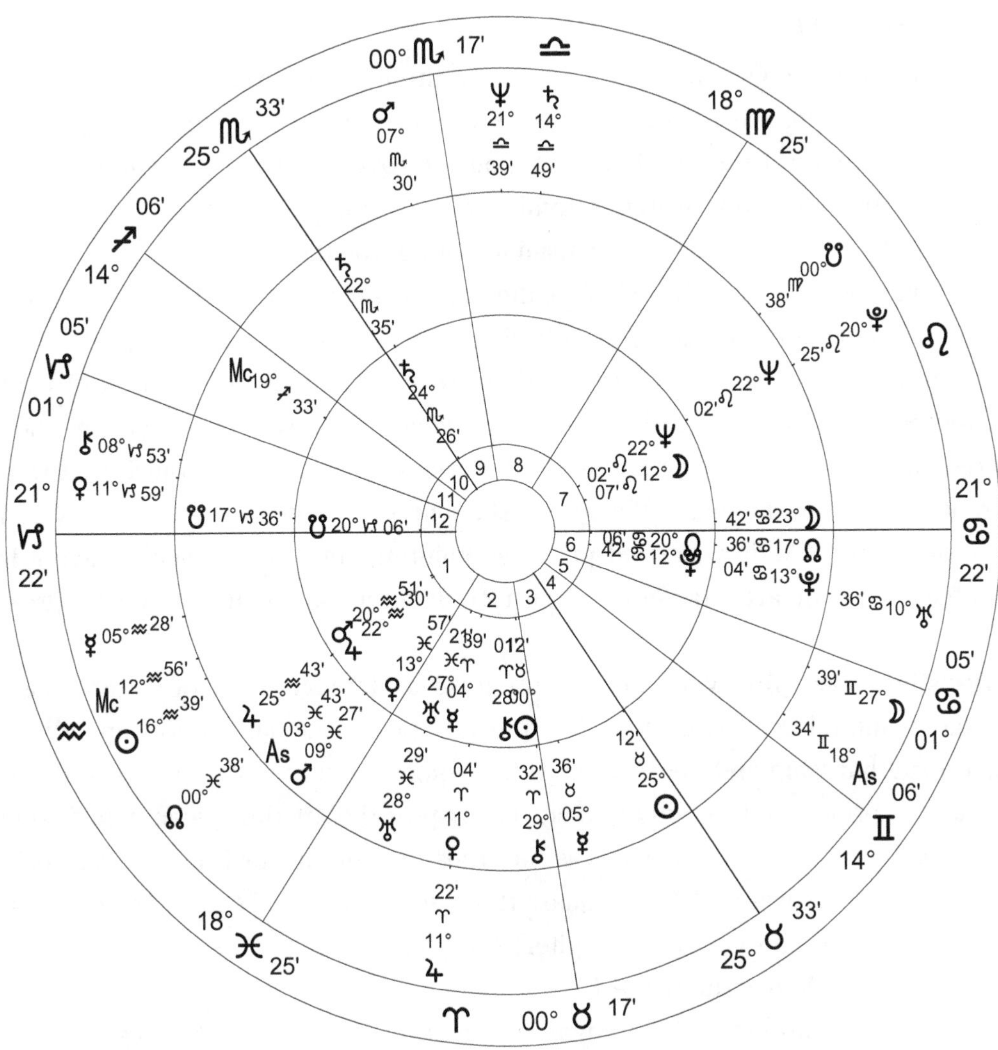

Chart 32:

Queen's Father's Death, Feb. 6, 1952, London, England, noon

The Great Fire

Forty years later, the Queen's castle caught on fire and suffered extensive damage. It began in her chapel after a spotlight set a curtain aflame. The fire spread quickly, burning out of control for nine hours. Ceilings collapsed, towers fell, and apartments were ruined by smoke and water. A total of one million gallons of water (some of it from the polluted Thames River) was used to put out the flames.

The south nodal solar eclipse before the fire was on June 30, 1992, at 8°56' Cancer, with the Moon (home) serving as the lord. The eclipse was square progressed Mars (fire). On the day of the fire (Chart 33) there was a mundane conjunction of Uranus and Neptune in Capricorn (sudden structural chaos) that was conjunct the Queen's progressed South Node and progressed Moon (loss in the home). Transiting Uranus–Neptune were opposite natal Pluto, a testament to the destruction. However, the Queen and Prince Andrew ferried priceless paintings out of the castle, saving irreplaceable pieces of art (transiting Saturn conjunct natal Venus sextile progressed Pluto).

Transiting Mars (fire) was conjunct progressed Mercury (ruler of the 8th house of devastation and rebirth). Transiting Saturn was opposite the natal Moon, an indication of emotional hardship and deprivation in the home. However, with progressed Venus conjunct the progressed Ascendant near the cusp of the 4th, the Queen would rebuild her castle. The timer for the event was the transiting Moon (lord) conjunct transiting Jupiter, opposite progressed Mars, square transiting Venus, and square the progressed Sun. This translated into a raging (Jupiter) fire (Mars) with the loss of personal (Sun) and real property (Venus ruling the 4th).

In declination, progressed Mars was contraparallel progressed Uranus, describing an accidental fire. In latitude, the progressed Moon was parallel natal Venus (and Chiron), transiting Mercury, and the Sun, angles, and nodes, which manifest as a wound to the home and the pocketbook.

Chart 33:

Queen's Castle on Fire, Nov. 20, 1992, London, England, 11.33 a.m. GMT

Death Of A Princess

A low point for the Queen and the British monarchy came in the wake of the untimely death of the 'people's princess,' Diana of Wales. The day after she died there was a north nodal solar eclipse at 9°33' Virgo, with Mercury (ruling the Queen's 8th house) serving as the lord.

At the time of the accident (Chart 34), transiting Venus was square the progressed nodes and progressed Pluto at the North Bending, symbolizing the death of the princess. Transiting Saturn was at the South Bending of the natal Nodes, and the Queen's restrained response brought her disapproval and condemnation.

There was a mundane transiting sextile between Uranus and Pluto, with the former trine progressed Venus, and opposite progressed Mercury, and the latter trine progressed Mercury and opposite progressed Venus. The Queen may have thought that a public statement was up to her discretion, but the public was enraged by her silence, and only after the Prime Minister intervened, did the Queen make a statement. Transiting Mercury was lost in the beams of the Sun, and square the progressed Ascendant and quincunx natal Mercury, which expressed first as silence, and then a forced eulogy.

Transiting Jupiter was opposite the natal Moon, marking a crisis for the Queen. According to the Prime Minister, the survival of the monarchy had never been in more danger. At the time of the accident, the transiting Moon was crossing the transiting IC, opposite transiting Jupiter, timing the event.

In declination, transiting Venus (Diana) was parallel natal Venus and contraparallel the progressed Moon, further describing the crisis in the monarchy and to the Queen following the death. In latitude, transiting Venus was parallel the Queen's natal Venus, Chiron, Sun, angles, and nodes, reflecting an outward wound and harm to the Queen's popularity.

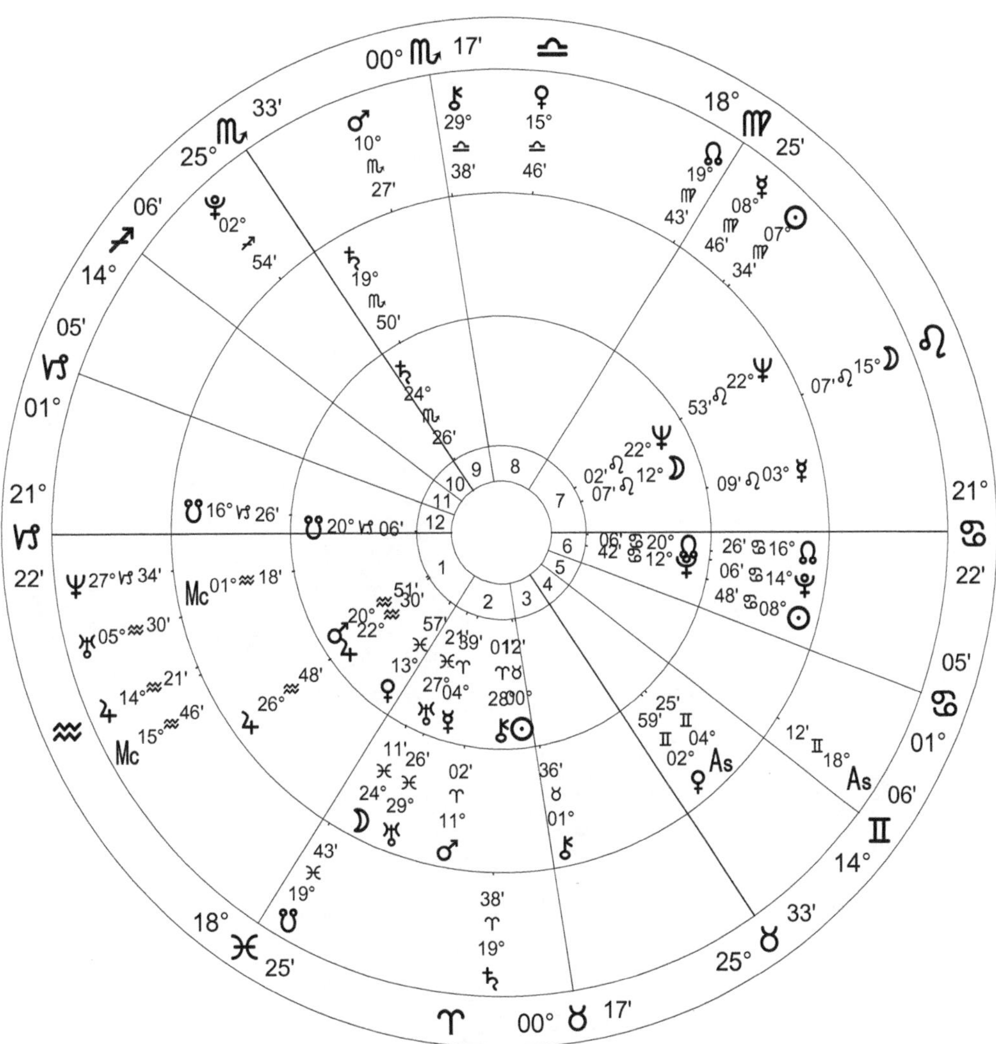

Chart 34:

Queen's daughter-in-law dies, Aug. 31, 1997, Paris, France, 0:27 a.m. CEDT

The purpose of life is not to be happy. The purpose of life is to matter, to be productive, to have it make some difference that you have lived at all. Happiness, in the ancient, noble version means self-fulfillment and is given to those who use to the fullest whatever talents God or luck or fate bestowed upon them.

— Leo Rosten

Chapter 10
Some Fairy Tale
Princess Diana

I cannot glance at the death of Diana without looking at the chart of the glamorous princess who bought into a fairy tale and found a nightmare. Growing up in a broken home, she was seven when her parents divorced after her mother had an affair. Her father won custody of the four children. The year before Diana was born, she had a brother who lived ten hours. When her mother was pregnant again, her parents expected Diana to be a boy and had no girl's name chosen at the time of her birth. Three years later the desired son was born. Four years after that, her mother left.

Diana attended boarding school where she showed a talent for dance and music, but not for academics. She failed high school, did not complete finishing school, and worked as a nursery school teacher. She had known Prince Charles from childhood and their romance blossomed in the summer of 1980 when she was nineteen and he was thirty-one. The royal family approved of the match and they became engaged in February 1981, marrying in July. By November, she was pregnant and soon had two sons. She was a hands-on mother and refused to defer to royal protocol or custom when it came to her children. As a member of the royal family, she was expected to involve herself in charitable work and she participated in over one hundred. Her primary interest was infectious disease afflicting children.

In the early 1990s, her marriage was unraveling. She learned about Charles' affair with Camilla weeks before her second son was born and sunk into a depression. In December 1992, as the palace press machinery painted Charles in the brightest light, the Queen granted permission for the separation. The sympathy of the public lay with Diana. Under pressure from the Queen, the couple divorced in August 1996. The following year Diana was dead, her life ending at thirty-six in a crumple of metal, in a Paris tunnel, on a dark August night.

Nativity

In overview, the nodal energy is linked with a three planet dispositor chain between the luminaries and Uranus, promising dynamic activity (Chart 35). Three configurations add a further testament to a life of great crises (a yod and a t-square), as well as great gains (a grand trine).

Sagittarius is rising, with Jupiter in Aquarius ruling the chart, giving universal generosity and largesse. Domiciled in the 2nd, Jupiter points to the importance of money and a focus on the accumulation of resources. There is a belief that money can change not only personal circumstance, but the circumstances of others (Jupiter in Aquarius).

The PNSE on February 15, 1961, was at 26°25' Aquarius and fell in the 2nd house, along with the South Node. The 2nd house of money was the arena which would expand greatly in her lifetime. The nodes were stationary at birth and would turn direct in five hours.

The Sun is in Cancer, and she was nurturing, motherly, and caring. With the Sun in the 7th, she was interested in partnership and marriage. In declination, the Sun is parallel the Descendant, which places the Sun on the angle, and actualized as a prince. The Sun rules the intercepted 8th, showing an interest in power and spousal money. She

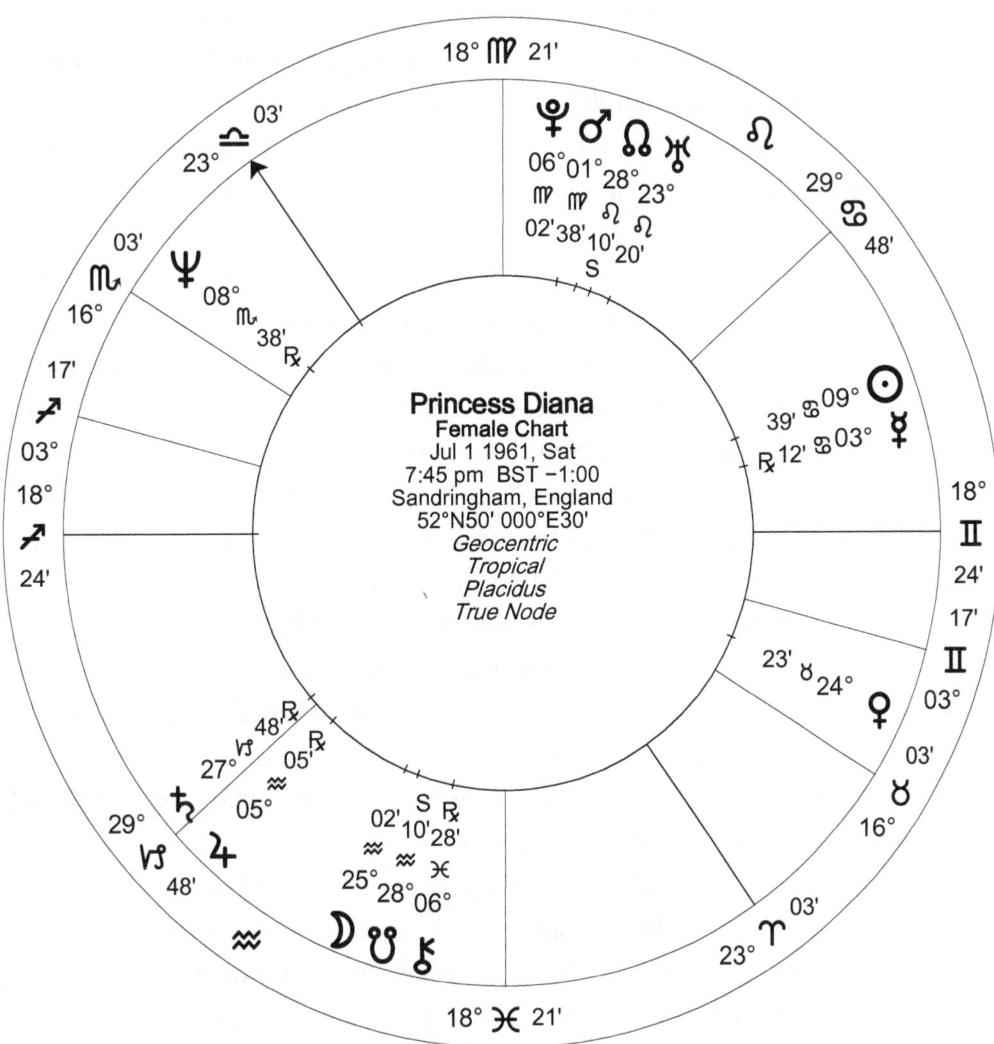

Chart 35:

Princess Diana Nativity

also suffered psychological trauma and transformed herself. The Sun rules the North Node, gaining inborn strength and wisdom through the association. She was given an opportunity to express herself outwardly in the world— and she took it. She was born to 'be someone' and innately knew how to hold power and behave in a manner that maximized her bearing. She became a big, bright star, and was adept at using the media for her own purposes (Sun trine Neptune in the 10th).

The Sun is disposited by an Aquarian Moon, which holds high ideals, mitigates emotional intensity, and gives concern not only for her own children, but for all children everywhere. The Moon is in the 2nd house, again pointing to an interest and need for financial security and the acquisition of resources. The Moon rules the 8th house, and shows money from the spouse coming to her. With the Moon conjunct the South Node, there is loss associated with the luminary. As a child, her mother abandoned her and she never received the amount of nurturing or love she needed. Upon her separation, she lost her children to the royal family. Their idea of shared custody was to give her fifty-seven visitation days a year. She also lost her royal title, the inheritance associated with the monarchy, and any prospect of becoming queen. To work optimally, it was necessary for her to use her Moon in service. Eventually she gave to others the maternal love and nurturing she never experienced. As a champion of starving, injured, maimed and diseased children throughout the globe, she devoted herself to numerous charities, giving her time and name to helping others.

The Moon is disposited (and opposed) by Uranus in the 8th house of inheritance and alimony. The opposition shows conflict with money that is emotionally upsetting. Uranus is in Leo, the sign of royalty, and she was a new kind of royal, one who was emotional and accessible to the people. Uranus is conjunct the North Node, denoting an influx of energy useful in the physical world, which manifest as a royal spouse who brought much money (Uranus ruling the intercepted 2nd).

However, Uranus rules the South Node, an indication this planet is also associated with loss. Upon marriage, she became public property and lost the right to be herself. After the breakup, there were bitter power struggles over money as the royal family fought to limit her alimony. With the ruler of the South Node conjunct the North Node, the losses pertaining to the South Node were expressed outwardly for everyone to see.

With the world watching the drama from the sidelines, she lost her royal title and the protection that went with it.

Venus is at the South Bending of the nodes, in a position of physical vulnerability and loss, but also inspired service. While dignified in Taurus, Venus is in a difficult t-square with the nodes, Moon, and Uranus. As the significator of love, she chose an admirable man, but one who didn't love her and 'did everything he could to knock her down.' Venus in the 5th and ruling the 5th, describes her royal children, whom she lost in separation and divorce. Venus rules the 10th house and she became famous through love, and later suffered as that love died publicly. She ultimately gave away Venus in service, working with numerous charities to raise money to help neglected and forsaken children. Venus is trine a dignified Saturn, which rules the 2nd house and is on the cusp of the 2nd, a testament to the wealth she accrued personally, and the money she made for her charities.

She has a yod with Jupiter at the apex, inconjunct a wide Mars–Pluto conjunction in the 8th, and a wide Sun–Mercury conjunction in the 7th. Mars–Pluto is a fighter without equal and the royal family had no idea what they were getting when they welcomed her into their fold. The Sun–Mercury pair describes what the royal family wished her to be—a partner who put family first and stayed at home (Cancer) and out of the spotlight, speaking only in support of her husband. But she had her own vision (Jupiter in Aquarius), and the yod was expressed as a battle of wills. In the end, she was beholden to the power of the crown (Mars, Pluto) and had her children to consider (Sun, Mercury), which prevented her from expressing her true self (Jupiter in Aquarius). The yod signifies profound disappointment, both received and delivered. She delivered disappointment from the day she was born, to parents who wanted a son, and later to a royal family who wished her to be subservient and acquiescent. She was disappointed by her husband who loved someone else, and a royal family who used their power to limit her influence.

A grand trine explains her popularity, and the addiction the press and the public had for her. The wide Sun–Mercury conjunction is trine an elevated 10th house Neptune and trine Chiron in Pisces. Her glamour healed the image of the stiff royal family. There was a public compulsion that knew no bounds in photographing her (Neptune) and reporting (Mercury) on her. In the public's eye, she belonged to them and there was no boundary they would not cross to delve into her private, personal life and present it to the world. Though glamorous, she was also manipulative and used the media for her own purposes.

In declination, Mars is parallel the North Node, an indication that the out-of-sign conjunction was active. (The mean node at 29°43' Leo, tightens the aspect further.) With the mean node in the regal degree of Regulus, what materialized through the North Node was a royal man. With Mars peregrine in Virgo, the prince was stodgy, critical, humorless and would not be king in her lifetime—if ever. But the Mars–North Node was also hers, and she was a formidable fighter. The Moon and Neptune are also parallel in declination, further indicating widespread popularity and boundless maternal compassion. The pair are parallel the South Node, and she was a mother to children throughout the globe. In latitude, Saturn is near the 0° line of the ecliptic and parallel the Sun, angles, and nodes, guaranteeing the outward appearance and inward experience of Saturnine circumstances.

A Royal Proposal

After what was at most a six month romance, the prince proposed (Chart 36). There was a solar eclipse two days before the event at 16°01' Aquarius that fell in her 2nd house of money and was trine progressed Venus and the Descendant (promise of a spouse and wealth). The lord of the eclipse was Uranus (excitement, change).

Progressed Mercury (ruler 7) was conjunct the natal Sun and trine Neptune, indicating that it was a dream come true. She did not heed the warning of the progressed Moon square natal Jupiter, calling for caution and more rationalization. The mundane conjunction of Jupiter and Saturn square her natal Sun was another warning that the responsibility would be a heavy burden to bear. However, with transiting Venus conjunct progressed Jupiter, she threw caution to the wind and accepted the proposal. Natal Neptune was at the North Bending of the transiting nodes, helping a fairy tale come to life. With transiting Pluto (conjunct the Midheaven) sextile transiting Neptune and in a yod with natal Venus, the prince may not have been the man she envisioned marrying, but she settled for power and a dream. Transiting Uranus was at the North Bending of the natal nodes, signifying surprise. Transiting

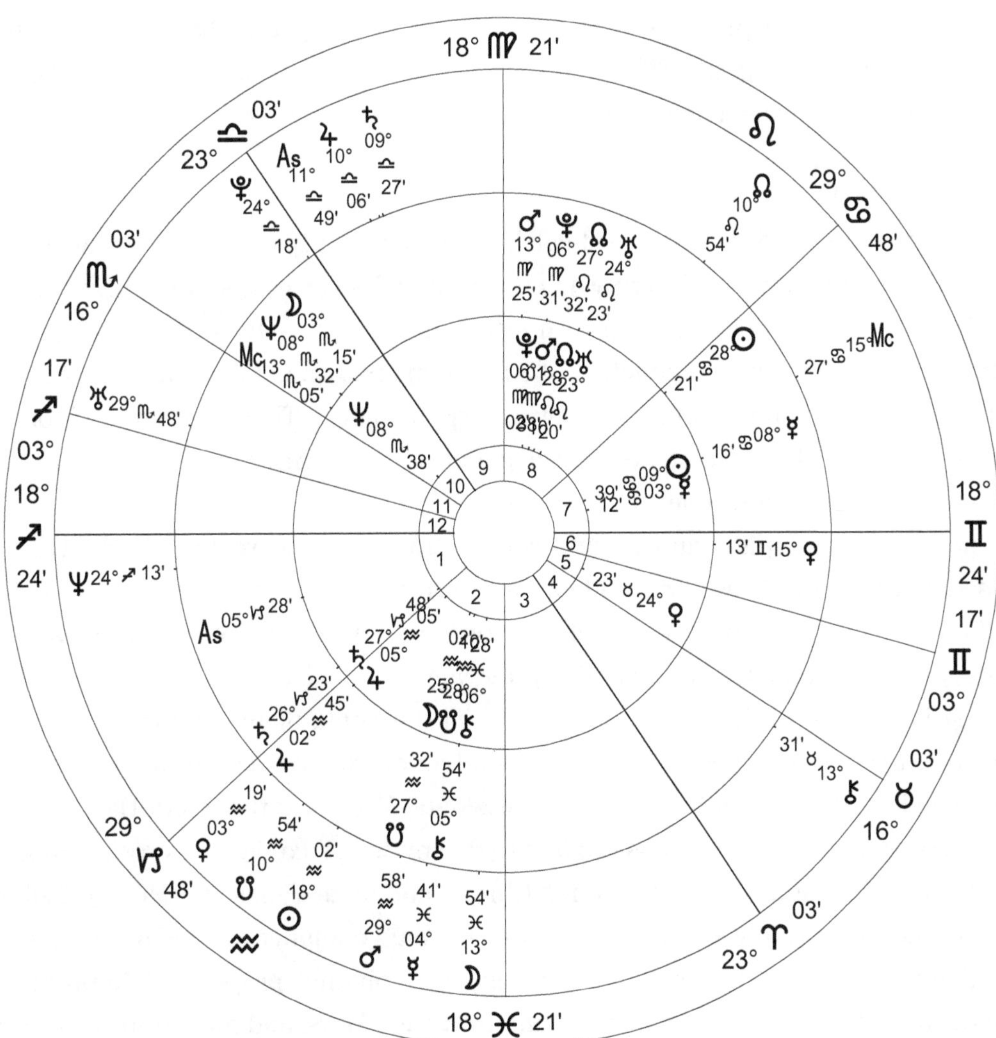

Chart 36:

Princess Wedding Proposal, Feb. 6, 1981, London, England, 10:00 p.m. GMT

Uranus was trine the progressed Sun and she was ready for change and financial security (Uranus ruling the 2nd). However, with transiting Mars conjunct the progressed South Node, the man would bring her suffering and loss.

The Wedding

Two billion people around the world celebrated as a twenty-year-old girl married into the royal family (Chart 37). There was a north nodal solar eclipse two days after the wedding at 7°51' Leo, that fell in her 8th house with the Sun as the lord. The eclipse was sextile a partile transiting conjunction of Jupiter and Saturn in Libra, that was trine her natal Jupiter (a new beginning of immense responsibility). The great conjunction was also parallel in declination, creating an occultation at the Aries Point, translating into an event that was witnessed around the world.

The transiting Jupiter and Saturn conjunction was square her natal Sun, progressed Mercury, progressed Ascendant and Descendant, and transiting Mars, indicating the enormous burden of responsibility for both her and the prince. The transiting South Node was conjunct progressed Jupiter, her chart ruler, and she was a sacrifice, and she knew it—'but her face was already on the china plates and the tea towels.' Transiting Uranus was now at the North Bending of the progressed nodes, reflecting change and wealth, but with Uranus opposite natal Venus (at the South Bending), she had reservations. However, it was too late to do anything (fixed grand cross comprised of transiting and natal Uranus, transiting Chiron, and natal Venus and Moon). Still, she bore her fate responsibly and bravely (transiting Mars conjunct natal Sun square transiting Jupiter–Saturn). The progressed Moon was conjunct progressed Neptune and trine the natal Sun, progressed Mercury and transiting Mars, and the world witnessed a romantic wedding—essentially even then, a glamorous deception. At least transiting Venus was conjunct natal Pluto and the certified virgin could finally have sex.

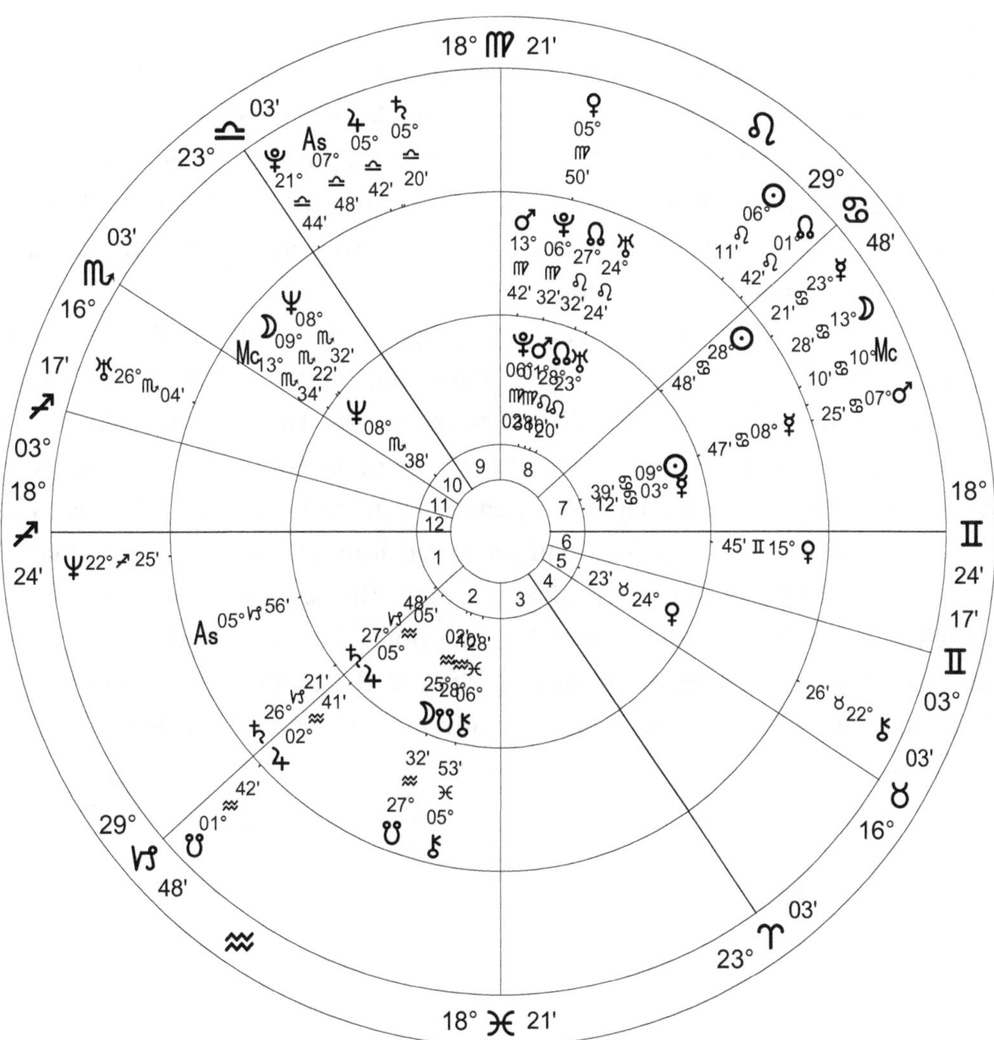

Chart 37:

Princess Diana's Wedding, July 29, 1981, London, England, 11.17 a.m. BST

An Heir

Prince William was born on the eclipse of June 21, 1982 (Chart 38). It was a north nodal eclipse at 29°46' Gemini, with Mercury as the lord. Transiting Saturn was at the North Bending of the transiting nodes, trine Diana's progressed Venus, (ruling the 5th) as the royal child was born. She was having a Venus return, which activated her natal t-square with Uranus and the Moon, and a son was given in sacrifice in the name of duty (Venus at the natal South Bending).

Transiting Mars was square the natal Sun, progressed Mercury, and the progressed Ascendant, symbolizing a long, hard labor. Transiting Jupiter was trine natal Mercury and the transiting Sun and Moon, alluding to happiness. However, transiting Jupiter was square progressed Jupiter, suggesting a loss of freedom, further shown by a square of transiting Uranus to natal Mars, and a square from transiting Venus to natal Uranus. Her role and opportunities had narrowed now that she was a mother. The royal family also had new leverage against her, since the baby was under their control. Nonetheless, transiting Neptune was in her first house in a grand trine with the natal IC and natal Uranus, and sextile transiting Pluto at the Midheaven, and she and the world bought into the fantasy of a perfect family, now blessed with an heir.

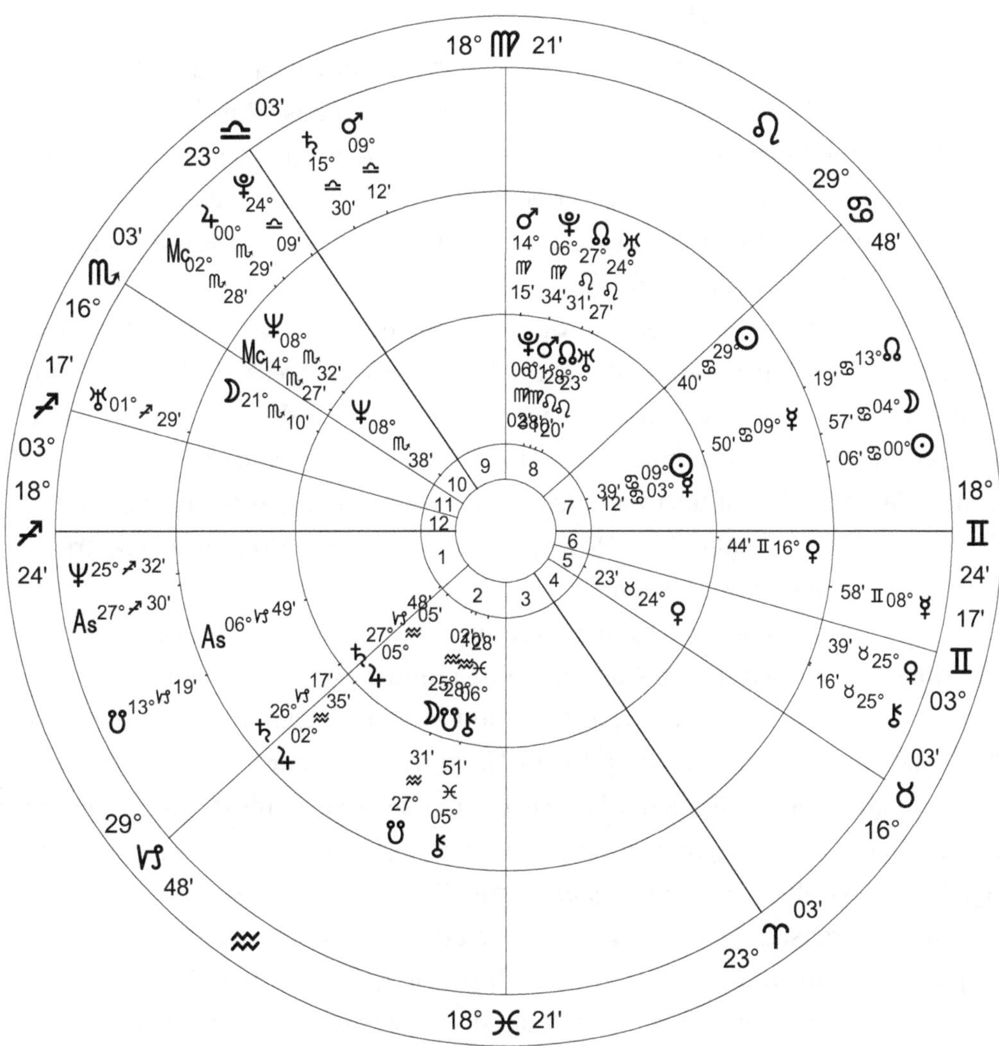

Chart 38:

Princess Delivers an Heir, June 21, 1982, London, England, 9:03 p.m. BST

A Marriage Crumbling

The fairy tale ended badly. On December 9, 1992, the day of a lunar eclipse at 18°10' Gemini, which fell across her Ascendant–Descendant axis, the Prime Minister announced what the tabloids had been reporting for weeks—the royal couple was separating (Chart 39). The north nodal solar eclipse two weeks later was on Christmas Eve at 2°27' Capricorn, with Saturn serving as the lord. The eclipse fell in her 1st house opposite natal Mercury, ruler of the 7th.

On the day of the announcement, the progressed Moon was conjunct the natal IC and in a t-square with progressed Saturn (lord) and progressed Mercury–transiting Mars, denoting emotional and mental sadness and anger at the end of the matter. The progressed Moon was inconjunct transiting Pluto–Mercury and the progressed Midheaven, reflecting difficult negotiations and a power struggle with the royals over the settlement and her official duties. However, the progressed Moon was also trine natal Uranus, bringing liberating freedom.

There was a rare mundane Uranus–Neptune conjunction, which literally translates as an awakening from a dream (nightmare). Conjunct her progressed Ascendant, she was affected personally. The transiting nodes were aligned across her Ascendant/Descendant, with the transiting North Node falling in her 1st, giving her strength. Public sympathy was on her side. For Diana, the separation must have been a relief. Transiting Venus was conjunct progressed Jupiter (where it had been when she got engaged nearly twelve years before), and transiting Jupiter was sextile the progressed Sun. However, transiting Jupiter was also square the natal Sun, and progressed Mars was square the transiting nodes at the South Bending. Despite new freedom, the royal family still had her constrained. Transiting Mercury was at the North Bending of the natal nodes, timing the announcement. The messenger was conjunct transiting Pluto and the progressed Midheaven, opposite natal Venus, and trine progressed Mercury–transiting Mars, describing the headline news that love had died.

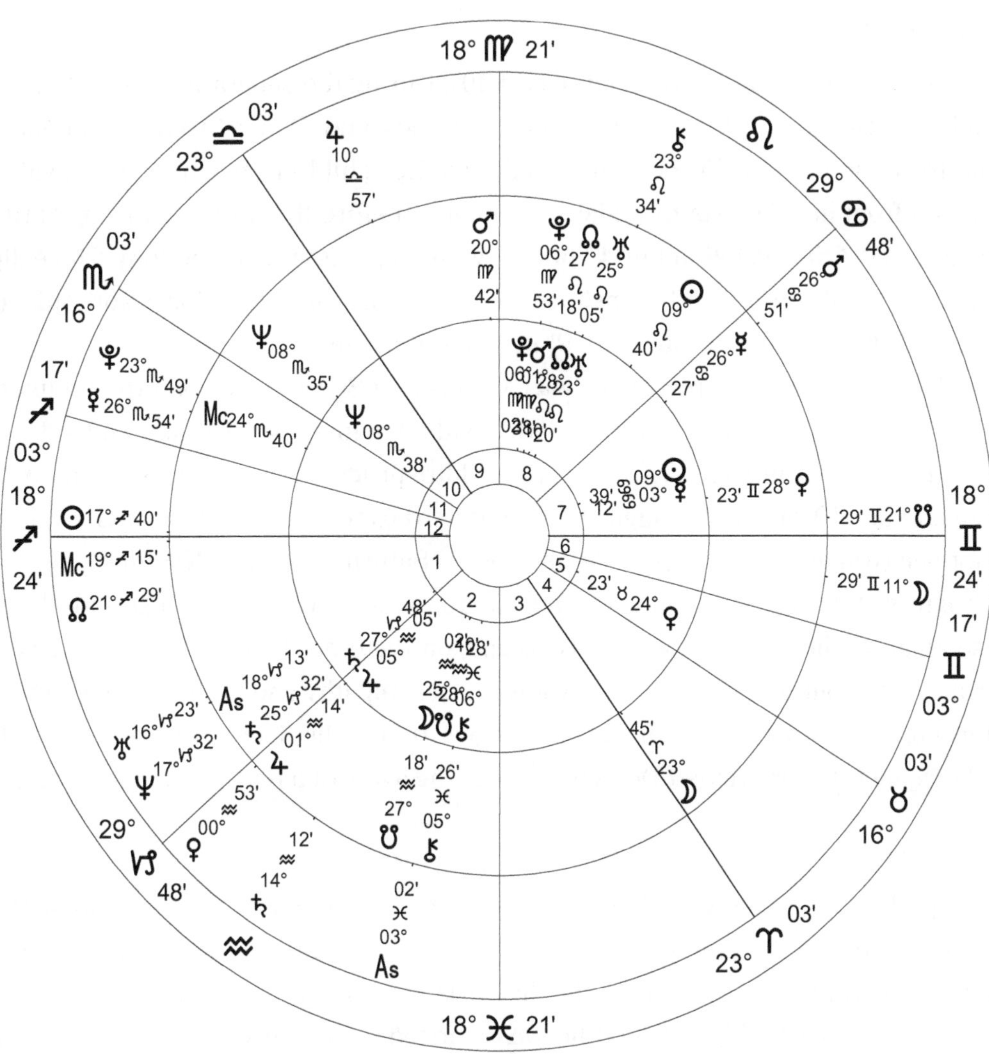

Chart 39:

Princess Separates, Dec. 9, 1992, London, England, noon

Divorce

Four years later the couple divorced (Chart 40). During the separation, leaked messages and secretly taped phone calls of both Charles and Diana brought scandal and shame to the monarchy. Diana had already lost her children, but now her royal title was taken from her. The south nodal solar eclipse before the divorce was on April 17, 1996, at 28°11' Aries. It fell in her 4th house, with Mars serving as the lord. The eclipse was square natal Saturn and transiting Neptune (loss of a kingdom) and quincunx progressed Midheaven and transiting Pluto (loss of a title).

At the time of the divorce, there was a transiting South Node–Saturn conjunction that was square her natal Sun at the South Bending, a low point for her, and a day she called the worst of her life. The transiting Pluto–progressed Midheaven conjunction was square natal Mars, and though she fought hard to retain her title, it was a fight she did not win (transiting Mars opposite progressed Saturn–transiting Neptune).

Progressed Venus was conjunct natal Mercury, symbolizing Camilla and Charles, whose affair did little for his popularity. Diana, on the other hand, brilliantly played the press and came out of the ordeal with widespread sympathy and her freedom (transiting Uranus conjunct progressed Jupiter). The trigger timing the decree was transiting Mars (lord) conjunct the progressed Descendant (cutting away of a partner in marriage).

Accident

Diana's problem was that even in divorce she was too popular, and more popular with the British subjects than the royal family. There was no place in the monarchy for the now single former princess. Before she died, Diana was afraid for her life and believed the royal family wished her dead. She was worried someone would tamper with her car and cause an accident. Specifically, she had pointed fingers at both Prince Charles and Prince Phillip. Two separate investigations, one in France, the other in Britain, place the blame for her death on a drunk driver and the paparazzi. However, the story is not so clear-cut.

While I do not consider myself a conspiracy theorist, I do not like inexplicable events or stories that do not make sense. As Charles Pidgen wrote, "To call someone 'a conspiracy theorist' is to suggest that he is irrational, paranoid or perverse. Often the

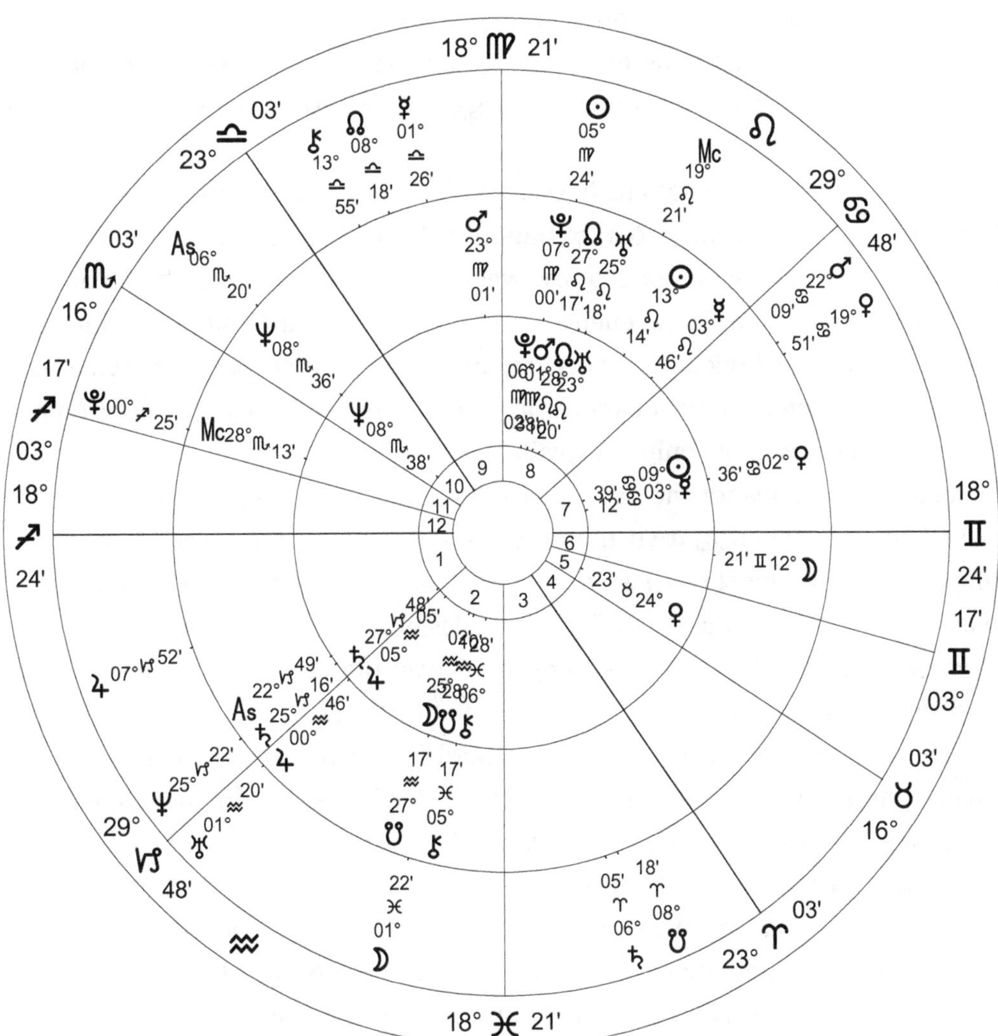

Chart 40:

Princess Divorce, August 28, 1996, London, England, noon

suggestion seems to be that conspiracy theories are not just suspect, but utterly unbelievable, too silly to deserve the effort of a serious refutation. It is a common ploy on the part of politicians to dismiss critical allegations by describing them as conspiracy theories."

Fifteen years after the fatal crash, conflicting stories abound about what happened in that Paris tunnel. According to information from online sources (I have read but not verified), the Mercedes was stolen a few weeks before the crash and recovered a few days prior to the accident in excellent condition. The onboard computer chip controlling the steering and brakes had been replaced. The British Secret Service has the technology to remotely control cars through a vehicle's onboard computer chip. Of a fleet, the stolen car was the only one available for use that night.

It took four minutes for the car to leave the Paris Ritz Hotel and reach the tunnel. The car had been tailed by two motorcycles traveling at high speed. Eyewitnesses driving through the tunnel reported seeing a bright flash of light with the intensity of a flare immediately before the crash. The Mercedes clipped a white Fiat Uno, which may have caused the accident. Diana's bodyguard was the only one wearing a seatbelt (later disputed), which investigators attribute to his survival.

The head of security at the Ritz Hotel, Henri Paul, was driving the car. Some people suspect he was working for M16, the United Kingdom's foreign intelligence agency. Starting nine months before the crash, large deposits were routinely made to Paul's bank account. At the time of the accident he was legally intoxicated, although video cameras show him leaving the hotel in an unimpaired state. Questions were raised about his blood tests and anomalies suggest that it was not his blood that was tested. Initial reports had him speeding 120 mph into the tunnel, which has a speed limit of 30 mph. He was later proven to be driving between 60–70 mph.

The crash occurred at 12:27 a.m. after Paul lost control of the car and hit a concrete pillar. Reports conclusively indicate he did not hit the brakes (an instinctive reaction even if drunk). A medical doctor chanced upon the scene and stopped to help. Diana was apparently conscious. Her lover and driver were dead. She was removed from the car at 1:00 a.m., transferred to an ambulance at 1:18 a.m., and taken to the hospital at 1:40 a.m. Although the hospital was four miles away, it took twenty minutes to get there. She arrived at 2:00 a.m., underwent emergency surgery, and was pronounced dead at 4:00 a.m. Questions have been raised and left unanswered, as to why it took so long to get her to the hospital.

She obviously died, but the question is, was it murder? A decade after her death, a retired M16 officer published the secrets of his trade for which he was, and still is, imprisoned. He disclosed a plot to assassinate Slobodan Milosevic in a car accident. According to the plan, a tunnel was thought to be the best place for the accident because the concrete would ensure maximum damage and limit eyewitnesses. A strobe light flashed from a car could be used to blind and disorient the driver. Alternatively, or in addition, M16 could remotely control the onboard computer chip to disable the brakes or the steering and cause the crash. Both the British Secret Service and the Royal Family have denied any collaboration or complicity in the accident. While the facts are murky, the astrology does not lie (although the symbols can be misinterpreted).

An event chart drawn for the time of the accident reveals the planetary energy of the moment (Chart 41). I read an event chart as I read a horary chart, and use the old rulers and Ptolemy's Table of Dignities to determine motivation as described by John Frawley in *The Horary Textbook*. I follow the chain of dispositors to find the connections between the players. In general, strong ties by dignity denote fondness, and debilitation indicates dislike.

In the event chart, Diana is represented by the 7th house, symbolized by Jupiter. The event Ascendant and Descendant are the reverse of her natal chart, so that her 7th house is rising, and her 1st house (she, herself) is setting. In the turned chart (counting the 7th house as the 1st), she is conjunct the 4th house and the end of the matter. It made no difference how long it took to get her to the hospital; she was close to death at the time of the accident.

Jupiter is in Aquarius and is peregrine (without dignity) and retrograde, an indication of vulnerability and weak standing. In the 9th house of the radical chart, Jupiter has accidental dignity and strength coming from position—she was, after all, the mother of the heir to the throne. She also had the love of the British people (Jupiter trine Venus in the turned 11th). However, Venus in Libra in the radical 5th also symbolizes her love affair, which according to then Prime Minister, Tony Blair, 'was a problem' for the royal family (Venus opposite Saturn).

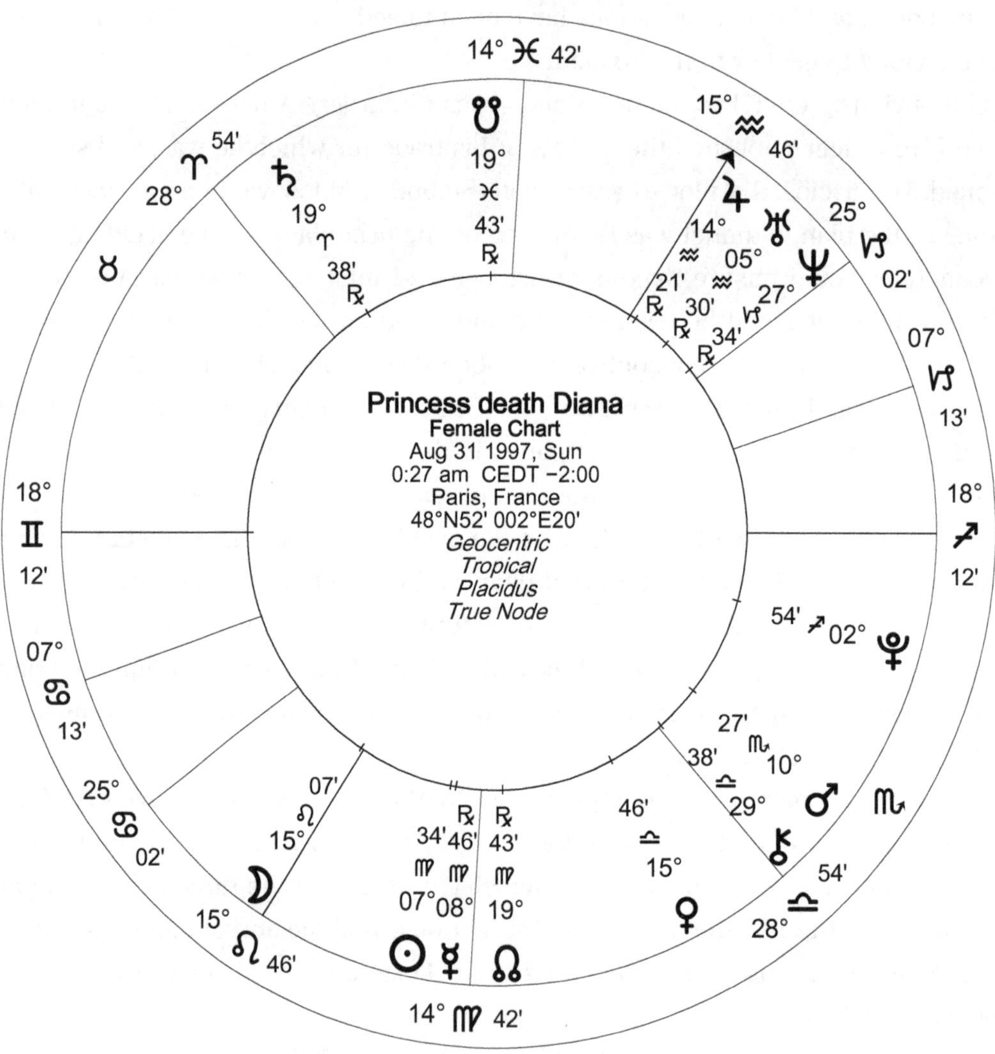

Chart 41:

Accident, August 31, 1997, Paris, France, 0:27:50 a.m. CEDT

Jupiter is opposite the Moon in Leo, which is conjunct the turned 10th house. In this context, the Moon in Leo represents the royal family, in particular the queen, who stood in opposition to the princess. The Moon rules the 8th house of death and the 9th house of foreign countries in the turned chart. The Moon in Leo is without dignity and in the triplicity and face of Jupiter, connecting the queen with the princess. Jupiter is in the sign of the Sun's detriment, repeating the connection, and indicating the strong dislike of the princess for the queen.

Gemini is rising, describing the accident and the short trip in the car. Gemini also rules chauffeurs and the press. The ruler of the chart is Mercury, dignified in Virgo, but retrograde and conjunct (combust) the Sun, which weakens it and suggests there is something wrong with either the driver or the car. The Sun conjunct Mercury could represent a blinding flash of light.

The Sun symbolizes the king and the kingdom, and is tied to the Moon through rulership (Sun rules the Moon). The Sun is directly connected to the car (Mercury) through aspect (conjunction) and dispositorship (Mercury ruling the Sun). With the Sun (royal kingdom) and Mercury (driver or car) in the sign of Jupiter's detriment, they have no love for the princess.

In a mundane chart, the 6th house represents the police. In the event chart, a dignified Mars in Scorpio in the 6th symbolizes an elite police force, such as M16. In its own sign, Mars answers to no one. Mars is sextile the Sun–Mercury conjunction directly tying it to the car. Mars is in the terms of Jupiter (linking it to the princess) and in the face of the Sun (connection to the royal kingdom).

Saturn in the chart represents the prime minister. He knew the princess was a political force, that she could use the press to her advantage, and that the royals were upset by her affair. Jupiter is in Saturn's sign, suggesting Diana may have felt he could protect her. However, in Aries, Saturn is in fall, showing essential weakness. Saturn is ruled by Mars, and the prime minister held no sway with M16.

In an event chart, as in horary, the fast moving Moon shows how the story unfolds. The following scenario is an opinion, based on and biased by circulating rumors. When the Moon entered Leo, the royal family decided something had to be done to refurbish a tarnished image of the monarchy and the problem of an independent ex-princess. The first aspect the Moon made was a trine to Pluto in Sagittarius, and the murder of the princess was tabled. The Moon then opposed Uranus and a plot involving an accident in a foreign country was suggested. M16 may not have been pleased (Moon square Mars), but was paid-off (Mars intercepted in the house ruled by Venus, showing the way out and onward). M16 tampered with the car (Mars sextile Mercury). In the event chart, Mercury is retrograde and the sextile had already perfected. The car was returned in a technologically altered state (Mercury quincunx Uranus). The crash occurred and the princess died (Moon opposite Jupiter), with the royals hoping to recoup the love (Moon sextile Venus) they believed she usurped. However, in their regal way, they maintained composed and said nothing while the country mourned. Four days passed before the prime minister personally intervened (Moon trine Saturn applying 4°), beseeching the queen to make a statement, which she did. After the trine to Saturn, the Moon went void-of-course, finishing with a quincunx to Neptune (an aspect not typically used in horary), but which symbolizes the cloud of suspicion shrouding the accident.

Death

Whatever the cause, the accident that led to Diana's death occurred at 12. 27 a.m. on August 31, 1997 (Chart 42). There was a north nodal solar eclipse two days after her death on September 2, 1997, at 9°33' Virgo that fell in her 8th house, with Mercury (cars) serving as the lord. The eclipse was conjunct her natal Pluto (death).

On the day she died, the transiting nodes were square her natal Ascendant at the North Bending, signaling an outer event for her physical body. Transiting Neptune was conjunct natal Saturn, bringing confusion and physical dissolution. The progressed Midheaven was at the North Bending of the progressed nodes conjunct transiting Pluto, indicating outward manifestation of death and public grief. Transiting Pluto was square natal Mars, describing the destruction and devastation. Transiting Uranus was opposite progressed Mercury and square natal Neptune and transiting Mars, reflecting the sudden car accident, trauma, and confusion. The transiting Sun was conjunct progressed Pluto and transiting Mercury and opposite natal Chiron, indicative of a fatal wound. Transiting Jupiter was opposite the progressed Sun and transiting Moon, pointing to stress for the luminaries and the chart ruler. Transiting Saturn was conjunct the 4th house cusp, quincunx the North Node, and trine the Ascendant: going to the grave.

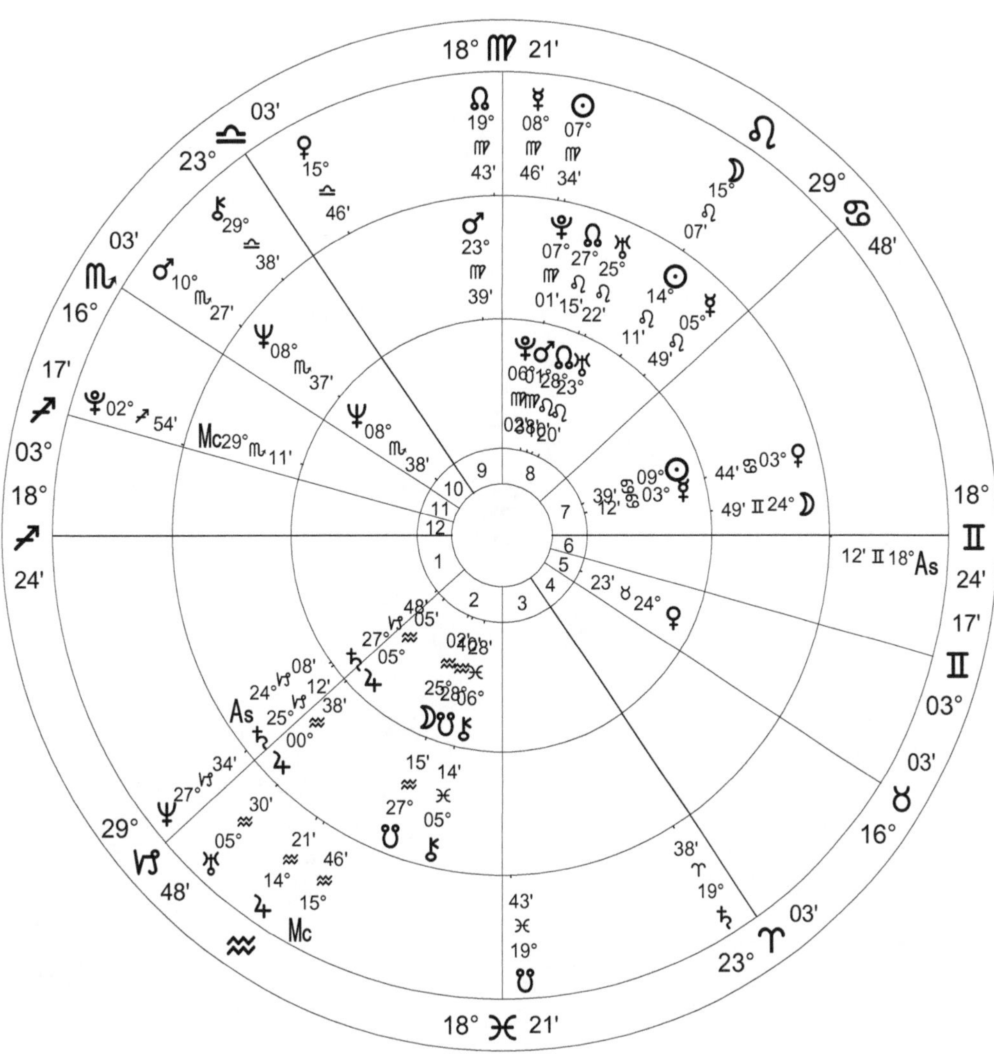

Chart 42:

Princess Death, August 31, 1997, Paris, France, 00:27 a.m. CEDT

The Great Spirit doesn't smile on those who dampen others and take the stars out of happy eyes.

— White Eagle

Chapter 11
The Fall
Dominique Strauss-Kahn

The North Node has a glowing reputation of bestowing wonderful gifts, but this next example shows how a dignified planet at the North Node can behave badly and bring harm. Dominique Strauss-Kahn has Mars in Aries conjunct the North Node in the 10th house and has recently been in the news for allegedly raping a hotel maid. He was expected to become the next President of France when this sexual scandal ended his public career.

Known in the French media as DSK (also, Dr. Strauss and Mr. Kahn), he is a lawyer, economist, and politician. He has been married three times, currently to a wealthy heiress and former TV news personality. His most recent position was as head of the International Monetary Fund (IMF), the largest financial institute in the world. DSK was a man of power who traveled the globe, stayed in two thousand dollar a night hotel suites, and made four hundred thousand dollars a year 'helping' the poor. His task was to arrange loans to impoverished countries to facilitate their development.

However, the loans come with high interest and enslave the borrower to the lender. When the loans go bad, the lender lays claim to the resources of the country.

DSK was in New York on a business trip, staying in a suite in an exclusive hotel, when he had sex with the maid who came to clean his room. He claimed the sex was consensual. Afterwards, he headed for the airport. He had a long-standing arrangement with Air France that he could fly business class on any flight, at any time, and he was in his seat, on the runway, headed for Germany to see the Prime Minister, when police stormed the plane. DSK was handcuffed, hauled off the plane, arrested, and imprisoned without bail. He denied the charges, but days later resigned from his post at the IMF.

As prosecutors looked into the allegations, news of his previous sexual encounters and offences came to light. In France, a thirty-two year old reporter said years earlier she too had been assaulted, and that a sexually aroused DSK was 'like a chimpanzee in rut.' The reporter's mother admitted she too had a tryst with DSK, and called the sexual encounter 'brutal.' DSK had a reputation as a 'great seducer' and told his wife that he'd had sex three times on the weekend of his arrest.

On August 23, 2011, New York prosecutors dropped the criminal charges and a judge ordered DSK to be freed after the physical evidence proved inconclusive and the maid appeared unreliable.

Nativity

DSK has a lucky chart (Chart 43) filled with a preponderance of sextiles and an angular Jupiter. He has a Taurus Sun in the 10th house conjunct (and parallel) a dignified Venus, fitting for a wealthy man who made a spectacular career out of managing money. The Sun rules the Ascendant, and the magnanimous expression of Leo was channeled through the career. With the chart ruler placed in the 10th, he was lifted to great heights. His one planetary square is between the Sun and Jupiter. This warns of hubris, a desire to be seen larger than life, and carries the risk of a great fall.

He has an Aries Moon, suggesting a fighter who enjoys competition. Placed in the 9th house, there is interest in law, higher education, foreign countries, and long distance travel. The Moon is disposited by the dignified 10th house Mars, and he

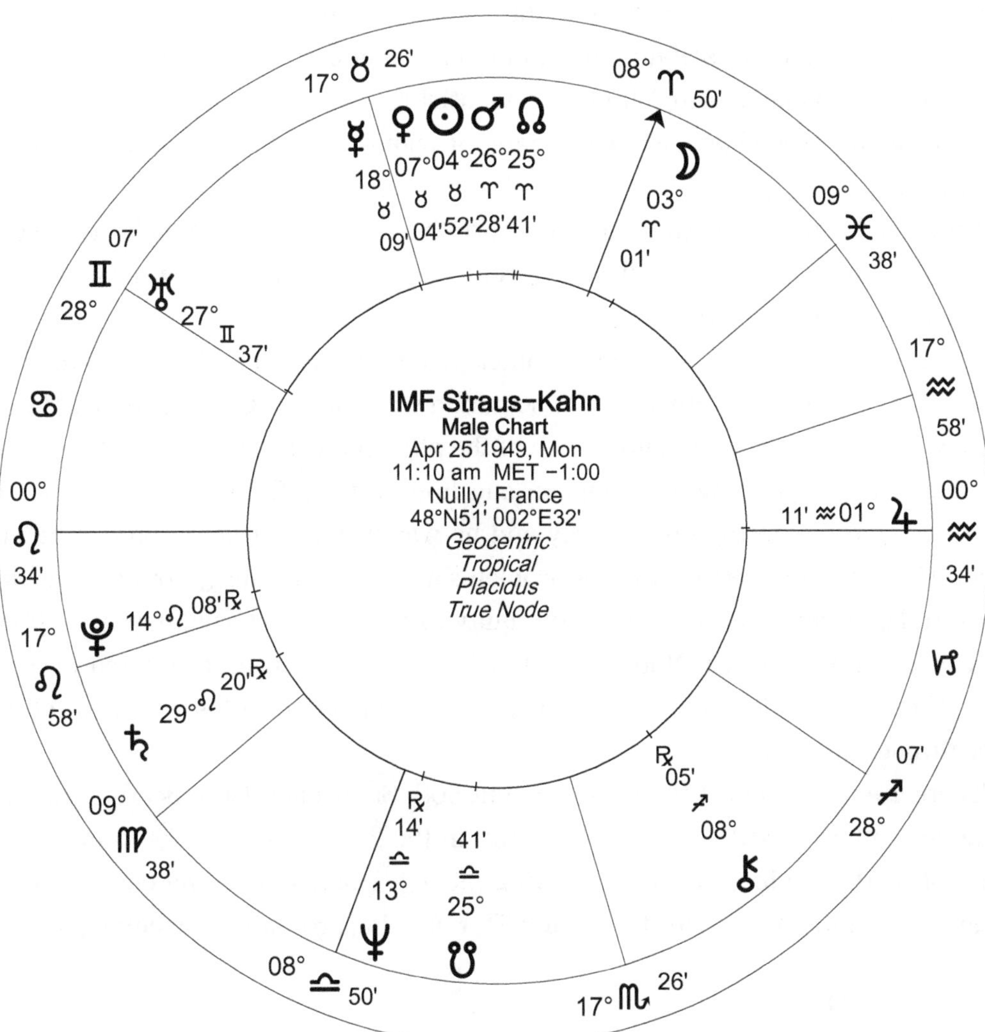

Chart 43:

Dominique Strauss-Kahn Nativity

channeled his ambition and aggression into his high profile career. The Moon rules the intercepted 12th house of self-undoing and hidden enemies. Many in France believe he was set up by his enemies to foil his presidential run. The Moon is sextile Jupiter and sextile/trine the Ascendant and Descendant, providing an outlet for grand passion and enthusiasm.

DSK was born three days before the April 28, 1949, north nodal solar eclipse that fell at 7°42' Taurus in his 10th house, the arena that would expand over his lifetime. His natal nodes are moving direct.

The North Node is in Aries and conjunct (and parallel) Mars, its ruler. Mars is dignified in Aries and empowered by its association with the energy of the node. Mars has innate wisdom, strength, and knowledge of the physical world. He came into the world knowing how to fight, how to compete, and how to win. The house Mars rules also benefited from the north nodal energy and he was triumphant and dominating in his career. However, Mars is not without problems and with the energy streaming in at the North Node, he shows little restraint or ability to manage his sexual impulses. If there is a caveat with the North Node energy, it is that there can be too much of a good thing. The South Node is ruled by Venus, and there have been losses and a fall from grace through women.

There are no planets at the bendings, but both Saturn and Uranus are sextile/trine the nodes and are sextile each other. Saturn in the 2nd house rules the intercepted 6th house of work, alluding to a job involving money. Uranus is on the cusp of the 12th (large organizations) and rules the 7th and 8th, reflecting profitable partnerships.

Alleged Rape

There was a south nodal solar eclipse two weeks after the incident on June 1, 2011, at 11°01' Gemini, with Mercury as the lord. The eclipse was conjunct DSK's progressed Mars–Mercury and fell in his 11th house of hopes and dreams (eclipsed).

On the day of the incident (Chart 44), transiting Jupiter was conjunct (and parallel) the natal North Node, conjunct Mars, and square progressed Venus at the North Bending, coinciding with an external event involving sex (Mars) and a cleaning woman (Venus in Cancer). The transiting South Node was conjunct natal Uranus, indicating

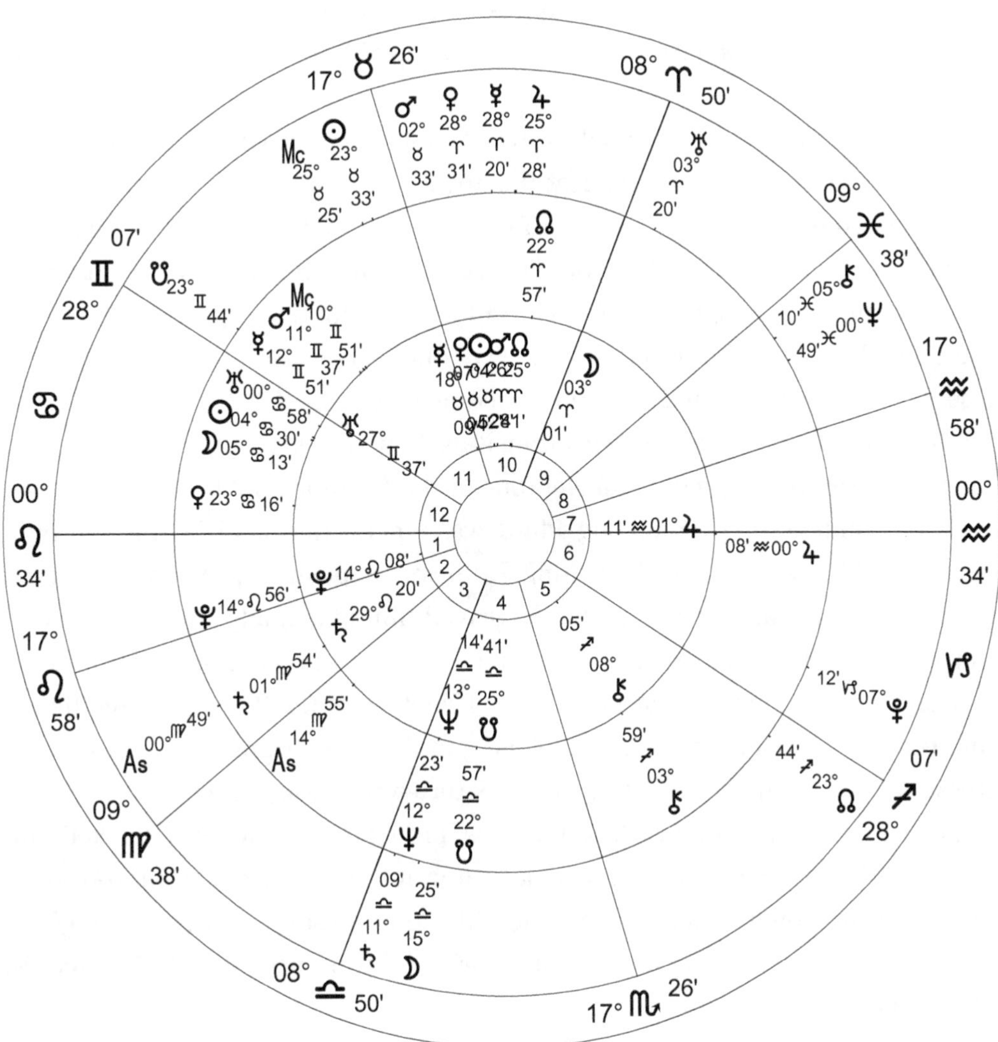

Chart 44:

DSK Alleged Rape, May 14, 2011, New York, NY, 1:00 p.m. EDT

shock and surprise—the world by his antics, and he by the world's upset. The transiting nodes were sextile/trine the natal nodes and natal Mars, enhancing sexual desire—to ruinous effect.

The loss of luck can be attributed to two interacting yods. One involves progressed Saturn and Uranus with natal Jupiter at the apex, which was set off by transiting Uranus, and describes his sudden legal difficulties, loss of freedom, and confinement. Transiting Uranus formed another yod and was conjunct the natal Moon, sextile natal Jupiter and quincunx progressed Saturn, reflecting emotional upset, intense frustration, and helplessness with no immediate way out. This is the problem with so many natal sextiles—at some point the sextiles become yods.

There was a double-whammy with transiting Neptune opposite progressed Saturn, and transiting Saturn conjunct natal Neptune at the IC, repeating the message that the career was disintegrating. Transiting Pluto was square the natal Midheaven and IC, reflecting a public sex scandal. Transiting Pluto was opposite a progressed Sun–Moon conjunction, an indication the scandal destroyed him personally. He was denied bail and thrown in prison. Transiting Pluto was also square the natal Moon and transiting Uranus, and square transiting Saturn and natal Neptune at the IC, suggesting the end of the matter for him and his career. This grand cross (transiting Pluto opposite progressed Sun–Moon, square transiting Saturn–progressed Neptune, and square transiting Uranus–natal Moon, describes his predicament. He was backed into a corner, alone in a prison cell on a suicide watch following a sexual impropriety that ruined him professionally. In the meantime, salacious gossip flew around the globe, as shown by transiting Saturn conjunct natal Neptune, trine progressed Mercury, Mars, and the Midheaven.

It is the soul's duty to be loyal to its own desires. It must abandon itself to its master passion.

— Rebecca West

Chapter 12
The Oracle of Omaha
Warren Buffett

In this example, the situation is similar to Dominique Strauss-Kahn, only in reverse, as here a dignified Venus in Libra is conjunct the South Node, which it rules. In regards to money, there was no loss for billionaire Warren Buffett. The CEO of Berkshire-Hathaway is currently worth fifty billion dollars. He was the world's wealthiest man in 2008, and the third richest in 2011. Buffett is frugal and still lives in a house he bought over fifty years ago for $31,500. He considers the house his third best investment—after two wedding rings. He married in 1952 and has three children. They attended public school and he jokes that if private schools were abolished, public education would improve because the rich would invest in it.

He considers his first wife, Susie, his hero, 'an incredibly wise and good person.' He doesn't think she got the credit she deserved for the influence she had on him. 'She put me together,' he says. 'She was a great giver.' She took him to hear Martin Luther King and Buffett was so inspired by King's statement, "It may be true that the law can't change the heart, but it can restrain the heartless," that he became more politically liberal, eventually becoming a Democrat. In 1977, after their children were grown, he and Susie separated. She moved away, but they remained close, never divorcing. She was worried about him and set him up with a friend who became his mistress. When Susie died in 2004, Buffett married her hand-picked successor.

In business, Buffett is a value investor. He buys stocks and companies that are selling for less than they're worth. He eschews debt and likes to keep ten to twenty billion of liquid assets. He recently caused a stir by calling on the wealthy to pay their fair share of taxes. He wants Washington to stop 'coddling the superrich.' He said, "I find the argument that we need lower taxes to create more jobs mystifying, because we have had the lowest taxes in the decade and about the worst job creation ever." He does not believe in the trickle-down theory of wealth creation, but rather in its opposite. Buffett thinks that if the government helps the masses become prosperous, their good fortune will trickle upwards. When he dies, he plans to leave ninety-nine percent of his wealth to charity.

Nativity

Buffett has a Virgo Sun, giving him a head for figures (Chart 45). In the 8th and ruling the 8th, he is interested in investment. He reads annual business reports for fun. The Sun is conjunct Neptune, indicating intuition and monetary growth without limit. The pair is trine Saturn, adding disciple and hard work.

The Moon is in Sagittarius, bringing a sense of optimism and a belief in luck. Conjunct the 12th, he is most comfortable behind the scenes. The Moon is in mutual reception with Jupiter, the chart ruler, reflecting his altruism and philosophy of fair play. Placed in the 7th, Jupiter describes his need of and affection for, his spouses.

The PNSE was on April 28, 1930, at 7°45' Taurus. The north nodal eclipse fell in his 4th house, along with the North Node (in Aries). The nodes are stationary and will turn retrograde in three hours.

Mars rules the North Node and is in detriment. In Cancer, Mars is cautious, and Buffett's investment strategy from which he has profited handsomely, is to minimize risk. The nodal influence may compensate for the planet's essential debilitation, as the

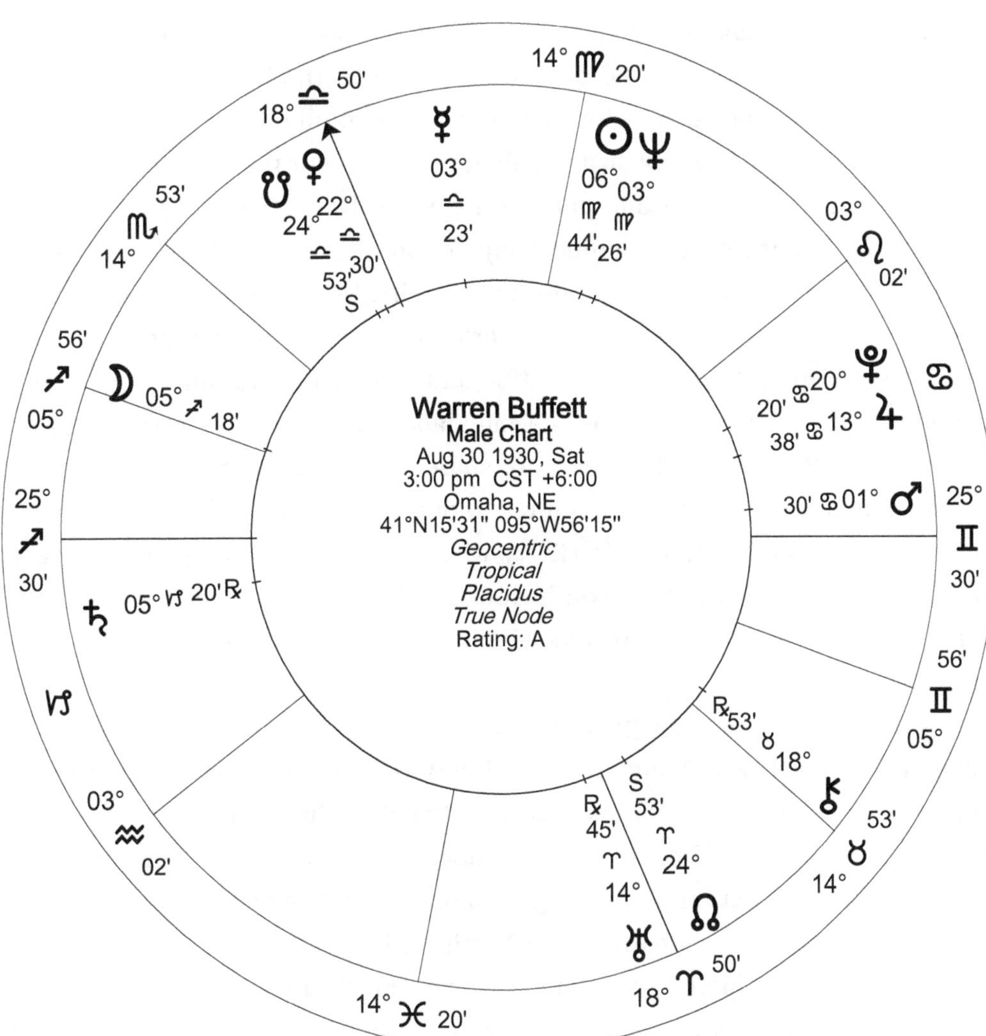

Chart 45:

Warren Buffett Nativity

warrior gains strength and practical wisdom from the association. Mars is in a t-square with Mercury and Saturn, and he is a logical, critical thinker, and a hard-working businessman with a long-term vision. The t-square also alludes to the loud and vehement protests of big business against his liberal ideas on fair taxation.

Venus is in Libra conjunct and parallel the South Node, acquiring a triple dose of south nodal energy through longitude conjunction, declinational parallel, and nodal rulership. This placement helps explains his frugality. He denies himself money for his own personal use, but gives it away to charity and noble causes (used in service to others). This set up bestows strong intuition and guidance regarding investment strategies and stock selection (Venus as the mundane ruler of money inspired by otherworld altruism). It attests to his belief in 'shared financial sacrifice.' He has a great ability to make money, but he does not do so out of greed or for his own selfish gain. Venus (women) also describes his (first) wife, the 'great giver' who never got the credit he thought she warranted (South Node rendering Venus invisible). Seven years after her death, he still could not talk about her without crying (grief from loss of love).

Pluto, the planet of big money, influence, and investment returns is near the North Bending of the nodes (wide), and in a position of maximum output. In his case, Pluto is related to the return of stock market investments, which has made him wealthy. Venus is square Pluto, and he frequently bemoans the unfairness of the American tax code and is indignant that his secretary pays more taxes than he does.

In declination, the Sun is parallel the North Node and empowered by the association. In latitude, Mars, Jupiter, and Pluto are near or on the ecliptic, and parallel the Sun, nodes, and angles, which bring energy, luck, optimism, generosity, and a talent for profitable investment.

Your future has nothing to do with getting somewhere you think you need to be. It has to do with the awareness that getting there means being here.

— Carl A. Hammerschlag

Chapter 13
The Microsoft King
Bill Gates

In an era when mainframe computers took up the space of a room, Bill Gates envisioned the day when every home would have a personal computer—and he made it happen. He was born into an upper middle class family. By thirteen, he demonstrated a talent for math. Fascinated by computers, he spent his high school years writing software code. He received a near-perfect score on the math SAT and went to Harvard. After one year, he dropped out to start his own company. He was nineteen.

Soon after, Gates picked up a magazine and saw an ad for a new, cheap computer chip that was ten times more powerful than the chip currently in use. He realized what the manufacturer of the chip did not, and that was that a powerful chip meant the bulk of a mainframe could be reduced without losing computing efficacy. This meant the size of a computer could be significantly deceased, along with its cost. He further realized that software had to be written to go with the chip. He wrote that software, which eventually became MS-DOS, the operating system sold on many first personal computers.

He started Microsoft when he was twenty-one. At thirty, he took the company public, selling Microsoft stock on the open market. That same day he became a millionaire. The following year he was a billionaire. Twelve years later, in 1999, he was worth $101 billion dollars. From 1995–2007, he was ranked as the wealthiest man in the world. He retired in 2008 as Microsoft CEO and Chief Software Architect, but remains the chairman. He now spends his time on his charitable foundation, largely dedicated to treating preventable infectious disease in developing countries. Thanks to his foundation and the research made possible by it, there is hope for a malaria vaccine, which has the potential to save millions of lives every year. On the grounds that it would relieve his children of the financial burden of managing his estate, he has pledged most of his wealth to charity.

Nativity

The astrological explanation for Bill Gates' phenomenal wealth and business talent is not obviously apparent (Chart 46). Half of his planets are either peregrine (Sun, Moon, Saturn) or in fall (Venus, Mars). Only Jupiter has dignity and that is by triplicity and terms. The majority of the planets are beneath the horizon, indicating a private, retiring person. He may have six angular planets (and one asteroid), but four of these are in a dark and private house. Yet, here is a man of exceptional success. With no planets conjunct the nodes or the bendings, the nodes would appear to have little influence. However, the rulers of the nodes are the keys to this chart.

Gates has a stellium in Leo (self-expression), Libra (intellect, relationship) and Scorpio (ruthless intensity). The Scorpio Sun gives focus, competitive drive, and executive ability. The Sun is in mutual reception with Pluto, which amplifies the desire for power and significance, and combines profitability with creativity (Sun ruling the 2nd and Pluto the 5th). The Sun is square Uranus in the 1st, giving a need for independence and freedom that has put him at odds with authority. Uranus in the 1st gives a propensity for computer technology and original thinking. He does things his own way.

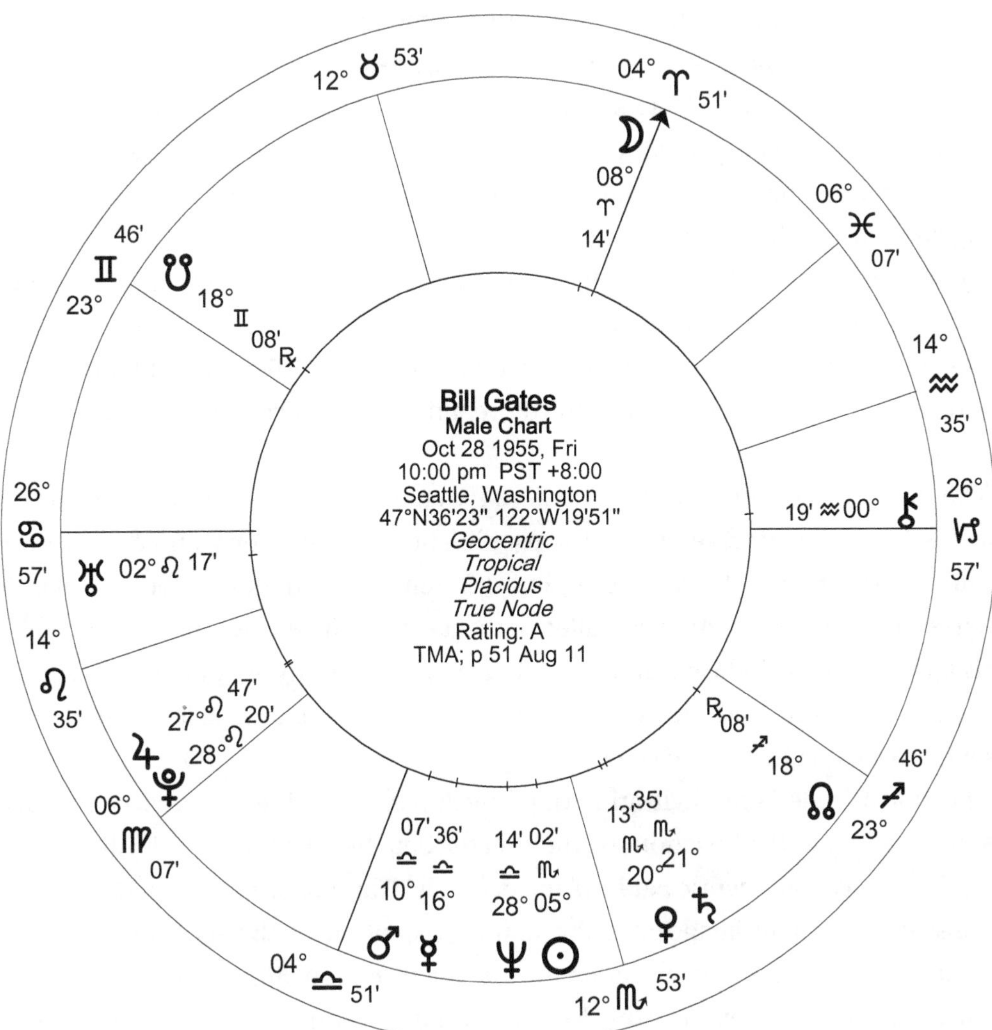

Chart 46:

Bill Gates Nativity

The Moon rules the chart and is in Aries conjunct the 10th cusp. At heart, he is a fighter, competitor, and pioneer. He is also an aggressive businessman. The chart ruler conjunct the Midheaven indicates a rise in station and rise he did. The Moon is opposite Mars, which adds to his combativeness and aggression. In meetings at Microsoft, he was known for his caustic remarks and outbursts (Mars in detriment in Libra behaving badly with others).

By traditional rulership, Gates has a mutual reception between Mars in Libra and Venus in Scorpio. With both planets in detriment, the help they afford each other is said to be limited. While Venus conjunct Saturn suggests difficulty and limitation with resources, in his case they are related to creating money through business—at which he was successful.

The PNSE was on June 19, 1955, at 28°04' Gemini. It was a south nodal eclipse that fell in his 12th house of large organizations, philanthropic missions, and creative visualization. The PNSE is in the same sign, but different house than the South Node. Here, the question of house system is called into question. In the Koch system, both the PNSE and the South Node are in the 11th house. In the Porphyry system, both are in the 12th house. Arguably, both houses expanded over his lifetime and it is difficult to assess which one dominated the other.

The North Node is in Sagittarius ruled by Jupiter, which energizes the expansiveness, luck, and practical wisdom of the greater benefic. With Jupiter in the 2nd house ruling the 6th, his daily work paid off handsomely. The nodal energy boosting Jupiter also assists Pluto, and invigorates the mutual reception of the dark planet with the Sun, and their drive for power and creative self-expression. Jupiter–Pluto is beneficial for business, and the sextile from Neptune brings vision and expansion, as well as profit without limit. Jupiter also relates to law, and Gates has been sued and called before Congress to answer antitrust and monopolization complaints (Jupiter–Pluto over-reaching and squashing the competition).

The South Node is ruled by an unaspected Mercury in Libra in the 4th house, which rules the 3rd and 12th. Mercury's association with south nodal energy brings the expectation of loss, and was related to verbal outbursts. He was too smart for his own good and had little tolerance for others who could not keep up with him mentally. However, Gates also gave Mercury away in service. His particular genius was writing computer code. Rather than protect his software through copyright, he made it available to other programmers who could build on it (opposite to the strategy of Steve Jobs).

In latitude, Venus is parallel the Sun, nodes, and angles, another indication of a potential to accumulate immense wealth.

Taking Microsoft Public

The initial public offering (IPO) of Microsoft stock was on March 14, 1986 (Chart 47). The previous solar eclipse on November 12, 1985, was at 20° Scorpio, with Pluto serving as the lord. The south nodal eclipse fell in his 5th house of stock-broking and risk, and was conjunct natal Venus–Saturn.

On the day of the IPO, the progressed Moon was opposite the November solar eclipse degree and natal Venus–Saturn, indicating the culmination and turning point of his business. Transiting Pluto (lord) was conjunct the natal Sun, trine transiting Jupiter, and sextile transiting Neptune, bringing luck and vast wealth, as well as personal power and influence. Natal Uranus was at the North Bending of the transiting nodes, and the output of Uranus was publicly traded computer stock. The transiting South Node was conjunct a progressed Mars–Neptune conjunction, signifying his loss of personal control over his corporation. There was a mundane transiting Mars–Uranus conjunction separating from the natal North Node, denoting an outward event related to personal computers—in this instance stock (Uranus ruling the 8th). The transiting conjunction was square the transiting Sun, which was trine natal Venus–Saturn, marking the time of change in the business.

Transiting Venus was conjunct the 10th house cusp on a profitable day. Transiting Venus was conjunct the natal Moon and trine a progressed Sun–transiting Saturn conjunction, testifying to a profitable business move. But with transiting Venus and the Moon opposite natal Mars and inconjunct natal Sun–transiting Pluto, the loss of personal control over his business would have been difficult to bear.

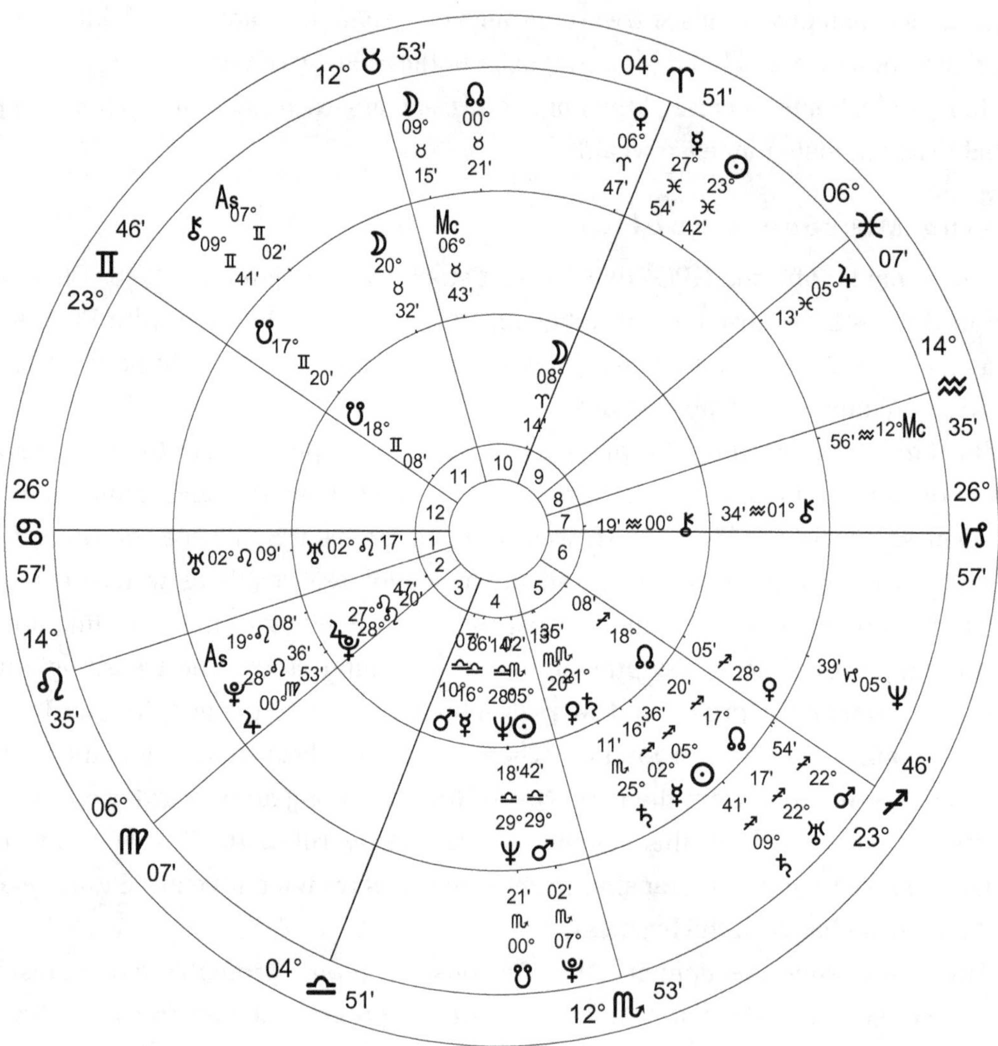

Chart 47:

Gates' Microsoft IPO, March 14, 1986, New York, NY, 9.30 a.m. EST

Marriage

Eight years later, there was another solar eclipse at 21°31' Scorpio, conjunct Venus–Saturn. This was a north nodal eclipse with Pluto as the lord, and fell in his 5th house of romance. The eclipse was related to marriage and at thirty-eight, Gates wed Microsoft employee Melinda French.

On the day of the Hawaii wedding (Chart 48), the progressed Moon was at the South Bending of the progressed nodes, as he gave himself up for love. Progressed Jupiter was at the South Bending of the transiting nodes, reflecting the ceremony and a partner in work. He married during the mundane conjunction of Uranus and Neptune that was sextile natal Venus–Saturn, suggesting that the marriage (or his wife) was good for business. There was a close four planet transiting conjunction in early Capricorn involving Venus, Mars, Mercury, and the Sun which formed a t-square with the natal Moon–Mars opposition, an indication that the marriage had a tempering influence, inducing him to be a better man (as he has said), and to fight and argue more fairly.

Transiting Pluto (lord) was conjunct progressed Saturn (ruler of his 7th), as he took responsibility for love. The pair was square transiting Saturn and square natal Jupiter–Pluto forming a stressful t-square, which suggests premarital negotiations and agreements regarding money and the ownership of the business. This message was repeated in secondary progression with a Saturn–Pluto square, as well as in declination with a parallel between the transiting South Node and progressed Uranus. He took steps to protect his money.

Chart 48:

Gates' Wedding, Jan. 1, 1994, Lanai, HI, noon

Stepping Down

Four months before he retired from Microsoft, there was a solar eclipse at 17°44' Aquarius on February 6, 2008, that fell in his 8th house (rebirth). It was a north nodal eclipse with Uranus serving as the lord (change).

On his last day of work at Microsoft (Chart 49), natal Venus–Saturn were at the South Bending of the transiting nodes trine transiting Uranus, marking a time of change when he would turn his attention (and money) and address overseas problems (transiting Uranus in the 9th house of far-off places ruling the 8th of big money).

Transiting Neptune was square natal Venus–Saturn, indicating mixed feelings of retirement. Regardless, with transiting Mars conjunct natal Jupiter–Pluto and square progressed Saturn, his work in the company came to an end (progressed Saturn conjunct the progressed IC). Transiting Pluto was conjunct the progressed Sun and trine natal Jupiter–Pluto as he reinvented himself as the world's greatest philanthropist.

In latitude, transiting Jupiter was contraparallel natal Venus at the 0° line of the ecliptic, symbolizing a largesse vision and the money to go with it, and describes his scientific foundation dedicated to enhancing the well-being of others.

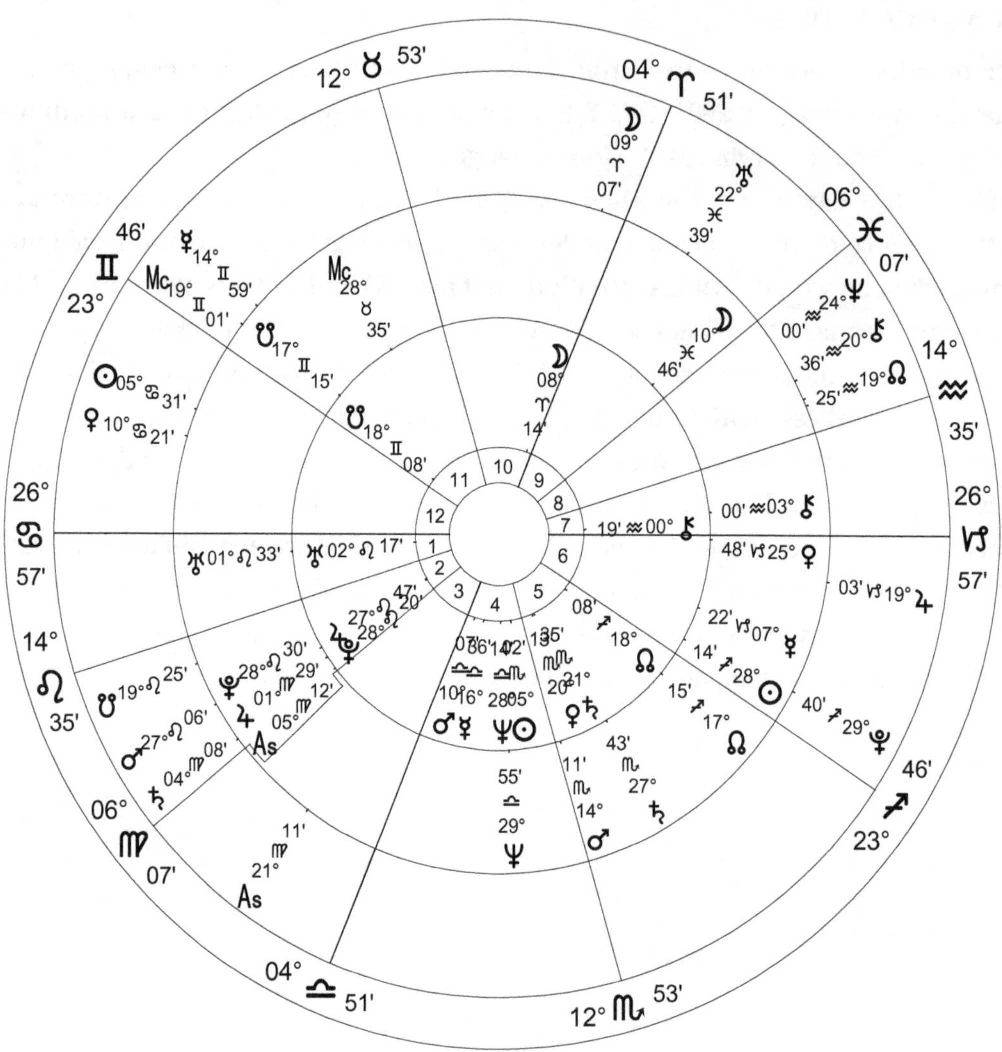

Chart 49:

Gates' Retirement, June 26, 2008, Bellevue, WA, noon

Every life is a mystery. And every story of every life is a mystery. But it is not what happens that is the mystery. It is whether it has to happen no matter what, whether it is ordered and ordained, fixed and fated, or whether it can be missed, avoided, circumvented, passed by; that is the mystery.

— *Cornell Woolrich*

Chapter 14
An Unlikely Corporate Superstar
Steve Jobs

Apple founder Steve Jobs followed a different business model than Microsoft. Whereas Bill Gates sought to make his computer software compatible with any hardware and thus available to everyone, Jobs worked to corner his market by controlling the software and hardware of his computers. Called a perfectionist, a visionary, a pioneer, and a genius, he was a leader in business, innovation, product design, marketing, and sales. He was no computer or software expert, but rather a master salesman who used 'magical thinking' to manifest his vision. During his life, he transformed six different industries: personal and tablet computing, animated film, music, communication and digital publishing. Coming out of a garage, the creator of the iPod, iTunes, iPhone, and iPad built a technological empire that changed the world.

He was adopted, given up at birth by a mother whose parents did not want her to marry a Syrian man. His adopted parents said he was chosen: 'we picked you,' and he grew up thinking he was special. He came of age in San Francisco at the height of the hippy counterculture. He was a gifted student with a dislike of authority. In high school, he worked at Hewlett-Packard where he met Steve Wozniak. Jobs went to college for a semester, then dropped out to take a spiritual pilgrimage to India. He experimented with psychedelic drugs, became a Buddhist, learned to trust his intuition, and to simplify. He returned to the U.S., and along with Wozniak, started Apple Computer Inc.

In 1984, Apple introduced the Mac, the first personal computer with a graphic user interface and a mouse. A year later, after falling profits, Jobs was fired from the company he started. He thought it was the best thing that happened to him. It removed the burden of success and allowed him the freedom to be creative.

That same year, Jobs bought what became Pixar. He began collaborating with Disney and produced computer animated movies. Ten years later, Apple bought Pixar and brought Jobs back. He was soon CEO. In 2001, Apple introduced the iPod and iTunes, which revolutionized the music industry. In 2007, he combined telephone communications with music and web browsing in the iPhone. In 2010, Jobs was estimated to have a fortune of 8.3 billion, and was listed as the 42nd wealthiest American. He was not known for philanthropy. At the time of his death, he was under investigation for securities fraud (back-dating stock purchases) and income tax evasion.

Jobs was married with four children. His oldest daughter was born out-of-wedlock when he was twenty-three. He long denied paternity and refused to pay child support. A private man, Jobs was especially secretive about his health. In October 2003, after suffering chronic gastrointestinal distress, he was diagnosed with pancreatic cancer. Refusing traditional medical care, he treated himself homeopathically. Nine months later when the cancer had spread, he had surgery. Six years later, he had a liver transplant, an indication the cancer had spread. It was a questionable treatment because long-term anti-rejection drugs depress the immune system, which is needed to keep cancer growth in check. In January 2011, Jobs went on extended medical leave. He stepped down as CEO on August 24, 2011, and died at home six weeks later.

Nativity

Jobs has a scattered planetary pattern dominated by an elevated Jupiter–Uranus conjunction (Chart 50). The Sun, Moon, and Mercury are unaspected (untethered and unrestrained). The PNSE before his birth was on December 24, 1954, at 2°58' Capricorn. The eclipse fell in his 4th house along with his natal North Node.

Jobs has a 6th house Pisces Sun (parallel Neptune in declination), and his forte was high vision and magical thinking that he applied in his every day job. The Sun rules the 12th house, and he used his imagination to channel the mystical realm of non-ordinary reality. In the 6th, Jobs used visualization in his work and in self-healing. The nodes are sextile/trine the Sun, empowering high insight. "Have the courage to follow your heart and intuition," he said. "They somehow already know what you truly want to become. Everything else is secondary." He also said, "You can't connect the dots looking forward; you can only connect them looking backwards. So you have to trust the dots will somehow connect in your future."

The Moon is in Aries, and he was combative and competitive (same Moon sign as Bill Gates). Placed in the 7th, Jobs needed relationships, but he was known to be coldhearted, callous, and abrasive. Ruling the 11th house of friends, Jobs went into business with friends, and also fell out with them (ruler 11 in the house of open enemies). The Moon rules the South Node and there were losses pertaining to family—he was abandoned by his birth parents, and he in turn abandoned his daughter and her mother. He refused to meet his father on the grounds he did not like what he had heard about him. Tapping into the higher side of the South Node, he learned to trust his instincts. If Pisces and Neptune symbolize inspired intuition, then the Moon's intuition is the instinct of the gut – the guidance of feeling. The Moon rules the public and Jobs served society by developing and selling products people did not know they needed—and eventually could not live without.

The Moon is widely square the nodes at the North Bending. However, in latitude, the Moon is at 5N02 approaching its maximum degree and thus near the bending. The

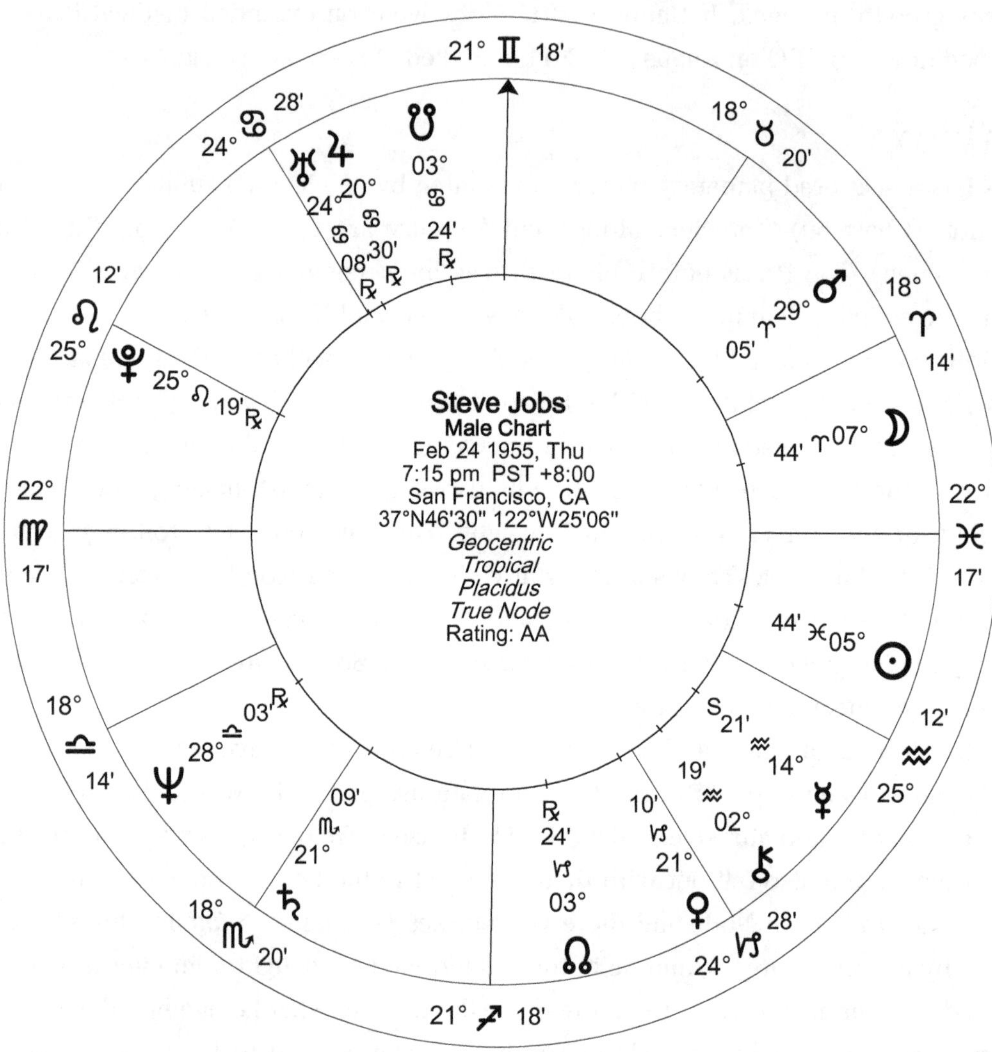

Chart 50:
Steve Jobs Nativity

symbolism of the Moon manifested outwardly. He used his intuition to see into the future (Moon ruling the 11th). However, the losses associated with the South Node ruler (multiple family abandonment) were also on public display. Nonetheless, he used the Moon in service, developing futuristic products for the masses. As Jobs said, "We're here to put a dent in the universe. ... We do things where we **feel** (emphasis mine) we can make a significant contribution. Our primary goal here is ... not to be the biggest or the richest."

Saturn rules the North Node and explains his business success. The association brings a mature business understanding, practical business sense, and easy acceptance of hard lessons. With Saturn in Scorpio, he was entrepreneurial, secretive in business, and transformed many industries. In the 3rd, he was a master manipulator of the press, who helped feed the mystique he built up around his products. Saturn is trine Jupiter–Uranus (seeing into the future of technology) and sextile Venus on the cusp of the 5th (stunning artistic design). Square Pluto, there were many power struggles and losses in business, which he took in stride, trusting that bad things happened for a reason and would work out for the best (faith in rebirth of a 12th house Pluto).

A stationary Mercury rules the chart and the Midheaven, and stands in the 5th house of creativity. About to turn direct (in seven hours), Mercury is brilliant in Aquarius, and brimming with new ideas and new ways to use old things, especially in regards to technology.

The elevated Jupiter–Uranus conjunction in Cancer is also parallel in declination, forming an occultation that strengthens the contact and the potency of the aspect. The conjunction bestows luck and a need to be true to the inner self. He said, "Your time is limited, so don't waste it living someone else's life. Don't be trapped by dogma—which is living with the results of other people's thinking. Don't let the noise of other's opinions drown out your own inner voice." Jupiter–Uranus defined Jobs' genius as a visionary who invented the future. Quoting hockey player Wayne Gretsky Jobs said, "I skate to where the puck is going to be, not where it has been." Jobs was guided by his vision of what technology could be. "Apple is about people who think outside the box, people who want to use computers to help them change the world, to help them create things that make a difference, and not just to get a job done."

Jupiter–Uranus is opposite Venus, expressed in his drive to create beautiful products. The opposition also describes his estrangement from his oldest daughter (Venus in the 5th) whom he denied, claiming in court that he was sterile (a unique legal defense). The opposition is eased by a sextile/trine to Saturn, and he ultimately accepted responsibility for his neglected child. He had a dislike of authority, but it worked out well for him (the trine). He said, "Here's to the crazy ones, the misfits, the rebels, the troublemakers, the round pegs in the square holes … the ones who see things differently—they're not fond of rules ...You can quote them, disagree with them, glorify or vilify them, but the only thing you can't do is ignore them because they change things … they push the human race forward, and while some may see them as the crazy ones, we see genius, because the ones who are crazy enough to think that they can change the world, are the ones that do." And he did.

Jobs has a Mars–Neptune opposition eased by a sextile/trine from Pluto. With Mars in its own sign, he was able to fight for his creative vision (Neptune). This vision gave him the power and means to transform the collective. The opposition also describes creative accounting and a sleight of hand when it comes to taxes and stockholder reports (Mars in the 8th). Pluto in the 12th in Leo, reflects his sense that he was chosen and somehow special. Pluto is square Saturn, an indication of ruthlessness in business, drastic business upsets, and trouble with authority and the government (tax evasion and stock fraud).

In declination, Pluto is parallel the Midheaven and the South Node, reflecting the humiliating losses he experienced in his career, but also a career that transformed the collective. The North Node is conjunct the IC, which indicates ultimate gain and benefit from the family. Jobs found his birth mother, developed a good relationship with his birth sister, and finally accepted his daughter.

Pancreatic Cancer

Since my interest lies more with medicine than business, in looking at events, my focus will be on the progressions and transits related to Job's health. Natally, health issues are shown by the 6th house, with periods of stress in general related to challenges affecting the Sun, Moon, Ascendant, and chart ruler.

Jobs has Aquarius on the 6th house cusp, ruled by Uranus in Cancer, conjunct Jupiter, and opposite Venus. This opposition defines his illness: insulin (Jupiter) producing cells in the pancreas (Cancer and possibly Jupiter, Virgo and Pluto) that metabolize sugar (Venus) became cancerous, eventually requiring a liver (Jupiter) transplant. With Mars opposite Neptune, and Neptune ruling the 7th house of his partner in health (his doctors), Jobs had a hard time following medical advice.

In October 2003, at 7.30 in the morning, Jobs was diagnosed with pancreatic cancer. He was forty-eight years old. A GI scan showed the islet cells of the pancreas that produce and secrete insulin had become cancerous. While pancreatic cancer itself is fatal and quick acting, the type of cancer Jobs had was more readily treatable by traditional medicine. However, he preferred self-healing and homeopathic remedies. There is a time, but not a date for the diagnosis and the chart is set for October 15, 2003 (Chart 51).

Four important events had transpired by progression. The progressed Ascendant had moved into Scorpio, making Pluto the progressed chart ruler. Natally, Pluto is on the cusp of the 12th house of hospitalization square Saturn (practical threat to life). The progressed exalted Sun was square natal Uranus (upsetting disruption of the life force) and trine progressed Pluto in Leo, leading him to believe he could heal himself. The nodes had progressed from Capricorn/Cancer into Sagittarius/Gemini, giving rise to new progressed nodal rulers—Jupiter and Mercury. Mercury, as the ruler of the progressed South Node is relevant to health issues because it is the natal chart ruler. Jupiter as ruler of the progressed North Node is important because it is conjunct Uranus, the natal 6th house ruler. The onset of the illness coincided with the exact progressed perfection of the natal Venus–Jupiter opposition.

The solar eclipse before the diagnosis was on May 30, 2003, at 9°19' Gemini, square the natal Sun. The lord of the eclipse was Mercury, the natal chart ruler, pointing to a potential for health issues. Since there is no date, I will ignore the fast moving planets and concentrate on the nodes and the outer planets. The transiting South Node was conjunct natal Saturn, indicating a loss and weakness of Saturn, in this case physical limitation. Progressed Pluto was at the North Bending of the transiting nodes and cancer manifested. There was a double-whammy involving Uranus and the nodes, with

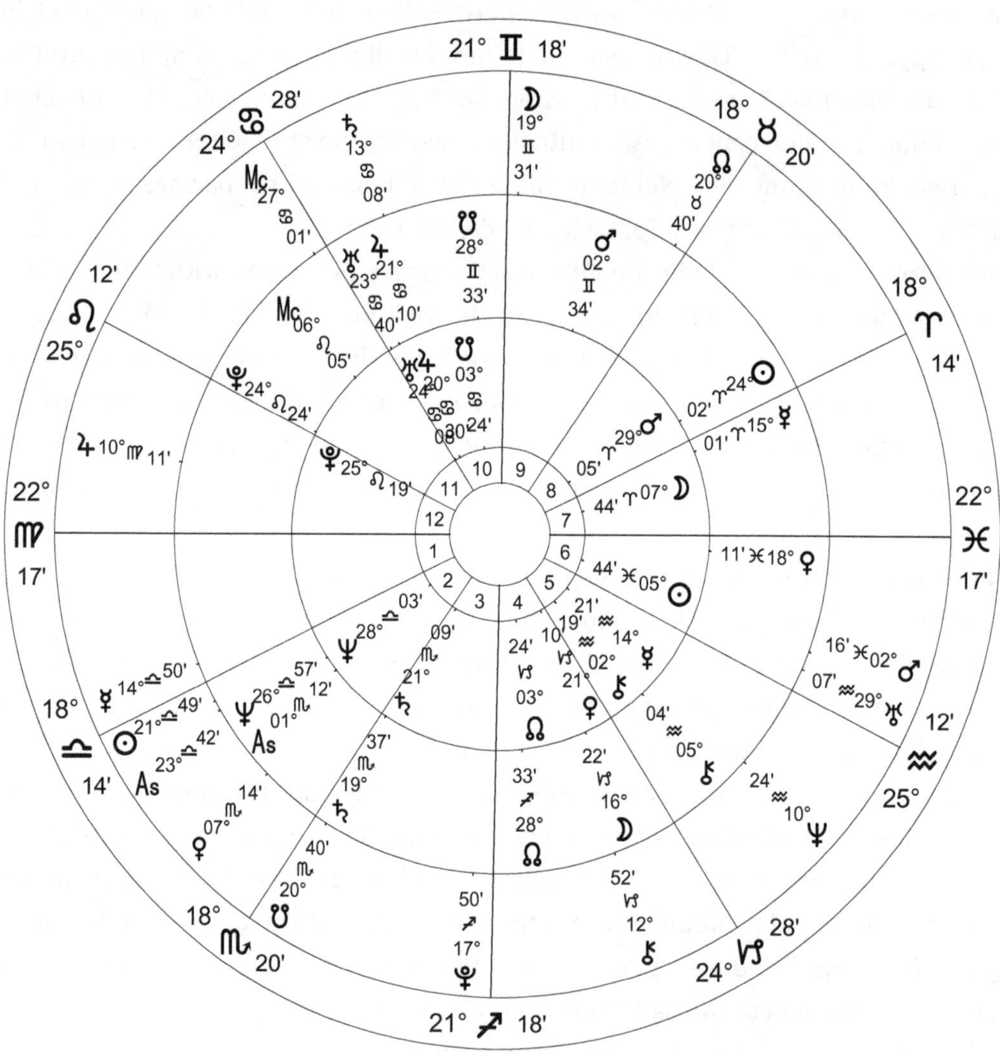

Chart 51:

Jobs' Cancer Diagnosis, Oct. 15, 2003, Palo Alto, CA 7.30 a.m. PDT

the transiting nodes sextile/trine progressed Uranus, and transiting Uranus sextile/trine the progressed nodes. With Uranus ruling the 6th house of health, the easy aspects suggest he may not have taken the threat to his health seriously. Transiting Saturn was square progressed Mercury and he ignored the advice of his doctors. Transiting Uranus had just entered the natal 6th house and was sextile natal Mars and trine natal Neptune and he believed he had the power to heal himself. Reinforcing this belief was the conjunction of transiting Neptune to natal Mercury (lord). Transiting Pluto at the natal IC had formed a yod and was quincunx natal Jupiter and inconjunct the transiting North Node (giving Pluto more power). He ignored the treatment of traditional doctors and the aggressive tumors spread (Pluto).

In declination, the progressed South Node was parallel progressed Pluto, suggesting loss from the dark planet. This aspect would remain in effect until his death.

Surgery

Nine months after the initial diagnosis, after a new GI scan showed the cancer had metastasized, Jobs accepted traditional medical intervention and underwent surgery. The right side of his pancreas, gall bladder, and parts of his stomach, bile duct, and small intestine were removed. The solar eclipse before the event was on May 4, 2004, at 29°49' Aries and fell in his 8th house of surgery conjunct natal Mars (the mundane ruler of surgery) and was opposite natal Neptune (crisis of faith). The lord of the eclipse was Mars.

On the day of the operation (Chart 52), transiting Mars was conjunct progressed Pluto on the cusp of the 12th house of hospitalization, activating the natal Saturn–Pluto square (surgery, death of tissue, and a fight for life). Transiting Uranus, ruler of the 6th house of illness was conjunct the natal Sun and square progressed Mars, another indication of surgery with unexpected results (partial loss of many organs). There was a Full Moon on the day of the surgery that fell across the progressed Midheaven-IC that was square the transiting nodes, with the transiting Moon, progressed IC and Chiron, all at the South Bending, signifying the wound that was made that day. Although the removal of tumors brought some healing, physiologically, portions of organs cannot be removed without consequence. Nonetheless, with the transiting nodes

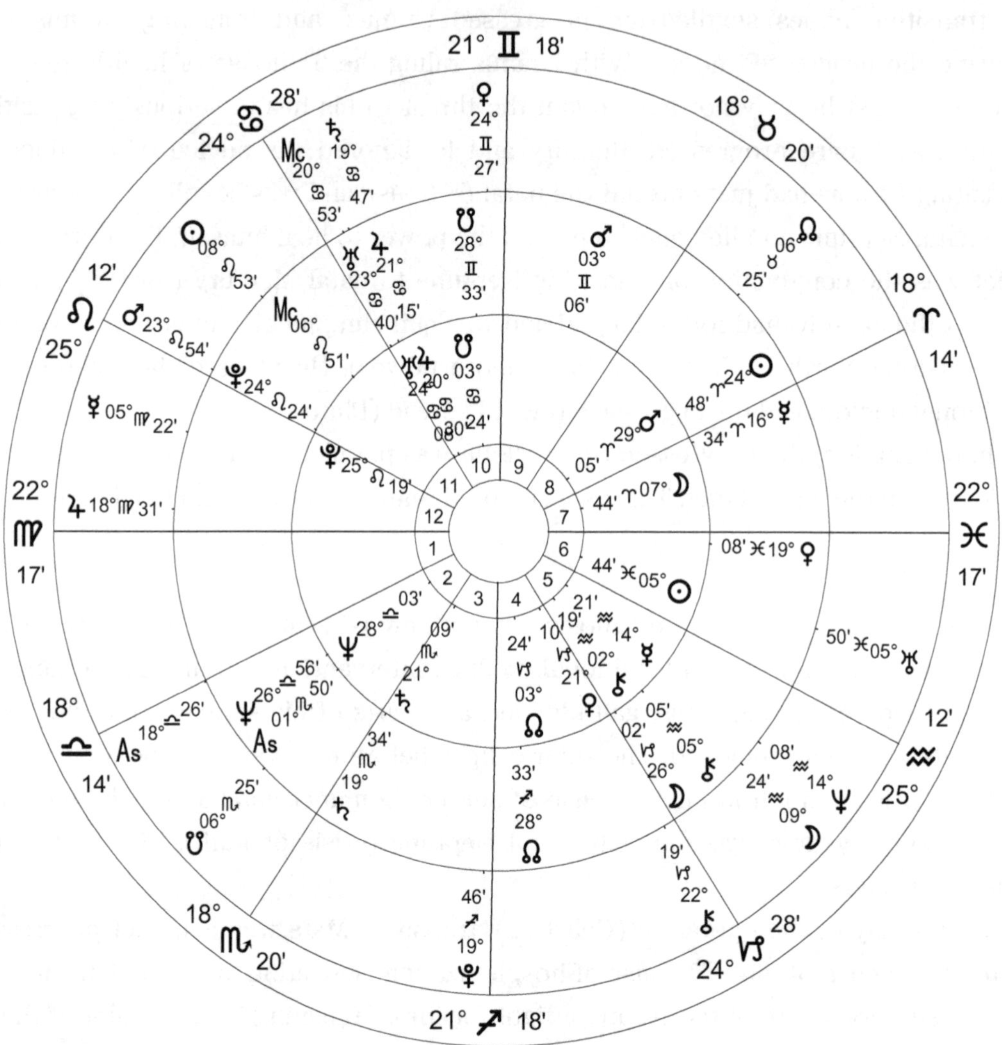

Chart 52:

Jobs' Surgery, July 31, 2004, Palo Alto, CA, noon

sextile/trine his natal Sun and transiting Uranus, along with a grand trine formed with progressed Venus, natal Jupiter, and progressed Saturn, Jobs was optimistic for his future. He declared himself healed. Although he was derided for his decision to treat himself holistically, the case cannot be made that medical science helped him.

Transplant

Five years later on Mar 15, 2009, Jobs received a new liver. The north nodal solar eclipse before the transplant occurred at 6°30' Aquarius on January 26, 2009, with Uranus as the lord.

On the day of the transplant (Chart 53), transiting Uranus was conjunct the natal Descendant, progressed Venus, and trine natal Uranus–Jupiter, and a donor was suddenly found and the transplant was performed. As seen previously, a planet crossing an angle can precipitate an event related to the planet and here transiting Uranus at the D.C. brought a compatible liver (trine natal Jupiter–Uranus). Transiting Pluto was conjunct the natal North Node (sextile the natal Sun), and there was death of the old liver, with regeneration made possible from a new liver.

The progressed Ascendant was square the transiting nodes at the South Bending, an indication of physical weakness and vulnerability. The progressed Moon was square the progressed nodes at the North Bending, suggesting outward relief, particularly for his wife. Progressed Mercury was opposite progressed Neptune, and prayers were answered. However, the opposition formed a t-square with progressed Jupiter and natal Uranus, and the science was unsound. With transiting Uranus inconjunct progressed Pluto; and transiting Neptune opposite natal Pluto; the transplant would be his death knell.

Jobs had his transplant and returned to work. From then until the end of his life, he was on immunosuppressant drugs to stop his body from attacking the donated liver. He remained at Apple for eighteen months.

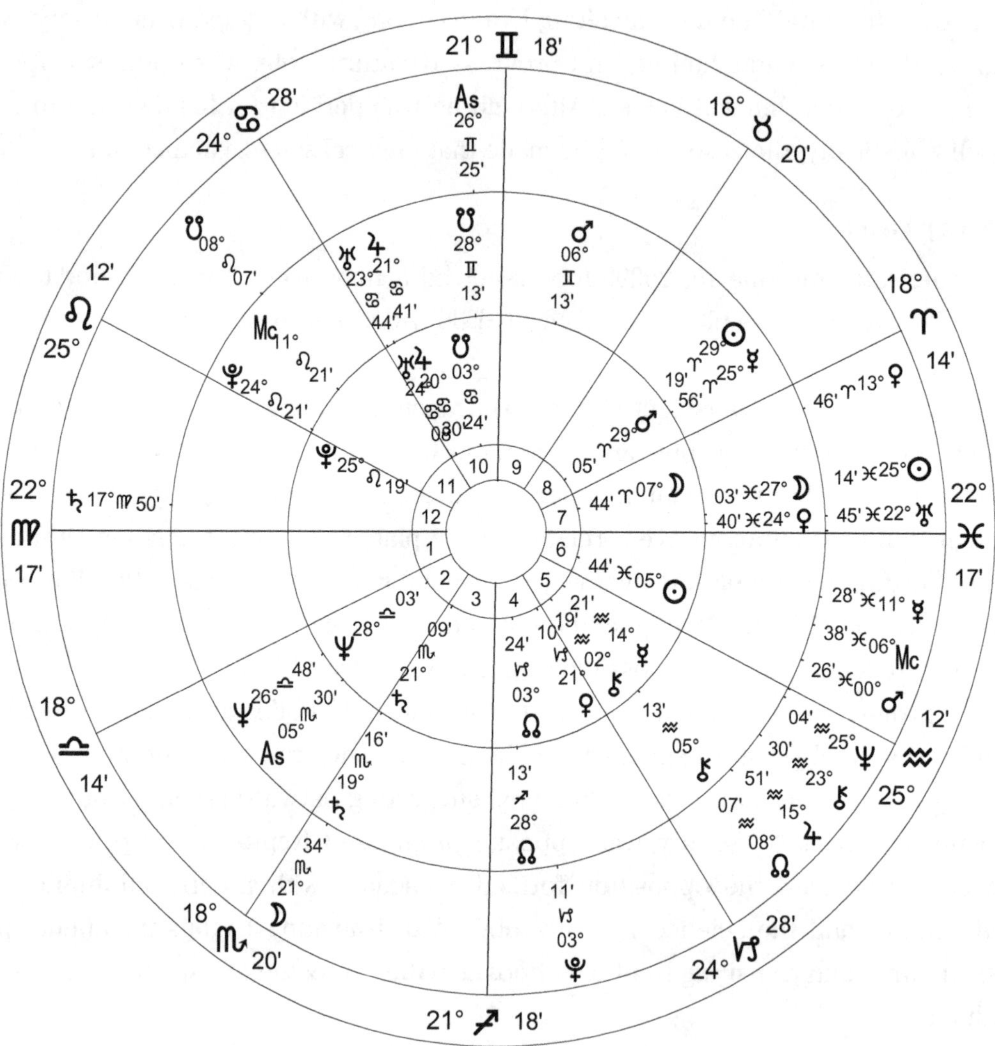

Chart 53:

Jobs' Liver Transplant, March 15, 2009, Memphis, TN, noon

Death

Steve Jobs died on October 5, 2011 (Chart 54). There were two south nodal solar eclipses before his death. The first was on June 1, 2011, at 11°01' Gemini, with Mercury as the lord, and the second was on July 1, 2011, at 9°12' Cancer, with the Moon as the lord. He had a progressed New Moon in Taurus in the 8th house (of death) in July.

On the day he died, transiting Venus was conjunct progressed Neptune and there was wonder. His last words were, "Oh wow, oh wow, oh wow." Progressed Venus was at the North Bending of the progressed nodes, and manifested a long journey (Venus ruling the 9th). Transiting Pluto was still conjunct his natal North Node (as it had been when he had his transplant), now bringing physical death. Transiting Pluto was square the natal Moon, trine the progressed Moon (mixed feelings, bitter and sweet), and square transiting Uranus at the North Bending of the natal nodes (the end coming suddenly). Transiting Mercury (lord 1) and transiting Saturn (the Grim Reaper) were square natal Jupiter and progressed Uranus, suggestive of unexpected physical weakness. The transiting Moon (lord 2) was separating from a square to the progressed Sun and Mercury, and in approaching square to the progressed Moon, transiting Jupiter and the progressed horizon, as hope set in the sky. The progressed IC had come to natal Mercury (lord 1 and chart ruler), signaling the end of the matter for his physical body.

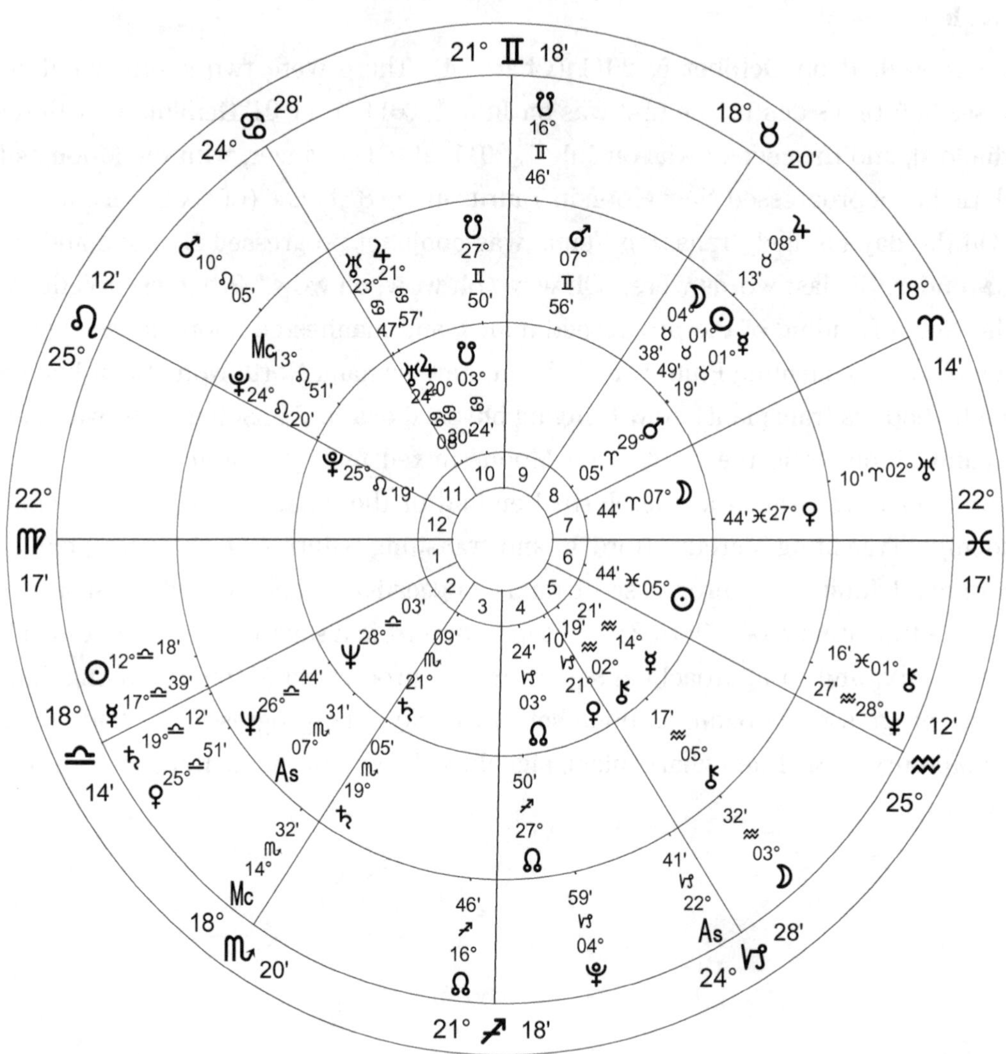

Chart 54:

Job's Death, Oct. 5, 2011, Palo Alto, CA, 3:00 p.m.

The essence of humanity's spiritual dilemma is that we evolved genetically to accept one truth and discovered another. Is there a way to erase the dilemma, to resolve the contradictions between the transcendentalist and the empiricist world views?

—*E. O. Wilson*

Chapter 15
An Unusual Scientist
Kary Mullis

My motivation for this project was an attempt to redeem the South Node. I thought it had acquired a bad reputation it did not deserve, and did not think the activity of its house should be ignored. I was wrong on both counts. South Node energy kind of *does* deserve its grim reputation, and, the focus *can* be taken off house position (along with the house position of the North Node). The research led me in a direction I was not expecting, which is usually the nature of research. I decided to publish what I had learned after reading an article on the Nobel Prize winning chemist Kary Mullis where the astrologer wrote that she hoped he would stop doing his 10th house South Node and focus on his 4th house North Node. I thought it was bad advice. People do what comes naturally. And, South Node energy works so long as it is used for a higher purpose, or serves a good that is greater than the self.

In his biography, *Dancing in the Mind Field*, Mullis wrote that he liked to blow things up. He was born knowing about circuit breakers, was playing with electricity at six, and received his first chemistry set at seven. He chose to study biochemistry in order to impress girls. He quit science to write fiction, but when he had to support himself waiting tables, he returned to research. He has been called "an impatient and impulsive researcher who avoids lab work and instead thinks about research topics while driving and surfing." He has been married four times and has three kids with two different mothers. He has used LSD and when it became illegal and unobtainable, he made his own—although one batch went bad and made him temporarily psychotic. He passed out after inhaling nitrous oxide and thinks an astral-traveler saved his tongue and face from frostbite. He believes he has been visited by aliens.

He won the Nobel Prize for developing the polymerase chain reaction (PCR), a technique that enables the rapid sequencing of DNA and has revolutionized biology. Two leading scientific journals had rejected his manuscript on this work. Publicly, he criticizes the government, pharmaceutical industry, and politically-backed scientific institutes like the NIH and CDC. He questions if HIV is the cause of AIDS, and if AZT has any value to anyone besides its manufacturer. He believes in astrology and says he chose to study biochemistry because, "With Mercury and Mars in conjunction in Sagittarius, I was not going to specialize in something well-defined and manageable. I didn't think of myself as a worker, or a specialist. I thought of myself as a man of deep science with a Gemini moon in my face and the cold, red winds of Mars in my hair. I wanted to see reality, if possible, and my Capricorn sun felt a strong need to make a living." While I question his delineation of Mercury and Mars in Sagittarius—his explanation seems more attributable to his 9th house Sun square Neptune—he is nonetheless open-minded and his research transformed the study of biology and all associated fields.

Nativity

Mullis' chart is dominated by two t-squares: one involving the Sun, Neptune, and Saturn; and the other the Moon, Mercury–Mars and Jupiter (Chart 55). Mercury and Jupiter are in mutual reception and they are the final dispositors of the chart. He was born

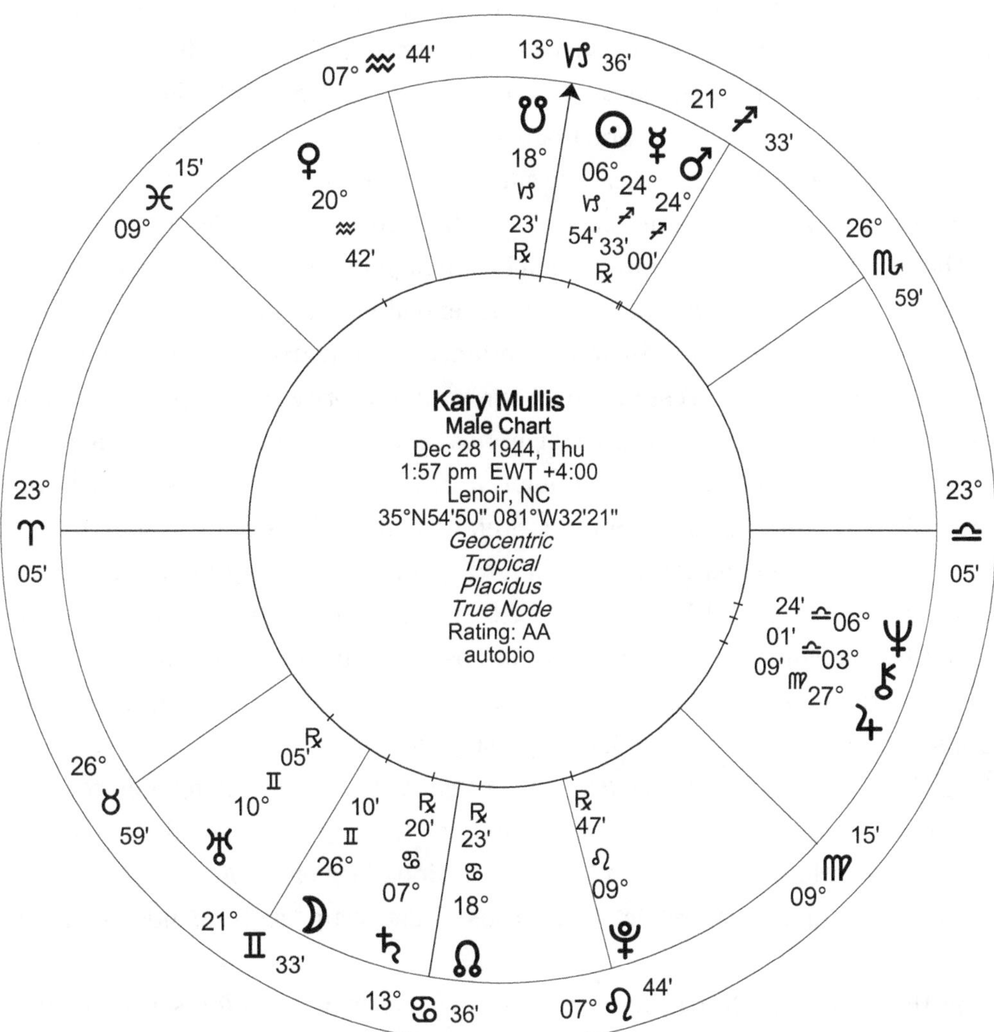

Chart 55:

Kary Mullis Nativity

within a day of a lunar eclipse at 7°47' Cancer that was conjunct Saturn. There was a solar eclipse two weeks later at 23°41' Capricorn. The eclipse fell in his 10th house of career and this was the house (containing the South Node) that expanded over his lifetime.

With a Capricorn Sun, he is practical, ambitious, and hard-working. In the 9th, this is expressed through higher education and advanced study. The Sun is the most elevated planet in the chart and he has elevated himself in the public eye. The Sun rules the 5th house of play and creativity, which he employed in research and was instrumental to his success. The Sun is square Neptune, explaining his desire to expand his mind with LSD, as well as his non-ordinary experiences with astro-travelers and aliens. The Sun is opposite Saturn, suggesting a problem with authority. The opposition is mitigated by the Sun's residence in Saturn's sign, but Saturn in Cancer is weak, and since it rules his 10th house, his career and reputation have suffered from his unscientific and far-out beliefs (Saturn square Neptune). Still, he achieved success through hard work and the use of his imagination rather than traditional laboratory methods. The Sun is in a yod with Uranus and Pluto, alluding to the trouble he had getting his research accepted by academia, and the trouble he has had with mainstream science for his unusual and outspoken ideas (Uranus in Gemini). He is far from the conservative, old-school scientist that a Capricorn Sun might suggest.

The Moon is in Gemini in the 3rd house of early education, giving a curious nature and a collector of facts and information. He likes to keep busy and ideas come to him when he drives. He thinks with his heart and rationalizes emotions. The Moon is ruled by Mercury conjunct Mars in Sagittarius, bestowing a tremendous drive for knowledge.

The Moon rules the North Node and acquires maturity, common sense, strong intuition and worldly experience through the association. He can 'feel' what information (Gemini) is missing and necessary for the big picture (Moon opposite ruler Mercury in Sagittarius), and what information doesn't fit and is misleading, irrelevant, or incorrect.

Saturn in the 3rd in detriment in Cancer rules the South Node and is equated with loss, vulnerability sacrifice, and service. He is out of favor with the scientific authorities and his reputation has suffered accordingly. In his autobiography, he never mentions his father (Saturn). In contrast, he mentions his mother frequently and lauds her support of his curiosity in his formative years (Moon in Gemini ruling the North Node). He may have gone into science to impress girls, but the aim and result of his research was to improve the plight of humanity (Saturn used in service). He was a theoretical scientist who discovered a practical application of molecular biology that has saved lives and enhanced the scope of biological research. His refinement of PCR and its practical use transformed biology and medicine.

With Mercury in Sagittarius and Jupiter in Virgo, the final dispositors are both in detriment. While traditionally this should weaken their influence, this was not the case as there was no hindrance to higher thought, or impairment of scientific research. It is possible the reception was helped by the house position of the planets (Jupiter in Mercury's house, and Mercury in Jupiter's house). The planets are also square, showing active tension and perhaps a lifetime of experience in learning how best to use the aspect for the least aggravation. With Mars the chart ruler involved, he is tireless in thought and expended much energy pushing forward the frontiers of scientific truth. The Moon's contribution in the t-square is the need to fight verbally for his brand of truth. The trouble with the t-square is related to his unorthodox beliefs.

In declination, Pluto and Mars are out of bounds, alluding to his near-death experiences, and wild, unrestrained actions. The pair are contraparallel, giving a talent for investigative research and a tendency to undermine his credibility with extreme viewpoints and behavior. Saturn and Uranus are parallel the North Node, which enable scientific expression and explain his innate understanding of circuit breakers and electricity. In latitude, Uranus is parallel the Sun, angles, and nodes making the genius of Uranus personal.

Polymerase Chain Reaction (PCR)

Driving down a highway one night, Mullis was pondering ways to find specific genes in DNA. DNA is a long strand of bases (sugar-like molecules) strung together to form genes. Genes are strung together to form a chromosome. Many chromosomes (in humans there are 46) make up the total DNA. To find a specific gene in this mix, he imagined a solution similar to the 'find function' in computer word processing programs that detect a given word in hundreds of pages of text. For example, to find the word 'explain', the letters 'ex' or 'pl' will locate that one word in a text containing hundreds of thousands of words.

Mullis' insight was to use a primer as the 'find function'. A primer is a stretch of DNA about twenty bases long that is specifically designed to recognize a gene that might be ten thousand bases long. DNA is designed to be copied. It is double-stranded, with one strand complementary to the other. It is made of four bases, abbreviated as "A", "T", "C", or "G". Since "A" always combines with "T", and "C" always combines with "G", knowing the linear sequence of one strand, automatically describes the sequence of the complementary strand.

In PCR, high temperatures are used to separate the DNA chains. Primer is added and combines with the desired gene. DNA synthesis is initiated, which copies the gene. The resultant copy can be copied, and those copies can be copied, thereby amplifying the DNA of that one gene. This is the technology that made possible the DNA sequencing of the human genome.

Used in medicine, PCR enables doctors to determine the genetic basis of some diseases. It also enables doctors to determine which treatments are most effective for some diseases, and which diseases a patient is most susceptible to (a technology now in its infancy, but certain to become more prevalent). In forensics, PCR is used to amplify minute samples of blood and semen that serve as biological fingerprints. PCR is used in microbiology and immunology to identify bacteria and viruses, and to track their evolution over time.

As he drove down that highway, Mullis realized the implication of the technique immediately and thought, "There are pressing reasons to want to read this molecule. Children are born with genetic defects, sometimes with tragic consequences like muscles that wither and die. Such things could be predicted and averted if we could read the DNA blueprints." He also recognized "... the looming but not so pressing reasons for knowing DNA—the ones that extend out to horizons mankind has not yet reached—the potential of gaining control over DNA and thus life."

According to his autobiography, the idea for PCR came to him late one Friday evening in early May. Arbitrarily I picked May 6, 1983, and 11 p.m. as the date and time of the chart located in Mendocino County (Chart 56).

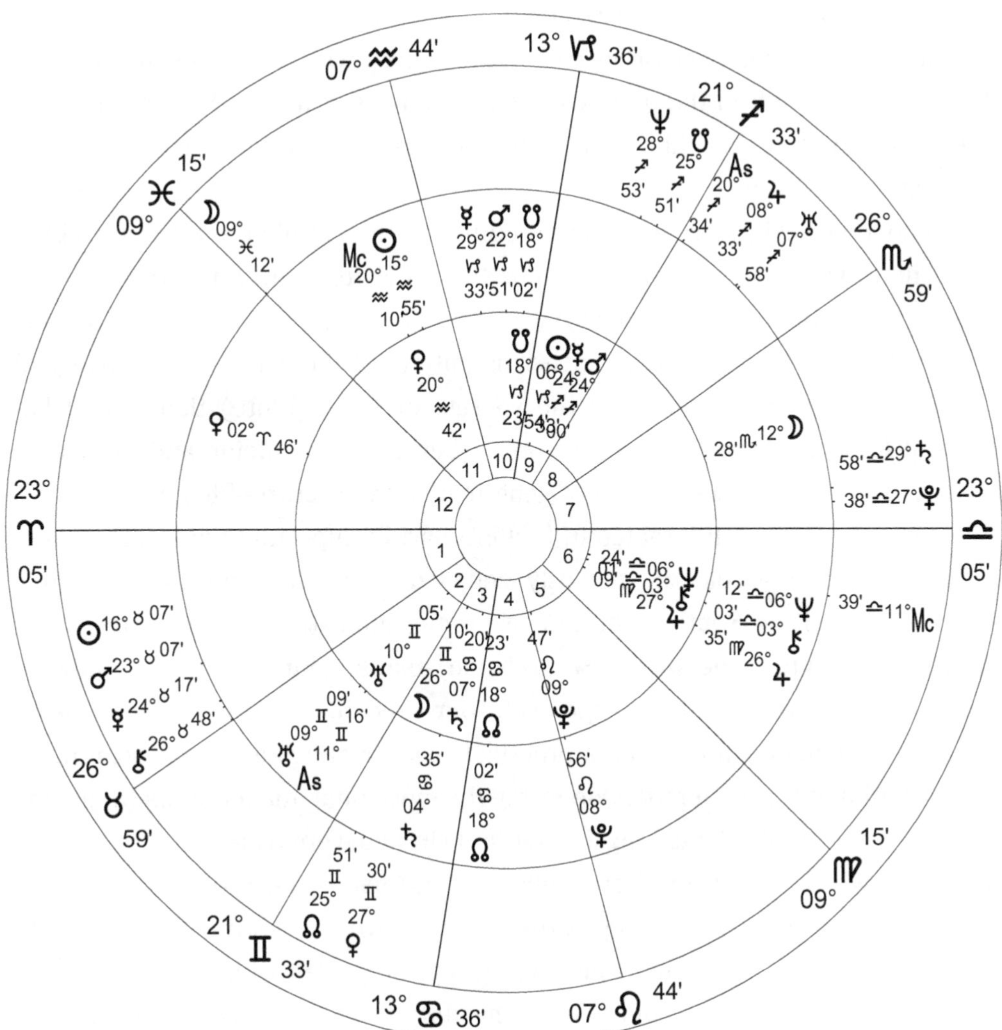

Chart 56:

Kary Mullis' PCR Insight, March 6, 1983, Andersonia, CA, 11:00 p.m. PDT

The prior solar eclipse was on December 15, 1982 at 23°4' Sagittarius. It was conjunct natal Mercury–Mars, activating the natal t-square with the Moon and Jupiter. The south nodal eclipse fell in the 9th house, with Jupiter serving as the lord. The eclipse foretold a period of intense 'higher thought,' and an influx of illuminating and inspirational ideas.

By mundane transit, there was a great conjunction of Jupiter and Uranus at 8° Sagittarius. There was an even greater conjunction of Saturn and Pluto that was sextile Neptune, and sextile/trine the transiting nodes, giving the conjunction more punch. These mundane aspects characterize the magnitude of the scientific discovery (Jupiter–Uranus) arising from unlocking the secrets of DNA (Pluto) that would have a widespread (Neptune) practical applicability (Saturn) to medicine and the treatment of disease, forensics, and the control of genetic material (Saturn–Pluto).

The mundane aspects interacted in Mullis' chart in important ways. Transiting Saturn and Pluto were sextile the recently eclipsed natal Mercury–Mars, which were conjunct the transiting South Node and Neptune, indicating far-reaching (Neptune) inspired ideas from the otherworld (South Node) enabling him to dream up news ways to manipulate DNA for practical purposes. Progressed Jupiter (lord) was at the North Bending of the transiting nodes and a practical vision manifested. The transiting North Node was conjunct the natal Moon, denoting the emotional impact of his thoughts, and their public applicability. Transiting Jupiter and Uranus were trine natal Pluto opposite natal Uranus when he realized how science could usurp the properties of DNA for humanitarian purposes. Transiting Saturn and Pluto were trine the natal Moon–transiting North Node and square progressed Mercury, describing his excitement at the implication of the science, but also his hesitation that if the solution was so obvious to him, that surely others had thought of it first and saw some problem he couldn't see (Saturn square Mercury).

Nonetheless, on Monday he was back at work and soon obtained permission to research PCR full-time. He assembled his reagents and began the lab work in September.

PCR Revolution Begins

By Christmas, Mullis had amplified the world's first DNA of a targeted gene. He ran the experiment in the afternoon on Friday, December 16, 1983, and it was dark outside by the time he developed the radiography that told him the experiment worked. The chart is set for 6 p.m. (Chart 57).

The result was obtained two weeks after a south nodal solar eclipse at 11°46' Sagittarius, with Jupiter serving as the lord. The eclipse fell in his 8th house of mysteries, opposite natal Uranus and conjunct transiting Uranus and the progressed Descendant. The timing of the discovery coincided with the breakup of a relationship as his girlfriend moved out of his home and out of state.

On the evening of the successful result, there was a transiting Sun–Jupiter–Neptune conjunction that was conjunct natal Mercury–Mars, setting off the natal t-square, which expressed as successful research with the promise of more work to come. Transiting Mercury was conjunct the progressed South Node (inspired ideas) and square transiting Mars at the North Bending of the natal nodes when research bore weighty fruit. Transiting Mars was also in a grand trine with the progressed Sun and transiting North Node, transiting Mercury was conjunct the Midheaven, and the progressed Midheaven was conjunct natal Venus; and Mullis knew the research would make him famous. The transiting North Node was conjunct the progressed Ascendant and natal Uranus (widely), attesting to the scientific results that would bring him money and fame.

In connection with the breakup of his relationship, transiting Uranus conjunct the progressed Descendant and the transiting South Node indicated the loss of a partner. Transiting Venus was conjunct transiting Saturn (also parallel) and square natal Pluto, as transiting Pluto was square progressed Mercury, and progressed Venus was square progressed Saturn, denoting a sad, dark and lonely space after his girlfriend moved away, leaving him alone at Christmas.

In declination, transiting Uranus, Neptune, and the South Node were parallel and parallel progressed Mars and contraparallel progressed Uranus, indicating the far-reaching effect of the research. In latitude, transiting Uranus was contraparallel natal Uranus at the 0° line of the ecliptic, parallel the Sun, nodes, and angles at the birth of the PCR revolution.

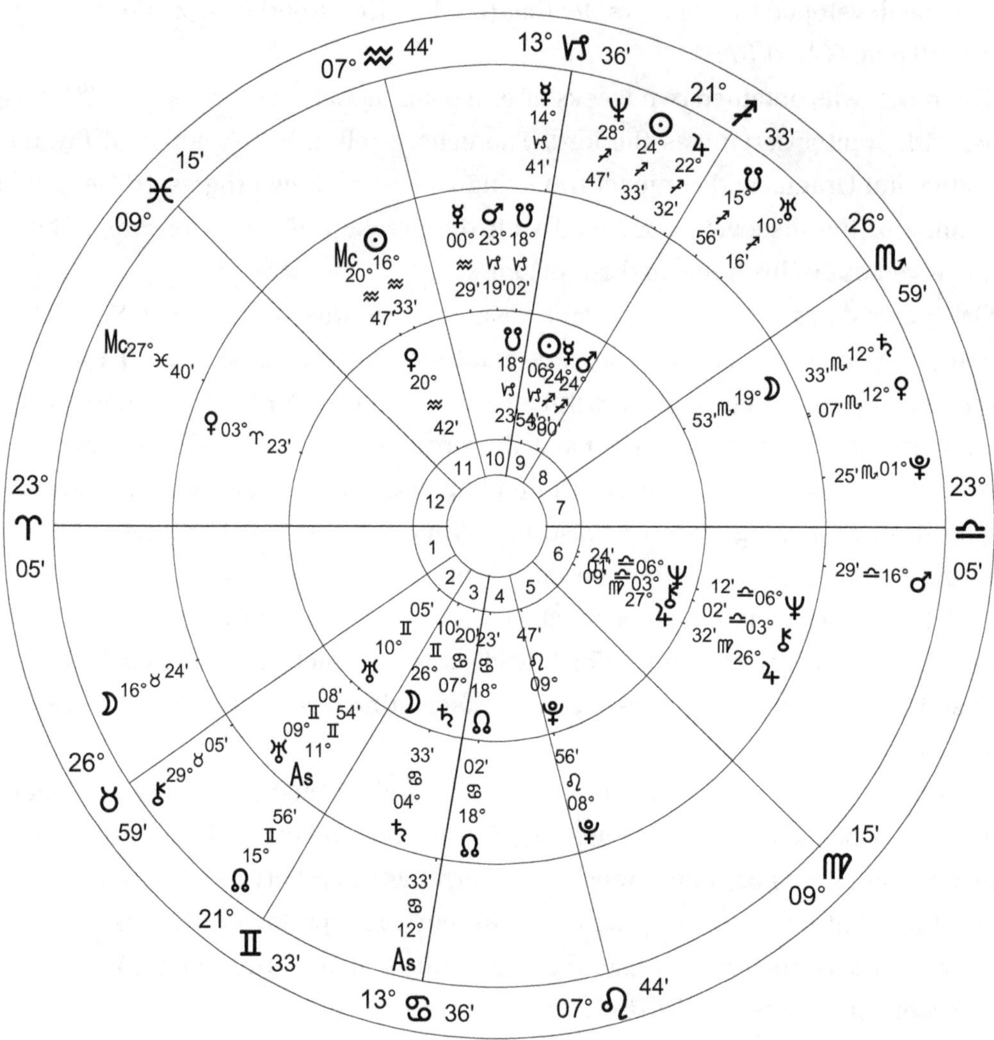

Chart 57:

Mullis' PCR Revolution, Dec. 16, 1983, La Jolla, CA, 6:00 p.m. PST

Nobel Prize

Ten years later, Mullis was awarded the Nobel Prize for his PCR research. He received the call in the morning of October 13, 1993, while he was on his way to go surfing. The chart is set for 6:15 a.m. (Chart 58). The previous south nodal solar eclipse was on May 21, 1993, at 00°31' Gemini that fell in his second house of money with Mercury serving as the lord.

The progressed Midheaven was at the North Bending of the transiting nodes denoting professional accomplishment. Transiting Mercury (lord) was sextile the natal Midheaven when he received word of the prize. There was a mundane conjunction of transiting Uranus and Neptune at 18° Capricorn that was conjunct his natal South Node and square transiting Sun–Jupiter and the natal Descendant at the North Bending of the natal Nodes, describing outward recognition from an esteemed group for service to science that enhanced the scope of biological research. Transiting Saturn was conjunct the progressed Sun and natal Venus, trine transiting Sun–Jupiter, and trine natal Moon, highlighting professional accomplishment and great happiness. However, Saturn, Sun, and Venus were square transiting Pluto, which was quincunx the Moon, at the same time transiting Mars was square natal Pluto, indicative of upsetting power struggles, as well as problems with newfound fame, and a loss of privacy due to the intrusion of the press.

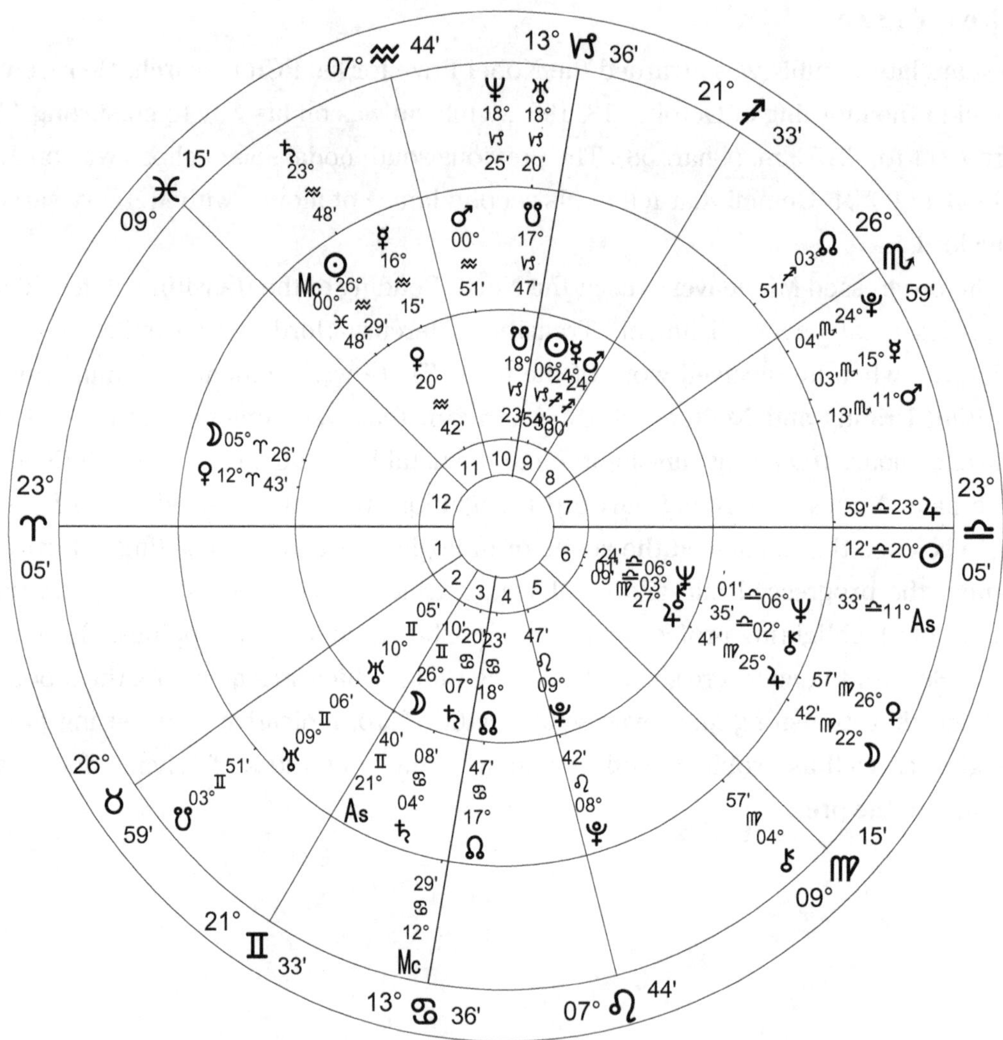

Chart 58:

Mullis' Nobel News, Oct. 13, 1993, La Jolla, CA 6:15 a.m. PDT

In my life's chain of events nothing was accidental. Everything happened according to an inner need.

— Hannah Senesh

Chapter 16
An Unusual Medical Doctor
Michael Crichton

Michael Crichton (rhymes with frighten) always wanted to be a writer, but he did not think he would make enough money to pay the bills, so he decided to become a doctor. He went to Harvard Medical School and did not like it. He wanted to drop out from the beginning, but the dean convinced him to persevere. He wrote an award-winning novel in his final year of medical school. The following year he began a post-doctoral fellowship at the Salk Institute. He finished that and started writing full time. He was a swift and prolific author, writing novels in as quickly as a weekend. He also wrote screenplays, directed movies, and along with Stephen Spielberg, created the story line of ER. A dominant theme of his work concerns the morality of science.

He was interested in metaphysics and the occult. His autobiography, *Travels*, details his skeptical foray into the field of psychic phenomena. In 1978, while directing *The Great Train Robbery* in London, he visited psychics daily, secretly studying their methods and accuracy. He was disturbed about their insights into the future because he could not see a mechanism that enabled it. He understood they could tell him about his past and things he had forgotten, but since the future had not yet happened, he thought it was impossible to know. Over the next decade his interest in and research of the occult continued as he studied energy work, telepathy, channeling, and shamanism. While he was open-minded about the occult, he maintained a state of constant scientific vigil less he believe something without evidence.

He admits to having difficulty with social relationships, and spent years in therapy trying to improve his 'karma.' As a youth, he felt awkward around people due to his height (6'9), and later as an adult, because of his high intellect. He was married five times, had one daughter, and was expecting another child when he died of throat cancer on the day of the 2008 presidential election.

Nativity

There were two north nodal solar eclipses before Crichton's birth. The first was on August 11, 1942, at 18°45' Leo and fell in his 1st house. The second was on September 10, 1942, at 17°17' Virgo and fell on the cusp of his 3rd house. Both houses expanded during his lifetime. Quite literally, his physical body grew, giving him an abnormally tall height, and his mind grew, giving him high intellect. As a successful author, he became larger than life. The North Node is in the sign of the 2nd eclipse, but not in the house of either eclipse.

The Scorpio Sun is in mutual reception with a rising Pluto, giving an interest in the occult and an investigative ability (Chart 59). The Sun rules the Ascendant and is square to it, an indication of difficulty in self-expression, compounded by the secretiveness inherent in Pluto and Scorpio. The Sun is sextile/trine the nodes, acquiring added punch and emphasis. Despite the Scorpio influence, his fate was to be a star. He was born within an hour of a Full Moon and the opposition between the luminaries denotes difficulty in simultaneously fulfilling the will of the ego and the emotional needs of the Moon.

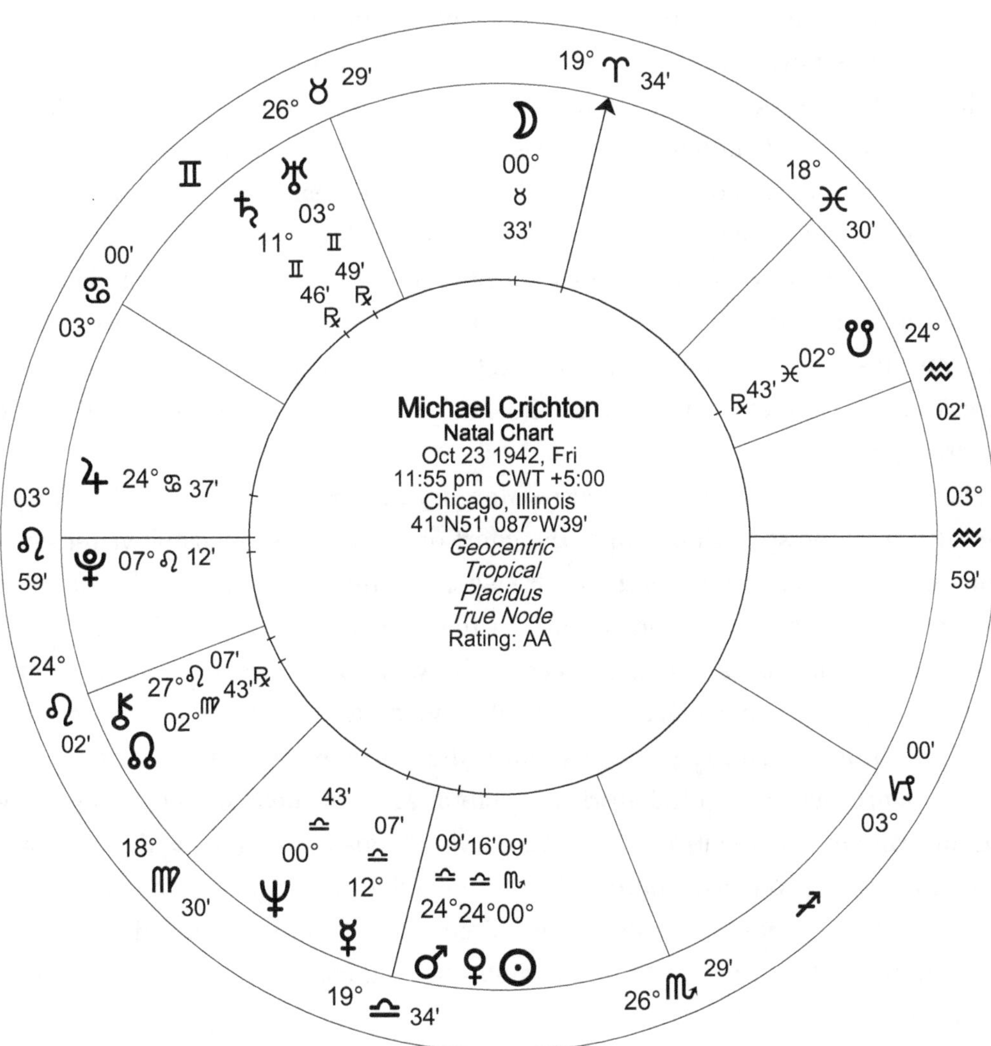

Chart 59:

Michael Crichton Nativity

The Moon is elevated in the chart and visible in the 10th house. Exalted in Taurus, the Moon seeks physical comfort and wishes to avoid unpleasantness. The Moon is sextile/trine the nodes, which adds to her power and therefore her influence: his emotions were strong but difficult to express (Moon square the Ascendant and opposite the Sun). Fortunately, in declination, the Moon is tightly parallel the Midheaven, giving it an outlet in the profession. He expressed his feelings and emotions vicariously though characters who acted out his own plutonic struggles on the page and on the screen. The first house Pluto came to life as inner beasts projected outwardly as dinosaurs, and diseases that threatened to destroy the world. The Moon rules the 12th house, which describes his work in the hospital, and as a writer of imaginative fiction and screenplays.

The North Node is in Virgo ruled by Mercury in Libra in the 3rd. While Gauquelin found the Moon was instrumental in the chart of writers, a successful writer needs a strong Mercury. Mercury rules the 3rd house of writing and is placed in the 3rd, emphasizing writing and communication. As the North Node ruler, Mercury can get things done and is wise and experienced in the ways of the world. A strong Mercury brings words, logic, and clarity of thought, necessary for high quality writing. A published author since his youth, Crichton did not need a steep learning curve in order to figure out how to tell stories. In Libra, Mercury has an ability to juxtapose ideas in brilliant combination. With Mercury's dispositor conjunct Mars, he was a rapid writer with productive output. Mercury is trine Saturn in Gemini, and in order to write so well so fast, he must have edited as he wrote. In latitude, Mercury is contraparallel Saturn, further strengthening the contact and adding the moral overtones evident in his work.

Neptune rules the South Node, and he used his imagination in service to edify the masses. With Neptune in the 3rd trine Uranus, the public learned about science and hospitals through his books, films, and TV shows. He personalized medicine, opening the eyes of the public to the quackery of medical science and the humans (not gods) who practice it. The South Node energy, representing inspiration, filled his books with ideas, characters, and storylines. However, there is always loss associated with South Node energy, and in his case the harm was compounded by a quincunx between the ruler and the node. Crichton was a hypochondriac (irrationality of Neptune), and he thought himself stricken with every disease that he studied—unhelpful for a physician.

Uranus is at the South Bending of the nodes, a placement that inspires on the inner plane and needs to be used in service on the outer plane. Uranus in Gemini gives an ability to communicate scientific ideas, and the trine to Neptune adds imagination, which was expressed in fiction. He wrote in his autobiography that he knew he would not be a good medical doctor because when patients mentioned their symptoms, he wondered how he could use the disease in a novel.

Crichton has a Libra conjunction of Venus and Mars, which are also parallel, forming an occultation that doubles the power of the aspect. Aside from the Sun–Pluto mutual reception, Venus is the dispositor of the remaining planets. However, in the conjunction, Mars at the lower position in longitude dominates Venus at the higher position, and 'wins the war' (according to Vedic theory). Mars in detriment in Libra explains his difficulty in relationships (too much me), and his effort to stick it out in medical school (force of will over-riding personal happiness). Nonetheless, Mars benefits from its conjunction with a dignified Venus. Ruling the 10th, Mars is concerned with professional achievement, and his work ultimately brought fame and wealth in a Venus-ruled career in the arts.

Mars and Venus are square Jupiter, another indication of tension between art and medicine. Jupiter in the 12th is a signature of a physician. In declination, Jupiter, Saturn, and Uranus are parallel, showing talent for conventional medicine. In the end, the pull of Venus was stronger, and medicine was practiced in art rather than on patients. Writing enabled him to work at home, which the Sun, Venus, and Mars in the 4th preferred. However, he traveled whenever he had writer's block (Venus–Mars square Jupiter). In latitude, Jupiter and Uranus are contraparallel near the 0° line of the ecliptic and parallel the Sun, angles, and nodes, an indication that one way or another, science would manifest in his life.

An Award Winning Novelist

In the summer before the start of his fourth year of medical school when he was twenty-five, Crichton published his novel *A Case Of Need* under the pseudonym Jeffery Hudson. The date of the copyright was August 5, 1968 (Chart 60). The solar eclipse before the book's debut was on March 28, 1968 at 8°19' Aries, which fell in his 9th house of publication. The eclipse was a north node eclipse (gain) and the lord was Mars (ruler 10).

When the book first came out, transiting Saturn was in the 10th house square natal Jupiter, as transiting Jupiter was square progressed Saturn, forming a double-whammy associated with a crisis in his career: he had published a promising book, but he must return to medical school. The transiting North Node was conjunct the progressed Moon and trine transiting Mercury, timing the publication of the book. The transiting South Node was conjunct natal Mercury, implying loss, which in this case was the writing that was not done while he was working at the hospital. With transiting Neptune conjunct the progressed Sun and Venus, and trine both natal and progressed Jupiter, it was a happy, euphoric time. The following year, while transiting Neptune crossed the conjunction, he finished medical school and the novel won the 1969 Edgar Allen Poe Mystery Award, a prestigious prize bestowed by the Mystery Writers' of America. Despite this success, Crichton moved to California and started a post-doctoral fellowship.

A Dinosaur Romp

Twenty-five years and many books later, the film *Jurassic Park* based on Crichton's book was released to great fanfare and triumph and launched him onto the world stage. He was fifty years old. The month before the movie's release there was a solar eclipse at 0°31' Gemini that fell in his 11th house of goals, conjunct progressed Uranus (science). The lord of the eclipse was Mercury.

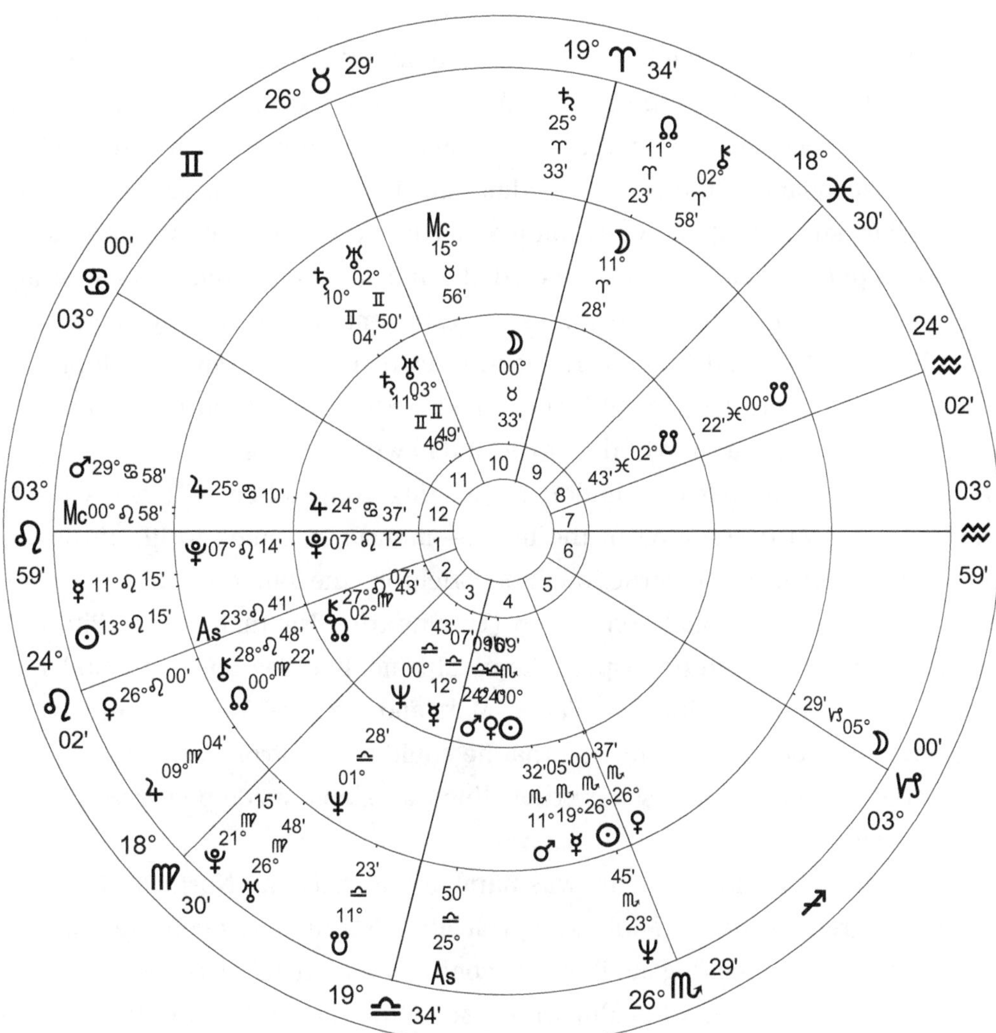

Chart 60:

Crichton's Award Winning Novel, Aug. 5, 1968, Boston, MA, noon

On the day of the movie's release (Chart 61), there was a double-whammy with transiting Saturn conjunct the natal South Node, and the transiting South Node conjunct natal Saturn (and the progressed Midheaven), which expressed as creative work given in service. The transiting nodes were square the progressed horizon, with the progressed Ascendant at the South Bending and the progressed Descendant at the North Bending, suggesting that Crichton may have felt invisible and in the shadow of his friend Stephen Spielberg who directed the movie. Progressed Mars was at the North Bending of the progressed nodes, a testament to professional achievement (Mars ruling the 10th) and hard work bearing evident fruit. Transiting Jupiter was conjunct natal Neptune, trine natal Uranus, and sextile progressed Pluto and the Ascendant, indicating the success of the movie and newfound fame.

Jurassic Park was released under a transiting conjunction of Uranus–Neptune sextile Pluto; an apt description of the movie—monsters coming to life through science, bringing chaos and destruction. For Crichton, the outer transiting planetary combination repeats the natal connection (Uranus trine Neptune sextile Pluto). The transiting configuration did not aspect the natal trine, but was opposite natal Jupiter and formed a grand cross with natal Venus–Mars and the natal Midheaven/IC, suggesting a creative collaborative production that he could not control. With transiting Mars (sextile natal Venus and Mars) square transiting Pluto, an outside power was hampering his creativity.

In declination, transiting Uranus was parallel the transiting North Node and contraparallel progressed Jupiter–Midheaven; transiting Neptune was contraparallel natal Jupiter–Uranus; and transiting Jupiter was contraparallel natal Neptune; corresponding to the outer expression of a film with a scientific theme. In latitude, progressed Mars was at the 0° line of the ecliptic parallel natal Jupiter, contraparallel natal Uranus, and parallel the Sun, angles, and nodes, describing public acknowledgment for a scientific tale.

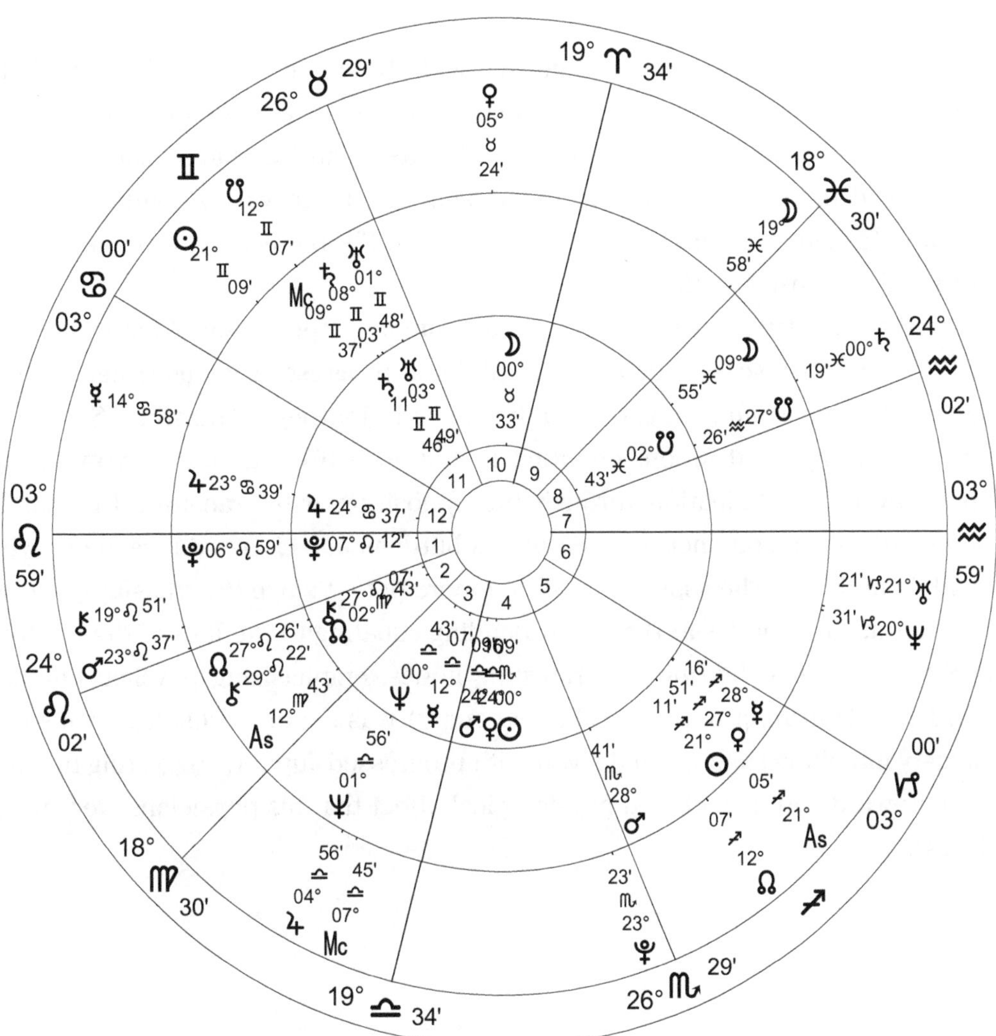

Chart 61:

Crichton's *Jurassic Park*, June 11, 1993, Hollywood, CA 8:00 p.m. PDT

Death

A long-time smoker, Crichton was diagnosed with throat cancer in early 2008. He had been undergoing chemotherapy and was expected to recover, when he died suddenly at age sixty-six. His baby was born three months later. The fact that he had cancer was not announced until after his death. In the summer, there was a south nodal solar eclipse at 9°32' Leo in the first house conjunct natal Pluto (secrecy, birth, and death). The lord of the eclipse was the Sun.

He died on the day (Chart 62) of the exact mundane opposition of Saturn and Uranus at 18°57' Virgo–Pisces, which was sextile/trine progressed Venus (ruler of the 4th house and the grave) and transiting Jupiter (a long journey). Transiting Saturn was conjunct the progressed Moon, denoting limitation, suffering, and sorrow brought unexpectedly to a culmination through the opposition with transiting Uranus. The transiting Sun was inconjunct natal Saturn (a burdensome circumstance about which he could do nothing). The aspect was all the more potent since the transiting Sun was square the transiting nodes at the South Bending equating to the loss of the life force, while Saturn was sextile/trine the transiting nodes, emphasizing physical limitation and hardship. Transiting Neptune (chemotherapy) was sextile transiting Venus (pain and anxiety inhibitors) and formed a yod with progressed Jupiter, suggesting the drugs had an untoward and unexpected physiological effect that his physicians were unable to address.

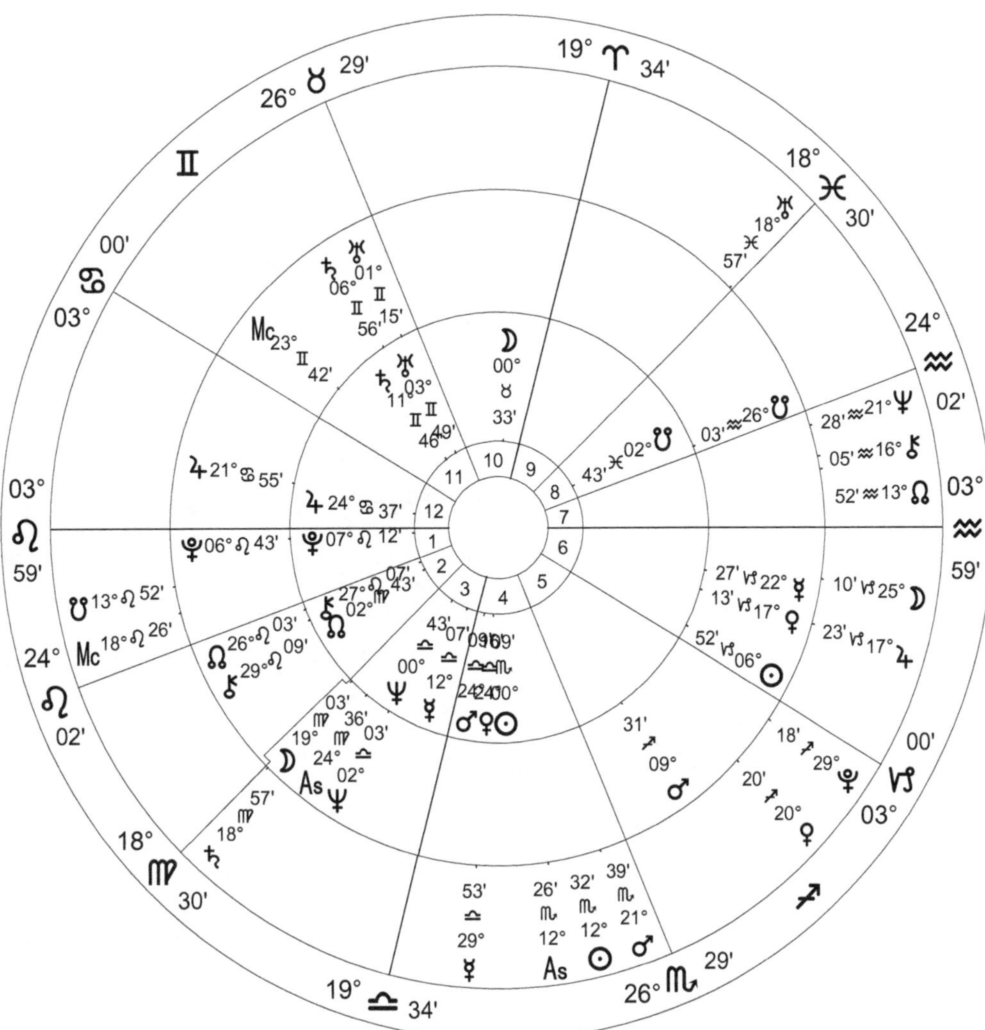

Chart 62:

Crichton's Death, Nov. 4, 2008, Hollywood, CA 6.20 a.m. PST

But when worlds collide ... I'm going to give you some terrible thrills ...
—from 'Science Fiction,' Rocky Horror Picture Show

Chapter 17
Master of Horror
Stephen King

Stephen King is another successful writer who is no stranger to the dark side. Raised by a poor, single mother, he was two when his father went out for a pack of cigarettes and never returned. At five, King went out to play with a friend who was hit by a train. King went home and never said a word and has been accused of writing about the incident ever since. From the time he was a child, he knew he wanted to be a writer. He held fast to that vision and despite numerous setbacks, he never gave up on his dream.

He studied creative writing and film at university and after graduation became a grade three teacher. He had a child and got married. He was living in a trailer with the phone disconnected for non-payment, when a manuscript his wife saved from the trash was accepted for publication. He soon quit teaching to write full-time.

He began drinking heavily and taking cocaine. His usage escalated along with his rising fame. Sober three hours a day, he wrote during black-outs. His wife would find him passed out in the morning with his face covered in vomit and blood. A decade passed and after a family intervention, he quit drinking on his 40th birthday. His worst fear was realized—he could not write sober. Writing had been his tool to keep fear at bay for he believed that anything he wrote down could not come true. Gradually, he was able to write again, but not at his previous prodigious rate.

In July 1999, King was taking an afternoon walk when he was hit by a car. After numerous surgeries, he recovered and resumed writing. In 2002, he tried to retire but he could not stop writing. He is still at it, with sixty-three books in print at this time. Along with his wife, he is a philanthropist and donates his name, money, and time to numerous charities.

Nativity

Similar to Michael Crichton who was five years older, King has a Libra stellium, Pluto rising, a Gemini Uranus, and a debilitated Mars that rules the 10th. Their Ascendant degree differs by four, although different signs rise. Eight of twelve houses have the same cusp sign. While King was no scientist, he wrote about a killer virus that nearly decimated the population of the world. His books articulate nightmares and the personification of evil.

Every planet in King's chart is moving direct (Chart 63), as are the nodes. He has a preponderance of sextiles and trines, including a grand trine formed between the Moon, Pluto, and Midheaven. The one major hard aspect is a square between the Sun and Uranus. The PNSE was on May 20, 1947 at 28°41' Taurus, which fell in his 11th house along with the North Node, and promised expansion related to goals, groups, and friends.

He has a 3rd house Virgo Sun, giving an orderly critical mind, and in an interest in writing and communication. The Sun is sextile Jupiter (publications), sextile Mars (energy), sextile/trine the nodal axis (solar accentuation and emphasis), sextile the Ascendant (outlet for the ego), and square Uranus (genius). The Sun's aspects appear in his writing: unusual stories about seemingly innocuous, non-threatening strangers (human and otherwise) coming to town (Mars in Cancer) who are actually from hell and wreak utter evil (Jupiter in Scorpio) and upset (Uranus). The Sun's square to Uranus indicates that the order he tries to create for himself is easily shaken.

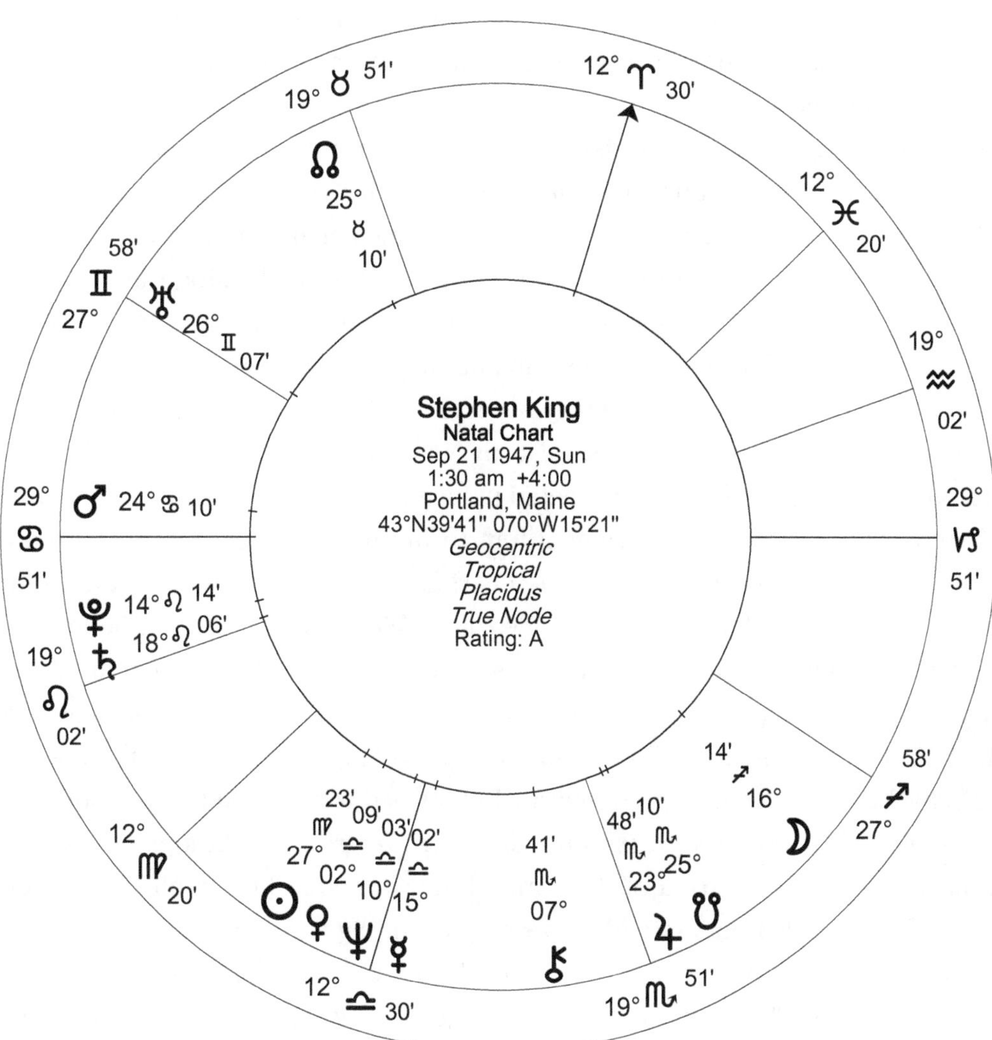

Chart 63:
Stephen King Nativity

Unexpected disruptions hamper his writing. The Sun rules the 2nd house of money and he made an exorbitant amount. However, with Saturn in detriment on the cusp of the 2nd, he also knew poverty.

The last degree of Cancer is rising, with the Moon ruling the chart in Sagittarius, suggesting he needs something to believe in. With the Moon's dispositor in Scorpio, what he believes in is hell. The Moon is out-of-bounds giving vulnerability and excessive emotionality, which were expressed in his creative work (Moon in the 5th). The Moon is sextile Mercury (signature for a writer), sextile Neptune (imagination and creativity), and trine Saturn–Pluto (determination, perseverance).

Both the Sun and Moon are heavily aspected and together contact every planet in the chart, except for one—Venus the North Node ruler—and final dispositor of the chart. She is dignified in Libra, unaspected in longitude, parallel the Sun in declination, and strong at the Aries Point, bringing him to the notice of the world. As the final dispositor, ultimately every planet in the chart answers to her, and benefits from her strength (in dignity and as the North Node ruler). With Venus in the 3rd, he loves writing and understands the art of fiction. He is a clear thinker with a logical mind and an ability to weave compelling, yet terrifying stories. When asked why he wrote, King replied, "The answer is fairly simple—there was nothing else I was made to do." (Unlike Michael Crichton who wanted to write but instead went to medical school).

The ruler of the South Node is Pluto, implying loss from the dark planet. Most children have fears and are afraid of the dark, of monsters that lurk in closets and under the bed, but they also understand, especially in the light of day, that their fears are baseless. There was no light of day for King. To him, the monsters are real, threatening, and terrifying (Pluto conjunct Saturn). He said he was afraid of others, afraid for others, afraid of the dark, of insects, rats, snakes, enclosed spaces and death. However, he learned early on that he could deal with his fears by writing about them and purged himself through creative projects (Pluto ruling the 5th).

Jupiter is conjunct the South Node, indicating a loss or sacrifice of Jupiter. In his early books and up until the time he quit drinking, there was no positive thinking, no enlightened beliefs that would bring a sense of well-being and safety. His only salvation was the daily work of writing (Jupiter ruling the 6th). However, Jupiter, through its contact with the South Node, was in a position to be inspired, to receive otherworld assistance, to regenerate and transform (in Scorpio), and learn new beliefs that would be supportive rather than terrifying.

Uranus in Gemini rules the 8th house and is on the cusp of the 12th, mixing the mental anguish of hell (8th) with the unreasonableness of the unconscious (12th). Answering to Mercury through dispositorship, this irrationality streams into his rational mind and keeps him constantly unsettled and on edge. Writing was his only strategy to deal with his fears, which is why he has not been able to stop.

Carrie

King's first novel, *Carrie*, was published in 1974 when he was twenty-seven. He was given an advance of $2,500 for the manuscript, He never liked the book: "My considered opinion was that I had written the world's all-time loser." Soon after when he sold the paperback rights, he received an advance of $400,000.

The solar eclipse before the publication was on December 24, 1973, at 2°40' Capricorn with Saturn serving as the lord. The north nodal eclipse fell in his 6th house of work square natal Venus. During the weeks leading up to the release, he worked all day teaching, then spent his evenings tweaking a novel he didn't like in preparation for publication.

On the day of the novel's release (Chart 64), transiting Mercury was at the North Bending of the transiting nodes (manifestation of a book) and formed a grand trine with natal Jupiter–South Node (his unhappiness with the story), and natal Mars (ruling the 10th), signaling a coming-out for him professionally. Transiting Neptune was conjunct the progressed Moon, a sign the book would be well received by the public, despite his doubts (the pair square transiting Jupiter). Transiting Mars was conjunct the transiting South Node, square transiting Mercury, and quincunx natal Jupiter, reiterating his misgivings regarding the book's worth, and suggesting personal powerlessness in regards to his publisher.

Transiting Uranus was conjunct the progressed Sun, alluding to a time of immense change, perhaps unwelcome (square natal Mars), and precipitating new fears (Uranus ruling the 8th). There was a progressed Saturn–Ascendant conjunction sextile transiting Mars–South Node pointing to a time of increased responsibility and hard work.

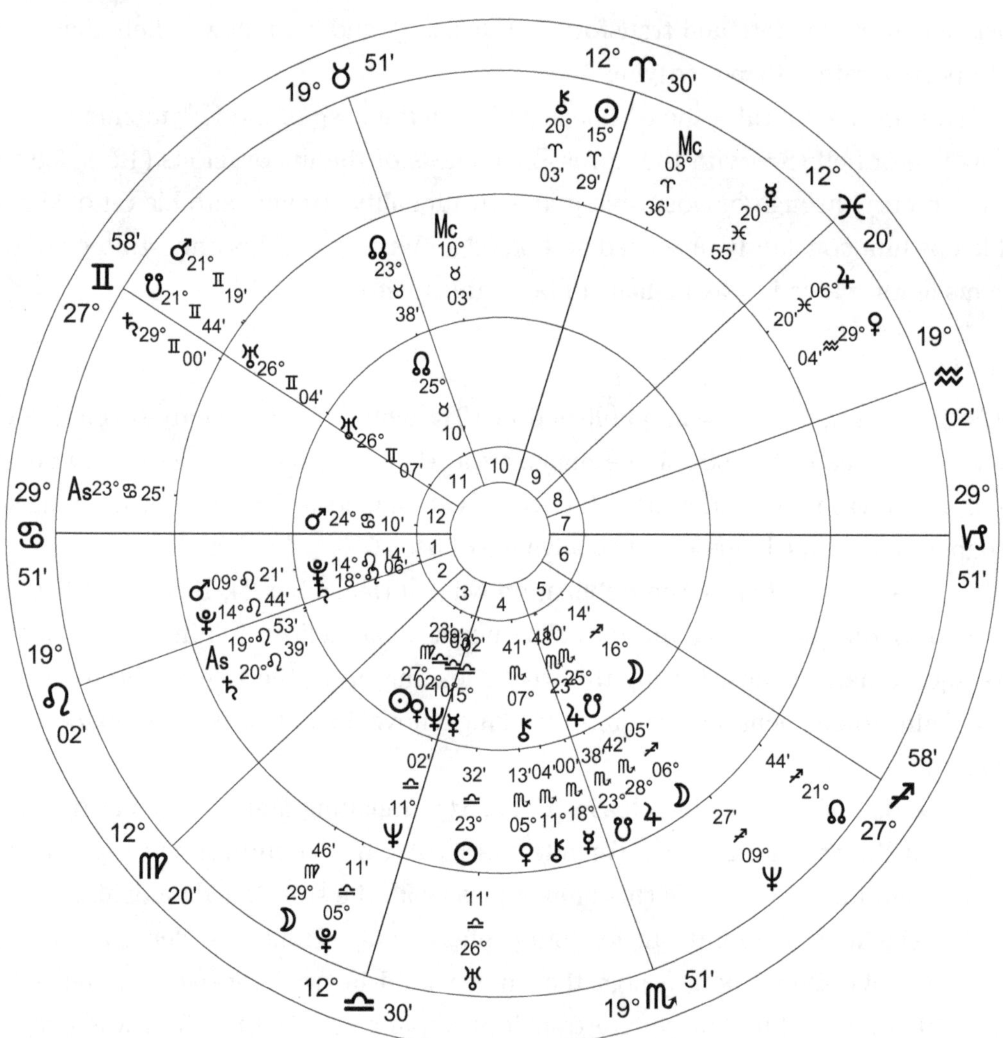

Chart 64:

King's *Carrie*, April 5, 74, Portland, MA, noon

Despite his dislike of the book, it would have been a happy time (transiting Jupiter trine progressed Venus) with talk of a movie and the wide distribution of a paperback (transiting Neptune trine progressed Mars). In any event, the book came out to reviews that were better than those King gave himself. It was an instant hit.

In declination, the transiting South Node was parallel transiting Saturn and contraparallel progressed Uranus–Pluto, describing the book—a shockingly dark tale of cruelty and revenge. By progression, Mars was parallel the North Node (wide) and contraparallel Jupiter, denoting a manifest published work.

Quitting Drinking

Thirteen years later, on the evening of his fortieth birthday, King took his last drink. He quit drinking (Chart 65) on the day of a south nodal (loss) solar eclipse at 29°34' Virgo, with Mercury serving as the lord. The eclipse fell in his 3rd house conjunct his natal Sun and square natal Uranus, which foretold a crisis in consciousness necessitating drastic change.

The progressed Moon was conjunct the progressed North Node and square progressed Saturn at the North Bending, and his wife (Moon and ruler 7) took outward action to stage an intervention that forced him to confront his addiction. Progressed Venus was conjunct the progressed South Node, while transiting Venus was (widely) conjunct the transiting South Node and natal Venus, producing a triple-whammy: profound loss of happiness. With progressed Venus–South Node conjunct natal Jupiter, he had reached the bottom of the bottle. However, transiting Neptune the planet of spirituality, was at the South Bending of the transiting nodes in a placement of maximum otherworld receptivity. The aspect was personalized through the conjunction between the transiting South Node and natal Venus (square transiting Neptune); down and out and faced with the impending loss of his family (Venus ruling the 4th) he was forced to address his addiction. Transiting Neptune was also sextile the progressed Sun and transiting Pluto, allowing for a spiritual transformation of the ego.

Progressed Jupiter had recently moved out of Scorpio into its own sign of Sagittarius, opening up the possibility of new beliefs and philosophies. In essence, Jupiter got a ticket out of hell. Progressed Jupiter was sextile/trine the transiting nodes boosting its power (new beliefs), and with a sextile to natal Venus, a road to happiness was opening up. Transiting Saturn was conjunct the natal Moon, marking a time of heightened self-discipline. Transiting Uranus was opposite natal Uranus and trine progressed Saturn, bringing a practical awakening. He was able to forge new routines and free himself from old ruts and entrenched habits. However, with progressed Mercury square natal and progressed Saturn, he could not write.

Car Accident

King was seriously injured after being hit by a car on June 19, 1999 (Chart 66). The south nodal solar eclipse before the accident was on February 16, 1999, at 27°08' Aquarius with Uranus (accidents) serving as the lord. The eclipse fell in his 8th house of death, and was at the South Bending of the natal nodes, forming a yod with his natal Sun and Ascendant, and alluding to a crisis not under his control (yod) that affected his physical body and his life. During the life-flight ride in the helicopter on the way to the hospital, King realized he was "lying in death's doorway. Someone is going to pull me one way or the other pretty soon; it's mostly out of my hands."

At the time of the accident, the two malefics (Mars and Saturn) were conjunct by progression and square the progressed nodes at the North Bending, indicating manifest injuries to the physical structures of the body, along with surgery to reset bones.

An encounter with death was shown through a t-square with transiting Venus conjunct transiting North Node and natal Pluto, square transiting Saturn at the South Bending, and opposite transiting Uranus–South Node. A major, sudden, upsetting accident impacting the physical body was symbolized by transiting Mars square natal Mars, opposite transiting Jupiter, square the Ascendant, and trine natal Uranus. Transiting Pluto was square the progressed Ascendant and conjunct progressed Venus, and (widely) conjunct progressed Jupiter and the IC, bringing the deathly encounter. However, the two benefics at an angle brought protection. The medic who treated him at the scene told him, "perhaps someone is watching out for you … You're a lucky camper to still be with the program."

An indication of spiritual assistance was shown by transiting Neptune sextile/trine progressed Jupiter, Venus, and the IC; and progressed Neptune sextile transiting Venus–North Node. The progressed Moon was conjunct progressed Mercury and sextile

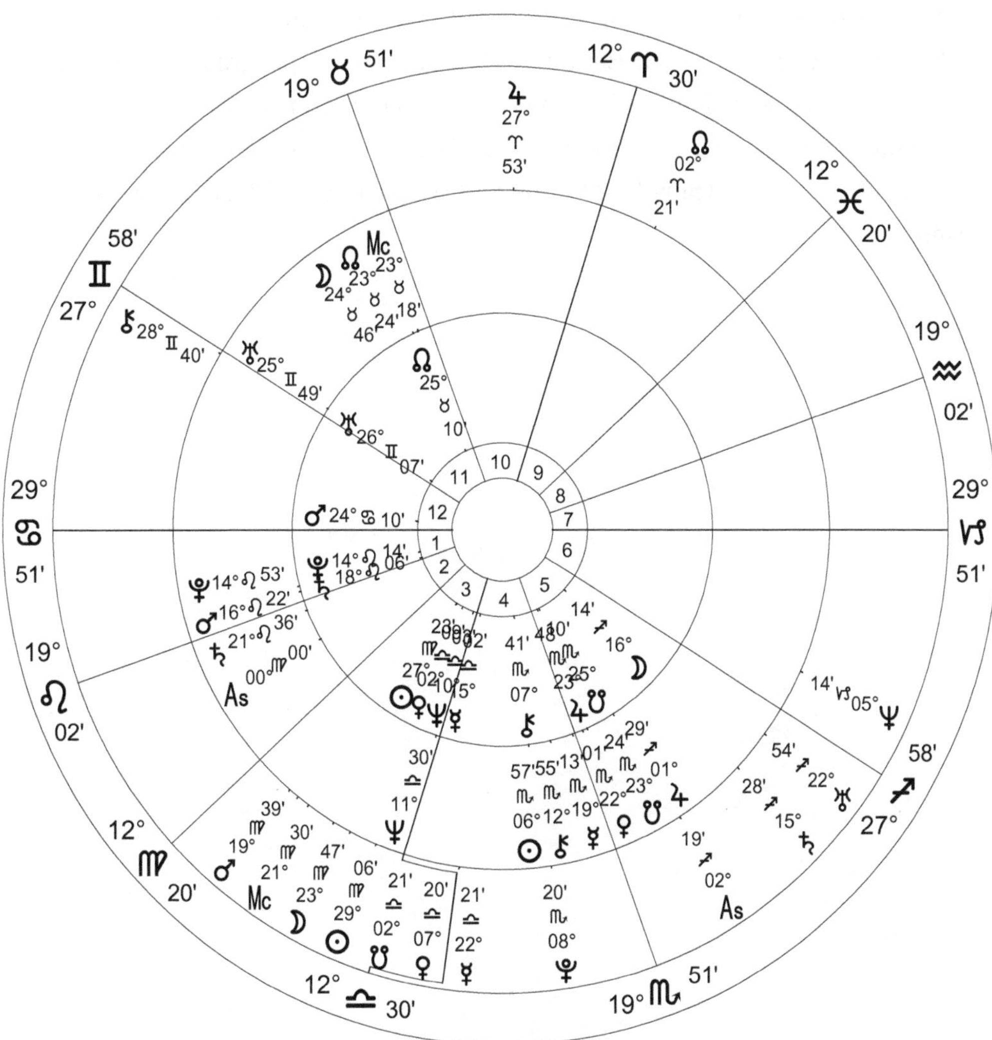

Chart 65:

King Quits Drinking, Sept. 22, 1987, Bangor, MA, noon

the progressed Ascendant, denoting further aid. At the moment of impact, the transiting Midheaven was at the North Bending of the natal and progressed nodes and had just crossed the progressed Mars–Saturn conjunction, triggering the event.

In declination, transiting Neptune was parallel the progressed South Node (spiritual aid), and contraparallel transiting Venus and the progressed North Node (outwardly expressed beneficence).

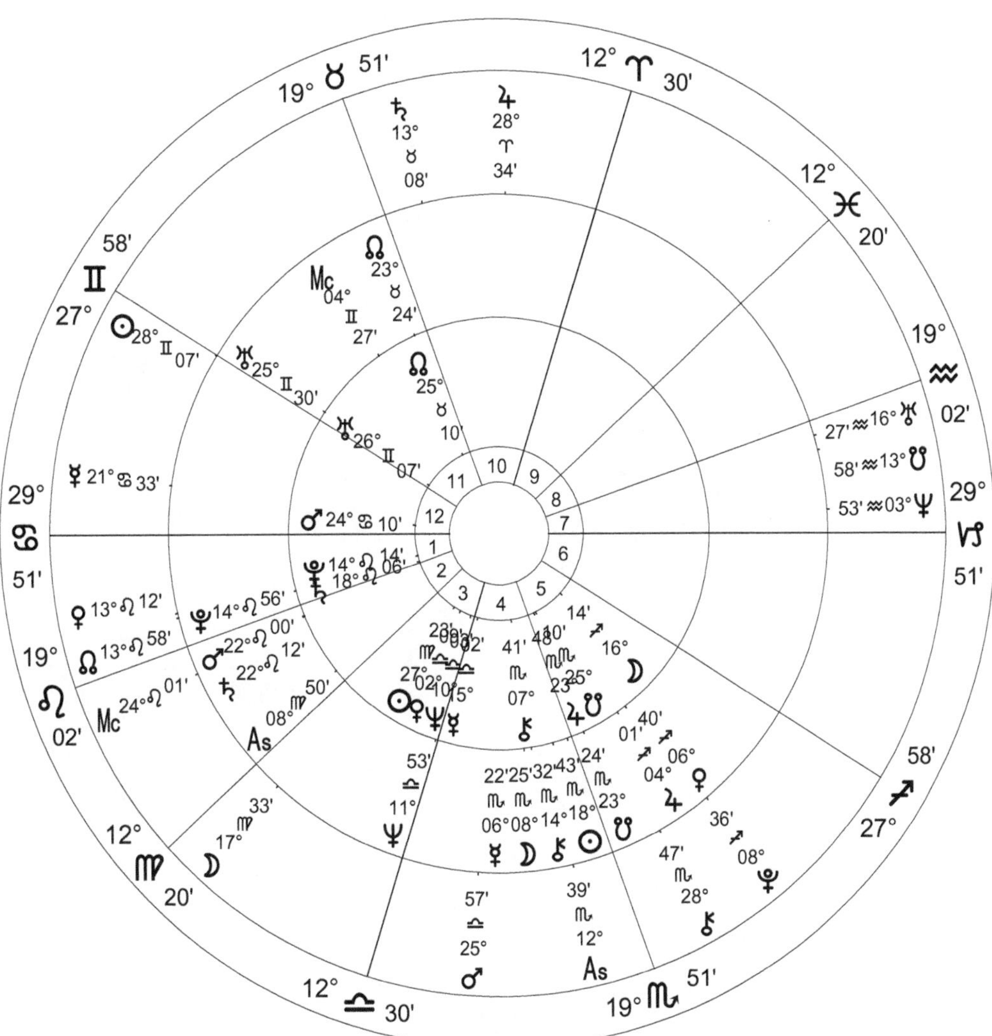

Chart 66:

King's Car Accident, June 19, 1999, Bangor, MA, 4:30 p.m. EDT

There's a bit of magic in everything, and some loss to even things out.

— Lou Reed

Chapter 18
A Super Hero
Christopher Reeve

Christopher Reeve was an actor, director, producer, screenwriter, and author who was best known for his role as Superman until a riding accident left him paralyzed. Although his parents divorced when he was young, he grew up in a well-to-do family. Academically and athletically, he excelled at school. He started acting when he was nine and knew he had found his calling. He studied piano, played tennis, skied, sailed, and rode horses. He attended Cornell University and the Julliard School of Performing Arts, where two thousand students had auditioned for the twenty available seats in the freshman class. Only two were accepted into the advanced acting program—he and Robin Williams. In 1978, the first Superman movie came out and Reeve achieved worldwide recognition.

He had two children but did not marry their mother. The relationship ended in 1987 after Superman IV was released. Five months later he met his future wife. They married five years later and had one son.

In 1995, during a riding competition where his horse froze, Reeve was thrown and severely fractured the C1 and C2 vertebrae of his neck, effectively dislocating his head from his body. Because he had been wearing a helmet, his brain was undamaged, but he was left a quadriplegic, unable to use any limb or breathe on his own.

He began intensive rehabilitation. In July 2003, he traveled to Israel for stem cell therapy. Awed by their success in treating spinal cord injuries, he returned to the U.S. and became an outspoken activist for stem cell research, which the second President Bush had banned. Although embryos created by *in vitro* fertilization were already routinely discarded, these could not be used for stem cell research using federal funds. Nine years after the accident, Reeve died at fifty-two after a bad reaction to antibiotics.

Nativity

There were two acts in the life of Christopher Reeve (Chart 67). In the first, he was Superman—a successful actor and competitive athlete. In the second, he was the antithesis—paralyzed, confined to a wheelchair, and fighting for innovative scientific research that could help him and others like him.

The PNSE was at 27°31' Leo and fell in his first house (along with the South Node), and what expanded during his life was the outward projection of the physical self, first in acting, and later as a functioning quadriplegic fighting for a cause. He was six-foot-four and there was no loss of height (vertical expansion of the physical body).

The lunar nodes lie across the Ascendant–Descendant axis, with the South Node conjunct the Ascendant and Pluto, and square Jupiter in the 10th at the North Bending. Neptune is in the degree of the nodes and sextile/trine them, Uranus is quincunx the North Node, and Mars is quincunx the South Node, giving a complicated and busy nodal influence. He has a Libra stellium and Venus is the final dispositor of the chart. In Libra, a dignified Venus brought high intelligence, grace, and honorable women. He showed the world how to live with dignity under trying circumstances.

With the South Node conjunct the Ascendant, there was weakness associated with the physical body. Growing up, he suffered from allergies and asthma, and later had alopecia where clumps of hair on his head fell out, leading him to shave it bald. With the South Node conjunct the Ascendant, service likely came naturally. For a time he was an

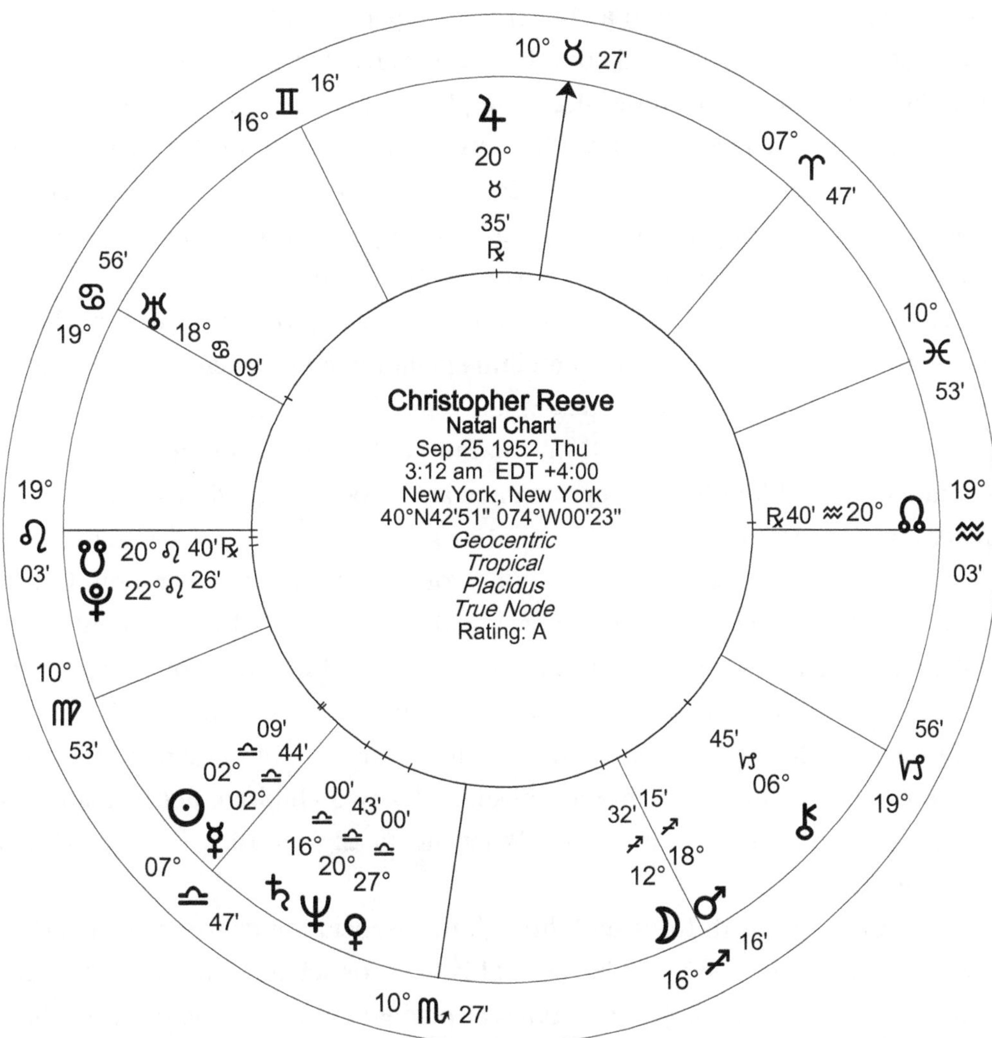

Chart 67:

Christopher Reeve Nativity

entertainer who lifted people into a greater archetypal realm for the length of a movie. After he lost the use of his physical body, he became an activist for stem cell research.

The Sun rules the South Node, suggesting loss for the Sun. He lost his father at a young age through divorce, and later lost his stellar acting career when he lost his physical vitality. Although the Sun in Libra is in fall, he had a strong personality, attributable to a strong dispositor. For his role as Superman, he brought a vulnerable sensibility (Libra effect) that was palpable on the big screen.

The Sun is conjunct Mercury, indicating a south nodal effect on Mercury, the planet related to communication and the cerebral-spinal nervous system. He used Mercury in service when acting, giving characters his voice. Later, when he lost his voice, he served as an advocate for others. Both the Sun and Mercury are at the Libra' Aries Point that connected him to a wider audience and brought him global attention, both as an actor and an activist.

Pluto conjunct the Ascendant is an indicator of profound regeneration. Conjunct the South Node, there was a loss of potency and power of the physical being, but also enlightened and empowering transformation. As he said in his autobiography, "I believe that it's what you do after a disaster that can give it meaning." With Pluto connected to the South Node and ruling the 4th, there was loss in the family. His parents divorced. He did not marry the mother of his older two children, and she took them with her when the relationship ended. When he finally married, he was paralyzed within three years.

Uranus rules the North Node and through the association gains wisdom and practicality. An accident also defined him, as did his fight for scientific research. Before the accident, Reeve was a pilot (Uranus rules airplanes), and for a brief period he had been a Scientologist (unusual beliefs). Uranus is inconjunct the North Node (adding frustration) and in a double yod with Mars (a sudden accident that ended his mobility about which he could do nothing), and Jupiter (he needed science to help him that was not forthcoming).

Uranus is square a Saturn–Neptune conjunction in the 3rd house. The combination of Saturn and Neptune is related to suffering, sacrifice, and structural decomposition. The square symbolizes the accident that ended a glamorous and successful acting career and left him paralyzed. He was also left depressed and suicidal.

Jupiter is at the North Bending of the nodes, elevated in the 10th house, ruling the 5th, and in a position that promotes the output and expression of all things Jupiter, such as early success and achievement in sports and higher education. Jupiter is square Pluto, which was related to the loss of his stellar career and his activism regarding stem cell research.

He had a Sagittarius Moon, known for its optimism, love of travel, higher education, and sports. He graduated from an Ivy League university and an elite acting school, and he lived overseas. When everything he loved to do became impossible he broadened his horizons and became an advocate for compassionate scientific research.

In declination, the Moon and Mars are way out-of-bounds, pointing to extreme emotional reactions and the impact he had on the public, as well as his determination to fight where others had failed. Uranus and Pluto are parallel, reflecting a transformational accident and a fight for reform.

Love

Reeve met his wife, Dana Morosini, during her performance in a cabaret on June 30, 1987 (Chart 68). There was a north nodal Solar Eclipse on March 29, 1987, at 8°17' Aries with Mars (will, desire) serving as the lord. The eclipse was conjunct his 9th house cusp, representing the second partner.

On the night they met, the transiting South Node was conjunct natal Sun–Mercury in Libra, indicating a loss of self (giving oneself up for another). Transiting Jupiter was opposite natal Venus and in a grand trine with progressed Pluto and transiting Uranus, describing a potent, unexpected sexual attraction. Transiting Saturn was conjunct natal Mars (lord) on the 5th house cusp, pointing to serious appeal. Transiting Mars (lord) was trine the progressed Moon and quincunx transiting Uranus, signifying a heart-felt response, but also likely a fear of commitment and loss of freedom (given his history, he was in no hurry to marry). The transiting Sun was at the North Bending of the transiting nodes opposite progressed Mars (lord) and transiting Neptune at the South Bending; suggesting an outer thrust of the ego, sexual tension, and a spiritual experience.

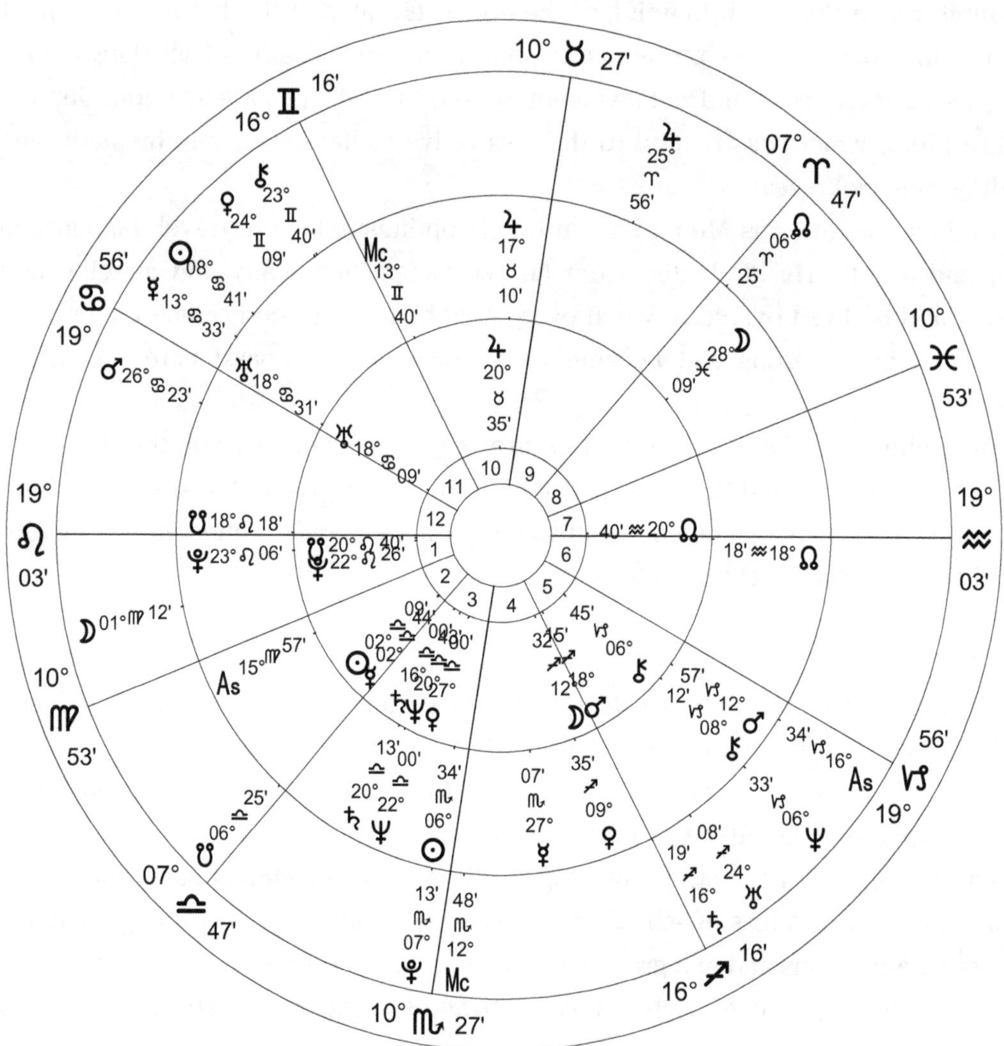

Chart 68:

Reeve Meets Dana, June 30, 1987, Williamstown, MA, 9:00 p.m. EDT

The Accident

Reeve fell from his horse on May 27, 1995 (Chart 69). A month earlier on April 29, there was a south nodal solar eclipse at 8°52' Taurus. Conjunct the 10th house cusp, the eclipse marked the end of his career. The lord of the eclipse was Venus, the final dispositor of the natal chart.

At the time of the accident, progressed Jupiter (horse) was at the North Bending of the progressed nodes (physical manifestation of the large animal), conjunct transiting Venus (lord), and opposite the progressed Sun (loss of vitality).

There were a staggering number of yods that emphasized the helplessness related to a sudden, devastating public accident involving a horse. Transiting Neptune was sextile transiting Saturn and quincunx natal Pluto–South Node–Ascendant; transiting Saturn was quincunx progressed Saturn–Neptune and quincunx natal Pluto–South Node–Ascendant (a near duplication of the previous configuration); transiting Jupiter was conjunct the natal Moon, quincunx progressed Moon–Uranus, and quincunx transiting Venus–Midheaven–progressed Jupiter; progressed Venus was conjunct natal Mars and quincunx natal Uranus, and quincunx natal Jupiter, activating the natal yod, which held the natal promise of an accident with a horse. Thus, there were four main yods, comprised of a multitude of planets and angles, which, when considered singly, totaled twenty yods.

In declination, progressed Jupiter was parallel the progressed South Node (the progressed pair are square by longitude) and contraparallel the progressed Sun, signaling personal loss from a horse. Destructive circumstances resulting in physical dissolution was shown by transiting Pluto parallel progressed Saturn and natal Neptune.

For nine years, Reeve lived with near complete debility. Nonetheless, through physical therapy and stem cell replacement, he reached a point where he was able to move a finger. This was the first time a patient with a C1–2 injury had managed to muster willful motor movement. During these years he started a foundation dedicated to spinal cord research. He tirelessly raised money for improved treatment and lobbied Congress to allow stem cell research. Twice Congress voted to repeal the bill, but Bush vetoed each successful vote.

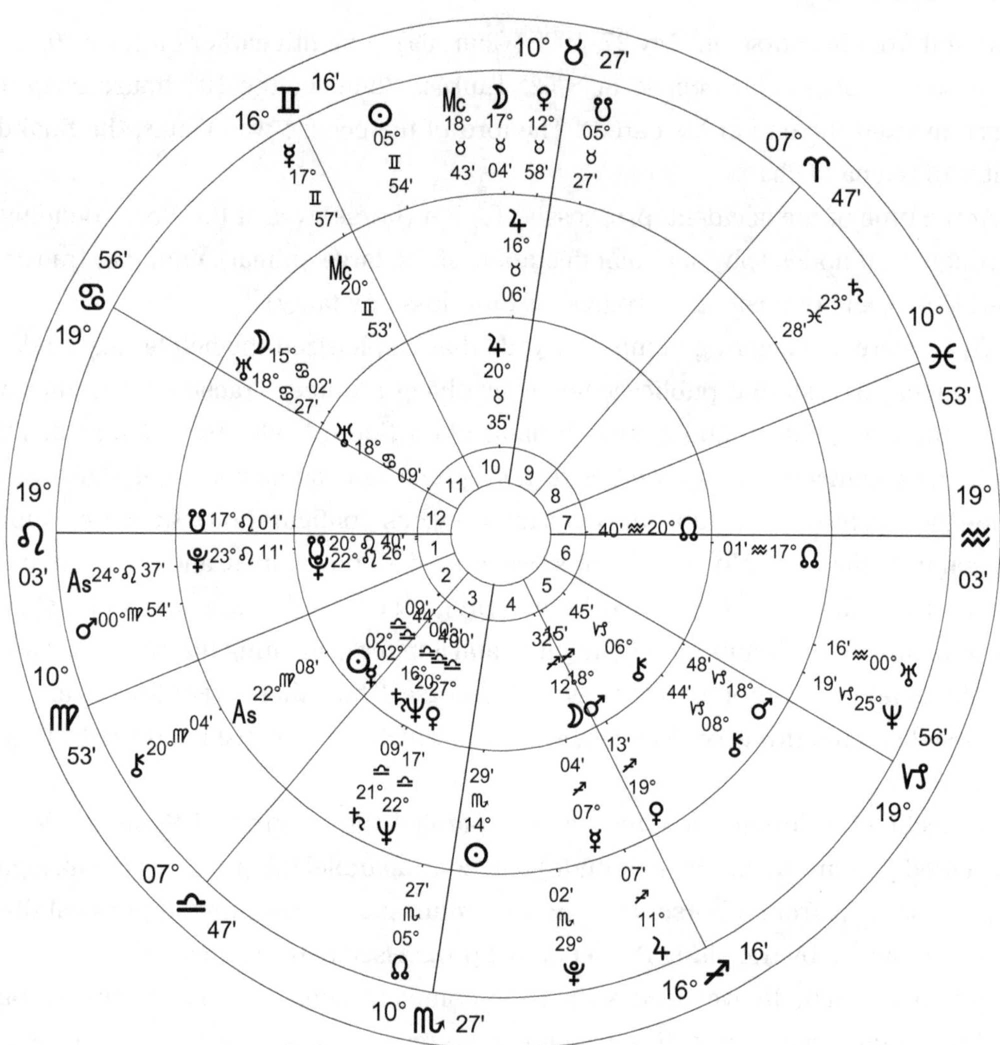

Chart 69:

Reeve's Accident, May 27, 1995, Charlottesville, VA, noon

Death

Reeve died unexpectedly on October 9, 2004 (Chart 70) after a bad reaction to antibiotics used to treat an infection. There was a solar eclipse three days after his death on October 13, 2004 at 21°05' Libra, with Venus (natal final dispositor) as the lord. The south nodal eclipse fell in his 3rd house conjunct a progressed Saturn–Neptune conjunction (infection and medication dissolving physical integrity).

Transiting Neptune was conjunct the progressed North Node (manifestation of infection and drug-induced chaos) and square progressed Jupiter at the North Bending (medical attention and a long journey). Transiting Pluto (death) was sextile/trine the nodes (acquiring power) and in two yods that attested to the hopelessness of the situation. Transiting Pluto activated the natal yod of Mars, Uranus, and Jupiter (sudden life and death crisis which cannot be fought), and transiting Pluto was conjunct natal Mars, sextile transiting Mercury and progressed Saturn–Neptune, and quincunx natal Jupiter (infection, dissolution, death, and a long journey).

Transiting Saturn was opposite progressed Mars (fever, inflammation) and square natal Venus (stress to the final dispositor and lord, weakening vitality). A life-threatening incident involving infectious bacteria and an unexpected response to medication was seen by the transiting Sun conjunct and parallel progressed Saturn–Neptune, which activated the natal square with Uranus.

There were a few nice aspects in play, indicating a measure of relief that came with release. Transiting Saturn was trine the progressed Sun (welcoming death) and transiting Neptune was sextile the natal Moon (acceptance). The progressed Moon was conjunct the natal IC and sextile transiting Venus (peace). Progressed Venus was trine the transiting North Node (gaining potency), conjunct the progressed IC, and sextile transiting Uranus; the end of the matter bringing happy liberation.

In declination, transiting Pluto was parallel the natal North Node and contraparallel progressed Jupiter (manifestation of death and a long journey). Progressed Mars was contraparallel progressed Uranus and Pluto (sudden fever and death).

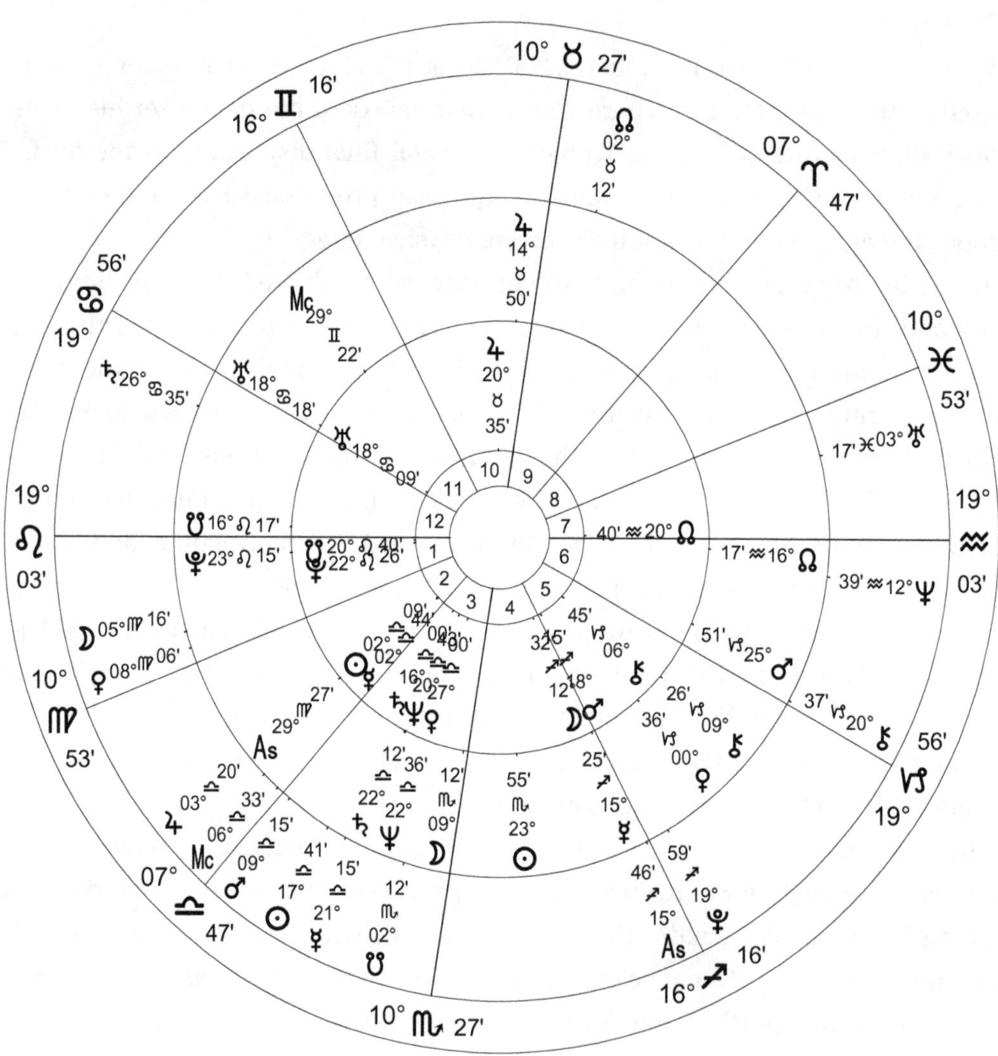

Chart 70:

Reeve's Death, Oct. 10, 2004, Pound Ridge, NY, noon

Miracles happen to those who believe in them.

— Bernard Berenson

Chapter 19
Hope and Change
Barack Obama

The 44th President of the United States is considered the first black American president even though he is of mixed-race. His mother was white and hailed from Kansas, while his father was a black African from Kenya who left for Harvard when Obama was young. His mother remarried and at seven Obama moved with his family to Jakarta where he lived for three years. At ten, he left his family and returned to Hawaii to live with his grandparents. During high school, he drank and used drugs in an effort 'to push the questions of who I was out of my mind.' He attended Columbia University and after graduation moved to Chicago and worked as a community organizer. In 1988, he went to Harvard Law School and became the president of the *Harvard Law Review*. He met his wife, Michelle, working in a law firm at a summer job. They married on October 3, 1992, and have two daughters.

After graduating from law school, he worked as a professor at the University of Chicago. He was elected to the Illinois State Senate in 1996, and in 2000 ran for a seat in the U.S. House of Representatives and lost. The winning incumbent was well liked and said Obama was 'blinded by ambition.' Although Obama proved to be good at fund-raising, he was not well known and he was viewed as inexperienced.

Obama learned from his mistakes and four years later after delivering a rousing speech at the Democratic Party Convention, he was elected to the U.S. Senate. Two years later he announced his presidential bid. He won the 2008 election and has been in office three years. He had been in office for less than a year when he was awarded the Nobel Peace Prize. Currently he is up for re-election and expects to raise one billion dollars for his campaign. He is not expecting an easy election as he has disappointed many by his willingness to compromise and he has reneged on previous campaign promises. At the moment, the political parties are deeply divided in ideology, yet almost indistinguishable in practice, with both parties serving wealthy donors at the expense of the electorate.

Nativity

Rex Bills gives the rulership of politics and politicians to the Sun, Leo, Saturn, Capricorn, and possibly Aries, Libra, Neptune, and the 10th house. Since south nodal energy is related to service, it should be prominent in the charts of politicians who genuinely seek to serve their constituents and the country. A strong ego and confidence are also a requirement.

Obama has a Leo stellium (Chart 71) with the Sun in Leo, the sign of the king. Placed in the 6th house, he is a natural leader, willing to work to improve the welfare of the kingdom. The Sun rules the 7th, denoting an interest in forging close relationships with (influential) others (dignified rulership). The Sun is separating from a square with Neptune, which describes his experience with drugs, and also his idealism, his 'audacity of hope', and his vision of a country driven by ethics and morals (Neptune in the 9th). After graduating from law school, Obama could have gone to any prestigious law firm, but instead, for little money, he returned to the lower west side of Chicago to work as a community organizer.

There was a solar eclipse a week after his birth on August 11, 1961, at 18°30' Leo. It was a north nodal eclipse that fell on his Descendant and promised the expansion of relationships during his lifetime. The natal nodes are retrograde, with the Sun ruling

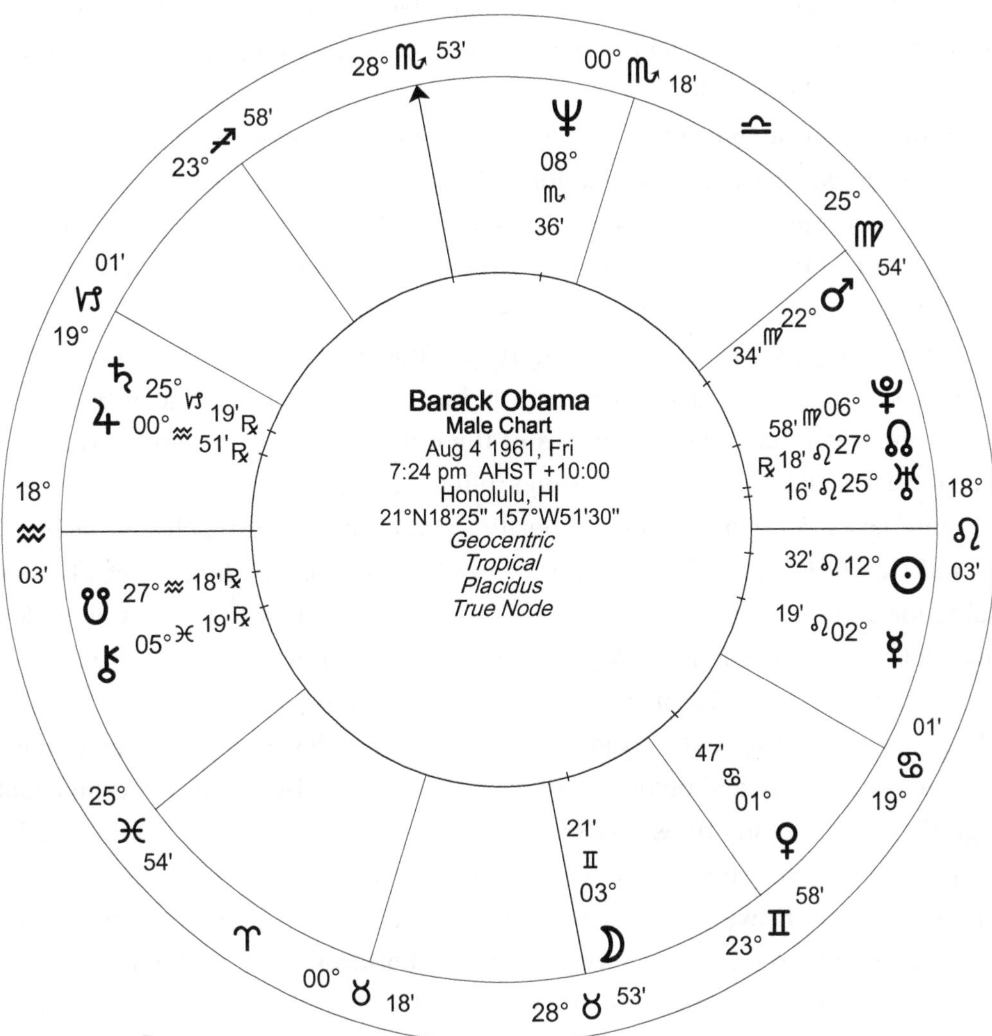

Chart 71:

Barack Obama Nativity

the North Node and acquiring know-how and wisdom through this rulership. He instinctively knows how to promote himself, and possesses great ambition, ego drive, and the desire for leadership.

The Moon is in Gemini sextile Mercury, giving him a way with words. He is an eloquent speaker, and as Hillary Clinton noted, he knows how to give a speech. The Moon is in the 4th, denoting a man whose heart lies in the home, and on a grander scale, the homeland. Ruling the 6th, his daily work involves improving the welfare of the country. The Moon is square Pluto, adding depth, secrecy, investigative prowess, as well as a public desire for power (Pluto ruling the 10th). With Pluto in the 7th, he has formidable partners and enemies. Though not evident in longitude, the Moon at a latitude of 5S14 is at the South Bending. There was loss of the mother (he left the family to return to Hawaii) and a need to be of service (Moon ruling the 6th).

Obama has a Mercury–Jupiter opposition which can over-reach and signify too much talk, too little action. The Moon is sextile/trine the opposition, which gives emotional tenor and passion to his speeches. There have been two Obama's in evidence: campaign Obama is a visionary, inspiring and grand (Jupiter in Aquarius), while President Obama is talk, conciliation, and acquiescence (Mercury).

Aquarius is rising, and Uranus in Leo rules the chart, describing a humanitarian desire to improve society and unique leadership capabilities. He is viewed as an agent of change (Uranus). Uranus rules the South Node, bringing potential weakness and vulnerability to the chart ruler. There have been questions about his birth and ignorance regarding his race. However, Uranus is strengthened by its conjunction to the North Node. This set-up strengthens the personality and affords an opportunity to manifest himself (and his ideals) outwardly in the world. His is a life of service, and with the South Node ruler conjunct the North Node, his willingness to serve has a direct outlet. When the nodes are tied to each other through the ruler of one, it is a mutual reception of sorts, bringing personal gain through willing sacrifice.

The Midheaven is at the North Bending of the nodal axis, aligning the culminating point in the chart with the nodal point of maximum fruition—bringing the promise of high social standing and prominence. With the North Bending here, energy flows into this point and boosts the power of any transits and progressions crossing or aspecting the Midheaven. His career is also helped by a sextile from Saturn in Capricorn to the

Midheaven and harmed by a square from impulsive Uranus to the Midheaven, which can want too much too fast. In addition, Mars is trine Saturn, which bestows a strong work ethic and a willingness to be of service.

The South Bending is conjunct his IC, indicating a loss in the home and family. He was abandoned by his father when he was an infant, and from age ten was raised by his grandparents. His family has also suffered from his political ambitions. While in the Senate, his family lived in Chicago and he lived alone in a cheap, rundown apartment in Washington D.C. However, the South Bending IC also indicates service at home. His current residence is the White House, where he lives and serves his country.

Obama has a five-planet configuration that is related to public service. The Moon is sextile Mercury (emotional speaking), square Pluto (striving to transform society), trine Jupiter (vision of utopia), and semi-sextile Venus (charm and money). As we shall see, this configuration is highly activated during election campaigns.

In declination, Neptune is parallel the South Node suggesting loss for Neptune (expressed as early escapism), but also service to an idealistic vision. Obama was born six months after a great conjunction of Jupiter and Saturn (symbolizing an ethical and just society), which occurred on February 18, 1961, at 25°12' Capricorn, the degree of natal Saturn. By the time of Obama's birth, the conjunction was separating in longitude, but parallel in declination, where it formed a complex with Mercury and Venus, tying him personally to the mundane conjunction. He is a voice for it and can establish the necessary powerful, influential and financial (Pluto also involved), relationships (Venus) needed to articulate (Mercury) a grandiose vision of society. What remains to be seen is whether he can act on his vision.

State Senate

A topical question as Obama enters his fourth year of office is whether he will win re-election. It is always instructive to study what happened in the past, in order to assess what may happen in the future. In addition, events that have already transpired help to reveal the meaning of natal placements, which makes prognostication easier.

On March 19, 1996, after fellow Democratic contenders dropped out of the race for the state senate seat, Obama became the uncontested Democratic candidate. He won

Chart 72:

Obama's State Senate Win, Nov. 5, 1996, Chicago, IL, 7:00 a.m. CST

the seat on November 5, 1996, in the same election that gave Clinton his second term in office. There was a north nodal solar eclipse prior to the election on October 12, 1996, at 19°31' Libra, giving Venus power as the lord.

On election day (Chart 72), the transiting North Node was conjunct transiting Venus and progressed Mercury, and trine the natal Moon, indicating outward expression of heartfelt happiness. Transiting Mars and Moon had formed a t-square and were conjunct natal Pluto and square an opposition of transiting Pluto and the natal Moon, suggesting a hard fought and hateful battle. Transiting Uranus was conjunct natal Jupiter, trine the natal Moon, and opposite natal Mercury, activating the natal five-planet configuration, bringing luck and an articulated expansive vision that was palpable to the public. Transiting Saturn was also activating the configuration and conjunct the progressed Ascendant (assuming responsibility), sextile transiting Uranus and natal Jupiter (luck), sextile natal Moon (hard work), and square natal Venus (high expense, running short of campaign funds, feeling a lack of love). However, transiting Saturn was also in a grand trine with transiting Pluto–natal Midheaven and natal Mercury, pointing to powerful speeches, success, respect and recognition.

Progressed Uranus (chart ruler and South Node ruler) was in partile conjunction with both the natal North Node and the progressed North Node as he won his first election (outward expression of service and sacrifice). Progressed Venus (lord) was conjunct the natal Sun, portending happiness and uplifting speeches (Venus ruling the 3rd).

In the sky, transiting Uranus–Neptune were conjunct and parallel, and aligned with natal Jupiter and Saturn, coinciding with luck and a utopian vision gaining the promise of expression through politics.

Congressional Loss

Three years later, while still in the State Senate, Obama ran for a seat in the U.S. House of Representatives. He lost the Democratic primary on March 21, 2000 (Chart 73). There was a south nodal solar eclipse on February 5, 2000, at 16°01' Aquarius, conjunct his Ascendant, with Uranus serving as the lord. Traditionally an eclipse is viewed as bringing a crisis and when the angles are eclipsed, this is especially so. An eclipse is a

Chart 73:

Obama's Congressional Loss, Mar. 21, 2000, Chicago, IL, noon

darkening, a loss of light, and when the eclipse is conjunct the Ascendant, it indicates a lessening of the projected self. It did not help that transiting Saturn was near the nadir and in a t-square with the Ascendant and natal Sun–progressed Venus, denoting burden and responsibility, coupled with insufficient confidence, charm and money.

On the day of the primary, the natal five-planet configuration was activated by the transiting nodes. The transiting North Node was conjunct natal Mercury, and the transiting South Node was conjunct natal Jupiter, signifying a gain of Mercury (name in the news and name recognition) and loss of Jupiter (denied an opportunity to serve in high office). A grand trine had formed between transiting Jupiter, the progressed Midheaven, and natal Pluto, suggestive of political power, but with transiting Jupiter opposite natal Neptune, the promise was denied.

The transiting South Node was quincunx natal Venus, indicating frustration with money, and a desire beyond his reach. Transiting Uranus (lord) was conjunct the Ascendant and quincunx the natal Sun and opposite progressed Venus, signaling an upset and helplessness that no personal effort could change.

However, what looks like a loss is not always a loss, and whether what happens is good or bad is not always immediately apparent. For Obama, Jupiter conjunct the transiting South Node brought the loss of luck and dreams (Jupiter ruling 11th), but with Mercury conjunct the transiting North Node, he gained public recognition. Analysts suggest that had Obama won the election and become a U.S. Representative, he would not have become president. With Uranus trine the progressed Moon, and transiting Pluto trine the natal Sun, Obama faced defeat and transformed himself. After the election he said he had to take a close look at himself and ask why he was running for office. Was it to get attention (Leo Sun and North Node ruler) or to help people (Uranus, the chart ruler and South Node ruler)?

National Senate Win

Three years later, Obama began campaigning for a seat in the U.S. Senate. He was selected to deliver the keynote speech at the Democratic Convention in Boston for John Kerry in the summer of 2004, a definitive moment that brought him to the attention of the world. A few months later, Obama was elected to the U.S. Senate. On

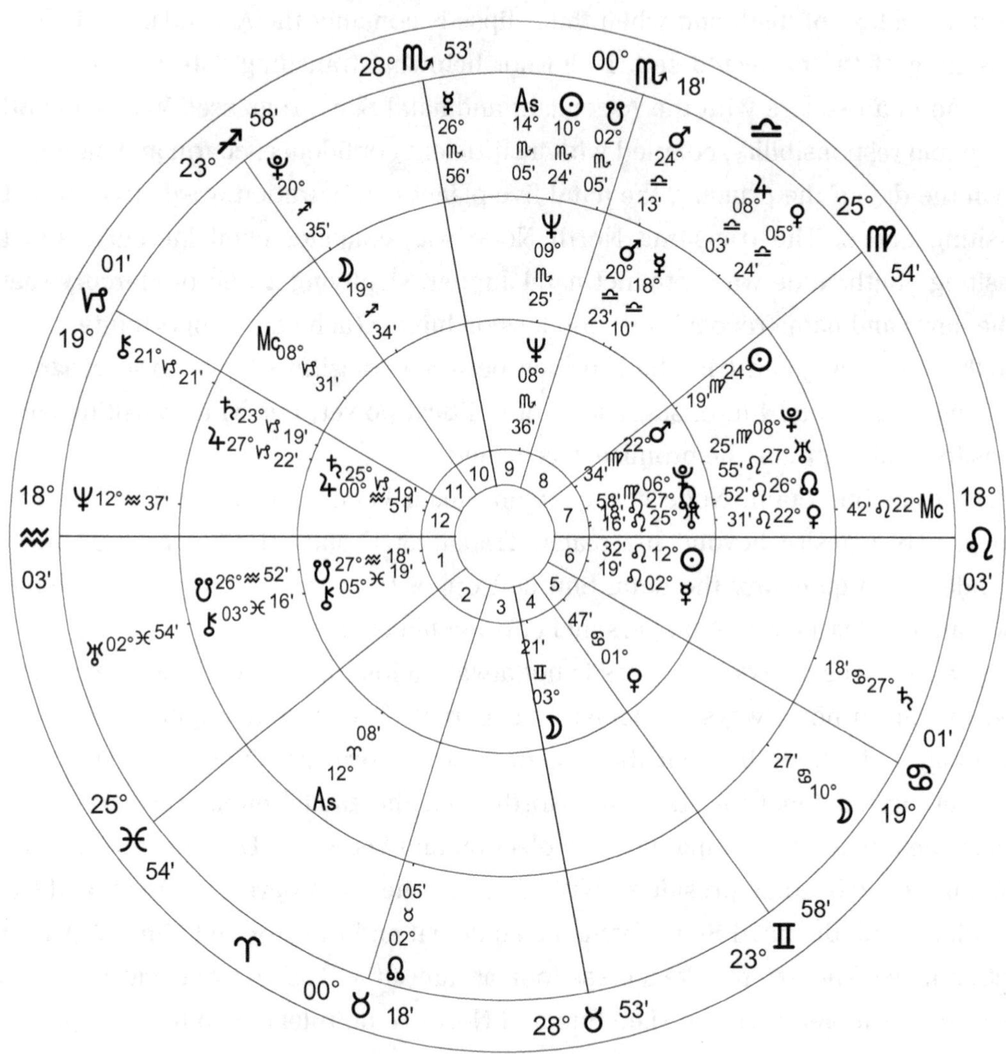

Chart 74:

Obama's U.S. Senate Win, Nov. 2, 2004, Washington, D.C. 7:00 a.m. EST

October 13, 2004, there was a solar eclipse at 21°05' Libra, which was within 2° of the north nodal solar eclipse of October 12, 1996, at 19°31' Libra that presaged his state senate win eight years earlier. The south nodal eclipse was conjunct progressed Mercury and Mars (battle with words), and had Venus serving as the lord.

On election day of 2004 (Chart 74), Obama's natal five-planet configuration was once again activated. The transiting nodes formed a grand cross with natal Mercury at the North Bending (verbal expression, much speaking) and natal Jupiter at the South Bending (inspiration and offering his vision in service to the state). In a double-whammy, transiting Mercury was at the North Bending of the progressed nodes, signifying the outer manifestation of Mercurial matters, which for Obama translated to speeches, a quest for power (8th house), risk-taking (5th house), and career visibility (transiting Mercury conjunct the 10th house). Transiting Uranus had formed a grand trine with the transiting South Node and natal Venus, and the win may have surprised him. Transiting Uranus also formed a t-square and was opposite natal Pluto and square the Moon, signifying the battle was fierce and hard-won. Other aspects indicating a happy professional outcome include: transiting Saturn trine the Midheaven (professional achievement); progressed Sun trine natal Saturn (attaining personal goals); and transiting Pluto conjunct the progressed Moon and sextile progressed Mercury–Mars (conquest in battle).

Presidential Election

Two short years into his tenure as senator, Obama announced he was running for president. He was elected on November 4, 2008 (Chart 75). There was a south nodal solar eclipse on August 1, 2008 at 9°31' Leo conjunct his natal Sun, with the Sun serving as the lord. Traditionally, similar to eclipses that fall across the angles, an eclipse on a luminary heralds a time of crisis. When Obama's Ascendant was eclipsed, he lost an election, but here with his Sun eclipsed, he won. The difference seems to be that in his chart the Sun rules the 7th house, representing his opponent. The eclipse weakened his rival, who was himself eclipsed by his running mate.

On election day, there was a double-whammy, with the transiting South Node conjunct his natal Sun, and the transiting Sun at the South Bending of the transiting nodes

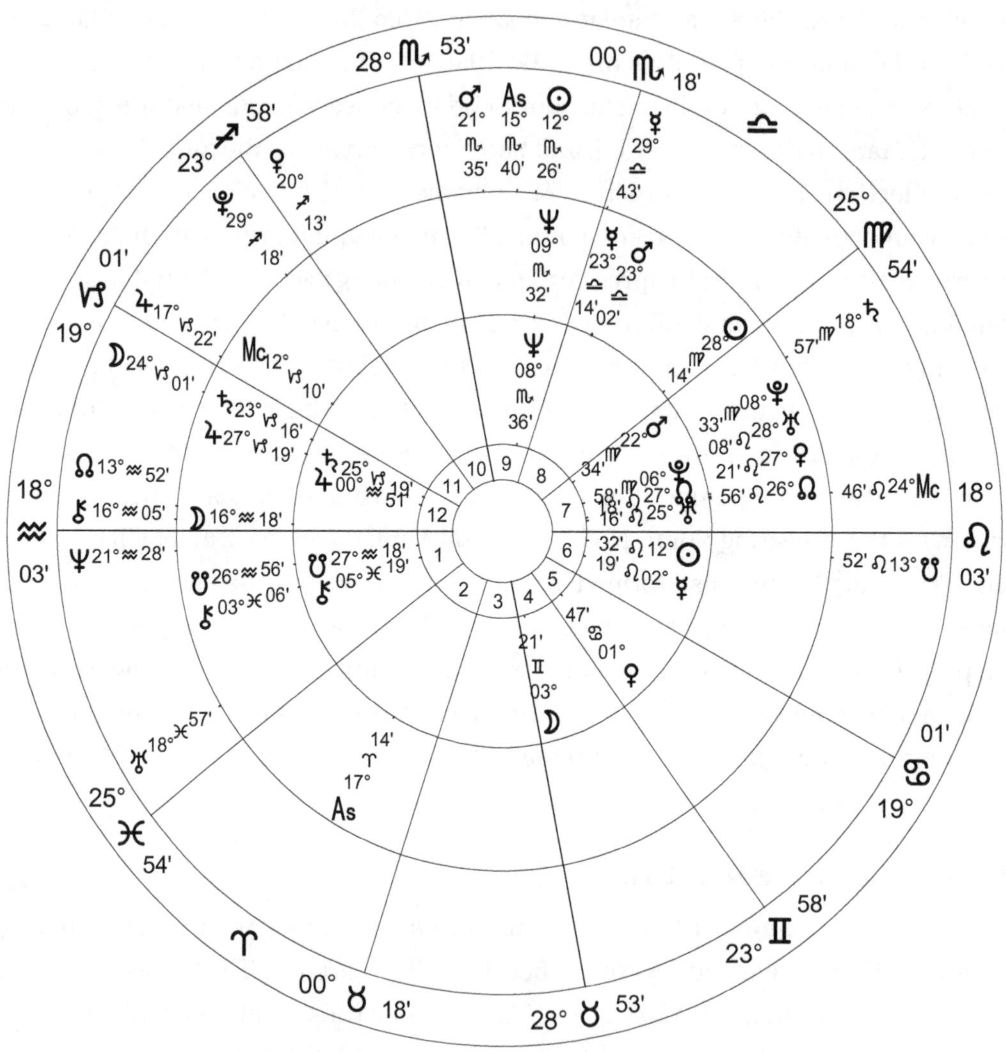

Chart 75:
Obama's Presidential Victory, Nov. 4, 2008, Washington, D.C. 7:00 a.m. EST

square his natal Sun, indicative of the vulnerability of his foe. The transiting North Node was conjunct the progressed Moon, describing a new home and a new job at the White House.

Transiting Mercury was activating the natal five-planet configuration with an out-of-sign square to the opposition of Mercury and Jupiter, as he smoothly spoke his way into office, offering the empowerment of many. Transiting Neptune was conjunct the Ascendant and trine a progressed conjunction of Mercury–Mars; articulating a vision (Neptune) he sought to enact (Mars). There was an exact transiting Saturn–Uranus opposition, with Saturn conjunct his natal Mars and trine transiting Jupiter, indicating good luck and hard work that paid off.

The progressed Sun was trine progressed Jupiter and both were sextile the Midheaven on a propitious day. However, the progressed Sun–Jupiter trine was about to end, and he would soon square-off against the establishment (transiting Pluto square progressed Sun). The progressed Mercury–Mars conjunction was perfecting a square with progressed Saturn, and he would find it difficult, if not impossible, to implement his promised agenda.

Election 2012

We have entered an election season and Obama knows he has an uphill battle. He has lost many of his grassroots supporters and a billion dollars of campaign contributions from big business might not be enough to win back disappointed voters. The origin of the Occupy Wall Street movement can be traced back to the last election and a promise of hope and change that went undelivered. Now Obama's best hope is that he will be a stronger candidate than his opponent.

Can he win? There is a north nodal solar eclipse on November 13, 2012, a week after the election at 21°56' Scorpio, with Pluto serving as the lord. Natally, Pluto is in his 7th and at this time will be trine transiting Pluto, indicative of powerful friends. Since Pluto rules his 10th house, this eclipse bodes well for him.

On election day (Chart 76) the transiting nodal axis aligns with Obama's natal Midheaven–IC, with the North Node conjunct the culminating point in the chart (flowering of profession). At the opening of the polls in Washington D.C., the transiting nodes are square the natal nodes, such that the natal North Node, natal Uranus, and the transiting Midheaven are at the transiting South Bending—an aspect suggestive of professional loss. However, given the aspect involves his 7th house, the message may be more relevant to his opponent.

Transiting Jupiter is sextile the natal Sun, sextile progressed Moon, and sextile/trine the Ascendant/Descendant, signifying benefactors and personal luck. The progressed Moon is also sextile/trine the Ascendant/Descendant, auguring personal and professional success, and an opponent who does not do him too much damage. Progressed Mars is strengthened by a sextile to the progressed North Node and a sextile to natal Uranus, indicating Obama's fight for utopia. The natal five-planet configuration is highly activated, with transiting Uranus sextile/trine the Mercury–Jupiter opposition (luck on his side). But transiting Neptune is square the natal Moon, and the public may be disillusioned. Transiting Mercury is opposite the natal Moon (the public have heard his promises already) and sextile/trine the Mercury/Jupiter opposition (still, he is talking a good talk). Transiting Saturn has formed a t-square with the opposition, and though it is a hard sell, he is trying, giving it his best shot for another chance. He likely has help from Michelle and the girls (progressed Venus sextile the natal Moon). There is also a grand trine with the progressed Sun, natal Moon and natal Jupiter, suggestive of success. Given these aspects, Obama looks strong, despite a jaded and disheartened public.

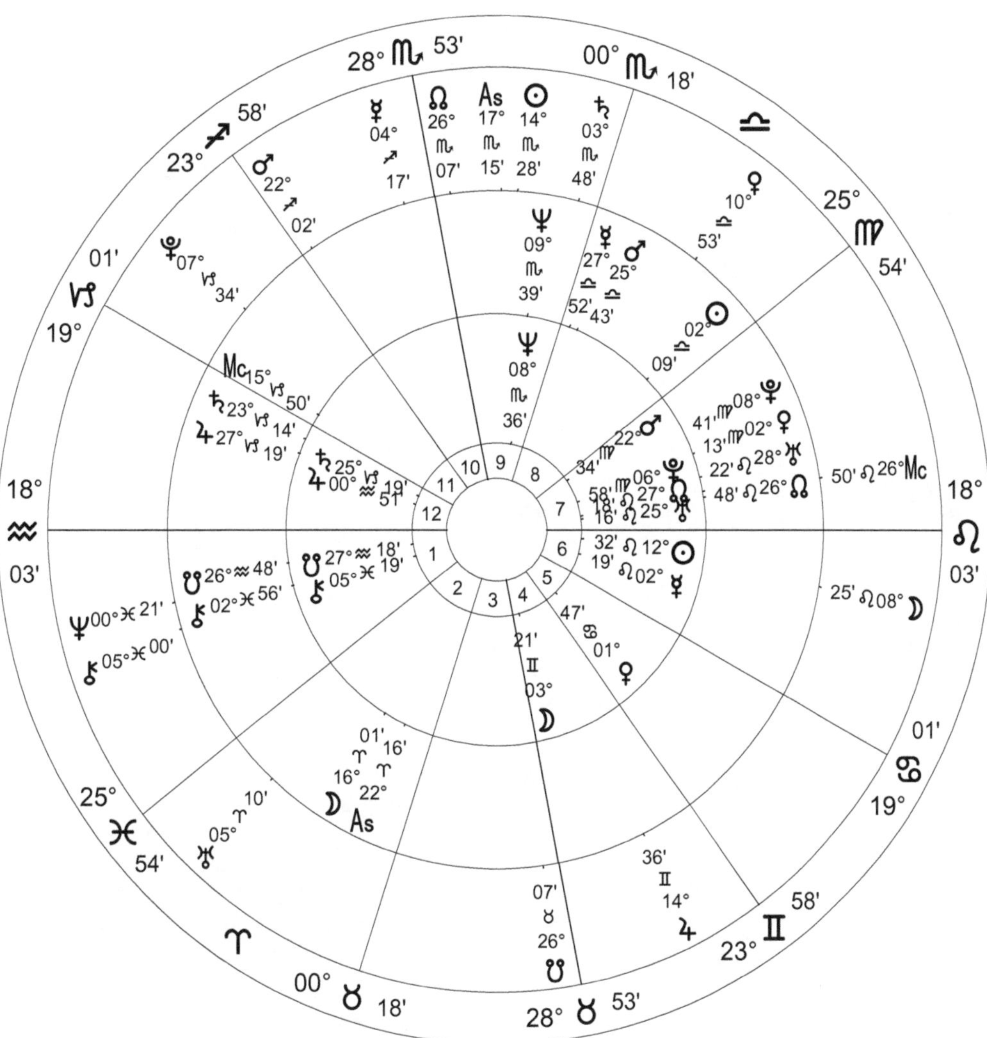

Chart 76:

Obama and 2012, Nov. 6, 2012, Washington, D.C., 7:00 a.m. EST

I don't know what your destiny will be, but I do know that the only ones among you who will be truly happy are those who have sought and found a way to serve.

— Albert Schweitzer

Chapter 20
2012 Presidential Challenger
Mitt Romney

At the time of this writing, the 2012 Republican presidential nominee appears to be Mitt Romney. He is a Mormon who as a young man did missionary work in France. He was a successful businessman and has amassed a financial portfolio estimated to be worth between $190–250 million. He organized the 2002 Winter Olympics in Salt Lake City. The following year he was elected Governor of Massachusetts and served one term. He ran in the 2008 Republican primary but was defeated by John McCain. He is the son of a former Michigan governor, is married, and has five sons.

Nativity

The PNSE was on November 23, 1946, at 0°49' Sagittarius. It was a south nodal eclipse conjunct the 7th house cusp, suggesting an expansion of close partnerships, both personal and professional during his lifetime. The natal nodes were stationary and would turn direct in fifteen hours.

Natally (Chart 77) Romney has a Pisces Sun, a sign whose positive attributes include altruism, compassion, and faith. Placed in the 11th house of goals, groups, and friends, he is personable and has friends and support in high places. Ruling the 4th, he has big dreams for his family, his home, and by extension, the homeland.

The Moon is in Scorpio giving intensity, depth, and a drive for power. With the Moon in the 6th house, these qualities are largely hidden and not overtly apparent. The Moon rules the 3rd house, and he is seen as a dispassionate speaker, which is not the case: his emotions run deep but are well-concealed. The Moon is exactly (within 3') conjunct and parallel Jupiter which gives emotional intensity and adds a religious and philosophical overtone that can border on self-righteousness and entitlement. Jupiter in Scorpio ruling the 7th and 8th (and conjunct the Moon) shows a need for power and influence. Venus at the Midheaven opposite Pluto further indicate an aspiration for power that is difficult to attain.

Romney has Gemini rising, and Mercury rules the chart. With the Sun, Mercury, Mars, and Uranus all in changeable signs, there is much mutability in the chart. Romney is a well-known flip-flopper, forever changing his positions in accordance with what he thinks people wish to hear. The universal health care plan he implemented in Massachusetts was the basis of Obama's health care plan, but the first thing Romney would do as president would be to repeal what he himself inspired.

Mercury also rules the North Node, and acquires wisdom, ease of expression, and accomplishment through the association. Because it is the chart ruler, the personality and outward projection of the self benefit and are strengthened as a result of the nodal influence. Mercury is retrograde and in Pisces, the sign of its detriment and fall, which would typically add weakness, but this effect appears to be mitigated by the influence of the North Node. Despite the emotional nebulousness of Mercury's sign, he is a smooth, concise, and unflappable speaker. There is an authentic belief in his faith, which goes largely unarticulated and which he tries unsuccessfully to hide (Mercury in a yod with Neptune and Pluto). In declination, Mercury is parallel the Sun, and speech and communication support the solar agenda: Romney has a message. I suspect he

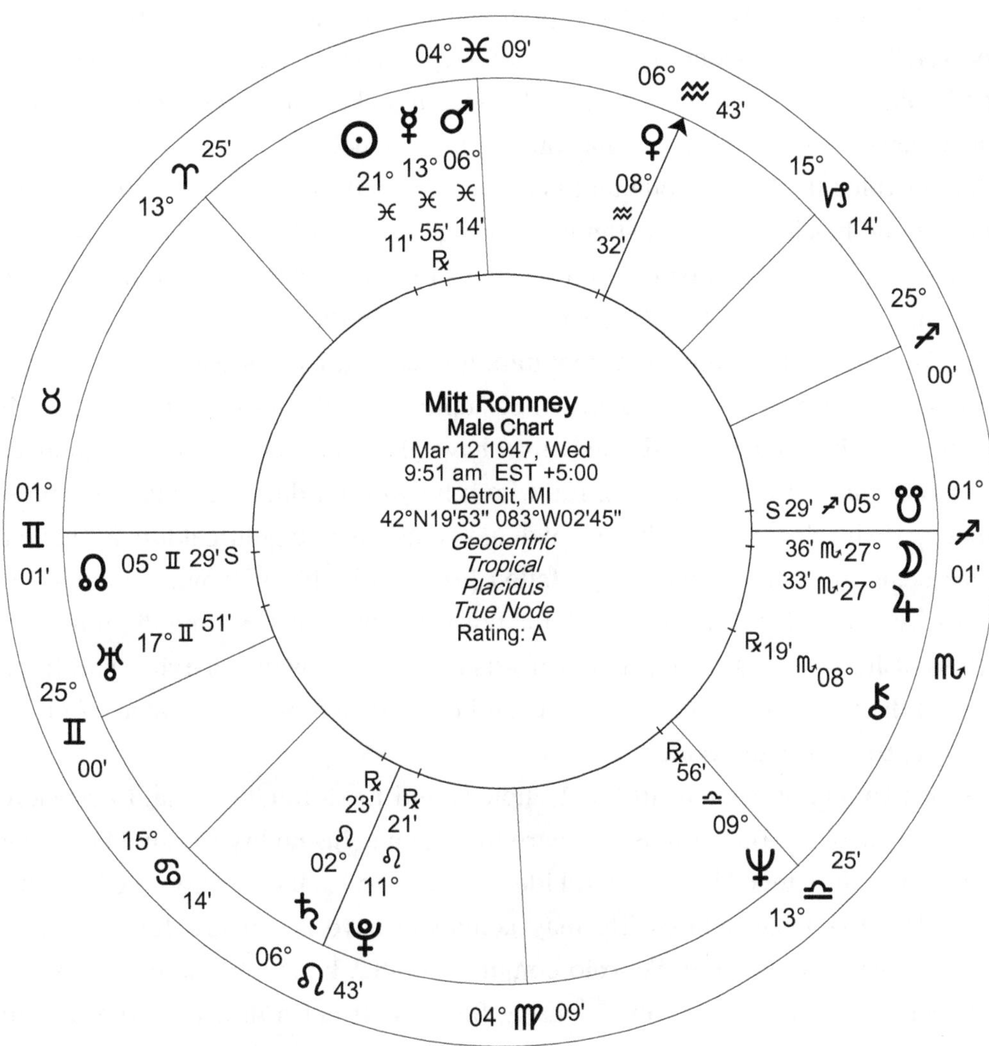

Chart 77:

Mitt Romney Nativity

would make a better preacher than a politician, but religion cannot satisfy his desire for power. The yod with Mercury, Pluto, and Neptune symbolize this unresolved struggle and point to the harm his spiritual beliefs have on his aspirations to power, as well as the damage his drive for power has on his spiritual beliefs.

Jupiter rules the South Node and is associated with weakness. As the significator of religion, he has lost political standing through his unorthodox religious beliefs. He has inaccurately tried to portray Mormonism as Christianity (loss of truth with respect to religion). Jupiter ruling the 7th suggests weakness in the spouse, and Romney's wife suffers from multiple sclerosis, a debilitating degenerative disease. Jupiter conjunct the Moon (wife) repeats this message, since Jupiter's weakness spills over to the Moon by virtue of their conjunction. Romney may have also had problems with a dominating mother (also shown by the Moon), for whom he worked during her failed senatorial campaign. He has had to live with the high expectations of a political family (his father besides being a governor, also had a failed presidential bid.) Romney attended both Harvard Law School and Business School, but went into business and did not practice law (loss of Jupiter). Optimally, Jupiter needs to be given away in service, and Romney organized the Olympics (a Jupiter event) and offered to forsake his salary if he could not turn a profit from the games.

He has Uranus in Gemini in the 1st house, and he is intelligent and occasionally surprisingly inspired. But Uranus is square the Sun and his ability to shine in conservative politics is threatened by his liberal ideas. Uranus rules the 10th house of career and recently this has been politics. He may genuinely have a concern for the common person, but with the Moon in Scorpio conjunct Jupiter, he is a friend of corporations, and sincerely believes that profit from big business trickles down for the benefit of everyone. In latitude, Uranus is in line with the Sun, angles, and nodes, further energizing the influence of Uranus. He is more of a humanitarian than his base can easily accept. He can be blunt and speak without thinking, innocently uttering contentious statements like, "Corporations are people, my friend. Of course they are." The multi-millionaire also erroneously views himself as a common man and once said, "We ought to provide help to the people who have been hurt most by the Obama economy … the great middle class—the eighty to ninety percent of us in this country."

He has Venus in Aquarius on the 10th cusp, a fortunate placement for success in business, as well as for looking good in public. Venus is sextile/trine the nodes, acquiring a boost from the association that has manifest as charm, good looks, and financial success in business. Nonetheless, the powerful far right base of the Republican Party does not like him (Venus opposite Pluto).

Mars in Pisces is at the South Bending of the lunar nodes. In this position, Mars cannot act selfishly without exacting considerable loss. Mars was expressed in his missionary work where he did service on behalf of his church. Mars in Pisces will also fight for spiritual beliefs, and with Mars ruling the 12th house of spirit, his work may be spiritually inspired. Mars can also be his undoing, which he may recognize, and in the current presidential debates, he refuses to get drawn into personal fights.

Il Est Mort

When Romney was twenty-one and on a two-and-a-half year religious mission in France, he was in a head-on collision that nearly killed him. Romney was driving with six passengers in an over-loaded vehicle when the car was struck by a Catholic priest who came driving over a hill in the wrong lane. Romney was knocked unconscious. The wife of the president of the Mormon mission in France was killed. A policeman at the scene believed Romney was dead and wrote on his passport: *Il est mort.* Romney was rushed to the hospital. His sister's husband, a medical intern, was sent to Paris to monitor his treatment. With time, Romney recovered. No charges were pressed against the priest in an effort to minimize tension between the two religions.

Three months before the accident there was a solar eclipse at 8°19' Aries, with Mars serving as the lord. The north nodal eclipse fell on Romney's progressed Sun, heralding a crisis for the ego. The eclipse was opposite natal Neptune (dissolution of the physical being). At the time of the accident (Chart 78), natal Mars (lord), which is physically weak at the natal South Bending, was in opposition with the progressed Moon at the North Bending of the natal nodes. With Mars ruling metal and cars, and the Moon ruling the 3rd house of cars and trips, there was a physical event causing loss through cars.

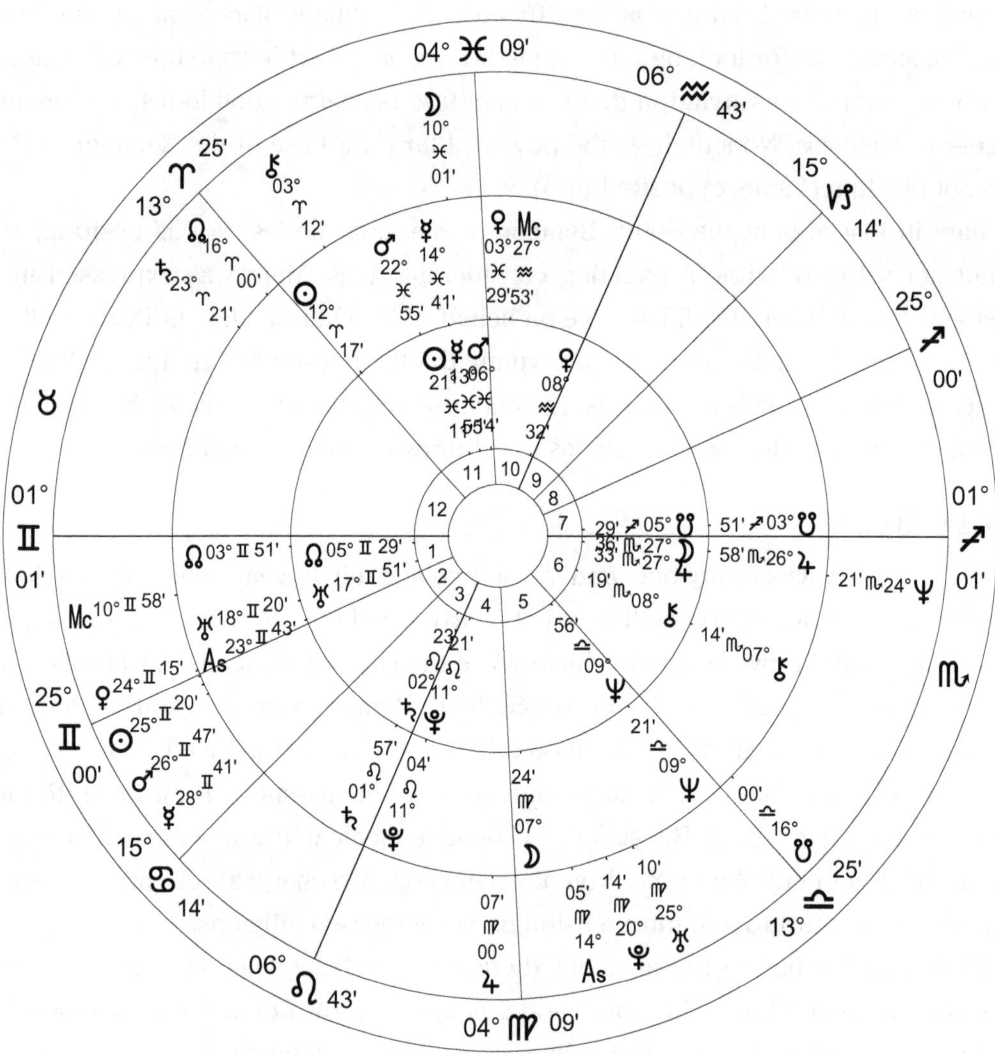

Chart 78:

Romney's Car Accident, June 16, 1968, Pau, France, noon

Transiting Neptune (chaos, dissolution) was conjunct natal Moon–Jupiter (inherently vulnerable due to the South Node rulership of Jupiter). The three planets were involved in two yods. In the first yod they were quincunx transiting Saturn in the 12th, and quincunx the progressed Ascendant and a quadruple transiting conjunction of Venus, Sun, Mars, and Mercury, signaling burdens, restriction, and surgery. The second yod comprised a sextile from natal Moon–Jupiter and transiting Neptune to transiting Uranus–Pluto, all quincunx transiting Saturn (a sudden encounter with death bringing limitation and hospitalization). A third yod (boomerang) was formed with transiting Uranus–Pluto quincunx the progressed Midheaven, quincunx transiting Saturn, and opposite a progressed Mars–natal Sun conjunction that was square natal Uranus, testifying to a serious, life-threatening accident and an assault on the health and physical body, which he was helpless to influence or control.

There was an opposition between transiting Jupiter (ruling the 7th and 8th houses) and progressed Venus (ruling the 6th house of illness and 12th house of hospitalization), which was square the progressed nodes. Venus in Pisces was at the South Bending (loss of health necessitating hospitalization) and Jupiter in Virgo was at the North Bending (physicians and medical treatment). The complex also describes Ann (Venus), his wife-to-be who was far away (Jupiter) in the U.S. converting to Mormonism when the overseas accident occurred. Working in his favor was a progressed trine between the Sun and Pluto (with the Sun exalted and Pluto in the Sun's sign) and Romney would recover.

Lost Senate Election

Romney's history of political wins and losses gives clues regarding his chances in the upcoming election. He ran against Edward Kennedy in the 1994 election for the Massachusetts senate seat and lost. There was a north nodal solar eclipse a few days before the election at 10°54' Scorpio opposite the progressed Sun and square natal Pluto (challenge to personal power). The lord of the eclipse was Pluto, making the square to Pluto particularly onerous.

At the time of the election (Chart 79), the progressed Sun was quincunx Neptune, suggesting a period of disappointment, helplessness, and unanswered prayers.

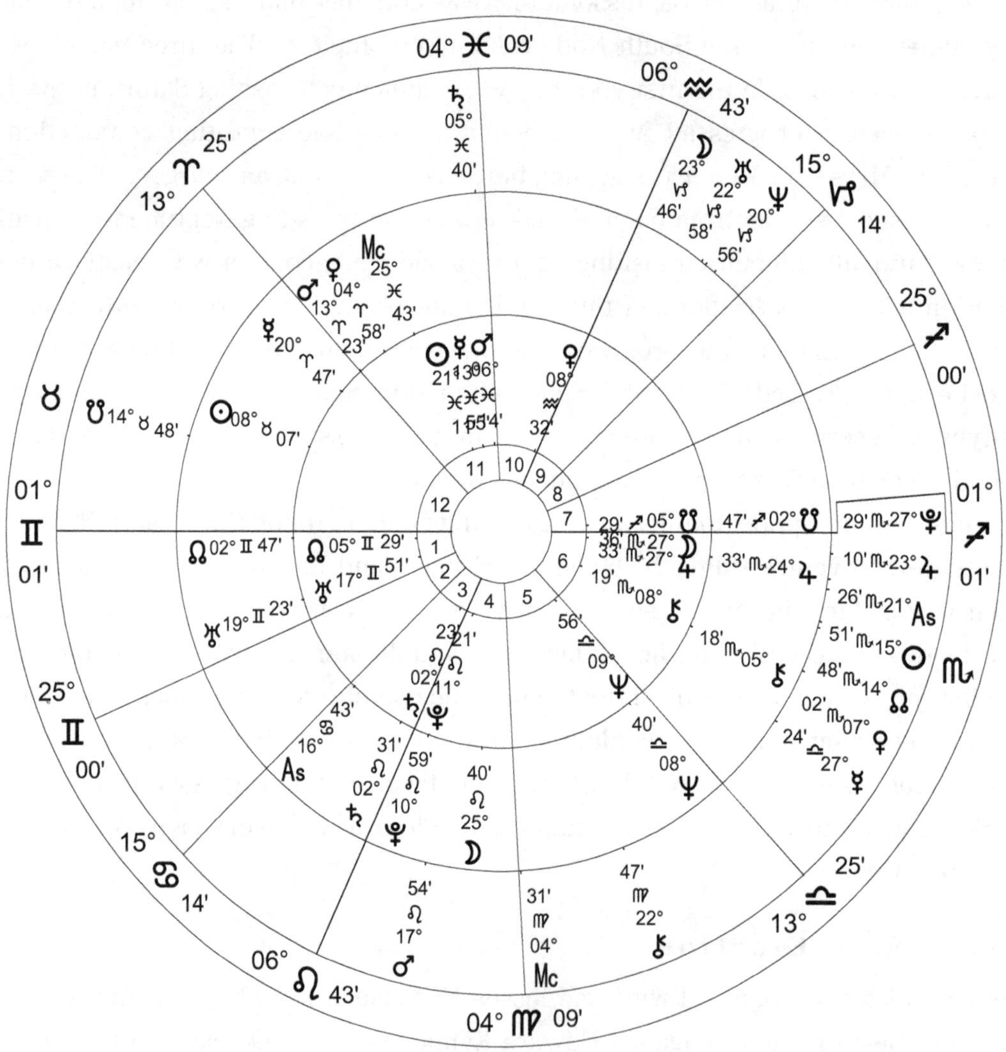

Chart 79:

Romney's Lost Senate Election, Nov. 8, 1994, Boston, MA, 7:00 a.m. EST

Transiting Saturn was at the South Bending of the natal nodes conjunct natal Mars and he experienced loss, a fall in standing. Progressed Venus was sextile/trine the natal nodes indicating that something good came from the failure. He found his calling and made new friends in high places (Venus in the 11th). The progressed nodes were sextile/trine natal Saturn, which translated as duty, responsibility, and national name recognition.

The transiting Sun was conjunct the transiting North Node and trine the important natal Mercury, but square (wide and separating) natal Pluto and quincunx Uranus, suggesting frustration concerning the formidable powers that stood against him.

The election occurred during the mundane conjunction of Uranus and Neptune in Capricorn that was sextile the natal Sun, but square progressed Mercury, giving a mixed message of hope and loss. The mundane conjunction also formed a yod and was quincunx progressed Uranus and quincunx transiting Mars, which expressed as high hopes that were unexpectedly dashed. Despite great assistance, as shown by transiting Pluto conjunct the natal Moon–Jupiter, transiting Jupiter nearing a return, and Pluto in his own sign trine the progressed Midheaven (though square the progressed Moon), there was not sufficient strength to bring about a win. All the family money, influence, and wealthy friends in the world could not help him.

The Governor

Eight years later, on November 5, 2002 (Chart 80), Romney was elected Governor of Massachusetts. There was a north nodal solar eclipse two weeks after the election on November 19, 2002 at 27°32' Taurus, making Venus the lord. The eclipse was opposite natal Moon–Jupiter, and with Jupiter ruling the 7th house, the competitor was eclipsed and weakened.

At fifty-five, Romney was approaching a nodal return, at the same time transiting Neptune was conjunct the Midheaven–natal Venus, and sextile/trine the natal and transiting nodes (boosting energy) and forming a grand trine with natal Neptune (spiritual assistance). The progressed nodes were still sextile/trine progressed/natal Saturn, as they had been eight years earlier during his defeat, signifying sustained duty, a struggle to become an authority, and hard labor.

A key factor at this time was the progressed Moon that was conjunct the South Node (service), sextile natal Venus (lord) and the Midheaven (helpful for appearance and professional prestige), and sextile natal Neptune (God listening and answering prayers). Progressed Mars was sextile progressed Uranus and he was viewed as a man who would fight for the people. Transiting Pluto was trine progressed Venus and sextile transiting Mars, suggestive of big money from influential partners.

In latitude, transiting Neptune was near the 0° line of the ecliptic, parallel natal Uranus and the natal Sun, angles, and nodes, indicating collective appeal from an electorate who viewed him as a man who would represent the interests and concerns of the common people.

At the time he was elected he was experiencing many horrendous transits. Transiting Pluto was opposite natal Uranus (power struggles affecting him professionally). Transiting Neptune was opposite natal Pluto (power eroding away). Transiting Saturn was quincunx natal Moon–Jupiter (high family expectations and necessary payback for election favors). Transiting Uranus was square progressed Jupiter, and transiting Jupiter was square the progressed Sun, reflecting hubris and untenable promises. There was a grand cross with transiting Neptune and natal Venus square both transiting Venus and progressed Mercury and widely opposite progressed Saturn, reinforcing the theme of boundless and appealing promises that sounded good, but could never be kept. Nonetheless, he won the election. The primary factors denoting a win appear to be the eclipse that favored him over his opponent and good aspects to natal and progressed Venus, the eclipse lord.

Presidential Election 2012

Should Romney be the GOP presidential nominee, how will he do in the election? It will be eighteen years after his failed run for the senate, the duration of time of a nodal cycle. On November 13, 2012, a week after the election, there is a north nodal eclipse at 21°56' Scorpio, with Pluto as the lord. The eclipse falls on progressed Jupiter, which rules the natal 7th, and indicates that Romney can eclipse his opponent. However, the eclipse is opposite the progressed Sun, which suggests that Romney himself is also weakened. The electorate may not view either corporate candidate with favor.

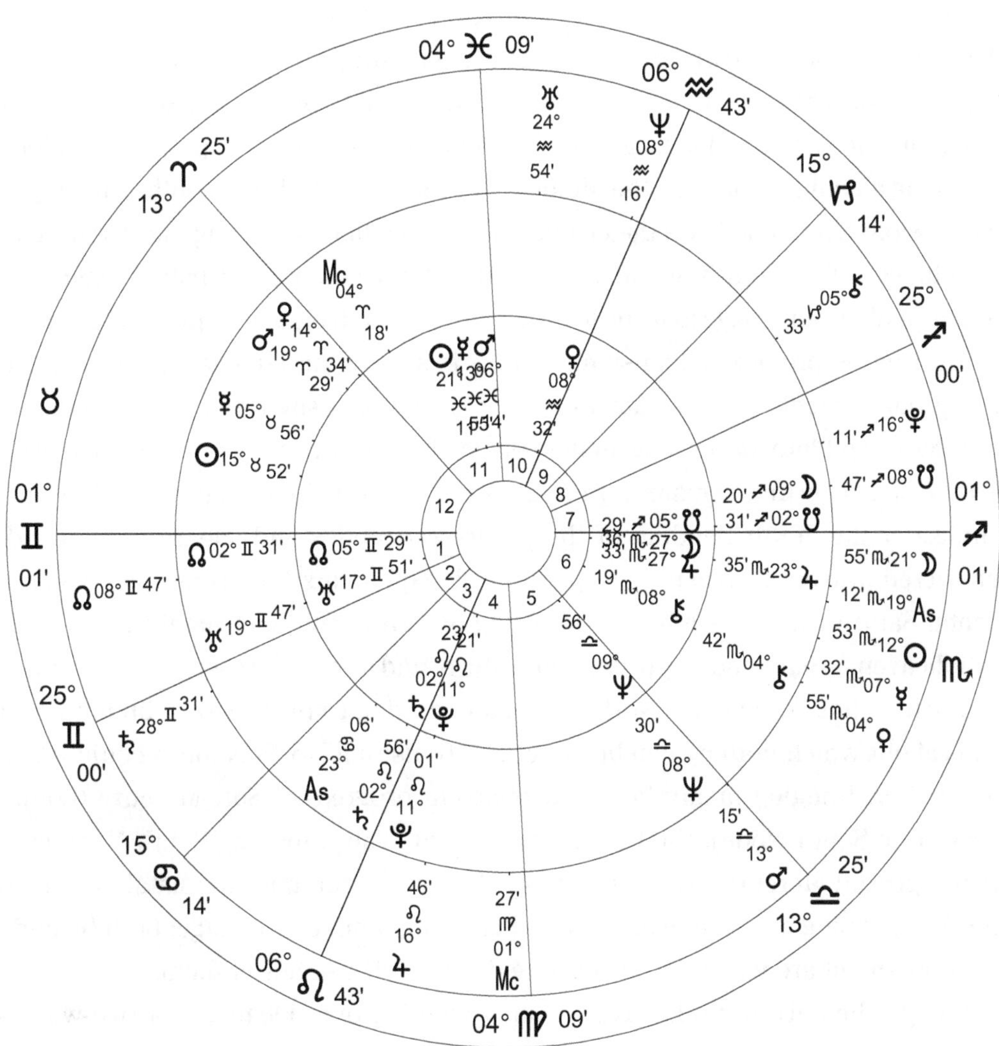

Chart 80:

Romney's Gubernatorial Win, Nov. 5, 2002, Boston, MA, 7:00 a.m. EST

On election day (Chart 81), Romney's progressed Moon is trine natal Pluto, suggesting his empowerment. However, the aspect is separating, an indication the influence is waning. The progressed Moon is also opposite natal Neptune and transiting Venus, bringing him close, yet as far away from a dream as possible. The progressed Moon is approaching a conjunction with the Midheaven (occurring in three months), highlighting the profession. Even if he loses the election, the race will be advantageous for his career and public visibility. Transiting Jupiter is in the 1st house conjunct natal Uranus which rules the Midheaven, suggestive of luck. However, a retrograde Jupiter often delivers less than what is promised. Transiting Uranus is sextile the Midheaven which it rules, also auguring for luck, but the planet of upset is also opposite progressed Neptune and square transiting Pluto, describing an unexpected battle with no clear path to victory.

Other disconcerting transits reflect a let-down. Transiting Neptune is late in the 10th house at the South Bending of the progressed nodes and square the Ascendant (unanswered prayers). Transiting Neptune is also quincunx the progressed Ascendant and natal Saturn (hopeless effort). Transiting Saturn is conjunct natal Chiron, square the Midheaven, square both progressed Saturn and the progressed Ascendant, and quincunx the natal Ascendant/ North Node, all pointing to professional limitations and wounds about which nothing can be done. The transiting North Node is conjunct natal Moon–Jupiter, bringing family help, but opposite progressed Sun–Mercury (conjunct the transiting South Node), the help is insufficient. The transiting South Node is conjunct progressed Mercury, while transiting Mercury is conjunct the natal South Node (in the 7th), forming a double-whammy and carrying a mixed message: both he and his primary opponent are weak. The electorate does not like either of them.

Although the current polls have Romney winning over Obama in a two-way race (statistically they are even), when considering the progressions and transits on election day, Obama appears stronger than Romney. As transpired eighteen years previously, if Romney is running in this race, he will likely lose. Does this mean a win for Obama? Possibly, since the President appears to benefit more from the eclipse and nodal placements. However, the activation of Romney's chart suggests that his opponent is also weak. Still, someone has to win. It is possible there is a third-party candidate in a three-way race, or that Romney is not the candidate and there is another Republican hopeful in the ring.

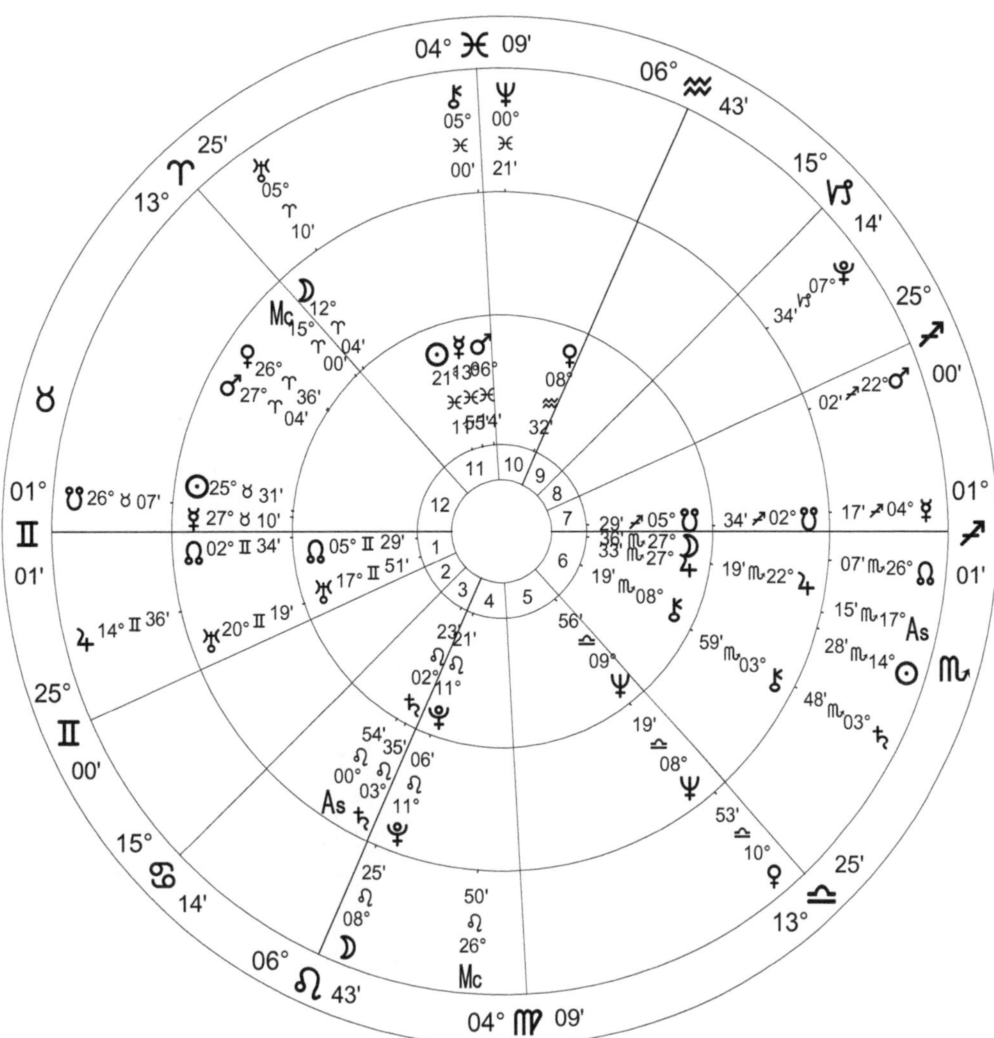

Chart 81:

Romney and 2012, Nov. 6, 2012, Washington D.C., 7:00 a.m. EST

Ignorance has always been the weapon of tyrants; enlightenment the salvation of the free.

— *Bill Richardson*

Chapter 21
Hero or Villain
Julian Assange

Julian Assange is the founder of WikiLeaks, envisioned as an intelligence agency for the people. Wikileaks is an internet site that accepts secret and restricted information and releases it into the public domain. Its mission is to "allow whistleblowers and journalists who have been censored to get material out to the public." Committed to freedom of information and protecting sources, WikiLeaks has obtained—and leaked—hundreds of thousands of confidential documents. In numerous instances, the documents contradict an official government line, and according to an editorial in *The Guardian*, they have "revealed wrong-doing, war crimes, corruption, hypocrisy, greed, espionage, double dealings, and the cynical exercise of power on a wondrous scale." Wikileaks has also published documents protected by court-ordered injunctions (gag orders that prevent the press from reporting on an ongoing court case), as well as super injunctions (which prevent the press from reporting on an injunction and the fact they have been gagged).

Raised by a single mother, Assange grew up a nomad in Australia. With his mother on the run, he had lived in fifty different towns and attended thirty different schools by the time he was fourteen. Highly intelligent, he taught himself computer programming, and at sixteen became a computer hacker. He lived by a hacker's code, taking care not to damage any computer, nor change any information on any computing site he breached. He has been called 'Australia's most ethical computer hacker.' He was arrested for hacking when he was twenty, but let off with a fine. He attended six universities, studying math and physics, but he never graduated. He had a son at eighteen, and when his relationship with the mother soured, he spent ten unsuccessful years fighting for custody. During that time he fought the restriction of child custody documents, and developed an intense dislike of censorship. His goal for Wikileaks is to force governments and corporations to be accountable through the threat of exposing unethical, criminal, and corrupt wrong-doing. He is currently under house arrest and wanted for questioning in Sweden for sex crimes. He has called the accusations politically motivated.

Nativity

Assange was born (Chart 82) born during a rare Jupiter–Neptune conjunction that was opposite Saturn and sextile Pluto. The opposition aligned with his Ascendant–Descendant axis, making the rare configuration personal. The aspect describes his search for truth (Jupiter) in a web of deceit (Neptune), and the revealing of secrets (Pluto) of those in authority (Saturn). In declination, Jupiter and Neptune are parallel (also parallel the Moon and Mars), all contraparallel Saturn, indicating authoritative opposition to his personal battle to expose the truth. Pluto is parallel the South Node, an indication of trouble from tyrants, as well as secrets disclosed in service.

There was a solar eclipse three weeks after his birth at 28°55' Cancer that fell in his 9th house and promised expansion of the house related to higher education, long distance travel, and a quest for truth. The eclipse was in the same house as the South Node, but in a different sign.

The Sun is in Cancer, giving a sensitive, emotional nature that is concerned with the home, which in his case assumed a broader meaning—home on earth. The Sun is

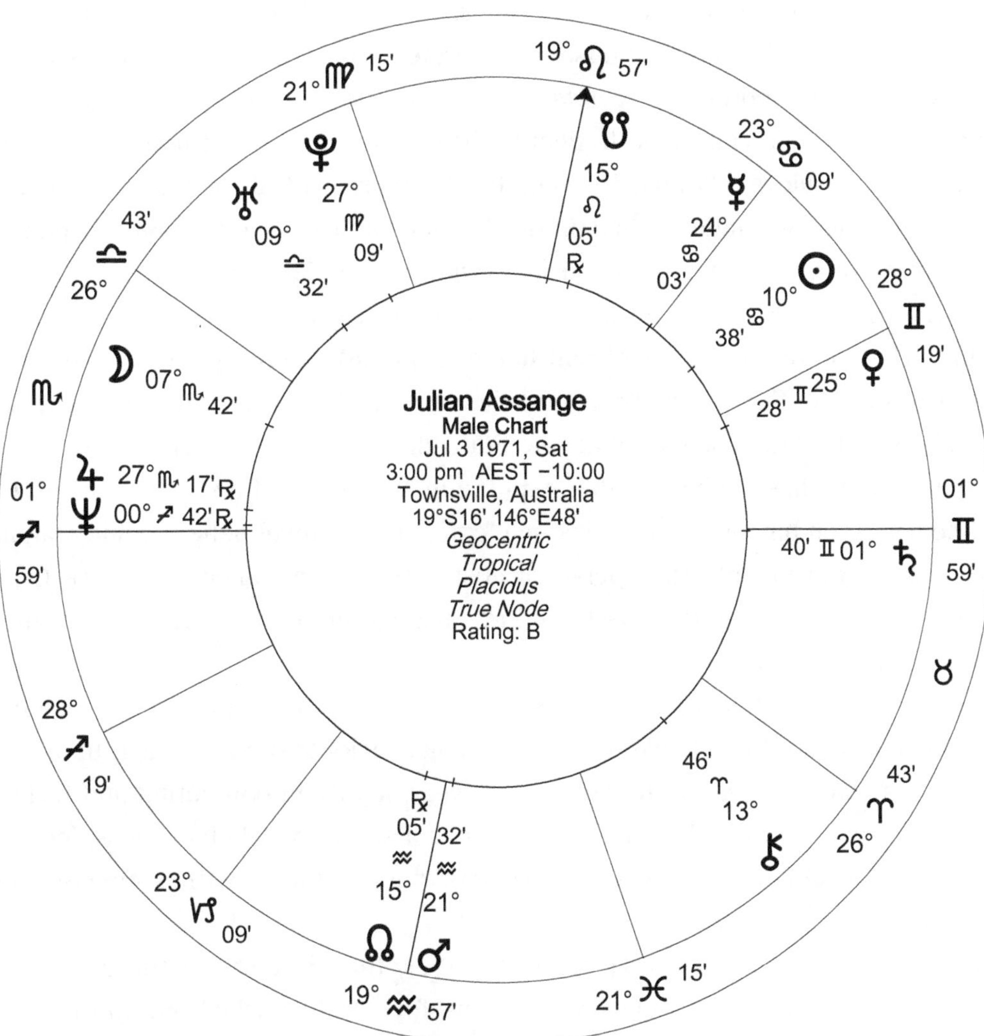

Chart 82:

Julian Assange Nativity

in the 8th house, alluding to an interest in unearthing what is hidden and buried, as well as in sex. The Sun rules the 10th house of the profession and his work involves publicizing government and corporate secrets. The Sun is trine the Moon in Scorpio, adding emotional intensity, a willingness to fight to the death, and a preoccupation with getting to the bottom of things. With the Moon in the 12th, there is idealism, but also a tendency to bring about his own undoing. In latitude, the Moon at 5S09 is at the South Bending. He grew up without a home and has had trouble with the law (Moon ruling the 9th).

As the ruler of the South Node, the Sun in Cancer is associated with vulnerability and loss. He did not have a permanent home as a child, did not grow up with his real father (loss of the Sun), and the courts denied him the right to behave as a father himself (loss of child custody). With the Sun ruling the 10th, he has had professional problems, and he has a tainted public reputation as a result of a sexual scandal. However, he has given himself away in service, compelling ethical behavior and standards from those in power—at grave personal cost. The Sun in Cancer is square Uranus, which shows a life of sudden upsets and an unstable home life (Uranus rules the 4th, Cancer's natural house).

Uranus rules the North Node and is associated with accomplishment, ease of expression, and innate knowledge. In Libra, Uranus seeks fairness through unorthodox means. This placement gives intellectual prowess, ability in computing and technology, unique and forward looking ideas, as well as a streak of rebelliousness, independence, and a dislike of authority. It also describes a talent with software, online interfacing, and computing.

With the two nodal rulers square each other, the difficulty of the aspect is increased. The weakened Sun causes problems for Uranus, which compromises the strength of the North Node ruler. However, over time, he combined his computing know-how with a life purpose to unearth the secrets of those in power.

Sagittarius and its ruler, Jupiter, are rising, denoting a seeker of truth. Jupiter is in Scorpio, describing his predilection for unearthing and disclosing secrets. Placed in the 12th house of the unknown, hidden enemies, and confinement, these activities have caused self-undoing. Jupiter is conjunct Neptune which adds an element of idealism, a message repeated with Neptune's domicile in Jupiter's sign. He believes full disclosure and transparency are best for everyone. However, those with the power to keep secrets do not appreciate this exposure, as reflected by Saturn's opposition to Jupiter and Neptune. He has made formidable enemies of those in authority who prefer to keep their secrets private (dignified Saturn on the angle trine Pluto).

Jupiter is sextile Pluto its ruler, and trine Mercury, which is sextile Pluto, forming a triangle that confers investigative prowess. He used his expertise to uncover secrets, which he then publishes. There is intensive reiteration in this triangle. Jupiter is in Scorpio, mimicking the Jupiter–Pluto sextile. Mercury rules the 8th house, which is Pluto's natural house. Pluto is in Mercury's sign and rules Jupiter. The repetition reinforces the symbolism of a determined and focused goal to publish untoward information that has been hidden.

Mars is conjunct the 4th house cusp, and at the core of his being he is a fighter. Trine Venus on the cusp of the 8th, he loves to expose secrets, which has been his undoing (Venus ruling the 12th). There have also been problems from women through sexual escapades.

Wikileaks

The birth chart for WikiLeaks is October 4, 2006, the day the internet domain was registered (Chart 83) and Assange launched his business. The preceding south nodal solar eclipse was on September 22, 2006, at 29°20' Virgo, conjunct natal and progressed Pluto, with Mercury in Scorpio serving as the lord.

The dominating configuration of the day was a transiting t-square composed of Jupiter (truth) square Neptune (deceit) and Saturn (authority). These are the same three planets aligned across Assange's horizon, and in the event chart straddled his Midheaven (Saturn) and IC (Neptune). Transiting Neptune was also conjunct his natal Aquarian North Node, progressed Mars and progressed Moon, reflecting his actions to use the internet to acquire and dispense state secrets.

The progressed Sun was conjunct the progressed South Node, indicating personal sacrifice. The transiting South Node was conjunct the progressed Midheaven, which was closing in on a conjunction to natal Pluto, describing a profession dedicated to revealing the secrets of those in power. With transiting Uranus trine the natal Sun (the two planets in natal square now coming together in easy aspect), he

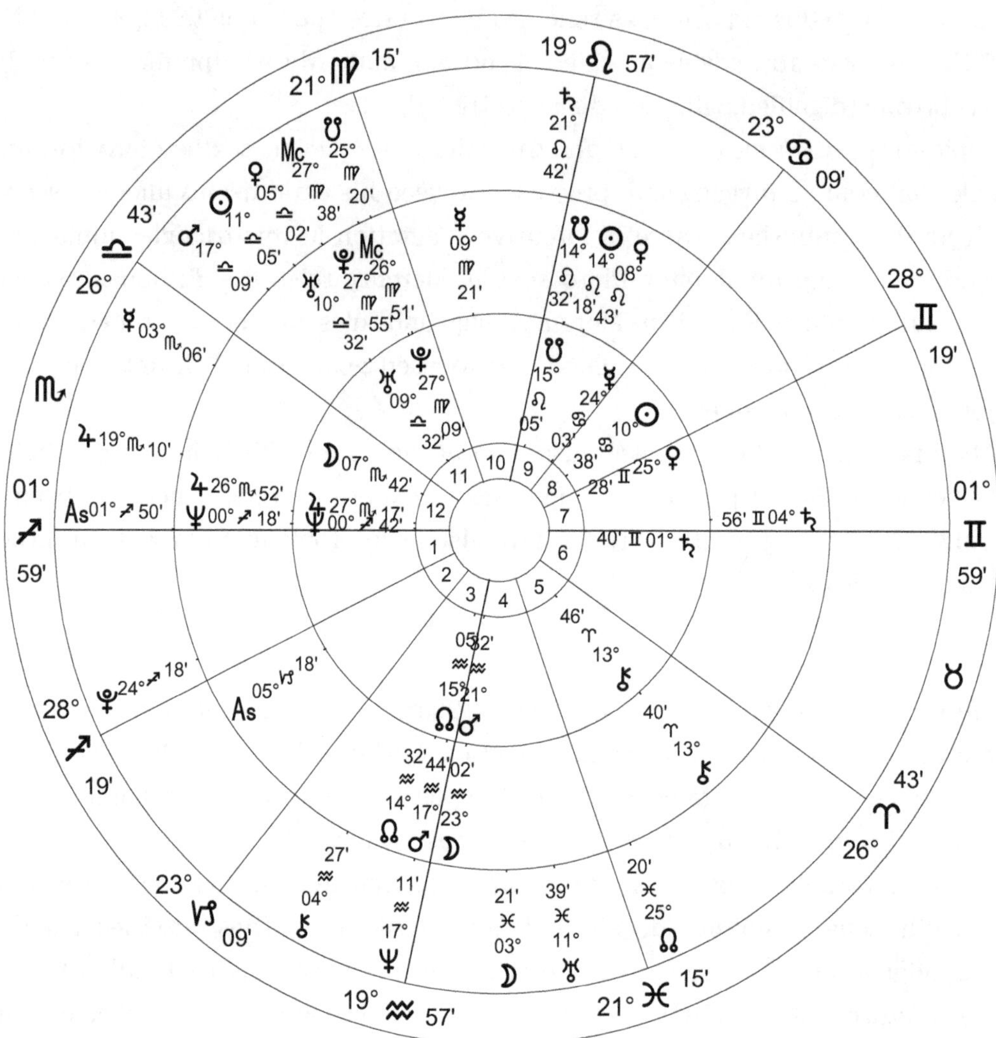

Chart 83:

Assange and Wikileaks, Oct. 4, 2006, London, England, noon

employed his computer skills in his life purpose. The transiting North Node formed a grand trine with natal Jupiter and natal Mercury, portending success in his quest for accountability.

Transiting Mars in Libra was sextile/trine the transiting Saturn–Neptune opposition, and trine progressed Mars, signifying a fight for fairness and a disclosure of lies and deception (Neptune) considered the right of kings (Saturn in Leo). There was a transiting Saturn–Pluto trine (repeating a wide out-of-sign trine in Assange's natal chart), suggesting an easy flow of secret information from those in high places. With transiting Pluto at the South Bending (leaking of secrets) of the transiting nodes, opposite natal Venus at the North Bending, the work began (Venus on the cusp of the 8th ruling the intercepted 6th).

Kenya Corruption Report

In 2002, the President of Kenya, Daniel Moi, retired after twenty-four years in office. He was long viewed as ruling one of the most corrupt governments in the world. He had backed the son of Kenya's first president as his successor, but Mwai Kibaki, running on an anti-corruption platform, won the election.

In 2003, President Kibaki fulfilled his campaign promise and commissioned an inquiry into the massive theft (estimated between $1.6–4.0 billion dollars) perpetrated by Moi and other former high government officials. The inquiry was to be the first step in recovering the stolen money and bringing it back for the people to whom it belongs.

The report was concluded and given to the government in 2004. Calling it 'incomplete, inaccurate and based on a lot of hearsay,' President Kibaki chose to ignore it. He made no attempt to repatriate the stolen wealth or prosecute anyone in Moi's regime. On August 28, 2007, four months before he was up for re-election, Moi publicly supported Kibaki's re-election. Three days later, Wikileaks published the secret document. The Kroll report revealed in detail the startling greed of Moi, his family, and his administration. Despite the leaked report making Kenyan and British headline news, Kibaki was elected for a second term.

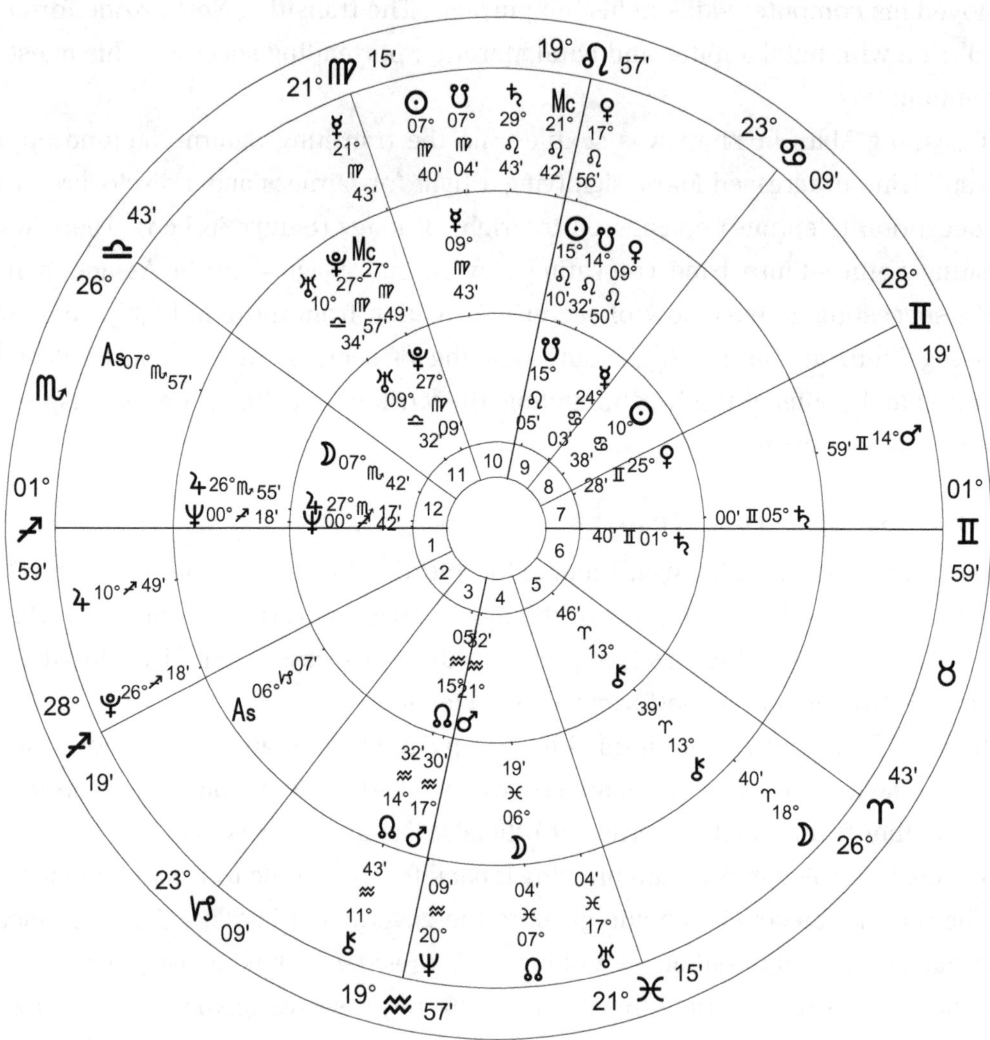

Chart 84:

Assange Kenya Corruption, Aug. 31, 2007, London, England, noon

The Kroll report was released on August 31, 2007 (Chart 84), ten days before the September 11, 2007, solar eclipse at 18°24' Virgo, which fell in Assange's 10th house, opposite transiting Uranus. The south nodal eclipse was ruled by Mercury (news).

On the day of the leak, transiting Saturn had formed a t-square with the natal opposition of Jupiter, Neptune and Saturn, reflecting the action taken against Kenyan authorities in the pursuit of truth. The progressed Midheaven was in partile conjunction with natal and progressed Pluto and sextile natal Jupiter, timing the expression of the natal aspect. Transiting Pluto was square progressed Pluto–Midheaven, activating the conjunction and suggesting a stressful response to the release.

The transiting North Node was conjunct the progressed Moon and in a grand trine with the natal Moon and natal Sun, suggesting that Assange felt he was taking the high road and doing the right thing. The progressed Sun was conjunct the natal South Node and transiting Venus, describing his work as a service that brought satisfaction. However, the transiting South Node was conjunct the transiting Sun and progressed Mercury, and the Kibaki regime dismissed the report. Transiting Jupiter was at the South Bending of the transiting nodes, denoting a loss of truth, or truth that carries no weight. Transiting Uranus was square transiting Mars (battle for liberation) and formed an inconjunct with the progressed Sun, natal South Node, transiting Venus, and an opposition with transiting Mercury, reflecting the risky but ineffectual action regarding news of stolen wealth that made no impact and brought no effective change.

War

For three-and-a-half-years, Wikileaks worked steadily to release confidential documents. The site made available secret and expensive Scientology manuals, published an order of a Somali opposition leader calling for the assassination of government officials, leaked Sarah Palin's private emails, and exposed the emails of scientists who questioned global warming. However, it was not until the release of the video *Collateral Murder* that Wikileaks caught the rapt attention of the U.S. government, and came into prominence.

The disturbing video was uploaded on April 4, 2010 (Chart 85), and showed a trigger-happy U.S. helicopter mission in Iraq where soldiers gunned down eleven civilians,

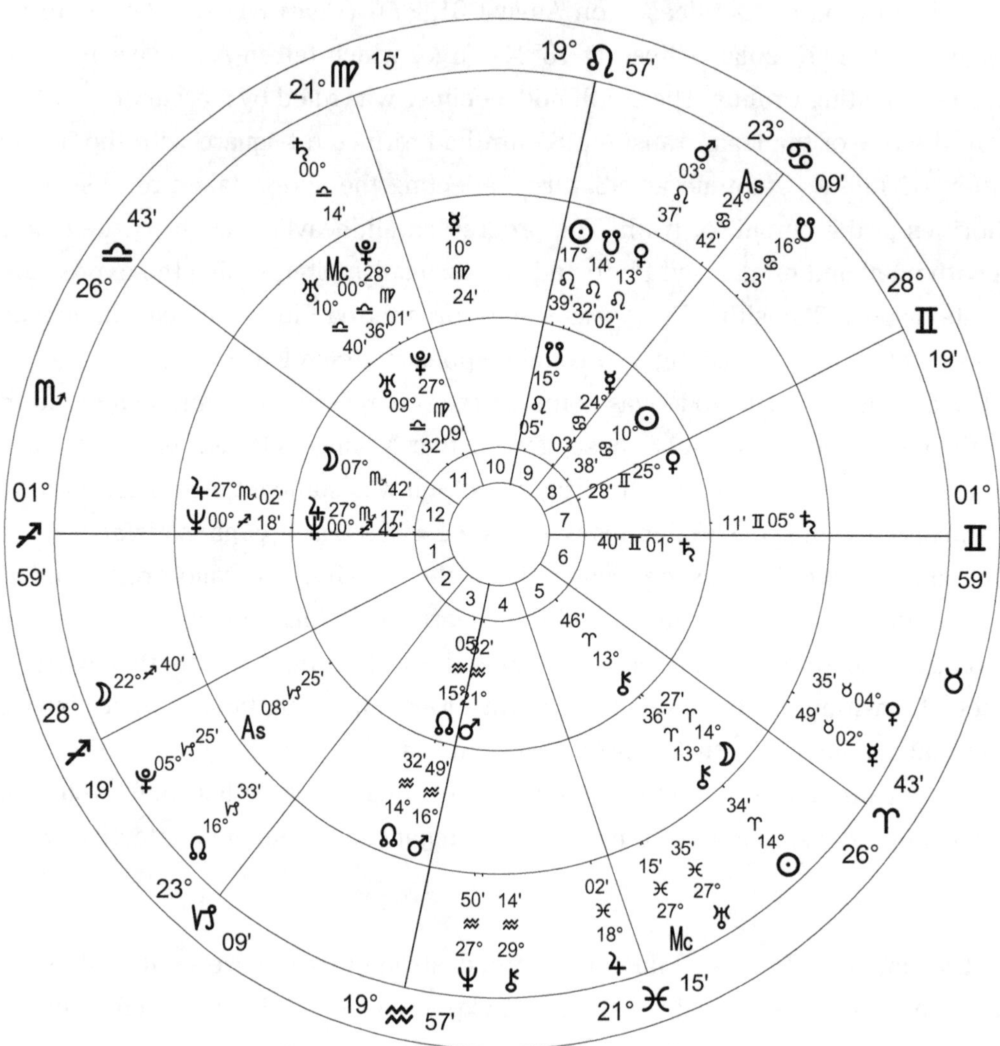

Chart 85:
Assange's War, April 4, 2010, London, England, noon

including two Reuters journalists. The U.S. military had labeled the attack as 'combat operations against a hostile force.' For months Reuters had been requesting the video footage, which the military had refused to release. Wikileaks did so.

There was a north nodal solar eclipse at 25°1' Capricorn on January 15, 2010, with Saturn serving as the lord. The eclipse fell on the cusp of Assange's third house of news. On the day of the release, transiting Saturn was at the Libra' Aries Point conjunct Assange's progressed Midheaven–Pluto, reflecting his public action taken to expose murderous military secrets to the world. Transiting Neptune was quincunx progressed Midheaven–Pluto and transiting Saturn, an indication the government could do nothing to prevent the release. Transiting Uranus was opposite progressed Midheaven–Pluto and transiting Saturn, and the release took them by surprise. The transiting Sun was at the North Bending of the transiting nodes conjunct progressed Moon–Chiron, suggesting Assange's indignation over the shooting. Transiting Pluto formed a yod with the natal Moon and progressed Saturn, describing Assange's outrage there was no pressure on the military to investigate the incident. However, with the progressed Sun opposite progressed Mars, his actions, once again, brought no effect.

In response, during the summer, Wikileaks began dumping documents in earnest. On July 25, 2010, it released 90,000 documents called the *Afghan War Diaries*, which indicated the war was not going as well as people had been told.

A Sex Scandal

In August 2010, Assange traveled to Sweden to attend a meeting on war and the media. During his visit, he had sex with two women who later accused him of rape. He called the sex consensual. The south nodal solar eclipse before the event was on July 11, 2010 at 19°23' Cancer. The eclipse fell in his 8th house, with the Moon serving as the lord.

On the night he arrived in Stockholm and had sex with his host (Chart 86), there was an applying conjunction between progressed Venus and the progressed South Node, portending loss through women. The aspect was activated by a sextile from the transiting Moon (lord), which formed a grand cross and was square the transiting nodes at the South Bending and opposite natal Chiron at the North Bending, implying a stuck situation, loss from women, and a manifest wound.

There was a transiting mundane t-square on the world axis that involved Jupiter and Uranus near 0° Aries, Saturn at 2° Libra, and Pluto at 3° Capricorn. The t-square aligned with Assange's natal Jupiter, Neptune and Saturn opposition, suggesting that he became an easy target for the authorities (transiting Jupiter–Uranus sextile/trine natal Jupiter–Neptune and Saturn, and transiting Saturn sextile/trine natal Jupiter–Neptune and Saturn). Transiting Pluto was quincunx natal Saturn, and sexual antics left him indefensible in the face of determined authorities. With transiting Jupiter–Uranus conjunct his progressed IC, unexpected issues with the law brought his downfall. Transiting Venus was conjunct Mars and both were conjunct natal Uranus (at the South Bending of the transiting nodes), and there was diminishment through unusual, sudden, or unexpected (Uranus) sex (Venus–Mars) that affected his life's mission and compromised his stature (all square natal Sun conjunct the transiting South Node, portending loss for the self).

Arrest

Two weeks after the two sexual encounters, Assange was questioned by police, and allowed to leave the country. He returned to the U.K. In September, the case was reopened in Sweden and Assange was wanted for questioning. He called the accusations politically motivated and a smear campaign designed to stifle WikiLeaks. He continued working. On October 22, 2010, the first of 392,000 classified documents on the Iraq War were released. The following month, 250,000 diplomatic cables were uploaded. Now, embarrassed governments around the world were furious. In a fit of hypocrisy, President Obama's press secretary said, "Such disclosures put at risk our diplomats, intelligence professionals, and people around the world who come to the U.S. for assistance in promoting democracy and open government."

Assange was labeled a criminal, a spy, and a terrorist. There were calls for his arrest and execution. The Department of Homeland Security requested Amazon cease hosting Wikileaks, and Amazon complied. Government pressure on PayPal led to the closing of the Wikileaks account. MasterCard and Visa ceased doing business with him, effectively blocking all donations. In protest, supporters of Assange retaliated and temporarily crashed the online sites of the three banks. Meanwhile, Congress investigated

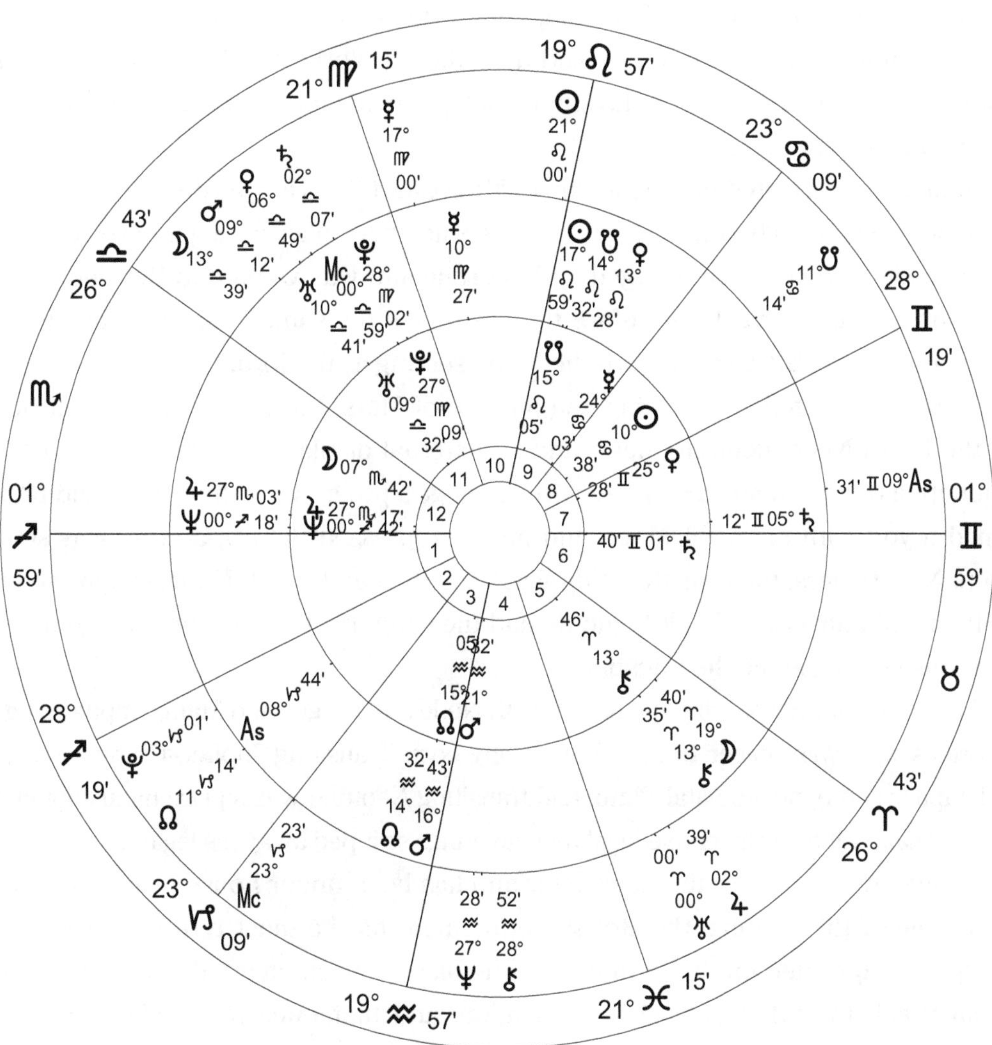

Chart 86:

Assange's Sex Scandal, Aug. 13, 2010, Stockholm, Sweden, 11:00 p.m.

ways to charge him under the Espionage Act. The law had been passed during World War I to suppress antiwar activists, and used during World War II to control criticism against the war. In principle, the law limits any political activity the government deems 'a clear and present danger.'

Assange was arrested on December 7, 2010 (Chart 87). He was denied bail and sent to prison, even though British legal experts said there was no legal case to confine him, since he had not been charged with a crime and was wanted in Sweden only for questioning. The solar eclipse before the event was the same eclipse of the summer, and occurred at 19°23' Cancer, with the Moon serving as the lord.

There was a running transiting conjunction of Mars, Pluto, Mercury, Moon (lord), and the North Node, denoting news and an external display of might and power. The conjuncting transits made a t-square with Assange's progressed Midheaven and IC, and formed a yod with his natal Moon and natal–progressed Saturn, and he was sent to prison. Nonetheless, the transiting Sun was trine the natal South Node, progressed Sun and the natal Midheaven (wide), and he had the support of many who came out to the courthouse to denounce the injustice.

Transiting Saturn was trine the natal North Node and progressed Mars, empowering the authorities who were eager to stop him at any cost. Transiting Jupiter–Uranus was trine natal Jupiter and opposite natal Pluto, and transiting Neptune was square natal Jupiter and quincunx natal Pluto, as inventive legal maneuverings stripped away his legal rights.

Assange was released nine days later and has been under house arrest ever since. At the time of this writing, the British court ruled that he must return to Stockholm. Assange has appealed on the grounds that he has not been charged with a crime, that he can speak to authorities while in London, and that once in Sweden he may be turned over to the U.S. on espionage charges.

Rather than address the incriminating information Wikileaks disclosed, the U.S. government has gone after the whistle-blower. The First Amendment of the U.S. Constitution protects freedom of expression from governmental influence and constraint. The general public (not only journalists) have the right to free speech and are protected by law against censure and punishment. Instead of addressing criminal behavior, the government has sought to make the *revelation* of criminal behavior illegal, using the law to protect liars and lies, and making the disclosure of truth an imprisonable offense.

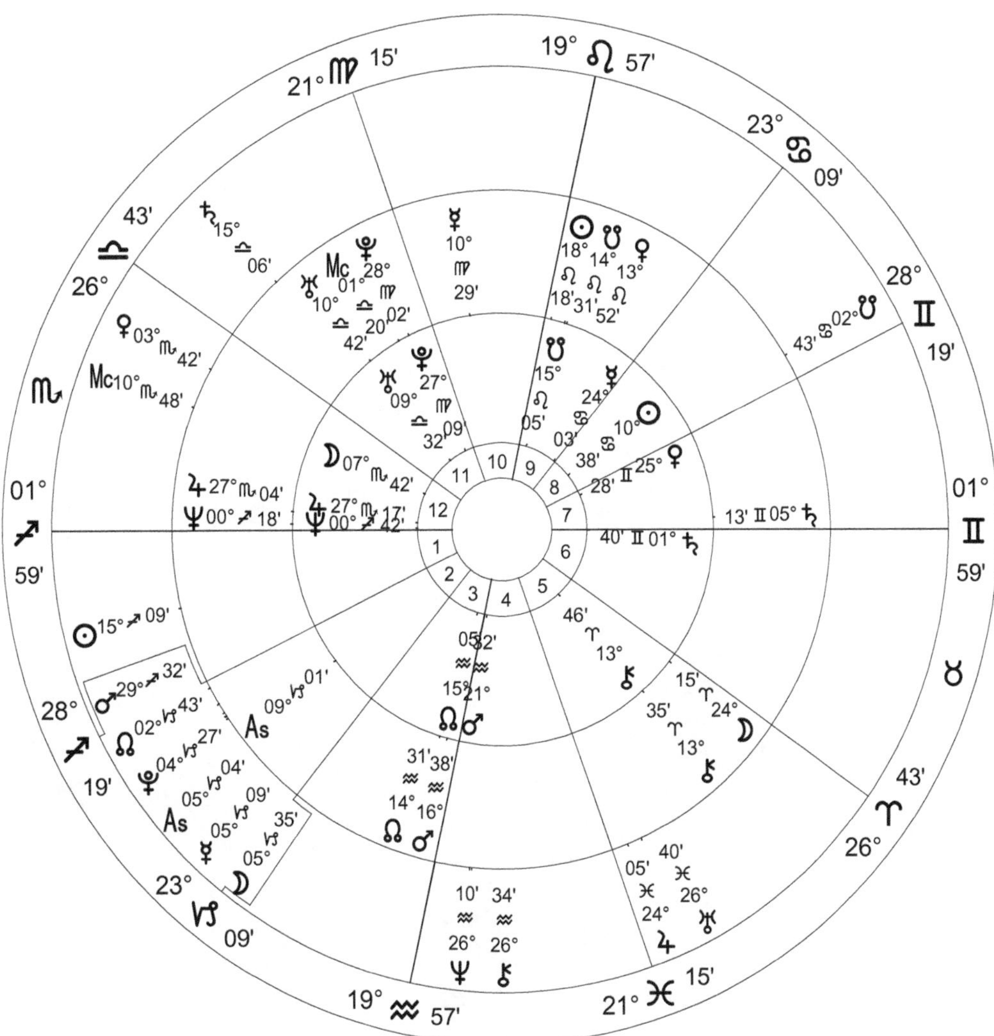

Chart 87:

Assange's Arrest, Dec. 7, 2010, London, England, 9:30 a.m. UT

Find a place inside where there's joy, and the joy will burn out the pain.

—Joseph Campbell

Chapter 22
U.S. Psyche

On July 2, 1776, in Philadelphia, the Continental Congress voted for the country's independence from Britain and outlined their reasons in the Declaration of Independence. The document did not create a government, but rather stated the role of a government that must answer to its people. It established the right to life, liberty, and the pursuit of happiness. The document was based on the Philosophy of Enlightenment, which acknowledged the preeminence of reason and science over superstition and challenged the divine rule of kings and clergy.

On July 4, 1776, the wording of the Declaration of Independence was agreed upon and the document was signed. Charts have been set on this date for near midnight, mid-morning, early afternoon and late afternoon. While there is a lively debate concerning which U.S. chart is most accurate, I use Ebenezer Sibly's chart set for 5.10 p.m. because it seems to work (Chart 88). According to Nicholas Campion, the chart is based on the Sun's June 1776 Cancer Ingress set for London, England. The Sibly chart uses the angles from the ingress and the positions of the planets at noon in Philadelphia on July 4, 1776.

Nativity

The solar eclipse related to the signing of the declaration was on July 15, 1776, at 23°32' Cancer. The eclipse fell in the 8th house (birth) conjunct the U.S. Mercury (written document). It was a north nodal eclipse, with the U.S. North Node (stationary) in Leo.

Sagittarius is rising, with Jupiter ruling the chart, reflecting the guiding philosophical principles of the document. Jupiter in Cancer alludes to a homeland ruled by ethics and reason. Jupiter is conjunct and parallel Venus, describing the 'pursuit of happiness.' The declaration outlines the American dream, and the hope of a better future and financial prosperity. Jupiter is in the 7th, along with Venus, Sun and Mars. According to Rex Bills, the 7th house rules agreements and dealing with the public, and the document was an agreement regarding the rights of patriots. To the early settlers, America was seen as a country where there was no religious persecution, behavior was guided by high ideals, and people could live together in peace.

There is a four-planet Cancer stellium. The Sun is in Cancer, pertaining to the goals of emotional serenity, security of home and family, and freedom from repression (square Saturn). At the time of independence, America was at war with the British who had closed the Boston Harbor and were taxing the settlers and giving nothing in return (taxation without representation). The Sun is conjunct the 8th house of birth, death, war, taxes, big money, sex, inner growth, and psychological healing. However, it is also the house of superstition and the occult, and the Sun posited here does not attest to a country solely under the dominion of reason and science. Interest in the occult lives on, but is underground (Sun hidden in a succedent house). The Sun rules the 9th, reflecting the country's philosophic principles, interest in religion, higher education, tolerance for foreigners, and proclivity for long distance travel. The country was to be guided by the rule of law rather than the will of a distant king.

The Sun rules the North Node and is empowered by the association. Since the Sun represents leaders in a mundane chart, the founding fathers were wise, practical, and successful. As a symbol of the life force of the country in general, this association bestows strong purpose, physical output, and manifest results. There is an inborn knowledge of what must be accomplished to achieve outward success.

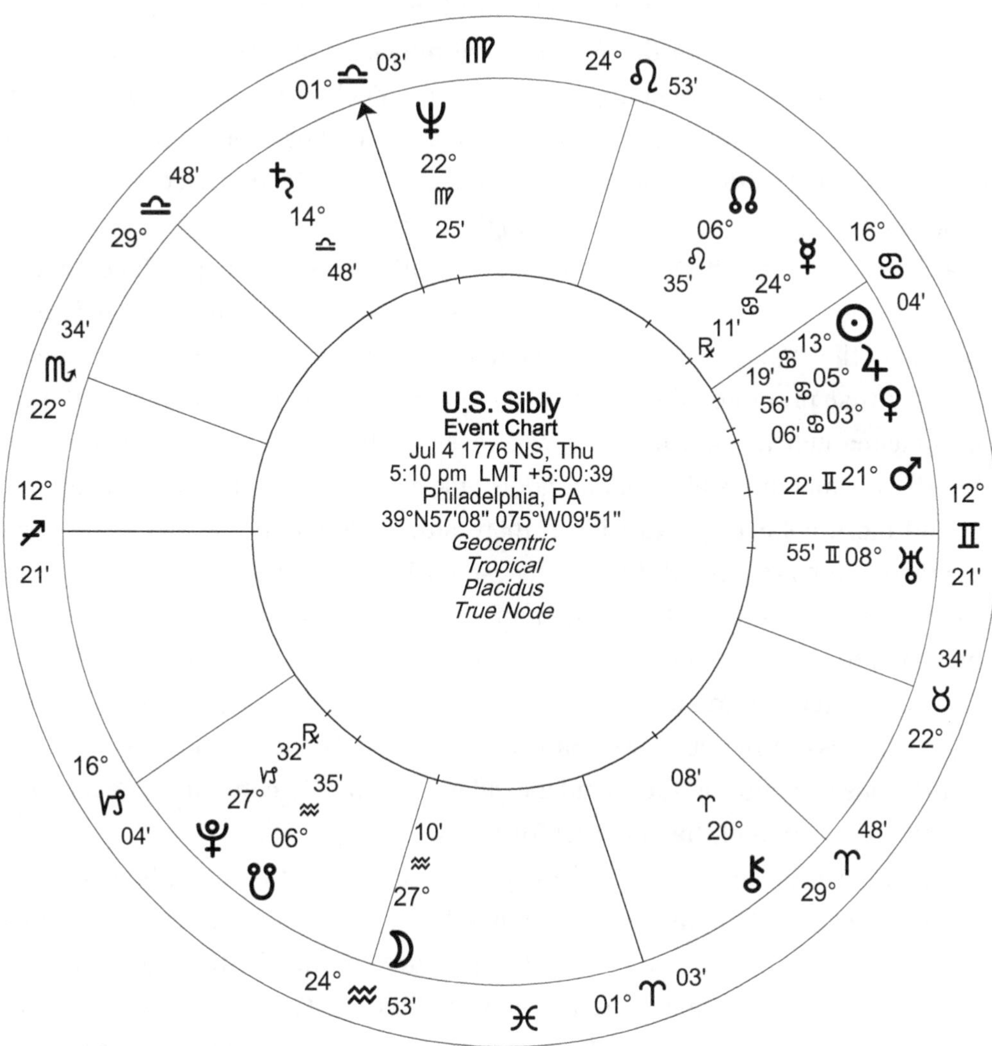

Chart 88:

U.S. Nativity

The Moon represents the emotional tenor of the country. In Aquarius in the 3rd, the settlers were concerned with the fundamental humanitarian values of independence, equality, and freedom, as eloquently outlined in the declaration. The 3rd house is related to news, communication, early education, cars, neighbors, and short-term travel—all interests of the American public. The Moon rules the 8th, adding emotional interest in the occult, big money, war, and psychological growth.

Uranus rules the South Node, alluding to problems with independence and freedom, as was the case and the reason the colonies were at war with Britain. Uranus in Gemini ruling the 3rd, also describes a document containing the guiding principles of a free society that promotes the greatest good for all people. Nonetheless, the south nodal influence indicates an inherent weakness of the Uranus principles of freedom and liberty. Uranus in Gemini talks a good talk, but the sign is flighty, at times two-faced, and more concerned with ideas than action. Freedom and democracy sound good in theory, but are difficult to actually establish and maintain.

The country's wealth is shown by the 2nd house. Capricorn on the cusp indicates money generated from business. Pluto in the 2nd describes big money made by corporations. An exalted Saturn in Libra rules the 2nd from the 10th, a placement which shows the success of big business (Saturn), and the influence of business on government (10th house). Venus as the mundane ruler of money is conjunct an exalted Jupiter, a further indication of the potential for wealth expansion.

There are five close longitudinal planetary aspects in the chart that denote the country's interests and character. The Venus–Jupiter conjunction describes a love of sport, entertainment, family, and romance. Mercury sextile Neptune gives a belief in dreams and idealistic thinking. Mercury opposite Pluto suggests the power to suppress free speech and information. Mars (armed forces) square Neptune indicates confused aggression, delusion in battle (especially when defending homeland) a police force of the universe, and a fight for religious faith (Neptune in the 9th). The Sun is square Saturn, reflecting leadership beholden to big business and financial interests. In his book *Time and Money*, Robert Gover equates these last two aspects with economic declines. He found that the activation of the Sun–Saturn square is related to financial depressions (downturn in business), while the Mars–Neptune square is related to stock market panics (Mars rules the 5th house of speculation and Neptune rules irrationality).

In latitude, Venus, Jupiter, and Uranus are near the center line of the ecliptic and parallel the Sun, angles, and nodes, suggesting luck, wealth, scientific innovation, liberty, happiness and freedom, as described in the founding vision.

A Defining Moment

On the morning of September 11, 2001, four planes with nineteen hijackers on a suicide mission flew into the World Trade Center, the Pentagon, and a Pennsylvania field, killing nearly three thousand people. Blamed on Saudi Arabian national Osama bin Laden and his terrorist organization al-Qaeda, the attacks were used to justify the wars in Afghanistan and Iraq. Closer to home, the 'war on terror' led to the passage of the Patriot Act, which legalized domestic surveillance, kidnapping, indefinite detention, and torture of American citizens. The behemoth Department of Homeland Security also came into being and was recently used to shut down Occupy Wall Street protests.

As I write this on the tenth year anniversary of the attack, there are more questions than answers about what happened that late summer day. While the mainstream media labels those who question the official account of 9/11 as irrational conspiracy theorists, about one half of the adult population in the U.S. believes the government has not told the truth about 9/11. In this next section, I digress (to remain silent on this matter, is to me immoral) and summarize some of the inconvenient facts of 9/11. The information is personally unverified, but derived from reputable sources (see references for relevant websites). My interest lies in the underlying story, motivation, and consequences of the attack, as shown by the event astrology.

Hours after two commercial planes struck the World Trade Center's North Tower (Building 1) and the South Tower (Building 2), both buildings lay in ruins. Later that afternoon, at 5:21 p.m., Building 7 collapsed, in what appeared to be a controlled demolition. However, at 4.54 p.m., twenty-six minutes *before* it fell, a BBC reporter standing in front of the building, reported that it had collapsed. Building 7 housed a CIA office on an undisclosed floor.

Engineers and scientists who studied the smoldering remains claim steel could not melt at the temperature that jet fuel burns. During the cleanup, instead of rigorously testing the steel, it was quickly sold and shipped out of the country. Chemical traces of explosives were found, leading to the suggestion that the buildings were blown up after the planes detonated laid explosives.

In the South Tower on the weekend prior to 9/11, there was a cable upgrade necessitating a thirty-six hour power-down in the building. On 9/11, minutes after the first plane struck, workers in Buildings 6 and 7 were evacuated, while those in the North and South towers were assured there was no danger and encouraged to keep working.

At the Pentagon, there was no evidence of a downed 747, and the hole in the façade of the newly constructed wing was too narrow to have been made by a large plane. According to a CNN reporter on the scene, "From my close up inspection, there's no evidence of a plane having crashed anywhere near the Pentagon." The previous day, the Secretary of Defense, Donald Rumsfeld, announced $2.3 trillion from the military budget was missing and could not be accounted for. The computers that could have tracked the money were housed in the portion of the Pentagon that was destroyed on 9/11. There were back-up files in Building 7 at the World Trade Center, but these were ruined when the structure collapsed. The missing trillions were not mentioned again.

An estimated sixteen million dollars was made in the stock market on 9/11 by speculators who placed bets that the stock prices of American Airlines, United, and other aviation related companies would fall. The week before 9/11, an incoming executive director of the CIA placed put options on aviation stocks and profited handsomely when the stock prices declined.

Following 9/11, a German company helped businesses housed in Buildings 1 and II to restore data on damaged hard drives. Information on thirty-two drives was recovered that suggested insider trading. In the early morning hours before the attack, suspicious transactions were made that resulted in a profit of over one hundred million dollars. This raised the suspicion that insiders with advance knowledge of the attack had made trades, and assumed the records would be lost. The FBI's response was that no computer hard drive could have survived the attack. Nonetheless, the possibility of insider trading prompted investigations both inside and outside the country. However, the reports were deemed too sensitive for the American public.

Due to pressure from the families of those who died, the government established a twelve member 9/11 commission. Although the government was in essence investigating itself, the White House was seen as uncooperative. It delayed the release of documents requested by the commission, while at the same time pushed the committee to publish its findings quickly. The President and Vice-President agreed to be interviewed, but refused to do so under oath. They insisted they be questioned together, but only off the record, and with no tape-recording of the proceeding.

After the commission report was published, panel members complained that what they had been told was 'far from the truth.' Senator Max Cleland resigned from the panel, saying, "It's a national scandal." Commissioner co-Chair Lee Hamilton said, "I don't believe for a moment we got it right. The commission was set up to fail ... people should keep asking questions about 9/11." What did happen that day? Although many questions remain, the astrology of the event shows the prevailing circumstances.

The first plane flew into the North Tower at 8:46:26 a.m. and the event chart is drawn at that time (Chart 89). From the perspective of America, the 1st house represents the country that came under attack from the 7th. The American people are represented by Venus (ruling the 1st) conjunct the 11th cusp of the future, hopes, and dreams. After this day, the future of the country will change. Venus also rules the 8th house, and lives will be transformed and death will come to many Americans through shocking events in the air (Venus opposite Uranus).

The 7th house shows open enemies and is ruled by Mars in Capricorn. Mars symbolizes soldiers and is exalted in Capricorn, suggesting an elite security force or military. Mars is conjunct the South Node, implying sacrifice and action taken for a larger cause. In declination, Mars is way out-of-bounds, indicating soldiers following an extreme agenda. Mars in Capricorn answers to Saturn, which is located on the 9th house cusp. At first glance this gives the impression the elite force owes its allegiance to a foreign power. However, Saturn rules the 4th house of the homeland, an indication that the authority is domestic but based overseas. The domestic authority has distanced itself as far as possible from the carnage (Saturn opposite Pluto).

Mercury on the cusp of the 1st house symbolizes the hijackers. In Libra, Mercury is peregrine and without dignity. The hijackers are wanderers, without strength. They are

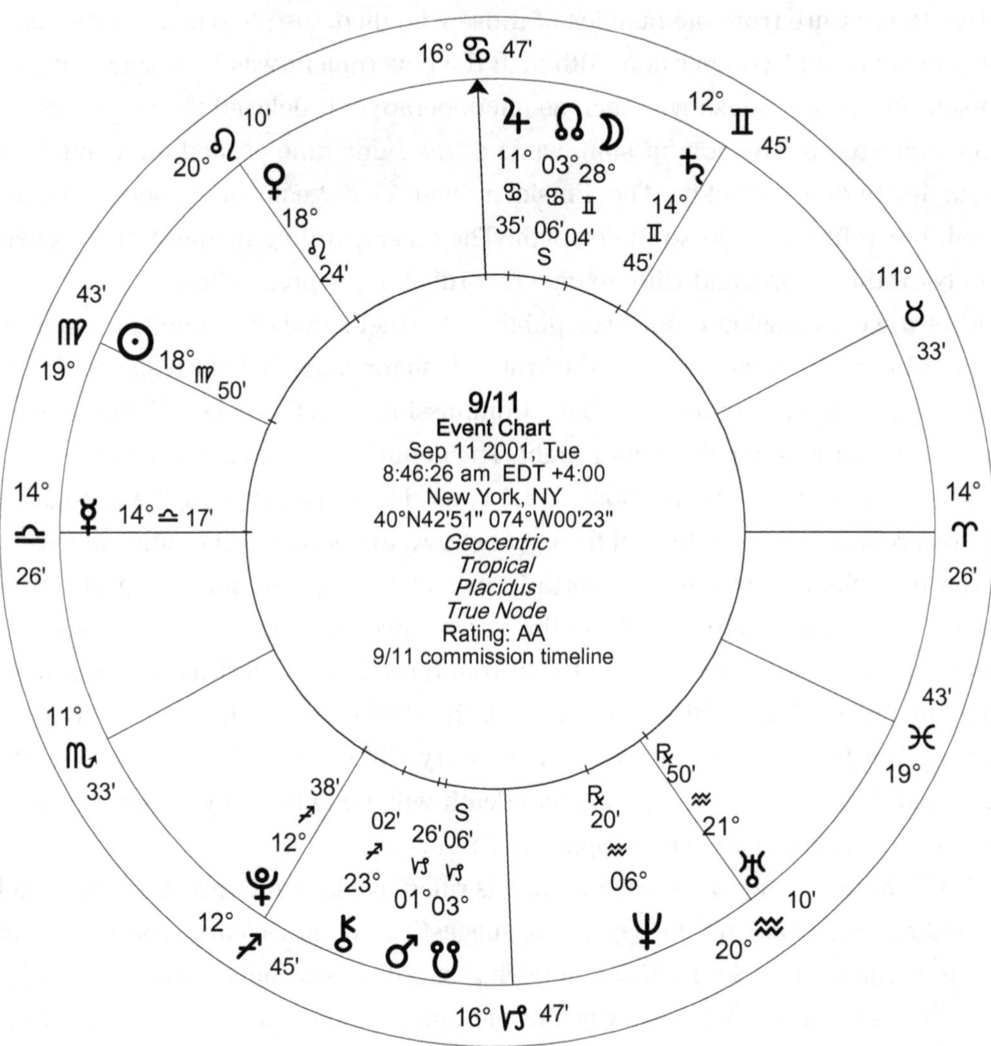

Chart 89:

A Defining Event

in America (conjunct the 1st) but have come from afar (Mercury ruling the 9th) with a hidden agenda (Mercury also ruling the 12th). Mercury in Libra suggests the hijackers have no hatred for Americans (Venus). After the fact, questions were raised as to how devout and religious the hijackers really were. Friends said they drank, went to bars, did cocaine, and visited prostitutes. Nonetheless, they readily killed (Mercury sextile Pluto) for religious beliefs (Mercury square Jupiter). Mercury is trine Saturn, an indication the hijackers are carrying out the agenda of the foreign-based domestic authority. While Saturn is hidden in a cadent house, Mercury is angular, with the ability and opportunity to act.

Saturn is in mutual reception with Mercury, further tying the two together through rulership and exaltation. The hijackers think highly of the foreign-based domestic authority (Mercury exalting Saturn). However, the hijackers do not hold the elite security force (Mercury in the detriment of Mars), or the U.S. leader (Mercury in the fall of the Sun) in such esteem.

In a mundane chart, the president is shown by the Sun, here in Virgo, in the sign of Mercury, connecting him to the hijackers. The Sun (President) is separating from a square to Saturn, the foreign-based domestic authority, which suggests a recent conflict between them. With Venus in the sign of the Sun, the people assume their leader is looking out for their better interests, but with the Sun in the sign of Venus' fall, the President is not acting in the best interests of the people. Did he know in advance about the attack? He claimed he did not (Sun on the cusp of the radical 12th house of unknowing). However, this was not the case (Sun on the cusp of the 3rd house of information in the turned chart using the 10th as the mundane house of the leader). According to The Center for Research on Globalization, the President had received at least twenty-eight advance intelligence warnings before 9/11, informing him of the possibility of bin Laden's attack.

Jupiter is culminating and exalted in Cancer. Jupiter is the chart ruler of the U.S. Sibly chart, and the mundane ruler of philosophy, and here represents the principles on which the country was founded (Jupiter in Cancer). With Saturn in the sign of Jupiter's detriment; Mars in the sign of Jupiter's fall; and Jupiter in the sign of Saturn's detriment and Mars' fall; the country's founding principles are at odds with the domestic overseas authority and the elite military. Given the Sun in the sign of Jupiter's detriment (and Venus's fall), the President also does not hold these principles in high regard. As for the American people, they are taking these principles for granted (Venus in Leo has little love for Jupiter, which has dignity in Leo only by face). In addition to lives, these philosophical principles were lost in 9/11—the right to life, liberty and the pursuit of happiness.

In the event chart, the fast moving Moon describes how the story unfolds. The following is one interpretation (biased by non-mainstream information) of the astrology. Upon entering Gemini, the Moon's first aspect was a trine to Neptune in Aquarius, representing a utopian view of freedom and individual rights. The Moon next came to conjunct Saturn and oppose Pluto: an authority decided this freedom was too great and could be undermined through an attack of terror. Such an assault was planned (Moon trine Mercury). Terrorized people will do anything and accept any hardship to enhance their security (Moon sextile Venus). What they would not allow was for their elected government to take their freedom for no reason (Moon square Sun). The attack provided the excuse to limit freedom in return for security (Moon trine Uranus).

The Moon went void and the attack transpired as planned. Some profited considerably from it. The government investigated itself and proclaimed itself guiltless. To prevent further attacks and protect the people, the new Department of Homeland Security was formed (Moon moved into Cancer and gained strength through dignity). The country went to war (Moon opposite a strong Mars). At home, the Patriot Act was passed, stripping American citizens of legally mandated rights and granting the government the unconstitutional power to control and imprison American citizens without judicial interference, as long as they were perceived to be a threat to the country's security.

This has been the fall-out of 9/11. America acquired a new philosophy of fear. A war has been waged against the rights of American citizens. Free speech is under attack. Obama's Information Czar has suggested the White House ban conspiracy theories. This would make it a crime for a person to express an opinion the government does not espouse. In a study prepared by the U.S. Army War College, the government was advised to prepare for 'purposeful domestic resistance,' which might be provoked in the event of an 'economic collapse,' and to stand ready to use military force *within* the country. Although there are other interpretations of the symbolism in the event chart, the fact remains that after 9/11, citizen rights have been eroded. The government has gained power and now has the legal authority to impose its might upon its people with impunity.

The Effect

A triwheel shows additional information regarding the impact of the event on the country (Chart 90). There was a solar eclipse on June 21, 2001, that fell on the world axis at 0°10' Cancer, portending an upcoming event that would have far-reaching ramifications. The north nodal eclipse fell in the country's 7th house of open enemies conjunct natal Venus. The lord of the eclipse was the Moon (people).

The mundane transiting opposition of Saturn and Pluto, a combination associated with death and destruction, aligned with the country's Ascendant and Descendant, making the attack personal for the nation. The close conjunction of Pluto to the Ascendant (within 17') described the fear and terror of the event (and for some verified the validity of the Sibly 5.10 p.m. chart).

The transiting North Node was conjunct the country's Venus–Jupiter conjunction, an indication of an outward event for the country. With transiting Mars conjunct the transiting South Node, opposing natal Venus–Jupiter, there was loss for the country through an attack. Transiting Mars–South Node formed a yod with a sextile to progressed Saturn and a quincunx to the progressed Moon in Gemini that was square progressed Mercury, alluding to the helplessness and suffering of the people from terrorists.

Transiting Neptune was conjunct the natal South Node, signifying the loss of humanitarian idealism, and the expression of the shadow side of Neptune (chaos, dissolution, delusion, and deceit). The progressed South Node was conjunct natal Pluto in Capricorn, reflecting the loss and destruction of physical structures. Progressed Neptune was trine the progressed South Node–natal Pluto, giving Neptune more power—fog thickening further. Progressed Saturn in Scorpio was sextile/trine the transiting nodes, acquiring more punch, and attesting to the profits that were made by some that day (Saturn ruling the 2nd). Authorities also gained power in response to the attacks. Transiting Uranus was conjunct the progressed Descendant (gaining expression through angularity) and in a grand trine with progressed Mars and natal Mars, symbolizing the sudden attack. Transiting Jupiter was conjunct the natal Sun, square natal Saturn and transiting Mercury, suggesting that truth would be limited.

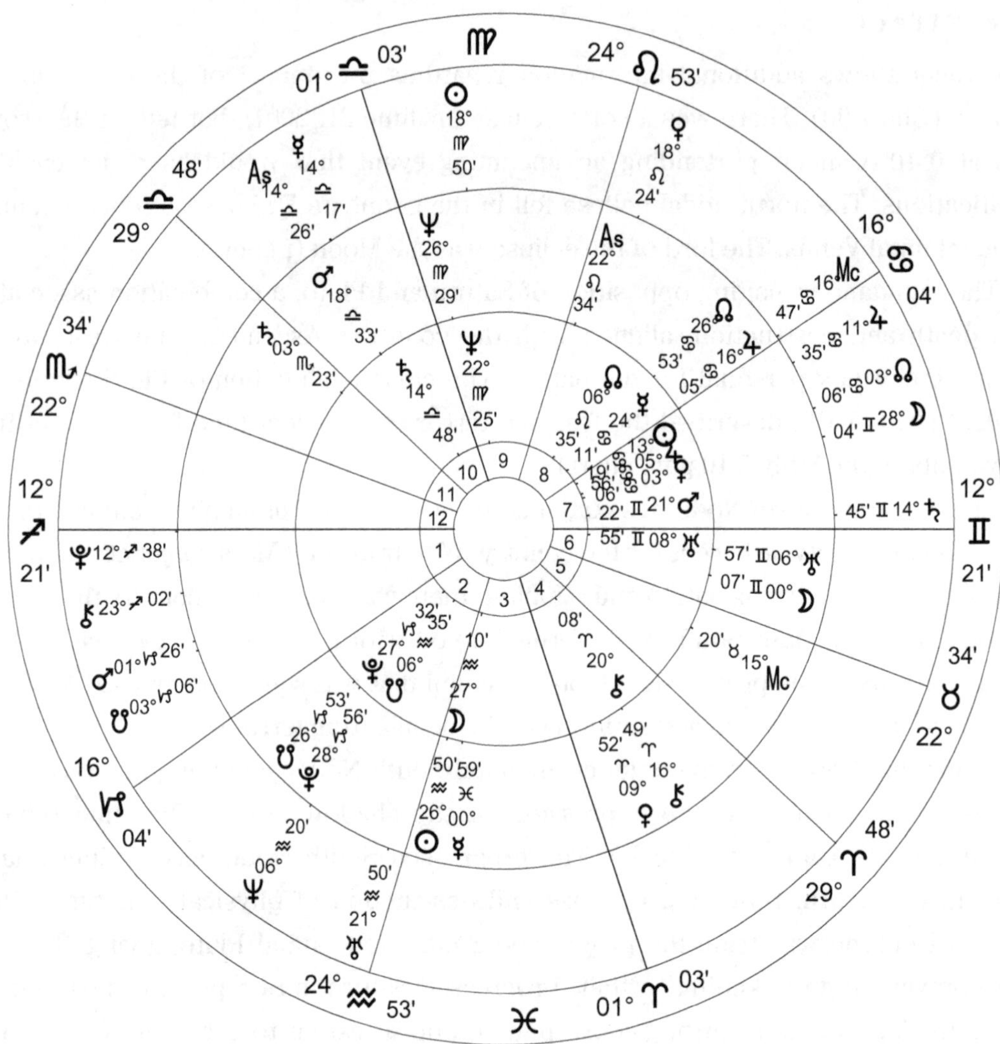

Chart 90:

U.S. Effect, Sept. 11, 2001, New York, NY, 8:46 a.m. EDT

Only the heart knows how to find what is precious.

— *Fyodor Dostoyevsky*

Chapter 23
Beating the Market

The nodes are useful predictors of the movement of the stock market. The market indicator used here is the Dow Jones Industrial Average (DJIA) which tracks the trades of thirty large U.S. companies on any given day. While I have had no luck predicting the daily gyrations of the market, in hindsight there are usually astrological indicators of market adjustments.

According to Louise McWhirter, the nineteen-year business cycle corresponds to the nineteen-year nodal cycle. She found that when the North Node was in Leo, the stock market was at its peak, and when it was in Aquarius, it was at its bottom. With the North Node in Scorpio, the market was normal but heading upwards (as the North Node retrograded towards Leo). When the North Node was in Taurus, stock prices were again normal, but moving down (toward their low in Aquarius). She found this trend was modulated ten to twenty percent through additional astrological factors.

The New York Stock Exchange was born in 1792 after twenty-four leading merchants in New York City signed an agreement to trade only amongst themselves. This formally established a marketplace where goods could be exchanged. Today, the goods exchanged are securities – the buying and selling of stocks, bonds, and notes of equity. Playing the market is gambling. There is a substantial risk, coupled with the potential for incredible gain.

Nativity

The McWhirter chart for the New York Stock Exchange (Chart 91) has 14° Cancer on the Ascendant and 24° Pisces on the Midheaven. McWhirter considered Mars the co-ruler of the 10th since Aries occupies most of the house. She found that aspects involving Mars and Neptune (both rulers of the 10th) were critical in timing market activities. These are the same two planets (in square) in the U.S. chart that Robert Gover found were related to stock market panics.

The solar eclipse before the market's inception was on March 22 1792, at 2°49' Aries. It fell in the 10th house, promising expansion of the enterprise, which in this case was a marketplace. It was a south nodal eclipse with Mars as the lord. On the day of the agreement, the South Node was in the eclipse degree, an indication the node marked a sensitive degree.

The South Node is in Aries, ruled by Mars, connecting the planet to loss and sacrifice. Placed in the 3rd, Mars in Virgo is related to data, information, and logic that in theory should guide investment. However, in practice, there is little logic in the marketplace (loss of critical thinking).

The North Node is in Libra, ruled by a dignified Venus in Taurus, the sign of money and physical resources. The association points to the output and successful manifestation of money. Placed in the 11th, Venus is related to money that makes dreams come true. Venus rules the 5th house of stock-broking and gambling, and alludes to money made through risk.

Cancer is rising in the chart, ruled by the Moon, and emotions move the market. The Moon is in the 10th in Aries, auguring for success and growth. The Moon symbolizes the public and most of the working population have their retirement and investment funds in the stock market. The Moon is trine Uranus in the 2nd, making for big money swings and people availing themselves of the flow. However, it is a ruthless game and the flow runs both ways. While much money has been made, much has also been lost. The playing field is not fair to the common investor.

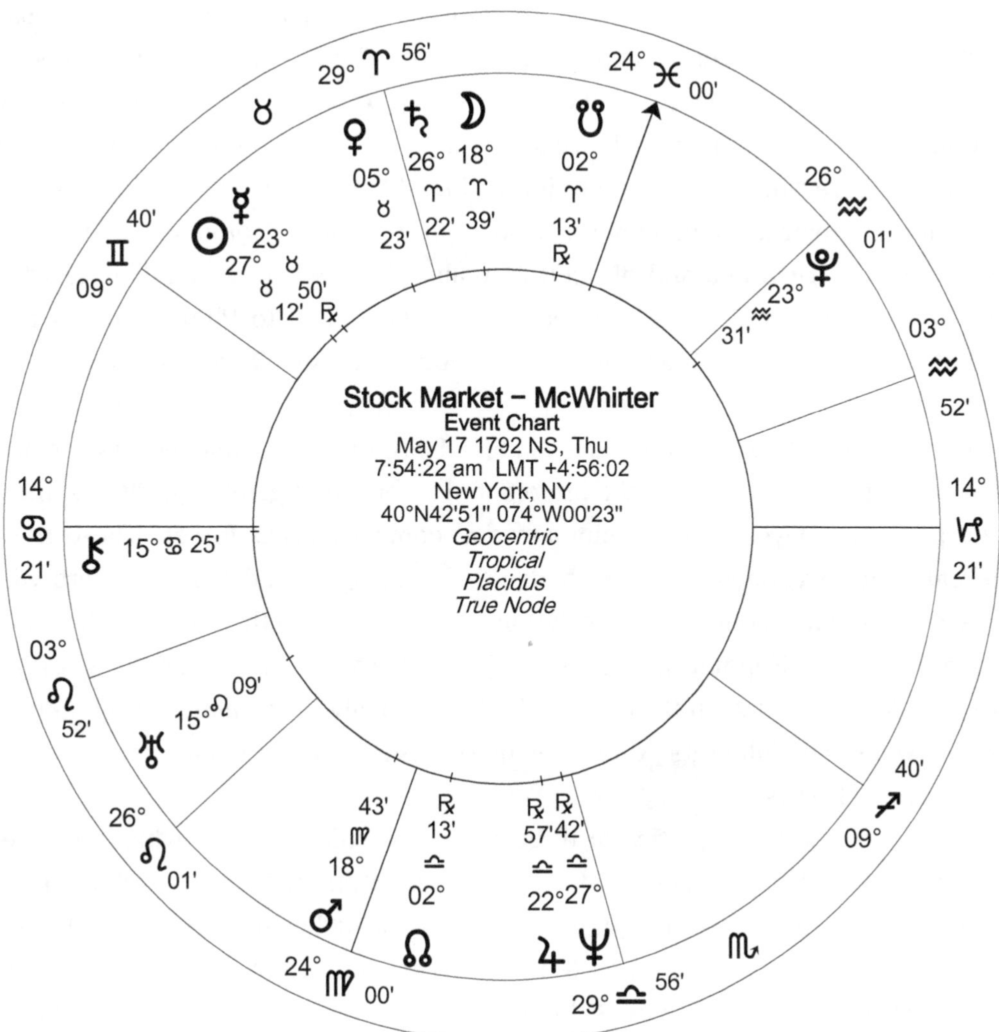

Chart 91:

New York Stock Exchange, May 17, 1972, NS, New York, 7:54 a.m. LMT

The 2nd house of money is ruled by the Sun, which explains McWhirter's observation that the Sun is related to daily market moves. The Sun is in Taurus, the sign of physical resources and money—the heart of the market. The Sun is in the 11th house of the future, connecting money with dreams. The Sun is conjunct a combust and retrograde Mercury (reason, logic), another indication of logic burned in the financial hopes of the Sun. The pair are inconjunct a wide Jupiter–Neptune conjunction, pointing to dreams that are frustrated and difficult to realize. The Sun in a mundane chart also symbolizes the government and the leader, and the square to Pluto indicates a government fighting the influence of big money without success (Sun inconjunct Jupiter–Neptune).

Central to the chart is Pluto, the planet of big money, domiciled late in the 8th house of investment, and ruling the intercepted 5th house of gambling. Pluto symbolizes the powerful players who manipulate and control market forces. These are the plutocrats, the investment bankers, hedge fund managers and stock brokers whose money and influence control the legislation (square the Sun) that governs the market. Pluto trine Jupiter–Neptune indicates the profitability of the marketplace – for the plutocrats. With Neptune on the cusp of the 5th, much about the market is clouded and obscure, which the plutocrats prefer. The market is a zero-sum game—for someone to win, someone else has to lose.

Saturn, the mundane significator of business is sextile Pluto, showing the close interaction between the plutocrats and big business. Saturn in Aries is debilitated, signifying weakness, which describes the vulnerability of big business in the marketplace. The opposition between Saturn and Neptune reveals loss from the invisible machinations of the market. However, with Pluto easing the opposition, business losses are mitigated and the plutocrats help big business prosper.

In declination, the Moon and Mars are parallel, which carries the vulnerability of the South Node to the chart ruler and bodes poorly for the general public playing the market. Jupiter and Saturn are contraparallel, denoting the tug of losses and gains that endlessly offset each other.

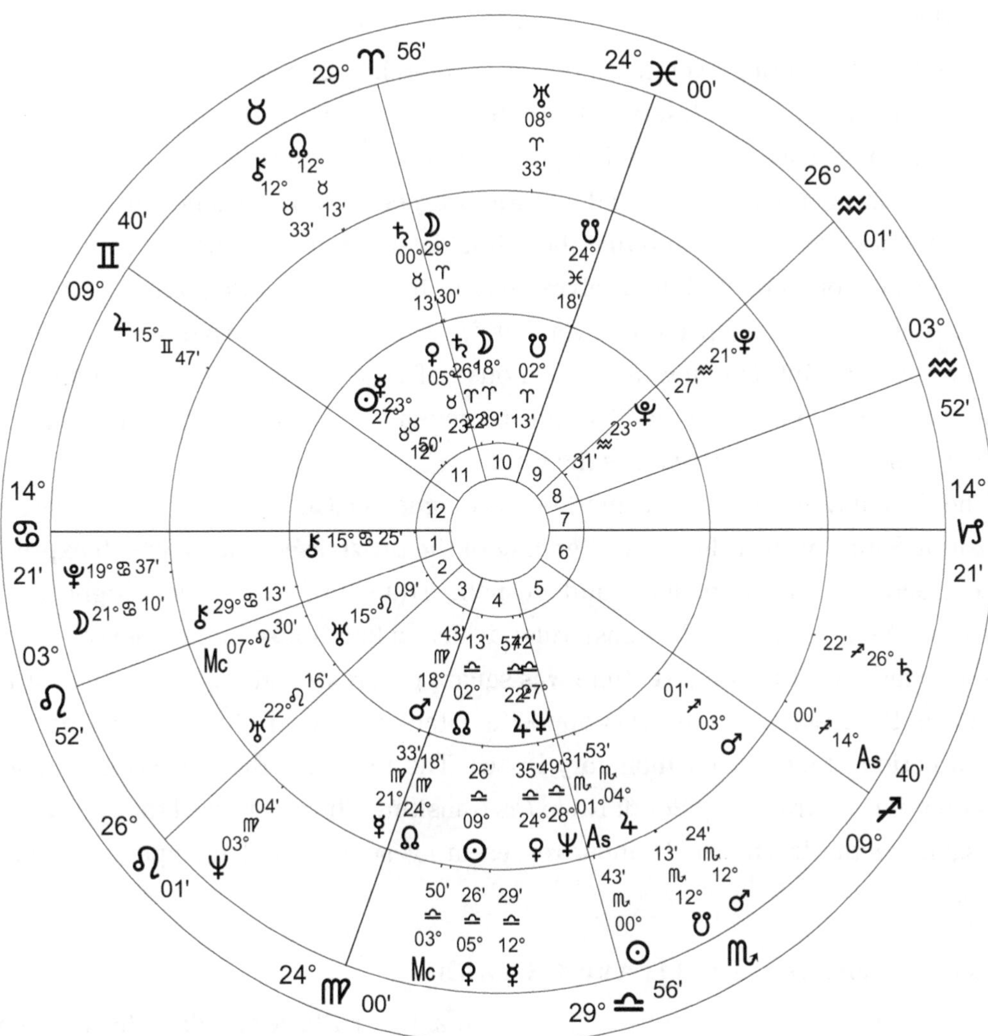

Chart 92:

Market Crash 1929, Oct. 24, 1929, New York, NY, 10:00 a.m. EST

The Great Depression

At the end of the roaring twenties, a period marked by rampant borrowing and market speculation, the Federal Reserve Board began contracting the money supply. The market crashed, ushering in twelve years of financial scarcity and distress. While publicly declaring the market sound, the Fed warned powerful friends in advance that the contraction was coming and that they should get out of the market. Later, hypocritical financiers congratulated themselves on their foresight in anticipating the crash.

There was a solar eclipse on November 1, 1929, at 8°35' Scorpio, a week after the market began to fall. Landing in the 5th house of risk, the eclipse was conjunct progressed Jupiter and opposite natal Venus, portending a crisis from risk. It was a south nodal eclipse, with Pluto serving as the lord.

The first day of substantial market loss came on October 24, 1929 (Chart 92). Transiting Saturn was at the North Bending of the progressed nodes, which expressed as contraction, restriction, loss, and despair. Transiting Uranus was opposite the progressed Sun, pitting the 2nd house ruler against a 2nd house planet, denoting stress related to money. Transiting Neptune was square progressed Mars, coinciding with the downturn. Progressed Uranus was opposite natal/progressed Pluto, describing a protracted period of significant monetary losses. The timer for the event was transiting Mars crossing the transiting South Node (as transiting Chiron crossed the North Node) and squaring the 2nd house Uranus, representing sudden and unexpected financial losses.

First Computer Instigated Crash

Fifty-eight years later, on October 19, 1987, on another Black Monday, the stock market crashed again. The market lost 508 points (22% of its value) in a single day. Analysts blame the crash on program trading, new at the time, which enabled computer programs to direct trades based on market activity. Once the market began to fall, automatic sell notices were executed, and caused further drops, which snowballed into the crash. There was a south nodal solar eclipse at 29°34' Virgo, highlighting Mercury as the lord.

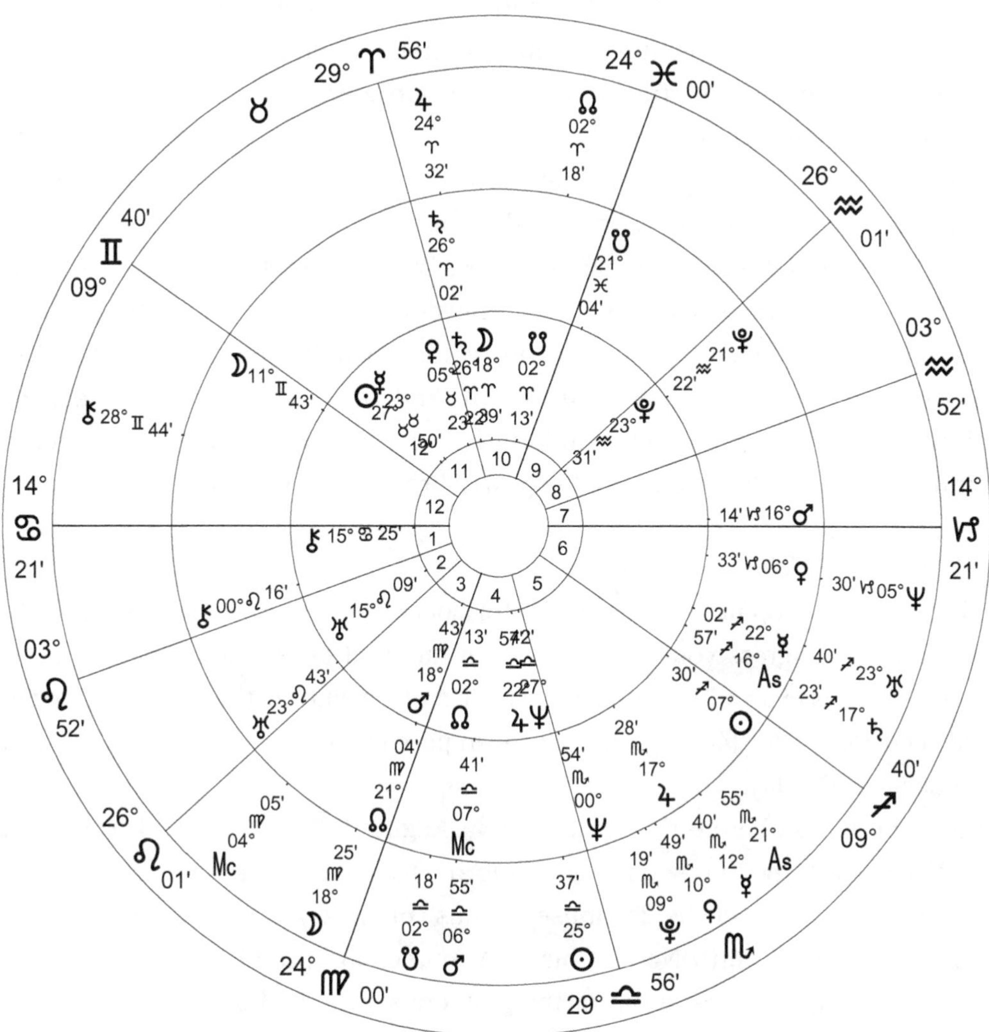

Chart 93:

Market Crash 1987, Oct. 19, 1987, New York, NY, 9:30 a.m. EDT

On the day of the crash (Chart 93), there was a half-nodal return within 5' of exactitude that was square a transiting Neptune–progressed Venus conjunction. This was a mixed double-whammy, with transiting Neptune–progressed Venus at the North Bending of the natal nodes (monetary chaos) and simultaneously at the South Bending of the transiting nodes (boundless money loss). Transiting Uranus was conjunct progressed Mercury (lord) at the North Bending of the progressed nodes, indicating the outward effect of automatic computer trades. With progressed Uranus square natal Mercury, the result was unexpected loss. Transiting Mars was square transiting Neptune and progressed Venus, again intimating widespread financial devastation. Transiting Jupiter was conjunct progressed Saturn, and opposite natal Neptune and the transiting Sun, indicating the magnitude of loss suffered by business. However, with transiting Jupiter sextile natal Pluto, the power-brokers profited from the crash.

No Bank Bailout

The single largest drop in the market's history occurred on September 29, 2008 (Chart 94), soon after Congress voted down a seven hundred billion dollar bailout for Wall Street in the aftermath of the housing crash and decline in the value of mortgage-backed securities. The stock market fell seven percent, losing 778 points ($1.2 trillion) in the course of the day.

The solar eclipse before the crash was on August 1, 2008, at 9°31' Leo that fell in the 2nd house, with the Sun serving as the lord. On the day of the vote, the transiting South Node was conjunct the 2nd house Uranus (monetary loss), opposite a conjunction of the transiting North Node, Chiron, Neptune, and progressed Pluto, signifying immense monetary decline—even for the plutocrats (who had precipitated the crisis). The crash was unexpected since many on Wall Street and in Congress thought the bill would pass. As in the fall of 1929, transiting Chiron was conjunct the transiting North Node and was expressed outwardly as a wound.

Transiting Saturn was conjunct the progressed North Node–natal Mars and opposite a conjunction of the progressed Moon–South Node and transiting Uranus, signifying sudden contraction, restriction, and loss for the public. Main Street, unhappy with the banks, refused to support the bailout and bombarded their representatives with angry complaints.

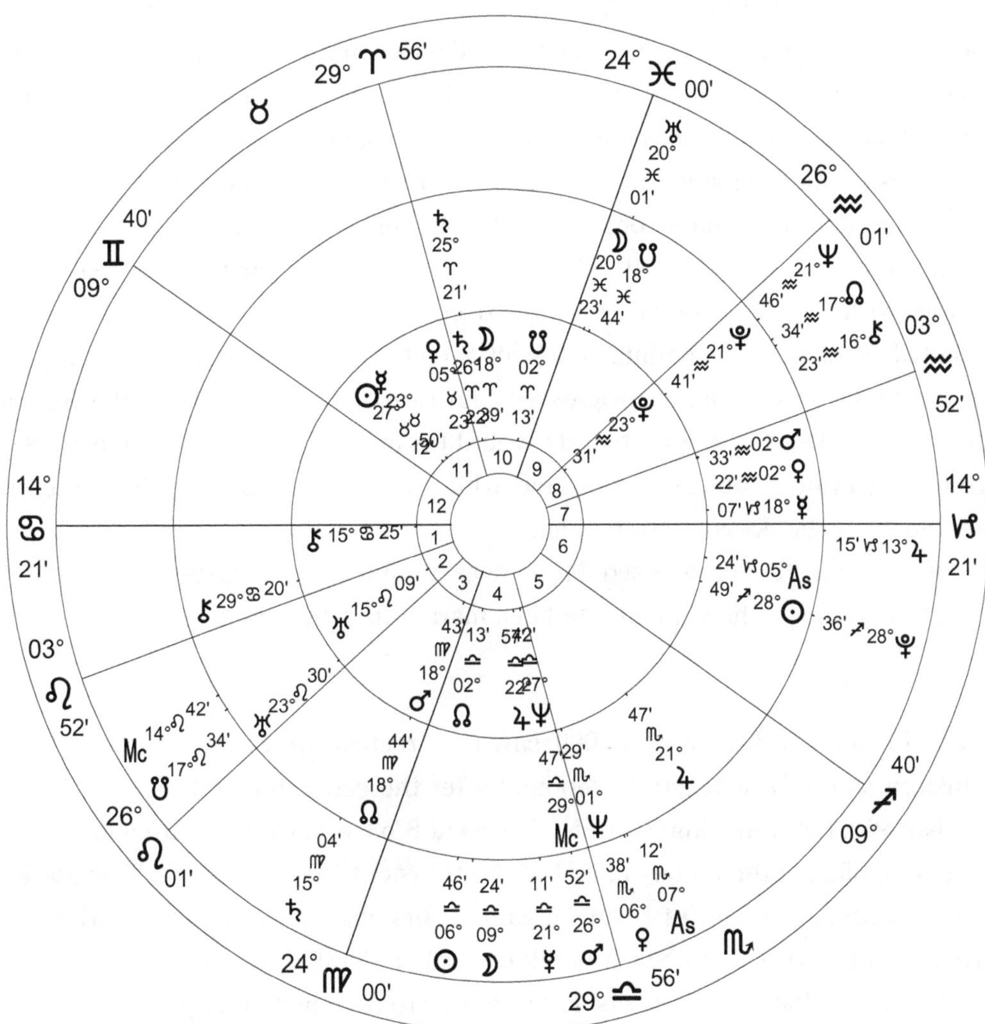

Chart 94:

No Bank Bailout, Sept. 29, 2008, New York, NY, 9:30 a.m. EDT

There was a New Moon early that morning, widely conjunct the natal North Node and square the progressed Ascendant–Descendant, forming a grand cross indicative of a tense, stuck position, with no one willing to budge. Progressed Venus was conjunct progressed Mars, sextile/trine the natal nodes, and square progressed Neptune, which expressed as a vast dissipation of wealth. McWhirter's two financial significators were conjunct, with transiting Mars conjoined natal Neptune (at the progressed Midheaven), describing the widespread crash. The conjunction was opposite natal Saturn, and correlated with a congressional inability to convince voters (two months before a presidential election) that bailing out Wall Street was in the voters' best interests. Transiting Pluto was conjunct progressed Sun (lord), an indication of the figurative death of the market. But the plutocrats would triumph, and with transiting Mars sextile transiting Pluto–progressed Sun, and trine natal Pluto, as a result of the stock market crash, the banks got their bailout.

In declination, the progressed Moon was parallel the progressed South Node, bringing loss to the public who invested in a market they thought was safe.

Market Rally

The period from March 1–June 1, 2009, saw the greatest three-month gain in the market's history as the Dow began to rebound after the economic collapse. On March 1, 2009 (Chart 95), the transiting North Node was at 8°53' Aquarius, square natal Venus at 5°27' Taurus, placing the money planet at the transient North Bending. This marked a period of maximum output of financial gain. Transiting Pluto at 2°59' Capricorn was square the natal nodes at the North Bending, further signifying the outward flourishing of big money and financial products. It was a time to reap monetary profit.

For three months the market rallied. It began as the transiting North Node (8°49' Aquarius) was within 4° of the square to natal Venus, and continued as the transiting North Node advanced to conjunct a progressed Venus–Mars conjunction at 2°53' Aquarius. By the end of April, the transiting North Node was at 6°57' Aquarius and would perfect the square to natal Venus that month. By May, the transiting node was at 4°4' Aquarius, closing in on the progressed Venus–Mars conjunction (energized output of money). At the end of the month, with the transiting North Node at 1°33' Aquarius,

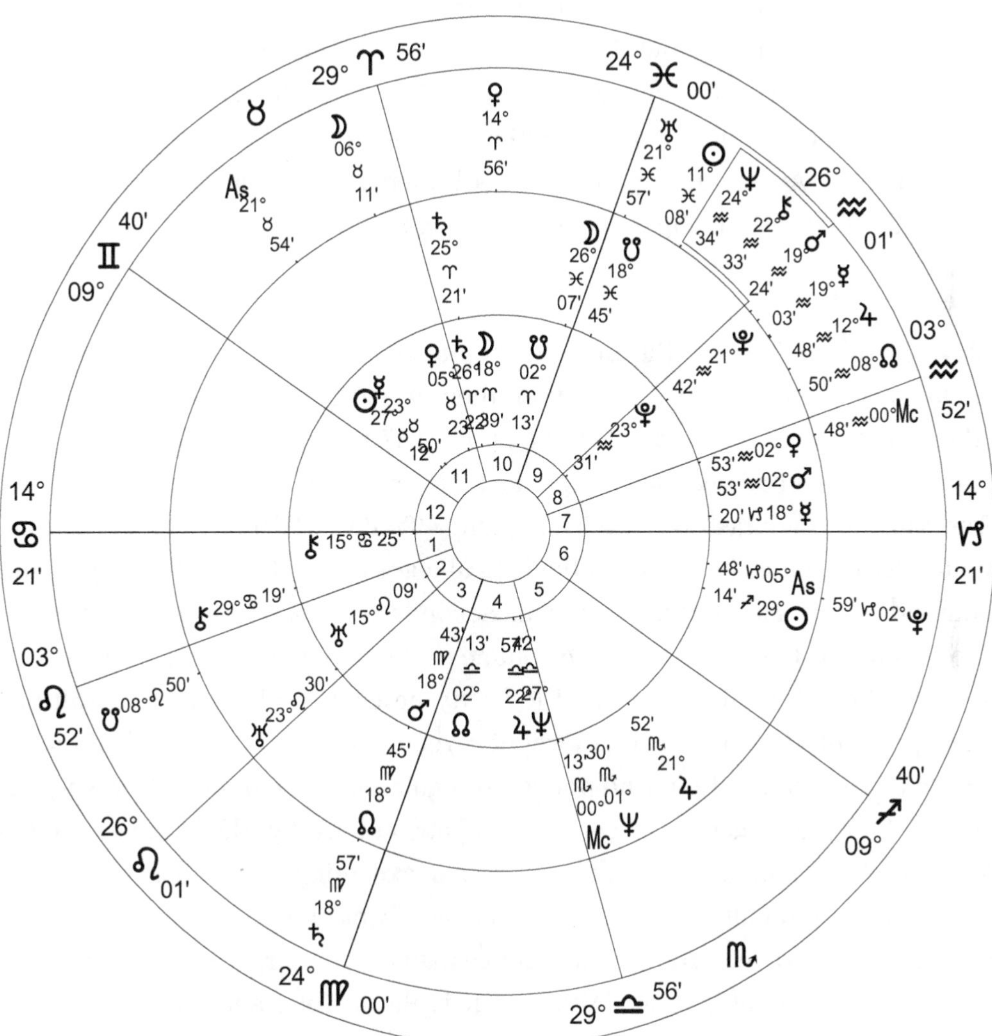

Chart 95:

Market Rally, March 1, 2009, New York, NY, 9:30 a.m. EST

separating from progressed Venus–Mars, and, separating from the square to natal Venus, the rally began to slow. During this period, transiting Pluto was trine natal Venus at the North Bending of the natal nodes. Pluto stationed retrograde in early April at 3°18' Capricorn and remained within a degree of the North Bending from May 11–June 23, 2009. At this time, plutocrats took their profits (big money manifesting), with the sell-off corresponding to the ensuing stagnation of market growth.

Flash Crash

On May 6, 2010, at 2.42 pm, the Dow Jones plunged suddenly, dropping six hundred points in five minutes (Chart 96). Up until then, it had been a bad day on Wall Street and the market had already lost 300 points. By 2.47 p.m. it was down 900 points. By 3.07 pm, the market had regained 600 points and went on to close that day down 320.

The cause of the crash was High Frequency Trading (HFT), which are automatic computer driven trades based on mathematical algorithms. HFT traders buy hundreds or thousands of stocks and trade them nanoseconds later for a return of as little as one tenth of a cent. Profit comes from high volume trades and high trading frequencies.

During 2009–2011, HFT accounted for sixty percent of all trades on Wall Street, netting a profit of $12.9 billion. This level of revenue caught the attention of the Stock Exchange Commission (SEC), who pondered regulating these trades. However, after a successful lobby and generous campaign contributions by HFT traders, the SEC backed off. With complex computer programs executing buy and sell orders, the transactions are difficult to trace. HFT enables 'front running,' a process whereby traders place an advance order for themselves ahead of a larger order, and receive a better price than the later order. Although it is illegal for traders to place personal trades ahead of other trades, when a computer is filling the orders, the deceit is not obvious.

At the time the flash crash began, the transiting South Node was conjunct the Ascendant, signifying loss for the market. The progressed Moon was at the North Bending of the transiting nodes, and the decline affected the public. Because of the crash, people became aware of illegal trading practices by market insiders (transiting Mercury conjunct natal Venus trine transiting Pluto). The progressed North Node was

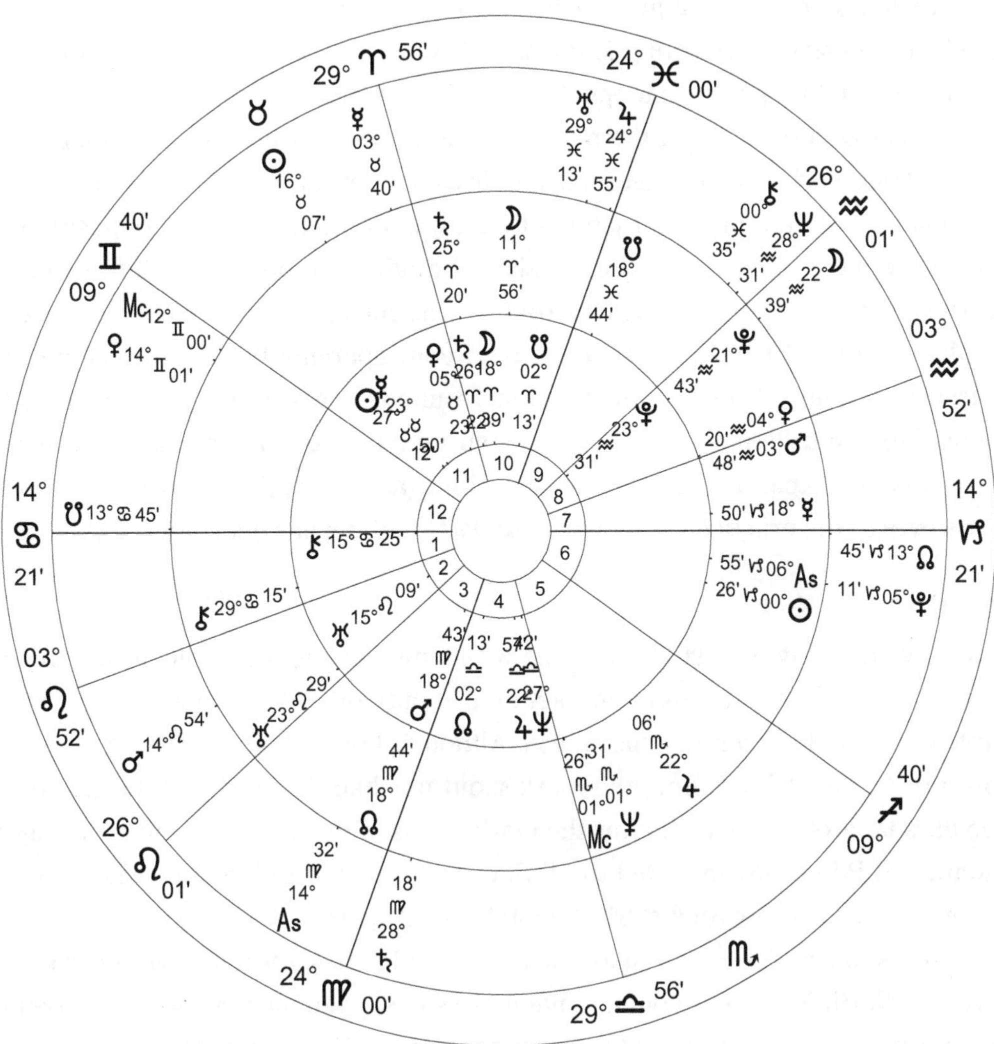

Chart 96:
Flash Crash, May 6, 2010, New York, NY, 2:40 p.m. EDT

conjunct natal Mars and in a grand trine with progressed Mercury and the transiting Sun, which was square transiting Mars–natal Uranus, a configuration suggesting computers caught up in repetitious loops they could not escape.

The event occurred during the mundane Saturn–Uranus opposition, which Robert Gover in *Time and Money* suggests symbolizes sudden upsets to the status quo and abrupt endings of systems or structures that are faulty. The mundane opposition was conjunct the natal lunar nodes (out of sign), bringing the opposition into manifestation. The volatility of computer-driven trading was shown by the conjunction of transiting Mars and natal Uranus, aggravated by a contraparallel between transiting Mars and transiting Pluto. The computer glitch resulted in a serious financial loss that amounted to one trillion dollars in twenty-four minutes. Also in declination, transiting Jupiter was contraparallel the progressed Moon and transiting Saturn, opening the public's eyes to the practice, about which to date, nothing has been done.

U.S. Downgrade

In late July and early August 2011, as the wrangling in Congress over raising the debt limit reached a climax, the stock market held steady on the anticipation that government leaders would reach a compromise. Although law-makers reached a deal hours before the August 2nd deadline, the market did not like the deal and fell 263 points. Three days later on August 5th, after the market closed for the week, the rating agency Standard and Poorer downgraded the U.S. economy from AAA to AA. When the market reopened on Monday August 8th, the DJIA fell 624 points (Chart 97).

The transiting nodes were square the progressed nodes, forming a grand cross. The progressed North Node was conjunct natal Mars (risk, gambles) at the South Bending of the transiting nodes, describing a loss of confidence. Transiting Mars was square the natal nodes at the South Bending (a double-whammy) reinforcing the message. Transiting Uranus was conjunct the natal South Node and square transiting Pluto at the North Bending of the natal nodes, signaling the loss of big money.

Transiting Mars was in a grand cross with the natal nodes, transiting Uranus, and progressed Sun–transiting Pluto, related to an impasse with significant financial consequences. There was a transiting Sun–Venus conjunction that was conjunct natal

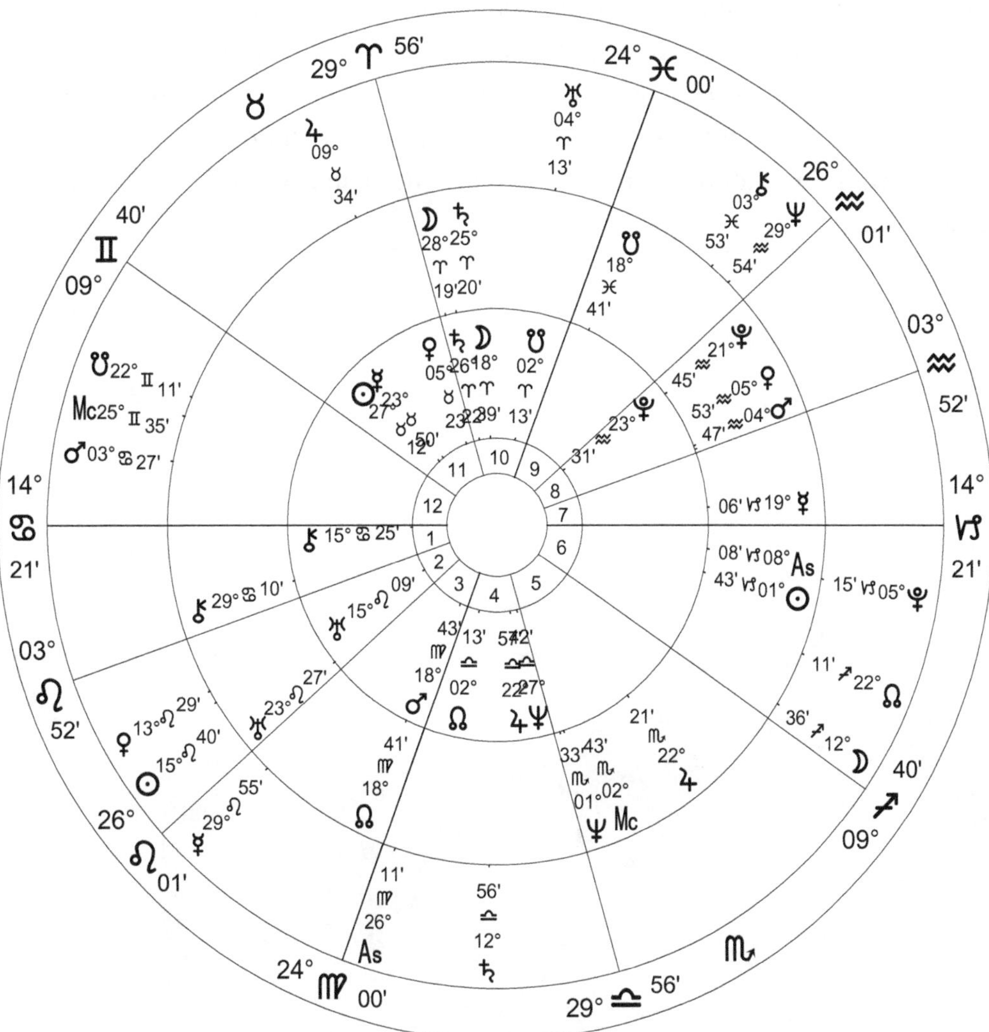

Chart 97:

U.S. Downgrade Effect, Aug. 8, 2011, 9:30 a.m. New York, NY EDT

Uranus and sextile transiting Saturn, as Congress voted to make no sweeping changes, and retain the status quo. Despite mathematic errors on the part of the S&P (transiting Mercury was retrograde and opposite transiting Neptune and square the natal Sun ruling the 2nd), the loss of the stellar rating stood. The reputation and standing of Congress fell (transiting Saturn at the nadir square the natal Ascendant–Descendant) as the market crashed.

And above all, watch with glittering eyes the whole world around you because the greatest secrets are always hidden in the most unlikely places. Those who don't believe in magic will never find it.

— Roal Dahl

Chapter 24

Easy Money

The Federal Reserve

The Federal Reserve, known as the Fed, is a for-profit central bank run by a private banking cartel that controls the U.S. economy. The Fed provides money and stability to other banks and financial corporations, determines the amount of money in circulation, sets the interest rate, and the fractional reserve rate. The central bank was created by the 1913 Bank Act, which was pushed through Congress three days before Christmas when most members were away on vacation. The stated goal of the Fed was to "harness the money trust, disarm its power [and] establish democratic control over money and credit ... [However], the results were nearly the opposite."

One hundred years earlier, British banker Mayer Amschel Rothschild explained the system. A central bank gives the "national bank almost complete control of national finance. The few who can understand the system will be either so involved in profits, or so dependent on its favors, there will be no opposition from that class, while on the other hand, the great body of people, mentally incapable of comprehending ... will bear its burden without complaint, and perhaps without even suspecting the system is inimical [opposite] to their interests."

What the Bank Act did was to take from Congress the congressionally mandated power to print money and give it to the banks. With this legislation, Congress could no longer mint its own money. Now it had to borrow it from the Fed with interest. It was no coincidence that the same year the Bank Act became law, personal income tax became necessary to repay the interest on government borrowed money.

One might wonder where the Fed gets the money it lends to the government, and where banks get the money they lend to consumers. The answer is: they create it out of thin air. In this age of electronics, once a loan is approved, the money appears through the push of a button as a ledger entry (in other words, a credit on a spreadsheet). This is how banks 'make' money. Once the U.S. went off the gold standard, money no longer had set value and could be created at will. In the current system, money is not traded for gold, but created through debt.

Right now, the U.S. is over $14 trillion dollars in debt. The interest paid on this debt in 2011 was $450 billion. It has been estimated that up to fifty percent of the cost of every government project is interest on borrowed money. For goods purchased by people every day, the interest contained in the cost of any item is about forty percent. For this reason, interest has been called a hidden tax—it is written into the cost of every item—but not easily seen.

The money supply is multiplied through the fractional reserve. It works like this: If the reserve is ten percent and you go to the bank and deposit one hundred dollars, the bank must keep ten dollars (the reserve percent). Assume the bank lends the other ninety dollars to Ann. When Ann deposits the ninety dollars in her bank, that bank must keep nine dollars. If it lends eighty-one dollars to Mary, you have a hundred dollars in your bank, Ann has ninety dollars in hers, and Mary has eighty-one dollars. As the process continues, the initial one hundred dollar deposit becomes one thousand dollars ($100 + $90 +$81 + $72.90 ... = $1,000).

For banks, the mortgage industry is especially lucrative. Take for instance, a $300,000 thirty-year mortgage at a five percent interest rate. After thirty years, the buyers own the house and would have repaid the bank $580,000—almost double what the house was originally worth. All this is given to a bank for a house it never owned, for money it never had. The banks would like customers to think they shift money from elsewhere in order to make loans, but the truth is, they never had the money to begin with. They create the money, charge interest on it, and then multiply it using the fractional reserve.

The problem with money expansion is inflation. The money created has no practical worth because it is not real. Printed money makes the money that is real, worth less. It's like putting Monopoly money into circulation with the legal mandate that it be treated as real under penalty of law. When Monopoly money (from the fractional reserve) is added to the money supply, the value of money is reduced by the same amount that is added. (For example, if the money supply is doubled, the value of money is half of what is was, because only half the money in circulation is real.) This is the cause of inflation: prices go up because money is worth less. Since the Bank Act was passed in 1913, the value of $1.00 (100 cents) has been reduced to 5 cents. I suspect this is what 'the great body of people [are] mentally incapable of comprehending'—that our political representatives can write and enforce financial bills that are so inimical to the economic prosperity of the country.

There is an easy solution. If Congress gave away its power to print money, it can take it back. There is no need for the Fed. The government can print money as easily as it can print an IOU (a government bond). When the government prints its own money, there is no interest, and no loan to repay. This is in fact the economic system in place in the state of North Dakota, which has its own central bank that serves the people. It is the wealthiest and most prosperous state in the country.

Nativity

The bill that created the bank became law on December 23, 1913 (Chart 98). A striking feature of the nativity is the number of planets that are either debilitated or peregrine (without major dignity). The Moon, Mars, and Jupiter are in fall. Mercury is in detriment. The Sun, Venus, and Saturn are peregrine. The net effect of so many debilitated planets is not that they are weak, but that they are generally up to no good and have difficulty fulfilling a high potential. A second feature is that the Midheaven, IC, Pluto,

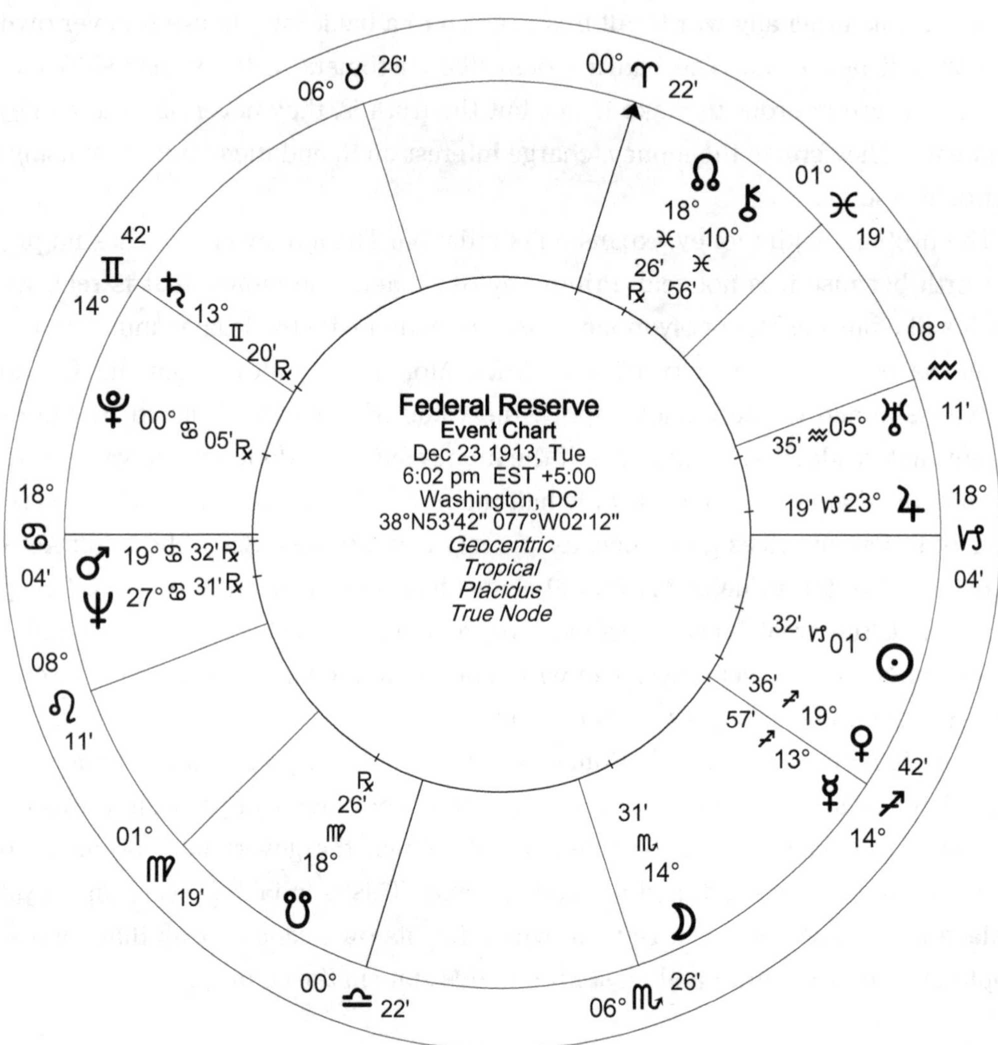

Chart 98:

Federal Reserve Nativity

and the Sun are all on the Aries Points, indicating the power of the Fed at home and around the world.

Venus is at the South Bending of the nodes, in a position denoting loss. The Fed is a bank that creates money out of nothing and cheapens the value of currency already in circulation. The net monetary effect of the Fed is a drastically devalued dollar.

The North Node is ruled by Neptune, rising in the chart, and shows the physical manifestation of the unreal—money created from nothing that is treated as if it were real. The association also describes the success of the Fed money cartel in shrouding itself in a cloak of invisibility. There is an inborn wisdom and knowingness in understanding how to deceive and disappear. For almost one hundred years, the Fed has successfully fought every attempt of an audit—and succeeded—up until now.

The South Node is ruled by Mercury, placed in Sagittarius in the 6th house of daily routine. Mercury rules the 12th house of illusion and the 3rd house of communication. The Fed is uncommunicative (loss of Mercury). Until recently, what exactly the Fed was and what it did, and at whose expense, was unclear. Many wrongfully believe it to be a branch of the U.S. government, rather than a for-profit commercial bank.

The Sun, the heart of any chart, is in Capricorn, the sign of government and big business. The Sun is in the 6th house of service, rules the 2nd house of money, and is opposite Pluto. One purpose of the Fed is to provide money for government and big business. Pluto, the planet of plutocrats and big money, stands in the 12th house of self-undoing, and rules the 5th house of creative efforts, alluding to the magical creation of money, which ultimately destroys the value of money and the economy.

The Moon is in Scorpio, giving a deep and secretive need for wealth and power. The Moon in the 5th describes an entity which creates money. The Moon rules the chart and provides the driving motivation of the Fed: to create, concentrate, and protect wealth, all while hiding what is going on. The Moon is in mutual reception with Pluto, and the two work together to create money, which is power.

Saturn in Gemini represents the government and big business, which are in hidden partnership with the Fed (Saturn ruling the 7th from the cusp of the 12th). The government puts up with the Fed because it can borrow money from the Fed surreptitiously, without regard for transparency. There is also a revolving door between the Federal Reserve, Wall Street, and the U.S. Treasury, with officials circulating between the three, pushing for policies that benefit big business and protect the power of the central bank. The Moon is quincunx Saturn, an aspect of frustration, related to the occasional attempts of some in Congress to reign in the Fed. With Saturn opposite Mercury, information about the bank is restricted and at a minimum.

Jupiter in the 7th represents the common people (Jupiter rules the U.S. Sibly chart and symbolizes the American people) who are (whether realized or not) the open enemy of the Fed. With Jupiter in Capricorn in fall, the American people have little power. Jupiter is opposite the 1st house Neptune and the Fed employs smoke and mirrors to mislead and confuse the public. Because Jupiter is disposited by Saturn, the people assume (incorrectly) that the government is on their side and will protect their better financial interests.

A fallen and retrograde Mars is rising, empowered by a sextile/trine to the nodes. Inborn in the Fed is the will to fight for its survival (Mars in Cancer). But it is a dirty fighter and uses the power of big money (Moon in Scorpio) as a weapon. Mars is quincunx Venus, and the Fed's activities erode the value of money. Mars is opposite Jupiter, which connects it by wide conjunction to Neptune, an inflationary aspect, as financial astrologer Bill Meridian has pointed out, with energy (Mars) fueling limitless (Neptune) growth (Jupiter). The configuration also testifies to secret (Neptune) actions (Mars) taken in self-interest (1st house) against the better interests of the taxpaying populace (Jupiter).

The placement of the 9th house ruler, Neptune, in the 1st indicates the degree of influence that outsiders have on the Federal Reserve: foreign interests are indistinguishable from the Fed's. Also, in a global economy, events overseas affect Fed policies.

The one dignified planet in the chart—Uranus in Aquarius, in its own sign, on the cusp of the 8th and ruling the 8th house of big money—has been used for no good. It represents the inspired innovations of the Fed and investment banks on Wall Street to create money, earn big profits, and protect the major banks, while shrugging the risk onto taxpayers through the Federal Deposit Insurance Corporation (FDIC) and bank bailouts.

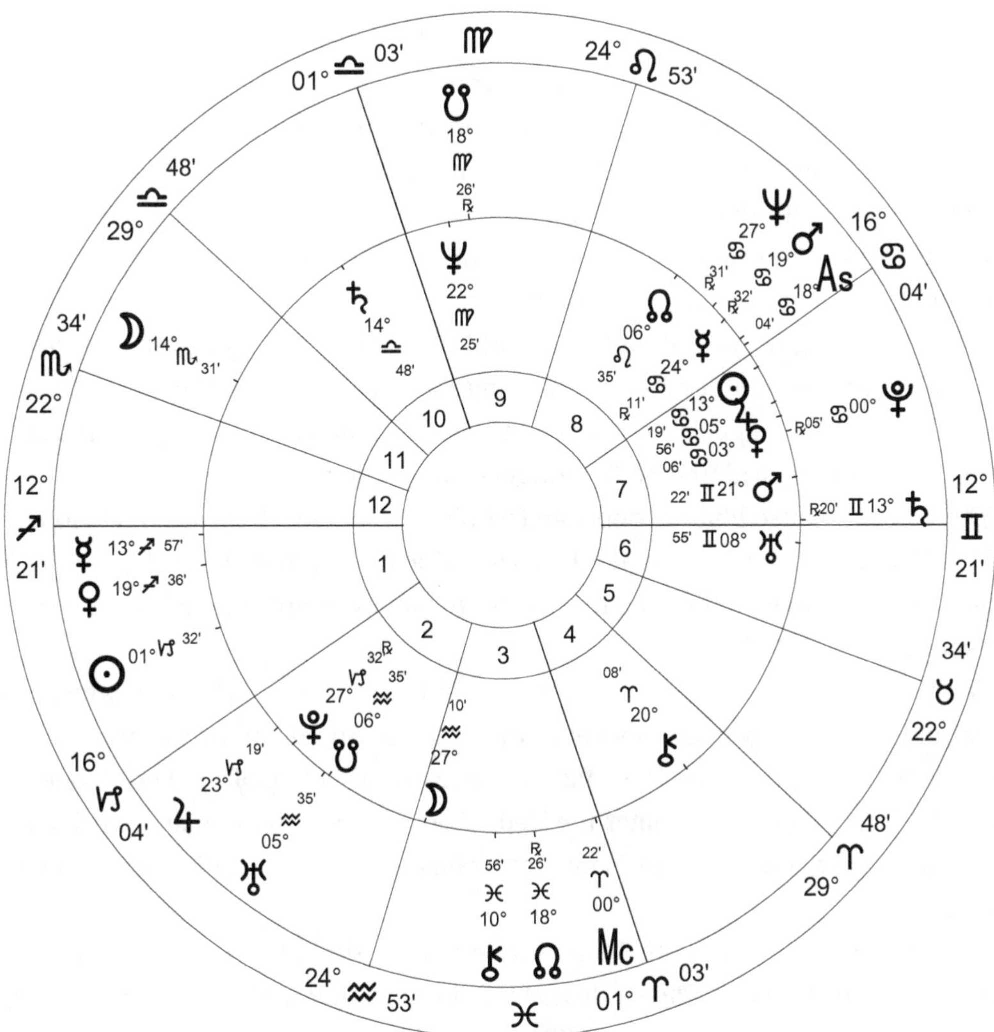

Chart 99:

U.S. and Fed: Dec. 23, 1913, Washington, D.C. 6:02 p.m. EST

U.S. Influence

An overlay of the Federal Reserve chart on the U.S. Sibly chart reveals the influence of the Fed on the country (Chart 99). The Fed's Mercury–Saturn opposition falls across the U.S. Ascendant–Descendant axis, an indication that the Fed's policy of limiting free-flowing information impacts the American people. The Fed and the U.S. MC–IC axes are flipped, with the Fed's IC conjunct the U.S. MC, and the Fed's MC conjunct the U.S. IC. With all four positions at or near the Aries Point, the transits to the meridian axis of one simultaneously activate the other, inextricably intertwining the affairs of home, country, government, and the world at large. In the U.S. chart, Capricorn is on the 2nd cusp, with the Fed's Saturn ruling the economy from the cusp of the U.S. 7th (open enemy). The Fed's Saturn is trine the U.S. Saturn, and the government and big business go along with the Fed's money-making scheme.

The U.S. 2nd house Pluto is opposite (within 1') the Fed's Neptune, and along with the U.S. Mercury, is caught up in the Fed's inflationary Neptune–Mars–Jupiter configuration. With Pluto now in the mix, there is more money, more secrecy, and more power at stake.

The Fed's North Bending Venus is in the 1st house of the U.S. chart, which on its own would show money in the pocket of the ordinary American. However, with Venus in a t-square and opposite the U.S. Mars (at the North Bending of the Fed's nodes) and square the U.S. Neptune (conjunct the Fed's South Node), there is an invisible (Neptune) attack (Mars) on the people's money (Venus) that has a negative outward impact on the country.

The Fed's Sun falls in the Sibly 1st house in opposition to the U.S. Venus–Jupiter conjunction and the Fed's Pluto, describing an economic policy whereby money is created through debt (Pluto) that inflates (Jupiter) and devalues the money supply (Venus). The Fed's Uranus falls in the U.S. 2nd house, conjunct the U.S. South Node, a further indication of the loss of value of money resulting from the Fed's policies.

No Bailout

As seen in the last chapter, on September 29, 2008, in wake of the housing crash and the fall of Lehman Brothers, the U.S. economy was in danger of failing. Under pressure from angry constituents, Congress voted to reject the Wall Street bailout that would save the banks. That day the stock market lost 1.2 trillion dollars and fell 778 points (Chart 100). In the Fed's chart, transiting Saturn was conjunct the Fed's progressed South Node, showing the weakness and vulnerability of big business and the government. Transiting Jupiter, empowered by a sextile/trine the progressed nodes, was opposite progressed Mars, and the American people (Jupiter), opposed the bailout and the will of the Treasury and the Fed. Transiting Uranus was conjunct the Fed's natal North Node, and there was outward surprise as the bill, which had been expected to pass, failed.

That morning's New Moon was opposite the Fed's progressed Sun, and for a moment it appeared a new day had dawned where the power of the Fed and the plutocrats would be challenged (transiting Pluto conjunct the Fed's natal Sun and opposite natal Pluto). A grand cross had formed with transiting Mercury opposite progressed Venus and square progressed Mars and transiting Jupiter, describing the stand-off and the opposition to the bill.

Mercury was retrograde, however, and three days after the market plunged, Congress changed its mind and the bill for TARP passed. Transiting Neptune was conjunct the transiting North Node and progressed Jupiter, sextile natal Venus, sextile progressed Venus, and trine progressed Saturn. In the wake of impending financial devastation and disintegration (Neptune), Congress (Saturn) gave the green light to use taxpayer money (Jupiter sextile Venus) to bail out Wall Street.

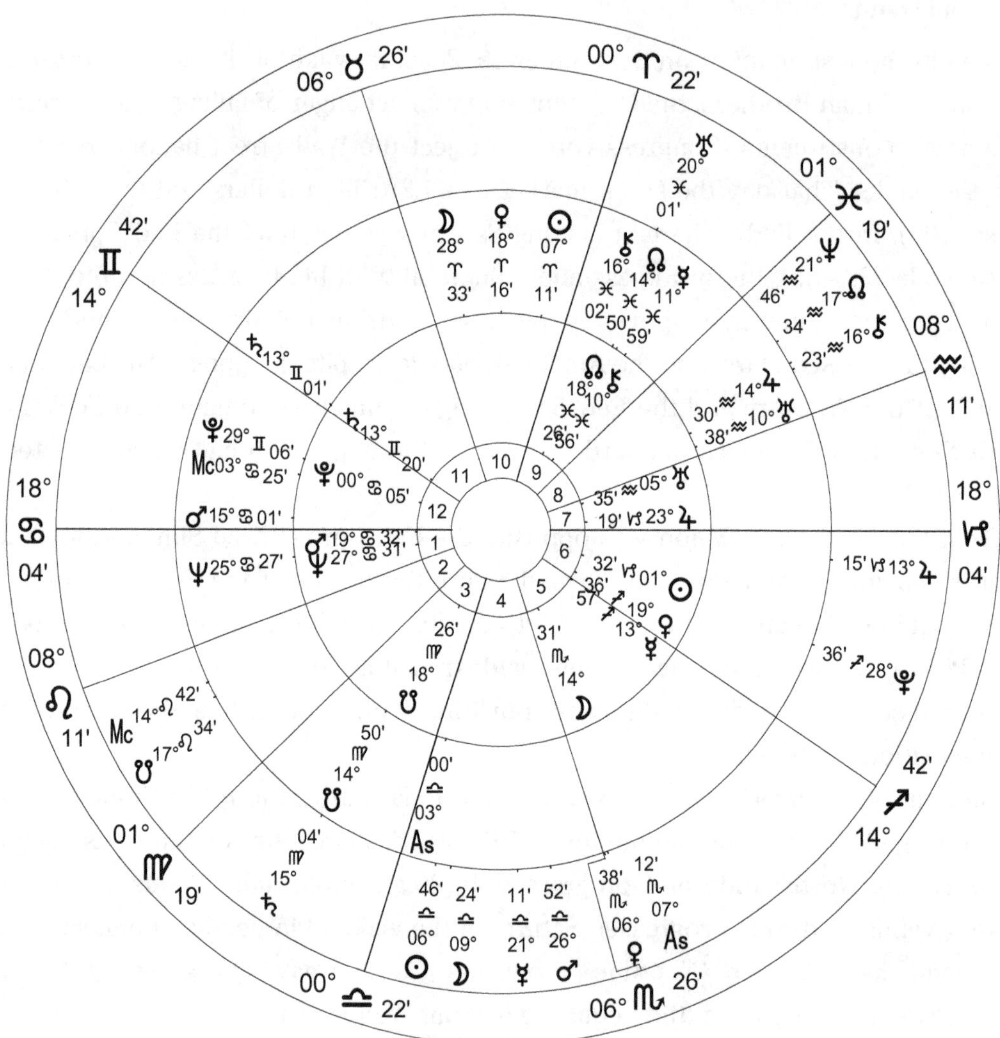

Chart 100:

Fed—No Bailout, Sept. 29, 2008, Washington D.C. noon

Trillion Dollar Handout

While the congressional battle for TARP involved a bailout of $700 billion for the troubled investment banks, two months later, in a single day, the Fed quietly and secretly created $1.2 trillion, which it gave away with no strings, and little or no interest, to its favorite friends on Wall Street. On this day, December 5, 2008 (Chart 101), transiting Pluto (big money) was at the Aries Point conjunct the natal Sun and opposite natal Pluto. With a global threat of recession looming, the Fed did what it was born to do, and that was to save the sinking banks. With the natal Moon at the South Bending of the transiting nodes, the Fed fulfilled its service.

Transiting Uranus (ruler of the 8th house of debt, Wall Street, and big money) was conjunct the natal North Node and the money was made and given away to corporate banks in the U.S. and abroad. There was a double-whammy, with the transiting North Node conjunct progressed Uranus on the cusp of the 8th, reiterating the theme of a secret bailout. Congress was kept in the dark, as shown by transiting Saturn in the 3rd conjunct the natal South Node and opposite progressed North Node and transiting Uranus. It is possible some in government knew, but could do nothing (transiting Saturn in a yod and quincunx progressed Venus and transiting Neptune). Publicly, the plutocrats claimed their banks were in great financial shape, and they were—after the Fed created 1.2 trillion dollars for them (transiting Sun–Mars conjunct natal Mercury, trine progressed Venus). There was a Jupiter return that day, with transiting Jupiter conjunct natal Jupiter and opposite progressed Neptune, and the American people did not see the handout that would cheapen the value of their money. But it would not remain invisible forever.

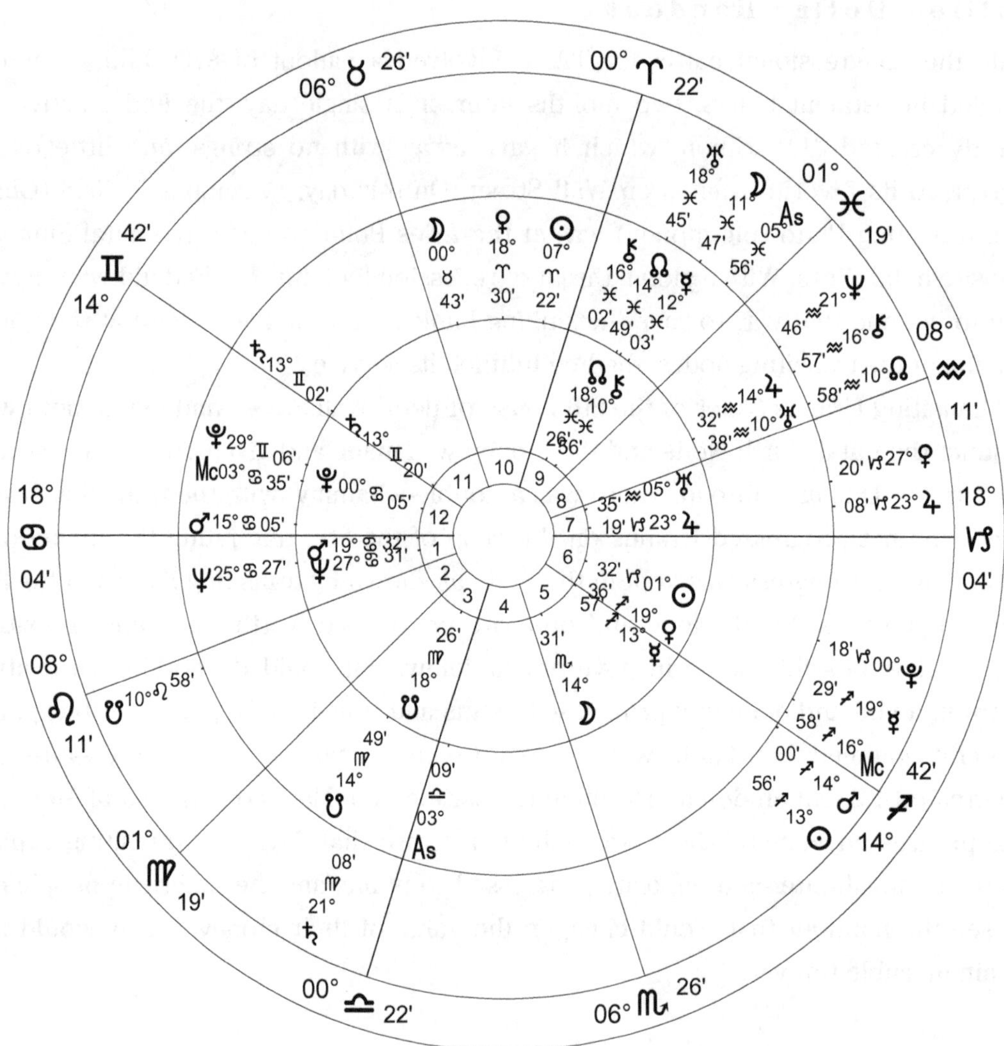

Chart 101:

Fed Handout, Dec. 5, 2008, Washington, D.C., noon

First Audit

Using the Freedom of Information Act, Bloomberg News requested details from the Fed of its 2008 corporate bailout. When the Fed refused, the case went to court. The Fed claimed the release of details would undermine trust in the financial institutes that were bailed out! The lower court of New York disagreed and the suit ended up in the Supreme Court, which declined to hear the case. This meant the ruling of the lower court stood and the Fed was compelled to release pertinent records.

On July 21, 2011, the GAO (Government Accountability Office) released the results of a limited audit, which indicated that between December 1, 2007, and July 21, 2010, the Fed created 16.1 trillion dollars that was used for emergency loans. Since the U.S. gross domestic product in 2010 was 14.5 trillion, the money the Fed created was more than the U.S. made in one year. According to Congressman Ron Paul, "When the Fed in effect doubles the worldwide supply of U.S. dollars in a relatively short time, it has the effect of stealing half your money through reduced purchasing power."

On the day that the audit of the Fed's 2008 secret bailout made the news (Chart 102), transiting Mercury was sextile/trine the nodes and sextile progressed Pluto. Progressed Mercury was conjunct the progressed North Node and quincunx transiting Saturn, and the information was released under duress and penalty of law. The scope of the secret bailout was breathtaking, as shown by transiting Neptune sextile the natal Sun and trine natal Pluto. Transiting Mars (ruling the 10th) in Gemini was at the North Bending of the natal nodes, as the activities of the Fed were made public. With transiting Mars conjunct the transiting South Node, the untoward action taken by the Fed was outwardly apparent (the pair at the natal North Bending). To quell public outrage, with transiting Saturn trine natal Saturn and opposite the progressed Sun, congressional leaders were calling for further audits and the need to curtail the action of the Fed.

The transiting North Node was conjunct natal Venus when the audit revealing the creation of $16.1 trillion was released. Transiting Venus was conjunct the Ascendant and natal Mars, and square progressed Venus, revealing the Fed's feelings (angst) regarding accountability. However, with transiting Venus quincunx natal Venus–transiting North Node, the Fed was forced to comply with the law and divulge the

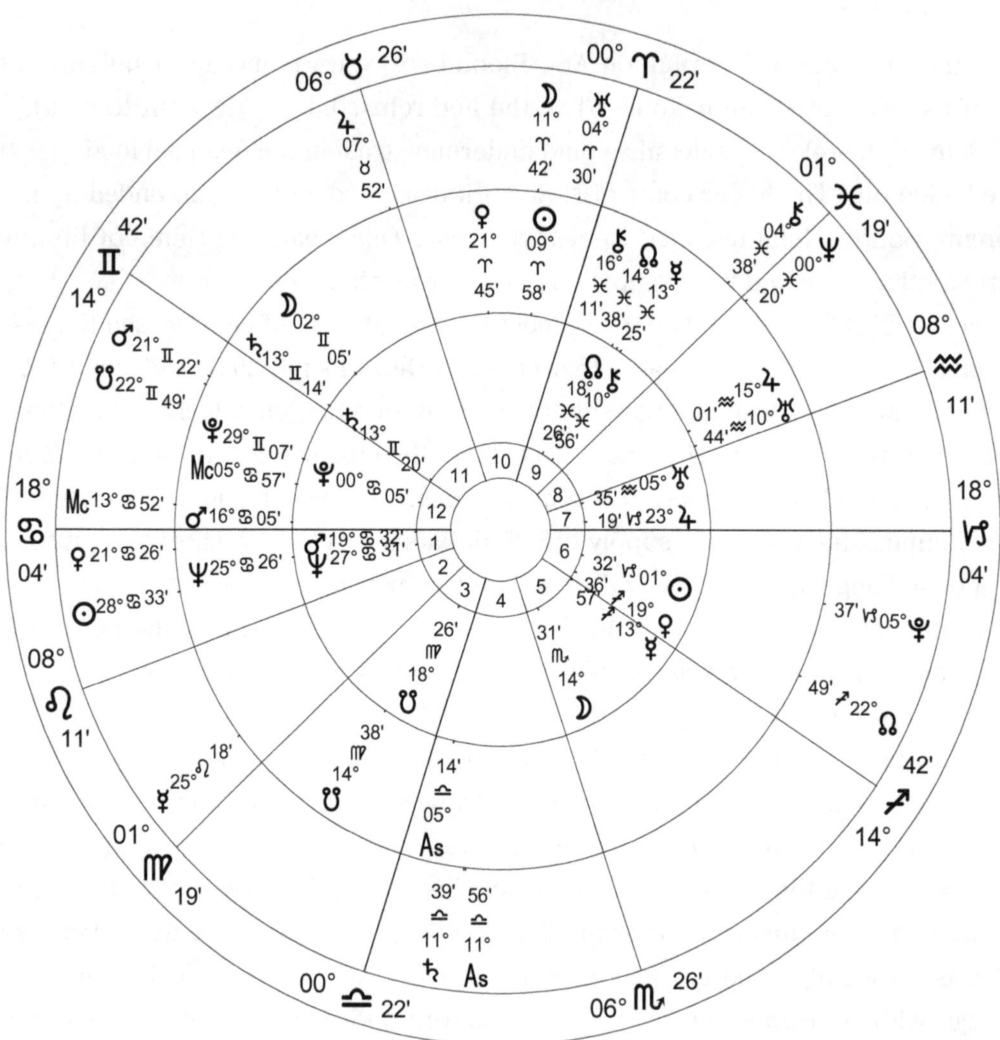

Chart 102:

Fed Audit, July 21, 2011, Washington, D.C. noon

money trail. There was no action it could take to prevent the audit (natal Venus opposite transiting Mars–South Node). According to Ron Paul, the details of the loans made it clear that "the Fed operates for the benefit of a few privileged banks, banks that never suffer for bad decisions they make. Quite the contrary—as we have seen since October 2008, under our current monetary system politically-connected banks are paid to make bad decisions."

We must remember that Satan has miracles too.

—*John Calvin*

Chapter 25
Acts of God

The nodes are markers of mundane catastrophes. The North Node energy describes the nature of the crisis, and the South Node energy indicates related effects and losses. While the transiting aspects in an event chart symbolically reflect the mundane event, the aspects are personalized through their interactions with a nation's nativity. The lord of the eclipse is frequently a trigger and directly involved in the astrological signature of the event.

Indonesian Tsunami

On Boxing Day 2004, two tectonic plates slipped, causing a 9.2 magnitude earthquake along a fault line on the Indian Ocean floor 1,000 miles long. The epicenter was 19 miles below sea level and 100 miles offshore of Sumatra in Indonesia. The slippage lifted the sea floor by several meters and generated tsunami waves almost 100 feet high. The waves stormed ashore and affected 14 countries, primarily Indonesia, Sri Lanka, India, and Thailand. More than 230,000 people were killed. Relief donations totaled $14 billion dollars.

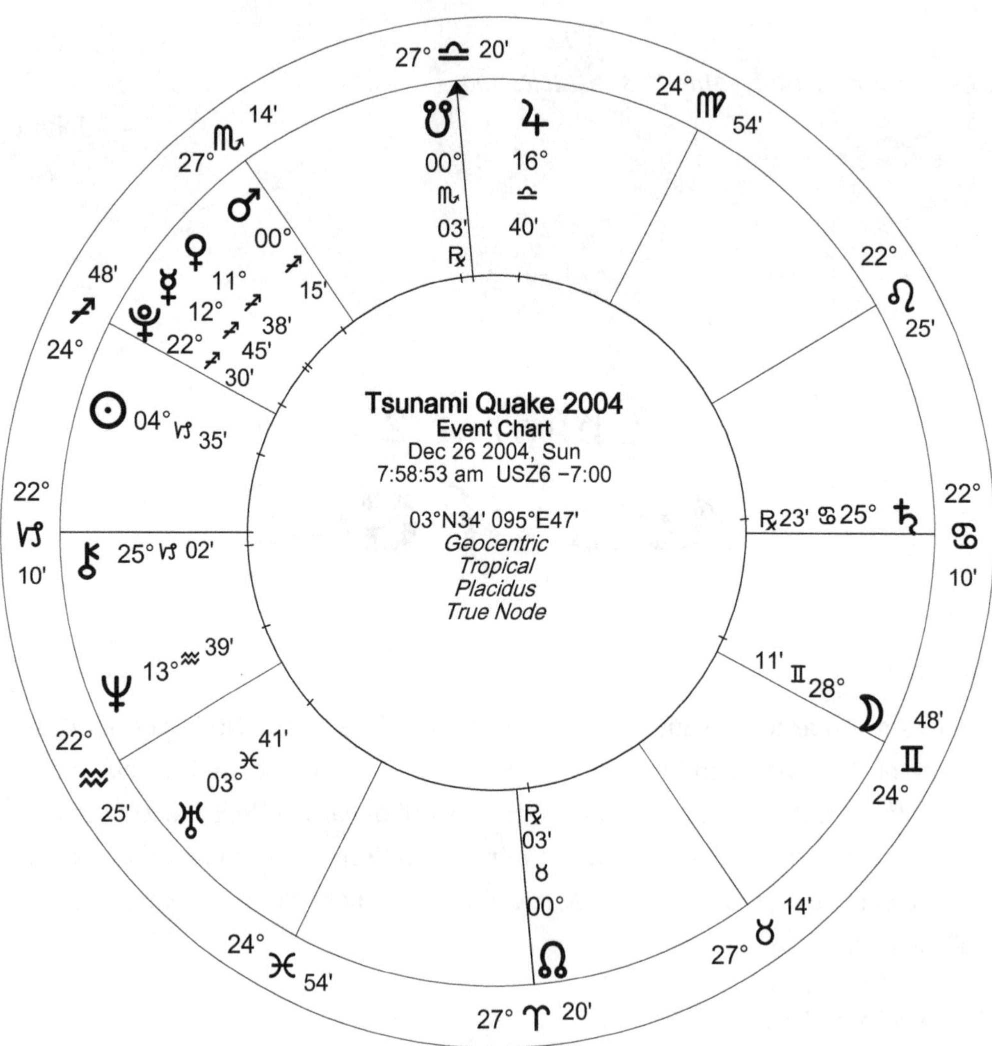

Chart 103:

Indonesian Tsunami Event

The solar eclipse before the tsunami was on October 14, 2004, at 21°05' Libra, directing attention to Venus (lord). On the morning of the quake (Chart 103), Venus was in mutual reception with Jupiter (expansion) and sextile Neptune (ocean). Neptune and Uranus were in mutual reception, describing a sudden and shocking oceanic event. Neptune was trine Jupiter, an indication of the immensity of the water and a wall of waves. Venus was in applying conjunction to Mercury, which was in detriment and moving slowly after a recent station. With Mercury involved and the earthquake occurring on the Pacific Rim of Fire, an underground volcano (Venus and Mercury in a fire sign) may have precipitated the earthquake.

Uranus was sextile/trine the nodes, gaining power. It formed an applying square to Mars, describing a violent shaking of the ocean floor. Mars in Sagittarius suggests an underground explosion, and flowing magma may have precipitated the seismic shifting of the plates. With Mars quincunx the nodes and Uranus sextile/trine them, the combined energy was especially destructive (1,500 times the energy of the Hiroshima atomic bomb). In declination, Uranus was parallel the South Node, an indication of loss through the sudden event.

The Moon was out-of-bounds, sextile/trine the nodes, void-of-course, and in applying quincunx to Mars, and no action could be taken to stop the rush of water. The Sun in Capricorn was sextile/trine the nodes, and sextile Uranus, describing a sudden shocking event that brought death (Sun ruling the 8th).

There was an exact Chiron–Saturn opposition across the event Ascendant–Descendant, denoting a physical wound. With Saturn in detriment, the wound was especially egregious, and not only homes, but entire villages and towns were obliterated by walls of water.

In latitude, Saturn and Neptune were parallel and contraparallel Mars, near the center line of the ecliptic, and thus parallel the Sun, angles, and nodes, attesting to a physically catastrophic energetic event in the ocean that brought devastation and suffering.

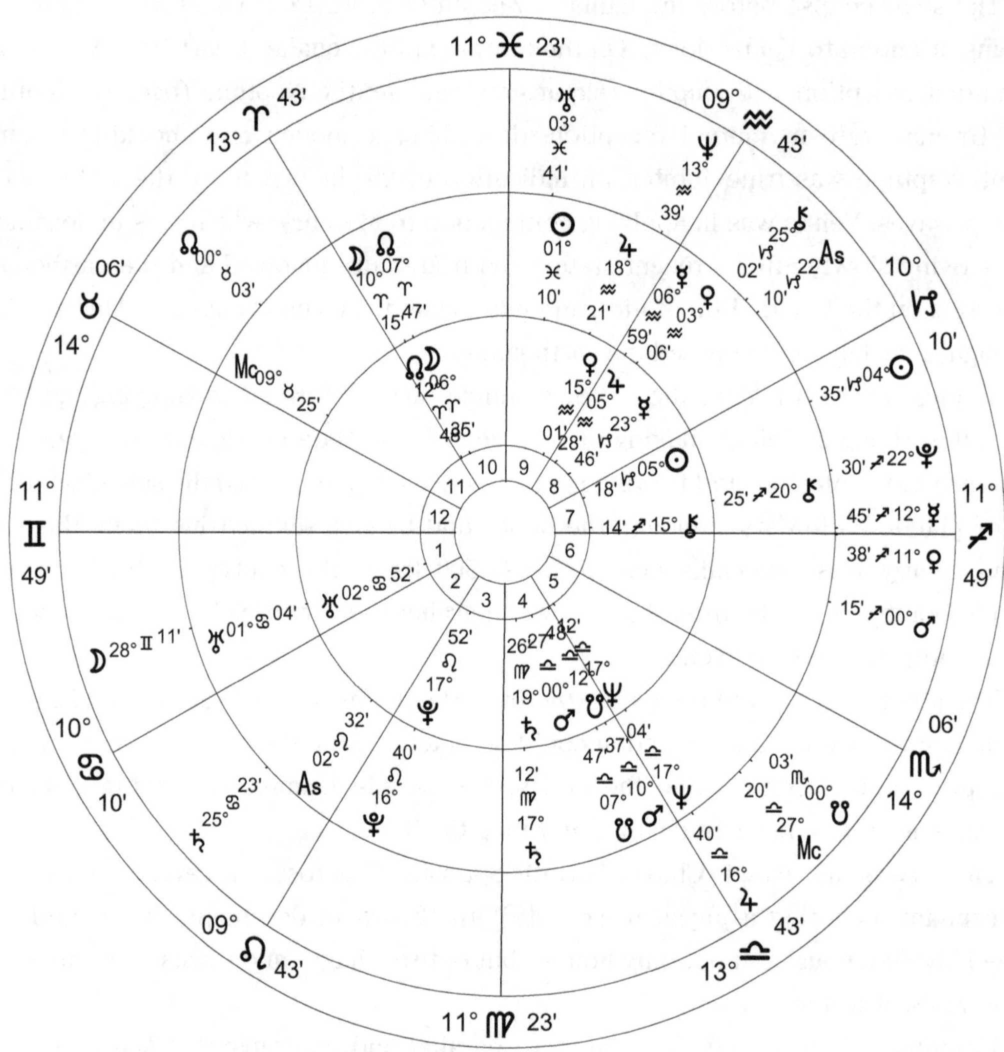

Chart 104:
Indonesian Flood Impact, Dec. 26, 2004, Jakarta, 7:58 a.m. USZ6

Indonesian Flood Impact

When viewed along with the nativity of Jakarta, Indonesia (Chart 104), transiting Jupiter was conjunct the country's Neptune (big water), trine progressed Jupiter and transiting Neptune; a double-whammy signifying and amplifying a message of torrential oceanic water. With transiting Jupiter sextile natal Pluto and trine transiting Neptune, the effect was massive death from drowning.

Natally, the country has a grand cross comprised of the Sun square Moon opposite Uranus and square Mars (at a cardinal point), symbolizing the promise of a sudden and destructive event, affecting leaders and the population, which will bring the country to the attention of the world. The configuration was activated on the day of the tsunami, with the progressed North Node conjunct the natal Moon, and the progressed Moon conjunct the natal North Node, forming a double-whammy indicative of an outward event affecting the people (Moon). Progressed Mars was conjunct the natal South Node, highlighting loss from destructive energy. It was a day of the solar return and the transiting Sun was conjunct the natal Sun, activating the potential of the natal grand cross. With the transiting Sun at the South Bending of the progressed nodes, there was loss for the country and the government. Transiting Uranus was conjunct the progressed Sun, trine natal Uranus, sextile the transiting Sun, sextile/trine the transiting nodes, and forming a yod with an inconjunct to the progressed Ascendant and a quincunx to natal Mars, suggesting a destructive accident that would strike without warning.

In declination, the natal South Node and Neptune were contraparallel, and at the time of the tsunami, transiting Jupiter was parallel Neptune, portending loss through expanding ocean waters.

Hurricane Katrina

In the last week of August in 2005, Hurricane Katrina formed in the Atlantic Ocean over the Bahamas. It passed over South Florida and crossed into the warm waters of the Gulf of Mexico, where it gained strength as it headed for New Orleans, a city in part below sea level. The massive Category 3 storm struck the port city at daybreak on August 29, 2005, bringing winds of 125 miles that spread out in a radius of 120 miles. The storm surge reached 14 feet, 8–10 inches of rain fell, 53 levees around New Orleans breached, and 80 percent of the city flooded. The death toll was 1,836, with property damage amounting to $81 billion dollars, making the storm the most costly to date in U.S. history.

The north nodal solar eclipse before the event was on April 8, 2005, at 19°05' Aries, with Mars as the lord. On the day of the event (Chart 105), Mars was in a t-square with Neptune (energetic water) and Mercury (wind). Jupiter was opposite the eclipse degree, and in a yod with Mars and Pluto (frustration and inability to respond to a mortal threat).

Venus was dignified in Libra and conjunct (and ruling) the South Node and conjunct Jupiter (immense monetary loss). Neptune (floods, water and confusion) was sextile/trine the nodes and Venus–Jupiter, denoting an unimpeded flow of water.

The Sun was opposite Uranus, and Saturn was quincunx Uranus, describing a federal government that failed to recognize the scope of the catastrophe. The Moon in Cancer was out-of-bounds (extreme response) and sextile-trine the Sun–Uranus opposition, and the people (Moon) bore the brunt of the government's inefficacy. Pluto was trine Mercury and sextile Jupiter, and the weather service (Mercury) accurately predicted the hurricane path and strength, but no timely action was taken in response (Mars in a yod and t-square). Uranus and Neptune were in mutual reception, with Uranus in Pisces and Neptune in Aquarius, repeating the theme of a sudden upset involving much water.

In declination, Neptune and Pluto were parallel and contraparallel Mercury, denoting a combination of wind, water, and destruction. Uranus was contraparallel the Sun, forming an occultation with the longitudinal opposition and strengthening both aspects, which translated to a government unprepared for a catastrophe. Venus, Jupiter, and the South Node were also parallel and formed an occultation, intensifying the aspect and the magnitude of loss.

Although not evident in longitude, the Moon at a latitude of 5N08 was at the North Bending, and in this instance was related to the extreme manifestation of torrential water.

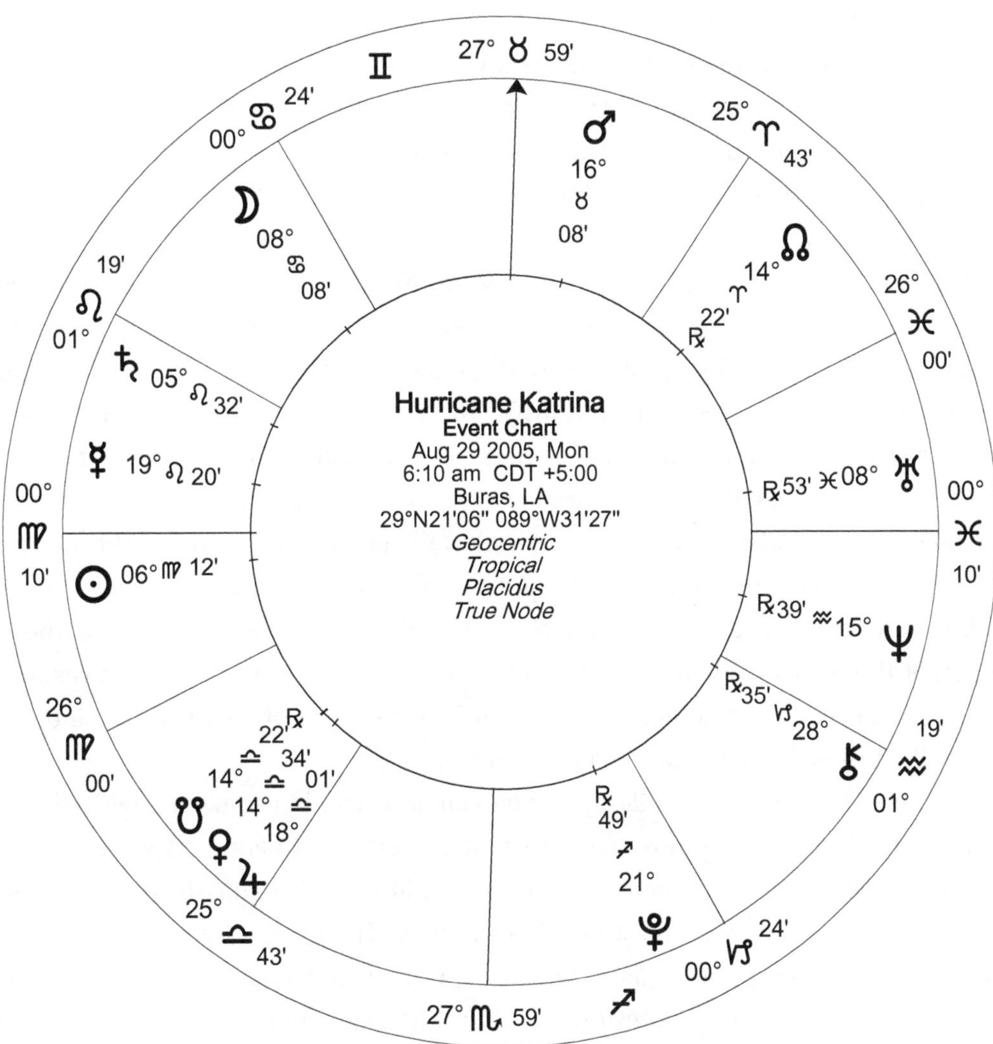

Chart 105:

Hurricane Katrina Event

U.S. Storm Impact

The mundane aspects operating universally at the time the hurricane struck were channeled by the planets and points in the U.S. birth chart (Chart 106). The solar eclipse prior the storm at 19°5' Aries, was conjunct natal Chiron opposite progressed Mars (lord), and trine transiting Pluto, portending a wounding act of carnage and destruction.

On the day of the storm, the transiting South Node was conjunct transiting Venus, Jupiter, progressed Mars, and natal Saturn, reflecting large (Jupiter) financial losses (Venus) related to inaction (Mars in detriment) and losses of physical structures, authority, and functional society (Saturn). The transiting North Node was conjunct progressed Venus, in detriment in Aries, in the 4th, denoting an outward event affecting the country that exposed an unprepared civil service (Venus ruling the 6th) and a president who was out of touch with his people (Venus ruling the 10th). The transiting North Node was square the natal Sun and progressed Jupiter at the North Bending, which manifested as a failure of leadership. With Saturn ruling the 2nd house, the conjunction of the South Node to natal Saturn reflected the loss of money and resources. Transiting Saturn was conjunct the U.S. North Node (a double-whammy), indicating outward limitation, restriction, shortages, and suffering.

Progressed Uranus was sextile/trine the natal nodes and in a t-square with the transiting Sun and transiting Uranus (facing sudden upset). Transiting Neptune was trine natal Saturn (and transiting South Node–Venus–Jupiter) and sextile the transiting North Node and progressed Venus, and water flowed easily. Transiting Pluto formed a t-square with the U.S. Mars–Neptune square, which expressed as a deadly flood accompanied with untoward action and confusion, resulting in death and decimation. Progressed Neptune was sextile/trine the progressed nodes and sextile the progressed Moon, a further indication of water flowing without restraint and the confusion of the public.

Gulf Oil Spill

On April 20, 2010 (Chart 107), the Deepwater Horizon oil well exploded in the Gulf of Mexico, killing eleven, wounding seventeen, and spewing crude oil into the gulf. Three days later the rig platform sunk, while underwater, oil continued to gush. Located fifty

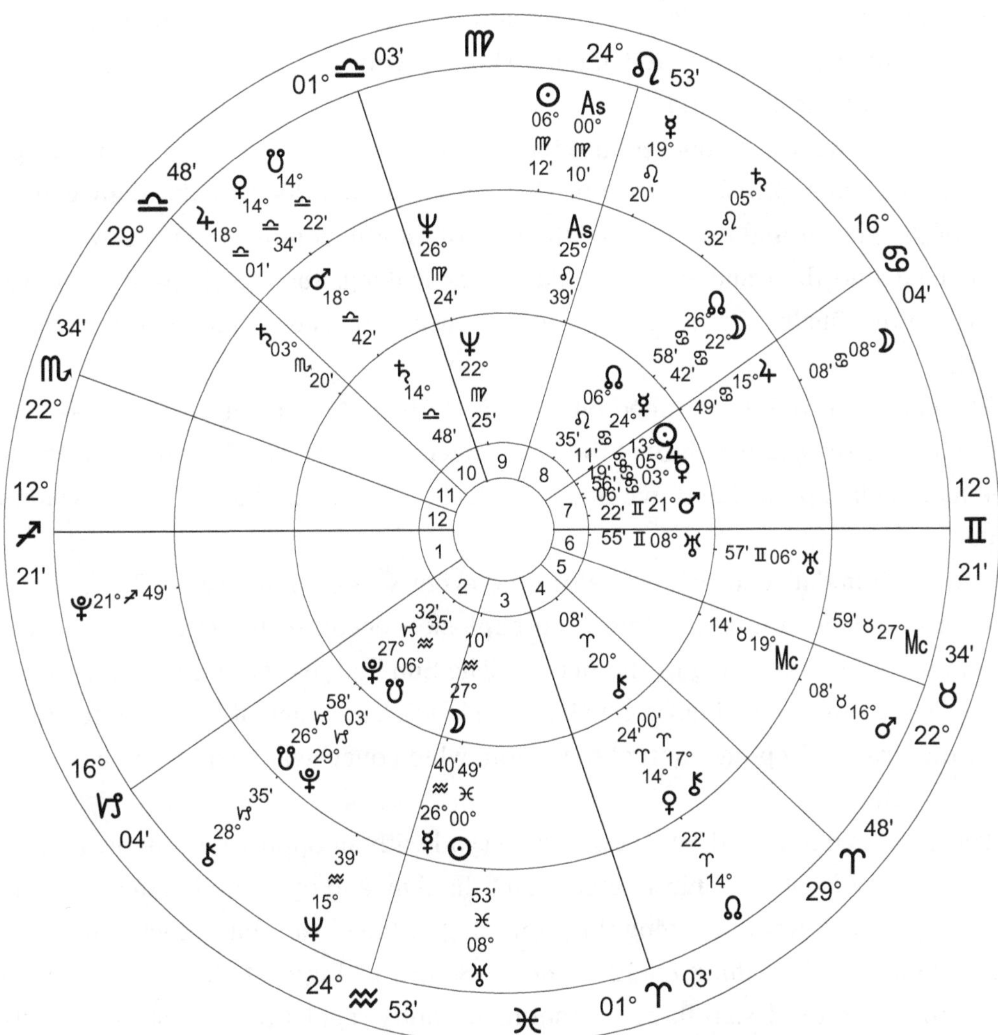

Chart 106:

Hurricane Katrina Impact U.S., Aug. 29, 2005, Buras, LA, 6:10 a.m. CDT

miles southwest of the Mississippi Delta and the Breton Wildlife Refuge, the oil contaminated surrounding flora and fauna. Those involved in shrimp, oyster, and fish harvesting lost their livelihood.

For thirty days, the oil poured into the gulf out of public view. After Congress pressured the oil giant British Petroleum (BP) to air its live feed of the damaged well, views of the gusher and estimates of the rate of oil effusion made daily news. At first BP claimed one thousand barrels a day were leaking, then perhaps five thousand barrels, before finally admitting fifty-three thousand barrels a day were pouring into the gulf.

The damaged well was capped on July 15, 2010, and it was permanently sealed by September 19, 2010, at which time the government declared it officially dead. By then, three months had passed and five million barrels of crude oil had soiled the waters of the gulf.

The north nodal solar eclipse before the event was on January 15, 2010, at 25°01' Capricorn, with Saturn as the lord. The explosion occurred hours after Chiron's ingress into Pisces (wounding of the ocean). The Sun had just entered Taurus and was sextile Chiron (the ocean injury translating to land). The blowout occurred toward the end of the Uranus–Neptune mutual reception, which once again expressed as a sudden oceanic event.

The chart is dominated by a boomerang (yod with an opposition) involving Saturn (lord) quincunx Neptune–Chiron, inconjunct the Sun, and opposite Uranus, describing a sudden physical event involving the wounding of the ocean that affected nearby life forms, about which nothing could be done. Saturn in Virgo at the apex of the yod, alludes to structural design flaws, questions of faulty regulation, and lax standards of safety that came to light after the explosion.

The Moon in Cancer rules the South Node and corresponds to a loss for the people. The Moon is trine Jupiter and sextile Venus, forming a deceptively insidious exalted configuration that describes an easy and massive flow of resources from beneath the ocean floor that appeared unstoppable.

In declination, Mercury and Pluto were contraparallel, relating to the (early) power of BP to control the news of the accident. The Sun and Neptune were contraparallel,

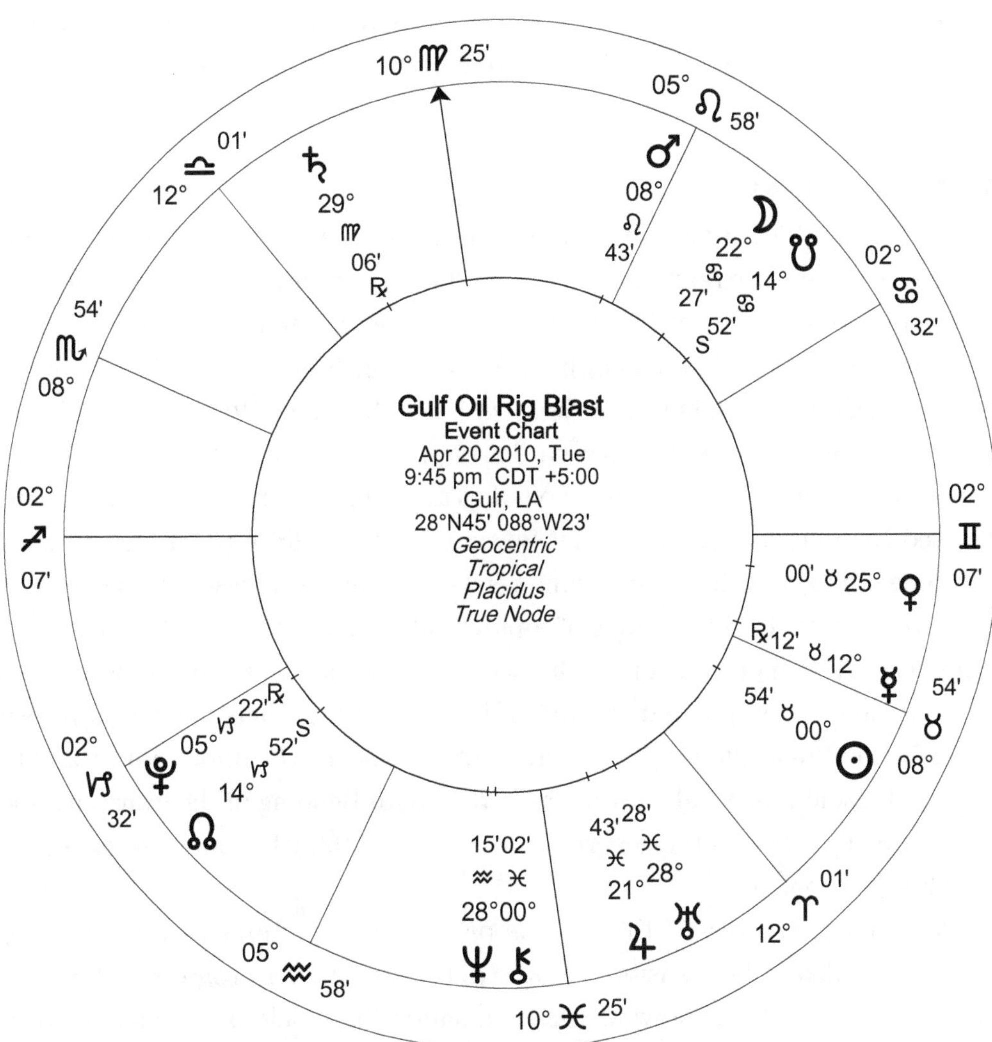

Chart 107:
Gulf Oil Rig Blast Event

indicating the government's (early) compliance with BP's analysis concerning the ocean's condition. The Moon and Mars were parallel, pointing to great public outrage over the accident.

U.S. Spill Impact

The solar eclipse (25°1' Capricorn) before the Deepwater Horizon blowout was conjunct the U.S. progressed South Node and U.S. Pluto, portending loss related to oil.

At the time of the incident (Chart 108), the U.S. progressed Moon was conjunct natal Neptune square natal Mars and opposite transiting Jupiter, symbolizing a massive oceanic explosion. Transiting Mars was conjunct the natal North Node, which expressed as an outward blast. Progressed Chiron was at the North Bending of the transiting nodes, indicating a manifest wound. Transiting Saturn (lord) was conjunct progressed Neptune and the U.S. Midheaven, trine the eclipse point and progressed South Node–Pluto, and trine transiting Venus and the progressed Midheaven. This configuration points to the attempt of a powerful business to limit the government's and the people's comprehension of the scope of the accident. The transiting South Node was conjunct progressed Jupiter and the natal Sun, and there was a loss of standing for the President and the government, who seemed without power and helpless to enact a solution. Natal Saturn was at the South Bending of the transiting nodes, repeating the message that the government could do nothing but stand aside and allow BP to solve the problem.

In declination, progressed Uranus was parallel the progressed North Node, symbolizing an accident. The transiting South Node was parallel progressed Jupiter and parallel the country's Sun, showing loss for a nation that could only watch as torrents of crude oil fouled the gulf waters.

Japanese Tsunami and Nuclear Meltdown

On March 11, 2011, with Uranus in Pisces minutes away from its Aries ingress, there was an 8.9 earthquake on the ocean floor that occurred two hundred and thirty miles northeast of Tokyo. The earthquake generated a tsunami that swamped the eastern coast of Japan. As in the Indonesian quake, the earth tremors were caused by a

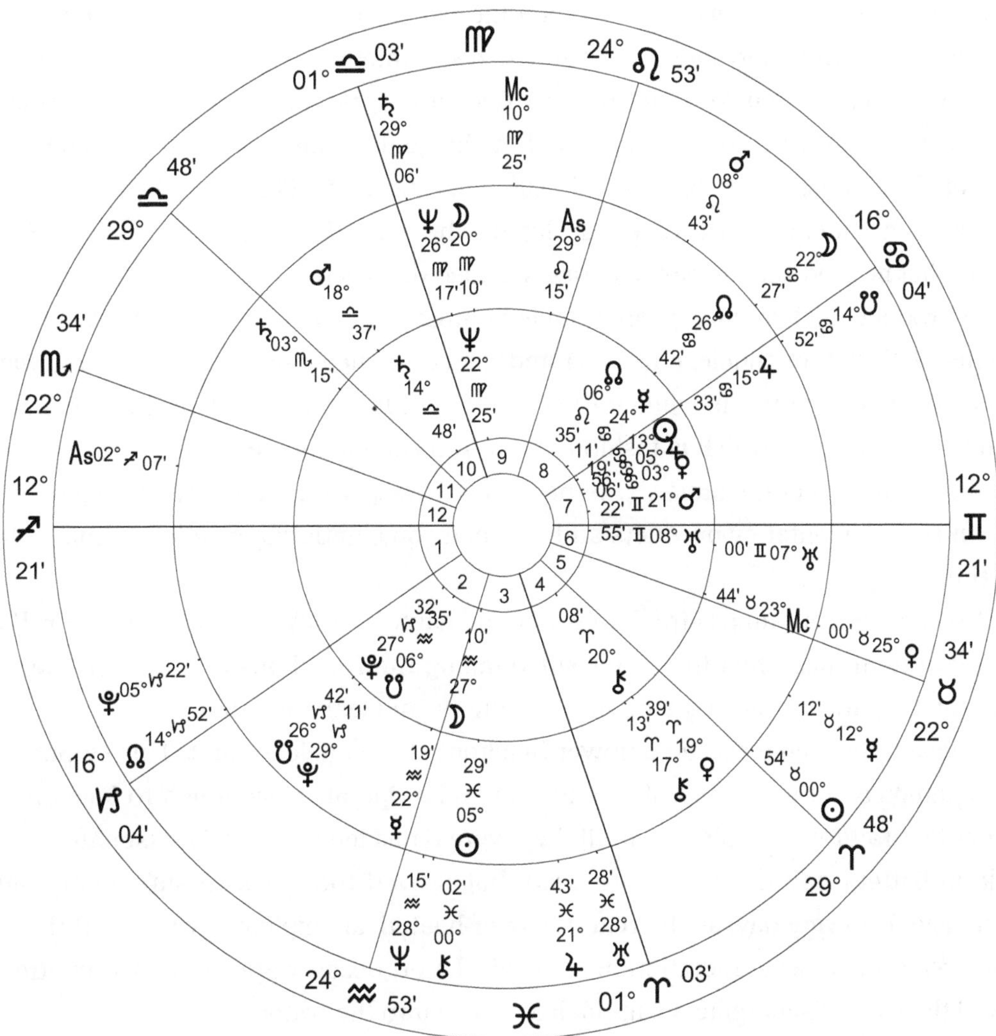

Chart 108:

Gulf Oil Blast U.S. Impact, Apr. 20, 2010, Gulf, LA, 9.45 p.m.

rupture in a fault zone between two tectonic plates. The rupture was 300 miles long and 120 miles wide, and increased the earth's diameter by 13 feet, speeding up the earth's rotation. The quake lifted the sea floor and generated tsunami waves that hit Japan's shoreline ten to thirty minutes after the quake. The waves reached as high as 130 feet. The tsunami left 16,000 dead, 5,000 missing, and 6,000 injured—a smaller toll than seen in Indonesia. However, in Japan, the Fukushima Daiichi Nuclear Power Station that housed six nuclear reactors was also damaged.

To produce nuclear energy, an atom is bombarded with a neutron, which splits the nucleus of the atom (nuclear fission) and generates heat that is used to boil water. This drives a stream turbine, generating electricity. In a nuclear plant, the bombarded atom is Uranium 235, which is fashioned into rods and immersed in a coolant of water and sealed in a steel container. One neutron reacting with Uranium 235 typically results in two elemental by-products and two neutrons, initiating a self-sustaining chain reaction.

Typically, water pumps circulate water and carry heat away from the reactor. If the coolant system fails, then the water surrounding the rods boils away. Once the rods overheat, they melt, breach their steel containers, and leak radiation.

In Japan, the quake caused a power blackout at the nuclear plant. This stopped the water pumps and the cooling of the nuclear rods. Operators switched to backup generators that ran for fifty minutes until they were damaged by forty-foot tsunami waves. Back-up battery power packs were used, but proved too weak to sufficiently pump water. The following day, as the reactors over-heated, an explosion ripped off the roof of one reactor, spewing radiation into the air. Later, ocean water was used in attempt to cool the rods, discharging spent nuclear waste into the water.

A month later, on April 6, 2011, there was a meltdown in one of the six reactors. Currently, the plant has been decommissioned and the true extent of the radioactive contamination is unknown. Experts believe the radiation will take decades to clean up.

The north nodal solar eclipse before the event was on January 4, 2011, at 13°38' Capricorn, with Saturn as the lord. On the day of the tsunami (Chart 109), Saturn was square the eclipse point, and quincunx Mars in Pisces, reflecting an underwater fracture of the tectonic plates that released uncontrollable energy about which nothing could be done.

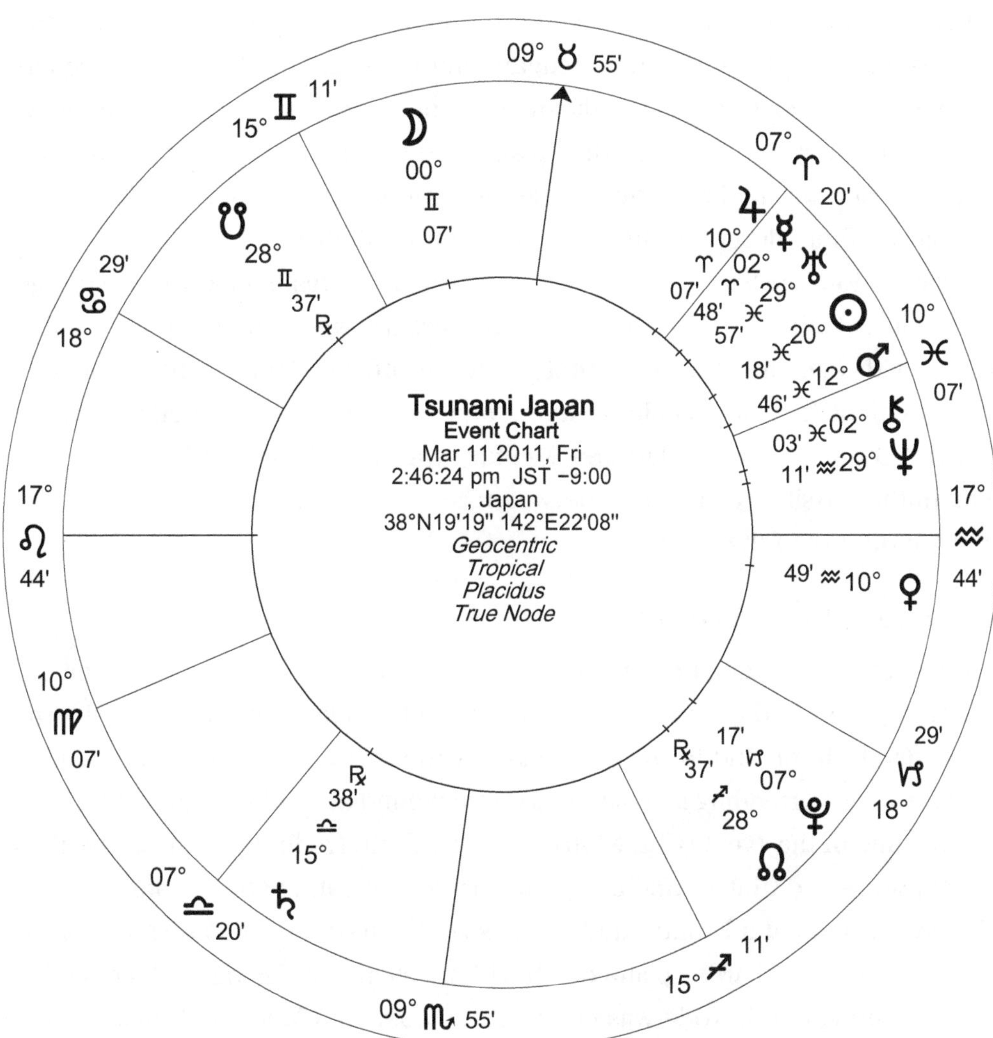

Chart 109:

Japanese Tsunami Event

At 29°, both Uranus (electricity) and Neptune (oceans) were in the last degrees of their signs, marking the end of their lengthy mutual reception. Uranus was square the nodal axis at the North Bending indicating the outward expression of Uranus, which manifested as an upset in an electrical plant following an underwater quake. Neptune was sextile/trine the nodes, showing the tsunami and an unimpeded flow of water. Jupiter square Pluto describes the crisis of radiation (Pluto).

In declination, the Sun and Saturn were parallel, suggesting a difficult struggle, affliction, and a lack of vitality. Uranus and Mercury were contraparallel, indicating problems with communication. At first Japanese officials labeled the severity of the nuclear accident four on a scale of seven, and were slow to move citizens at risk of radioactive contamination. In latitude, Mercury was near the center line of the ecliptic, leading to the possibility that an underwater current or sub-sea level air flow contributed to the rupture of the plates.

Japanese Flood Impact

As always, the connections of an event chart to a natal chart provide a channel for mundane aspects. In the Japanese nativity, the solar eclipse at 13°38' Capricorn, was conjunct natal Chiron and formed a t-square with natal Uranus and natal Saturn (lord and chart ruler), portending a crisis related to a wound at an electrical plant.

At the time of the event (Chart 110) transiting Pluto (radiation) was in the 1st house conjunct progressed Chiron, and in a grand cross with natal Saturn, transiting Jupiter–natal Mercury and natal Uranus, and progressed Venus–Sun, indicating a catastrophic nuclear event causing hardship and death with no clear way forward (all boxed in).

The transiting South Node was conjunct the country's Moon and square transiting Uranus at the North Bending, reflecting an electrical event causing loss for the people. Transiting Neptune was conjunct the country's North Node, sextile/trine the transiting nodes, and trine the natal Moon, describing a tsunami that drowned thousands. Transiting Saturn was conjunct natal Neptune and sextile progressed Moon–Pluto and natal Pluto, reflecting death from radiation and a destructive tsunami, with suffering compounded by government misinformation and denial.

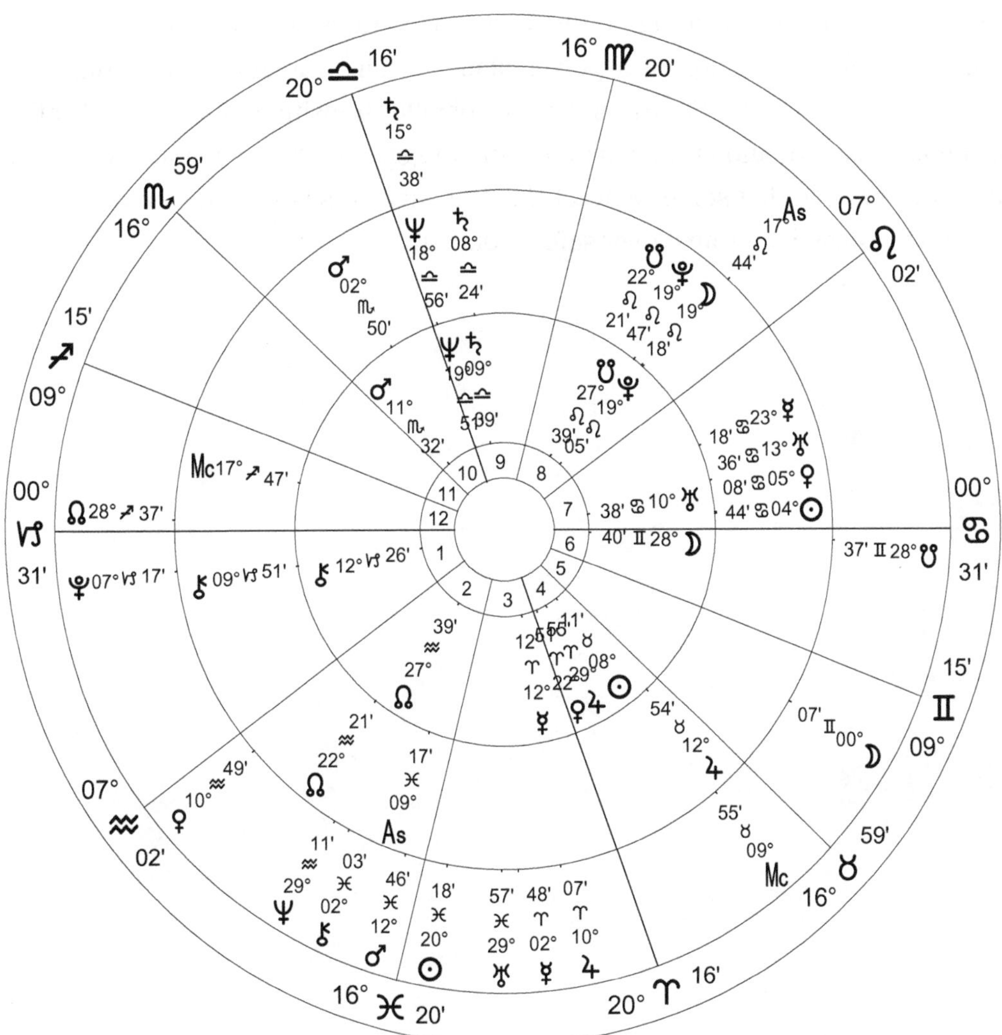

Chart 110:

Japanese Flood Impact, March 11, 2011, Japan, 2:46 p.m. JST

In declination, the transiting South Node was parallel progressed Pluto and natal Uranus, a simple description of a power planet leaking radiation. Transiting Uranus was parallel the country's Saturn and contraparallel transiting Mercury, indicative of misleading or lack of authentic communication regarding the accident. After the accident, news surfaced that some General Electric engineers who designed the plant had long before resigned in protest over safety concerns.

It is never too late to be what you might have been

— George Eliot

Chapter 26
Conclusions

In this text, no new keywords for the nodes were introduced. Astrologers working during the last century have clearly grasped the essence of the nodes. The problem is, the meaning of the nodes was reversed, the distinction between the nodes and eclipses was blurred, the significance of the bendings was ignored, and the house position of the nodes assumed undue importance. Not once during natal chart analysis were the houses of the nodes delineated. That is not to say that I did not look carefully at the house position during this study, or that this has no bearing on a chart—it is just not the dominant feature. When I ignored house position altogether, I achieved more consistent results.

Vedic astrologers view the nodes as physical bodies. However, astronomically the nodes are invisible points of intersection of two orbital planes. While western astrologers are cautioned not to mix the two systems, in the West, we have been treating the invisible points as if they are real: hence the attention to house position. However, only a physical body has the ability to act. The node itself is not active.

Early in the study, the importance of the nodal rulers became clear. As I considered an explanation for this, a return to astronomical principles led me to see that the nodes resemble an angle. I have long viewed the angles as a doorway through which the astrological force flows. However, angles are not active and require a planet for expression. This planet is the ruler, or, any planet conjunct the angle (natally or by transit).

The outward effect of a planet at an angle is well known—the planet is energized and guaranteed expression. So it was with the nodes. When a natal planet was conjunct a node, the planet gained significance. This was also observed with a transiting planet crossing a node, or a transiting node crossing a planet: that planet's symbolism was actualized into existence and gained transient observable expression. This helps explain why the natal houses containing the nodes (especially the house of the North Node) acquired such significance—at some point, a planet would conjunct the node, become energized, and activate the house. However, the action was incorrectly attributed to the node rather than the planet.

There is a distinct qualitative difference in energy between the North and South Node, as distinct, as say, the difference between Aries and Libra. The North Node pertains to the building of the ego (Aries-like), while South Node energy is connected to something larger than the self (Libra-like). While planets conjunct the North Node were considered to be well-behaved, too much energy can overpower a North Node planet, resulting in over-stimulation and over-use, which can cause problems. Planets conjunct the South Node were considered ruined, but this is not always the case. A South Node planet used for the greatest good can bring stellar effects. The defining feature is not the type of node (North or South), but how the nodal energy is used and for what purpose.

The bendings have been treated as if they are similar, but they are no more equivalent than the top of a mountain and the bottom of an ocean. The bendings are the zenith and nadir of the lunar orbit and represent the highest of highs (North Bending) and the lowest of lows (South Bending). There is a world of difference in the expression of a planet square the nodes at the North Bending and one square the nodes at the South Bending, a difference as stark as summer and winter.

The natal nodes point to the location of nearby eclipses. The PNSE activates the house where it falls, promoting the expansion of activities related to the house. In the event of a south nodal PNSE, the house with the South Node is activated. In a north nodal PNSE, the house of the North Node is activated. Here again, it is the house of the PNSE that is significant, rather than the house of the node.

However, the important factors in an eclipse (prenatal or transiting) are not the nodes, but the luminaries. It is the degree of the eclipse—not the degree of the nodes—that matters. A solar eclipse is powerful because it contains three repeating aspects of the luminaries: the longitudinal conjunction, the declinational parallel, and the latitudinal parallel. With the node in attendance there is a direct outlet of the luminary energies, which explains why eclipses are so reliable in forecasting.

The importance of the lord of the eclipse seems to have been, well, eclipsed. As the dispositor of the (eclipsed) Sun and Moon, the lord influences how the eclipse is expressed. In forecasting, the archetype of the lord of the eclipse is activated, such that the corresponding natal, progressed, and transiting planet appears equally dynamic. This provides a helpful tool in both timing and defining the meaning of a transit or progression. In addition, transiting inner planets (and at times outer planets) coming to an eclipse point, node, or bending, often serve as a trigger to precipitate events. Used together, the lord and the nodes are a potent forecasting tool.

The type of eclipse is another neglected feature of eclipse delineation. In looking at the events in this study, most of the eclipses were north nodal, in that the Sun and Moon were conjunct the North Node during an observable crisis. South nodal eclipses are less visible and relate to inner crises, but also periods of selfless service, the release of a great work, and marriage.

Nodal Energy

Throughout the text, I delineated numerous nativities to illustrate how to interpret the nodes. In natal delineation, I still give precedence to the Sun, Moon, and chart ruler. Next, I look at the nodal energy and examine the placement of the rulers with respect to planet, sign, house, and aspects. All things being equal, the North Node ruler strengthens the house where it stands and the house(s) it rules, and benefits planets that it aspects. The South Node ruler has the opposite effect (at least early on in life) and weakens the house where it stands, the house(s) it rules, and the planets that it aspects. There is some kind of problem related to the archetype of the South Node ruler, which improves over time, or once the planet is used in service for the greater good.

For an event, I look at the lord of the most recent solar eclipse (lords in the case of two solar eclipses) and examine that planet natally, by progression, and transit. I then go straight to the nodes, natal, progressed, and transiting, and look at the planets that conjunct and square these points. This is typically sufficient to describe the outward event.

A planet in declinational relationship with the nodes is in the same plane of the nodes above or below the celestial equator. Viewed as a conjunction, nodal parallels are easy to read since they combine only the meaning of the planet without the added context of sign and house. A planet parallel the North Node acts out the energy of the node in the service of the ego. A planet parallel the South Node is either detrimental to the ego, spiritually inclined, or provides a service to others.

Planets in latitudinal relationship with the nodes are on the ecliptic and form an aspect with the Sun and the four angles. Such a planet always has a latitude of (nearly) 0°, since this is the latitude of the Sun, angles, and by definition, the nodes—the intersection of the lunar orbit with the ecliptic. For this reason, a natal planet on the ecliptic, or one progressing to, or transiting over the ecliptic, is always important, because the contact with the angles and the nodes enables outward expression.

Nodal Myth

To date, astrologers have no Greek myth with which to understand the archetypal meaning of the nodes. However, there is one that appropriately describes their energy and expression. That myth is *Pandora's Box*, which explains how evil came to earth.

Pandora was created on the high order of Zeus after he had been tricked by the Titan Prometheus who stole fire from the gods and gave it to humankind. In retaliation, Zeus had Hephaestus fashion a perfect woman out of clay. Athena, the goddess of war, breathed life into her. Aphrodite gave her beauty, desire, and feminine wiles. Apollo taught her music, and Hermes gave her cunning and curiosity. Zeus sent Pandora (whose name means 'she who sends up gifts') to earth, along with a box she was never to open. Although Prometheus (whose name means foresight and who had the gift of prophesy) had warned his brother Epimetheus (whose name means after-thought) never to accept a gift from Zeus, when Epimetheus saw Pandora, he could not resist her, and they were married.

Pandora could not resist the temptation of the box. With time, curiosity got the better of her and she opened the lid, releasing every pestilence and horror imaginable: pandemics, illness, old-age, labor, pain, vice, passion, greed, poverty. Every possible evil afflicting humankind was let loose upon the earth. Too late, Pandora closed the lid, trapping only hope.

The myth describes the human predicament. We come to earth like Pandora, bearing gifts from the gods that are described by planets carrying North Node energy. These planets are endowed with wisdom and knowledge that facilitate their expression, bringing good results in the manifest realm. However, we also come with a box containing our own personal horrors that we unknowingly release, described by planets carrying South Node energy. These planets are vulnerable, weak and lack common sense regarding the physical world. Yet, they are attuned to the otherworld, spiritual in nature, and generous in service.

The myth is unique in that it has no ending. What happened to Pandora remains unknown. The story is still unfolding; the ending is still being written. The afflictions of Pandora's box are connected with the trials of human experience, the ordeals that assault the ego, yet strengthen the soul. The nodes help build both. Suffering stimulates inner growth that empowers and inspires the ego. The nodal energy describes the gifts and challenges that strengthen the ego and enlighten the soul, raising the personality up into the realm of the gods. Focus on their energy rather than their position and the nodes will breathe life into a chart, like Athena breathing life into clay.

Notes and References

Abbreviations and Terms

PNSE: Prenatal Solar Eclipse—the solar eclipse immediately prior to birth, or the solar eclipse falling within three weeks after birth.

Parallel: two planets or points that are on the same plane with respect to the celestial equator (declinational parallel), or the ecliptic (latitudinal parallel).

Contraparallel: two planets or points that are equidistant and on opposite sides of the celestial equator (declinational contraparallel), or the ecliptic (latitudinal contraparallel).

SP: Secondary progressions—shown in the middle wheel of the triwheel event charts. The angles are advanced using the Naibod rate in Right Ascension.

ADB: Astro-Databank is a collection of birth charts available free of charge at: www.astro.com

Double-whammy: a situation when an aspect is repeated, which doubles its power, and where the nodes are concerned, almost guarantees the manifestation of the involved planet's symbolism.

Inconjunct: an aspect (150°) similar to a quincunx only one of the planets is in a fixed sign, rendering the planetary combination more difficult.

Latitude: a body with 0° latitude is on the ecliptic since it is 0° North or 0° South of the ecliptic, which places it directly on the ecliptic.

Occultation: a set-up similar to an eclipse, except planets rather than luminaries are involved. The planets are either conjunct and parallel in declination, or opposite and contraparallel in declination.

Winning the War: a Vedic phrase indicating the power assumed by a planet at the lower degree in the case of a close conjunction.

General:

1. All charts were generated using Solar Fire Gold. When there is no verifiable time, noon is used. The software, by Astrolabe, Inc., Brewster, MA, is excellent and the tech support is superb. A special thanks to Madalyn Hillis-Dineen for the specialized uniwheel design.
2. In an event chart triwheel, the natal chart is shown on the inner wheel, the secondary progressed chart is shown on the middle wheel, and the transits are shown on the outer wheel.
3. Unless otherwise noted, the biographical information was obtained through Wikipedia. Rather than list all sites visited, type keywords or phrases from the text to locate the relevant websites.

Chapter 1: History

1. The Eastern perspective of the nodes and the quotations cited are from James Braha's book, *Ancient Hindu Astrology for the Modern Western Astrologer*, Hermetician Press, Hollywood, FL, 1986, p. 33–36.
2. The Hindu myth, 'The Churning of the Ocean,' was from *Myths and Symbols in Indian Art and Civilization*, by Heinrich Zimmer (ed. Joseph Campbell), Bollinger Foundation, 1975, (2nd printing) p. 175. In this text the title of the myth is 'The Face of Glory.'
3. William Lilly, *Christian Astrology, Book 1*, Astrology Classics, Abingdon, MD, 2004 (1st ed. 1647), p. 83.
4. Charles E.O. Carter, *Principles of Astrology*, Quest Book, Wheaton, IL, 1963, (1st ed. 1925), p. 30.
5. George White, *The Moon's Nodes*, AFA, Tempe, Arizona, 1989 (1st ed. 1928). The birth data of the newborn princess given on p. 86 is: April 21, 1926, 1:40 a.m. GMT.
6. Nicholas Devore, *Encyclopedia of Astrology*, Philosophical Library Inc., U.S.A., 1947, p. 266-268.

7. Ronald C. Davison, *Astrology*: *The Classic Guide to Understanding Your Horoscope*, CRCS Publications, Sebastopol, CA, 1987, (1st ed. 1964), p. 142.

8. Carl Payne Tobey, *Astrology of Inner Space*, Omen Press, Tucson, AZ, 1973, p. 320.

9. Dane Rudhyar, *The Astrology of the Personality*, Doubleday, NY, 1970 (1st ed. 1936). On pp. 289–299 he has a section on interpreting the North Node (destiny) and the South Node (human will). He delineates the planets in relation to the nodes using Mussolini's chart on p. 381.

10. Martin Schulman, Karmic Astrology, Vol. 1: *The Moon's Nodes and Reincarnation*, Samuel Weiser, Inc, NY, 1975. This is an entire book dedicated to the Moon's nodes, and I have through necessity hand-picked lines relevant to the discussion. He has a rich text which is not readily apparent in the two paragraphs of my text.

11. Zipporah Pottenger Dobyns, *The Node Book*, TIA Publications, Los Angeles, CA, 1979 (1st ed. 1973), p. 20.

12. Dane Rudhyar, *Person Centered Astrology*, Aurora Press, NY, 1980 (1st ed. 1976). On page 266–270 he discusses the nodes according to his revised delineation, whereby he attributes the North Node to the building of the personality, and the South Node to destiny. He does not mention this is opposite to what he wrote years earlier. However, later in the book, on p. 296, he said what he wrote previously 'was not logical, for the *nodes' motion is retrograde* (his italics), and that the nodes (in regards to Mussolini's chart) should be interpreted in a reverse manner.

13. Celeste Teal, *Eclipses: Predicting World Events and Personal Transformation*, Llewellyn, MN, 2006, p. 10.

14. Celeste Teal, *Lunar Nodes: Discover Your Soul's Karmic Mission*, Llewellyn, MN, 2008. p. XV.

15. Judith Hill, *The Lunar Nodes: Your Key to Excellent Chart Interpretation*, Stellium Press, 2009.

Chapter 2: Nodal Astronomy

Figure 1. The Lunar Axis: The diagram is a composite derived from the figure given by Celeste Teal in *Lunar Nodes* (p. 2) and by Dwight Ennis at: www.astrologyclub.org/articles/nodes/nodes.htm. This is an exceptional website about the nodes, their movement, and eclipses.

Figure 2. New Moon and Solar Eclipse: This diagram by Dwight Ennis can be found at: www.astrologyclub.org/articles/nodes/nodes.htm

Figure 3. The Ecliptic: The diagram is by Martin J. Powell and corrected for the precession of the equinox. The sine wave shows the ecliptic through the constellations. The straight line at 0° declination is the celestial equator (the Earth's equator extended into space). Longitude is shown by the star constellations along the x axis from Pisces to Aries.

Figure 4. The Great Circles: The diagram is adapted from Jeff Mayo in *The Astrologer's Astronomical Handbook*, Camelot Press, U.K., 1972, p. 13.

Figure 5. Declination and the tropics: The diagram is from:
www.bennettes.schools.pwcs.edu

Figure 6. Solar Declination and the Four Cardinal Points: Figure by Kathy Allan originally appeared in *The Mountain Astrologer*, Feb/Mar 2009, p. 51.

Figure 7. Lunar Latitude and the Four Nodal Points: Figure by Kathy Allan originally appeared in *The Mountain Astrologer*, Feb/Mar 2009, p. 51.

1. The Moon's orbital inclination varies from 5°01' to 5°17', with a mean of 5°08'. For more information see Deborah Houlding's site: www.skyscript.co.uk

2. Celeste Teal, *Lunar Nodes: Discover Your Soul's Karmic Mission*, Llewellyn, MN, 2008. Teal describes how the mean and true nodes are calculated on p. 3.

3. Robert Hand, *Horoscope Symbols*: Whitford Press, PA, 1981. On p. 90 he provides the maximum distance between the mean and true nodes.

4. Bernadette Brady, *Predictive Astrology: The Eagle and the Lark*, Samuel Weiser, ME, 1992. An outstanding book with comprehensive information regarding eclipses, Saros cycles, and longitudinal limits for total and partial eclipses.

5. Judith Hill, *The Lunar Nodes: Your Key to Excellent Chart Interpretation*, Stellium Press, 2009. p. 55.

6. Celeste Teal, *Eclipses: Predicting World Events and Personal Transformation*, Llewellyn, MN, 2006, p. 21.

7. Paul F. Newman, *Declination in Astrology*: The Steps of the Sun, Wessex Astrologer, U.K., 2006.

8. Dane Rudhyar, *Person Centered Astrology*, Aurora Press, NY, 1980, p. 253. Here the comparison between the Sun's movement in declination and the Moon's movement in latitude is described. For more detail see Dr. Lee Lehman's *Classical Astrology for Modern Living*, Whitford Press, PA, 1996, pp. 202–218.

9. Nicholas Devore, *Encyclopedia of Astrology*, Philosophical Library Inc., U.S.A., 1947, p. 267.

10. Robert Jansky, *Interpreting the Eclipses*, Astro Computing Services, San Diego, CA, 1979. On p. 60 he discusses how to interpret eclipses, and on pp.67–71 he explains the significance of the prenatal solar eclipse.

11. Jeff Mayo, *The Astrologer's Astronomical Handbook*, Camelot Press, U.K., 1972.

12. Maurice Lavenant, "Pluto in Capricorn", in *The Mountain Astrologer*, Feb/March 2008, p. 33.

13. For a superb discussion on the cardinal points from a declinational and Uranian perspective, Scott Silverman's four part series "Let's Get Lost in the Cardinal Cross" in the NCGR Declination SIG Journal *The Other Dimension* is highly recommended.

Chapter 3: Nodal Delineation

1. Paul F. Newman, *Declination in Astrology*: The Steps of the Sun, Wessex Astrologer, U.K., 2006, p. 61.

2. Ivy M. Goldstein-Jacobson, *Foundation of the Astrological Chart*, Pasadena Lithographers, Pasadena CA, 1973 (1st ed. 1959). On p. 5 she gives a Table of Digni-

ty where the outer planets are assigned rulerships. Uranus rules Aquarius, is exalted in Scorpio, in detriment in Leo, and in fall in Taurus. Neptune rules Pisces, is exalted in Gemini, in detriment in Virgo, and in fall in Sagittarius. Pluto rules Scorpio, is exalted in Aquarius, in detriment in Taurus, and in fall in Leo.

3. Carl Payne Tobey, *Astrology of Inner Space*, Omen Press, Tuscan AZ, 1973. On p. 365 he discusses the 12 different types of Aries' Suns.

4. Kt Boehrer, *Declination: The Other Dimension*, Fortuna Press, 1998 (1st ed. 1994), p. 65. This book, along with Leigh Westin's *Beyond the Solstice by Declination* present ground-breaking work in declination.

Chapter 4: Evangeline Adams

1. Evangeline Adams, *The Bowl of Heaven*, Dodd, Mead and Company, Inc., NY, 1970 (1st ed. 1926), p. 56. This book describes how a prominent astrologer viewed her business, how she worked, and how she saw astrology as a service.

2. Karen Christino, *What Evangeline Adams Knew*, Stella Mira Books, NY, 2004. A fascinating book that looks at the people and events in Evangeline's life through the lens of astrology.

3. Evangeline's nativity is from Karen Christino's *What Evangeline Adams Knew*, and is given on p. 3.

4. Evangeline's move and the start up of her practice is from Celeste Teal's *Predicting Events with Astrology*, p. 10. Evangeline wrote in her autobiography she moved mid-March and the date is an approximation.

5. Evangeline's marriage data is from Karen Christino's *What Evangeline Adams Knew*, and is given on p. 54, along with an absorbing account of the election chart.

6. Evangeline's death information is from her death certificate and is given by Karen Christino in *What Evangeline Adams Knew* on p. 142.

Chapter 5: C.G. Jung

Notes and References

1. C.G. Jung, *Memories, Dreams, Reflections*, Fontana Press, U.K. 1993 (1st ed. 1961). This text in Jung's own words describes his experiences throughout his life. In it he outlines his boyhood trauma, work at the asylum, friendship and falling out with Freud, and his travels, both inward and outward. He largely ignores personal details of his relationships involving his wife, lovers, and children.
2. Deirdre Bair, *Jung: A Biography*, Back Bay Books, NY, 2003. A comprehensive outsider's examination of Jung's life, which goes into great detail of events (along with dates) of his life and complicated relationships.
3. David Rosen, *The Tao of Jung: The Way of Integrity*, Arkana, NY, 1996. An intriguing book comparing Jung's philosophy with Taoism.
4. Jung's nativity birth data is from ADB (Rodden Rating C). I use a time of 7:24 p.m. given by Dr. Unger in *AQ* Fall 1956. Other times of 7:20 p.m., 7:29 p.m., 7.37 p.m. and 7:41 p.m. have been reported. ADB uses a rectified time of 7:29 p.m. Aquarius is rising in all these charts. In the two earlier timed charts, Scorpio is on the Midheaven, and in the later timed charts, Sagittarius is on the Midheaven.
5. Jung's father's death data is from *Jung: A Biography*, given on p. 38. There is no time.
6. Jung's starting date at the insane asylum is from *Jung: A Biography*, given on p. 55. There is no time.
7. Jung's marriage date is from *Jung: A Biography*, given on p. 81. There is no time.
8. Jung's first child's (Agathe) birth data is from *Jung: A Biography*, given on p. 83. There is no time.
9. Chart 7: Jung's second daughter's (Gret) birth data is from *Jung: A Biography*, given on p. 91. There is no time.
10. Jung's first meeting with Freud is given as 1:00 p.m. in *Jung: A Biography*, on p. 116. The day of the meeting is given on p. 114.
11. Jung's break up with Freud is from *Jung: A Biography*, with the date given on p. 238. There is no time.

12. Jung fell and broke his leg on his afternoon walk. The date is from *Memories, Dreams and Reflections*, on p. 496. The chart is set for 4:00 p.m.

13. Jung's wife's date of death is given in *Jung: A Biography*, on p. 561. There is no time.

14. Jung's death is from *Jung: A Biography*, on p. 623. The time given is 4:30 p.m. His thoughts on his mother's death are from *Memories, Dreams and Reflections* on pp. 345–346.

Chapter 6: Bill Wilson

1. *Alcoholics Anonymous* (also known as *The Big Book*), Alcoholics Anonymous World Services Inc, 1976 (1st ed. 1939), p. 83.

2. The concept of the 'planetary war' is described by James Braha in *Ancient Hindu Astrology for the Modern Western Astrologer*, Hermetician Press, Hollywood, FL, 1986, p. 61.

3. The 'Serenity Prayer' was written by Reinhold Niebuhr in 1943.

4. Bill Wilson's nativity birth data is from ADB (Rodden Rating B).

5. Bill Wilson's sobriety data is from ADB. An alternate date of Dec. 18, 1934, is also listed.

6. The day of the first AA meeting is from www.prohibitionists.org/Related_Orgs/History.htm There is some question about this date (ADB has it as May 12, 1935). Nonetheless, Bill W. and Dr. Bob treated June 10, 1935, as the founding day and celebrated it every year. The chart is set at 5:00 p.m. an approximation of the time they met, which was at the end of the work day.

7. Bill Wilson's death data came from ADB. He died enroute to Miami, FL. The chart is set for New York at noon.

Chapter 7: Ezra Pound

Ezra Pound's birth data is from ADB. Rodden Rating B.

Chapter 8: Albert Einstein

1. Michael D. Lemonick, *Right Again! New Satellite Findings Validate Einstein* www.time.com/time/health/articles/0,8599,2070438,00.html This *Time* article describes Einstein's theories in simple terms.

2. Walter Isaacson, *Einstein's Faith*
www.time.com/time/magazine/article/0,9171,1807298,00.htm

   This *Time* article is an excerpt from Isaacson's biography, *Einstein: His Life and Universe*. The article recounts Einstein's view of religion, and his belief that astrology was superstition.

3. Albert Einstein's nativity data is from ADB (Rodden Rating AA). The dates for the event charts were found on the internet.

4. Rex E. Bills, *The Rulership Book*, AFA, Tempe Arizona, 2001. Written as a dictionary, this is an excellent resource for planet, sign, and house symbolism.

Chapter 9: Queen Elizabeth

1. George White, *The Moon's Nodes*, AFA, Tempe, Arizona, 1989 (1st ed. 1928), p. 86.

2. The Queen's nativity is from the Clifford Chart Compendium and is rated AA. The dates for the other event charts were found on the internet.

Chapter 10: Princess Diana

1. John Frawley, *The Horary Textbook*, Apprentice Books, London, England, 2005, p. 71–83. The best explanation of planetary reception according to dignity to be found.

2. Princess Diana's birth data is from ADB and rated A. The dates for event charts were found on the internet.

3. The quote from Charles Pidgen came from:

   http://www.scientistsfor911truth.org/introduction.html

4. Other websites discussing the accident include:

http://www.londonnet.co.uk/ln/talk/news/diana_conspiracy_evidence.html

http://www.heureka.clara.net/sunrise/diconsp.htm

http://xymphora.blogspot.com/2005/06/henri-pauls-mysterious-payments.html

http://prisonplanet.com/articles/november2005/271105Diana.htm

5. In this website there is an interview with Richard Tomlinson, a former M16 agent, now imprisoned: http://www.dianaqueenofheaven.com/cgi-bin/forum.cgi?noframes;read=39

Chapter 11: Dominique Straus-Kahn

1. Christopher Dickey and John Solomon, *The Maid's Tale*, www.thedailybeast/newsweek/2011/07/24/dsk-maid-tells-of-her-alleged-rape-by-strauss-kahn-exclusive.html
2. Dominique Strauss-Kahn's birth data is from ADB and rated AA. The event data was found on the internet.

Chapter 12: Warren Buffett

1. Rana Foroohar, Mr. Sunshine: 'Warren Buffett puts his mouth where his money is', *Time*, Vol. 179, No. 3, January 23, 2012, p. 32.
2. Warren E. Buffett, *Stop Coddling the Super-Rich*, www.nytimes.com/2011/08/15/opinion/stop-coddling-the-super-rich.html
3. Warren Buffett's birth data is from ADB and rated A.

Chapter 13: Bill Gates

1. Bill Gates birth data is from ADB and rated A. The event data was found on the internet.

Chapter 14: Steve Jobs

1. Harry McCracken, Steve Jobs, 1955–2011: *Mourning Technology's Great Reinventor*, www.time.com/time/business/article/0,8599,2096251,00.html

2. Rana Foroohar, "What Would Steve Do?' *Time*, Vol. 179, No. 8, February 27, 2012, p. 18.
3. Steve Jobs birth data is from ADB and rated AA. The event data was found on the internet.

Chapter 15: Kary Mullis

1. Kary Mullis, *Dancing Naked in the Mind Field*, Vintage, NY, 1998. He has a chapter on astrology: p. 143–153.
2. Kary Mullis' provided his own birth data in his autobiography on p. 193.
3. Mullis on p. 1 describes the drive where he conceived the idea of PCR.
4. Mullis on p. 13 relays the date he received his first positive PCR results.
5. Mullis on p. 19 gives the date and time he received the call notifying him that he won the Nobel Prize.

Chapter 16: Michael Crichton

1. Michael Crichton, *Travels*, Pan Books, U.K. 1988
2. Michael Crichton's birth data is from ADB and rated AA. The event data was found on the internet.

Chapter 17: Stephen King

1. Stephen King, *On Writing*, Hodder and Stoughton, U.K. 2000
2. King's birth data is from ADB and rated A. The event data was found on the internet.

Chapter 18: Chris Reeve

1. Reeve's birth data is from ADB and rated A. The event data was found on the internet. The time on Chart 68 when he meets his future wife is a guess.

Chapter 19: Barack Obama

1. Justin A. Frank, M.D., *Obama on the Couch: Inside the Mind of the President*, Free Press, NY, 2011
2. Obama's birth data is from his birth certificate and rated AA. The event data was found on the internet. The election charts are set for when the polls open at 7.00 a.m. local time.

Chapter 20: Mitt Romney

1. David Von Drehle, 'Election 2012: Can Anyone Stop Romney?' *Time*, Vol. 179, No. 2, January 16, 2012, p. 24.
2. Romney's birth date is from ADB and has an A rating. The event data was found on the internet. The election charts are set for when the polls open at 7:00 a.m. local time.

Chapter 21: Julian Assange

1. There is some uncertainty as to Assange's time of birth. Early reports suggest that he was born at 2:08 pm. However, in his autobiography, he wrote he was born 'around three p.m.,' which is the time the nativity is set. Rodden Rating B.
2. The event data was found on the internet.
3. Editorial, Wikileaks: *The Man and the Idea*, www.guardian.co.uk/commentisfree/2010/dec17/wikileaks-man-idea-editorial-assange
4. Xan Rice, *The Looting of Kenya*, www.guardian.co.uk/world/2007/Aug/31/Kenya.topstories3

Chapter 22: U.S.

1. Nicholas Campion, *The Book of World Horoscopes*, The Wessex Astrologer, U.K. 2004, p. 363. From p. 348–376 there is a fascinating account of American history along with the associated charts.

2. Robert Gover, Time and Money: The Economy and the Planets, Hopewell Publications, N.J., 2005, p. 40 (depressions) and p. 58 (panics)
3. Jesse Ventura, *American Conspiracies*, Skyhorse Publishing, NY, 2010
4. Theiry Meyssan, *The Big Lie*, Carnot, U.K. 2002
5. The following quote is from:
   http://www.scientistsfor911truth.org/introduction.html

   "To read the newspapers or listen to the radio, one would think that questions about the official account of events of September 11, 2001 come only from a fringe group. But this is an illusion, consciously propagated, we believe, by government agents and their mouthpieces in the mainstream press. In a series of public opinion polls, roughly half of Americans were shown to doubt that the government is telling us the truth about 9/11, and the numbers are growing each year. The truth is that among independent scientists with no axe to grind, a large proportion of those who look into the 9/11 evidence find grounds for doubt. A few have put their reputations and careers at risk in order to speak out about that evidence, and what they see. In 2010, larger numbers of scientists have joined together and contributed their expertise to create this web site. It doesn't take a PhD to understand that the official account of the 9/11 attacks contains contradictions and physical impossibilities. One of the strongest reasons for doubting the official version is common sense. Still, sometimes our common sense can fool us, and, especially where such serious charges are being levied, it is wise to consult scientific expertise as well."
6. The following websites and the quotation below were given by Peter Tatchell in:

   http://www.guardian.co.uk/commentisfree/2007/sep/12/911thebigcoverup

   "I prefer rigorous, evidence-based analysis that sifts through the known facts and utilizes expert opinion to draw conclusions that stand up to critical scrutiny. In other words, I believe in everything the 9/11 Commission was not. Tatchell directs interested readers to the following four sites and the information given here is his:

   Scholars for 9/11 Truth 'which includes academics and intellectuals from many disciplines.'

250+ 9/11 'Smoking Guns': 'a website that cites over 250 pieces of evidence that allegedly contradict, or were omitted from, the 9/11 Commission report.'

911 Truth Campaign 'that, as well as offering its own evidence and theories, includes links to more than 20 similar websites.'

Patriots Question 9/11, 'perhaps the most plausible array of distinguished US citizens who question the official account of 9/11, including General Wesley Clark, former Nato commander in Europe, and seven members and staffers of the official 9/11 Commission, including the chair and vice chair. In all, this website documents the doubts of 110+ senior military, intelligence service, law enforcement and government officials; 200+ engineers and architects; 50+ pilots and aviation professionals; 150+ professors; 90+ entertainment and media people; and 190+ 9/11 survivors and family members. Although this is an impressive roll call, it doesn't necessarily mean that these expert professionals are right. Nevertheless, their skepticism of the official version of events is reason to pause and reflect.'

Tatchell also writes: 'There are many, many more strange unexplained facts concerning the events of 9/11. You don't have to be a conspiracy theorist to be puzzled and want an explanation, or to be skeptical concerning the official version of events. Six years on from those terrible events, the survivors, and the friends and families of those who died, deserve to know the truth. Is honesty and transparency concerning 9/11 too much to ask of the president and Congress?'

7. www.globalresearch.ca/articles/SM1402A.html

Chapter 23: Beating the Market

1. Louise McWhirter, *McWhirter Theory of Stock Market Forecasting*, AFA, Tempe, Arizona, 2008, (1st ed. 1938). The birth data for the New York Stock Exchange is on p. IX. The chart with the angles is shown on p. 96. She uses a range for the Ascendant (14–17° Cancer) and a range for the Midheaven (24–28° Pisces).

2. Robert Gover, Time and Money: The Economy and the Planets, Hopewell Publications, N.J., 2005.

3. The dates of the market's highs and lows were found on the internet. The time is set for when the New York Stock Exchange opened. The highs and lows refer to the gains and losses of the Dow Jones Industrial Average on any given day.

Chapter 24: Federal Reserve

1. The chart data is from Bill Meridian and uses the recorded time Woodrow Wilson signed the act into law. (www.billmeridian.com/articles-files/fed-new.htm)
2. The biwheel shown in Chart 99 has the U.S. Sibly chart on the inner wheel and the Federal Reserve chart on the outer wheel.
3. For more information on the federal budget and sources of debt: www.federalbudget.com
4. G. Edward Griffin, *The Creature from Jekyll Island*, American Media, CA, 2002, (1st ed. 1994).
5. Ellen Hodgson Brown, J.D., *The Web of Debt: The Shocking Truth About Our Money System and How We Can Break Free*, Third Millennium Press, LA, 2010 (1st ed. 2007).
6. Ron Paul, *The Fed is Stealing the People's Money*, www.ronpaul.com/2011-04-05/ron-paul-the-fed-is-stealing-the-people's-money/

Chapter 25: Acts of God

1. The epicenter of the underwater earthquake was: 03°N34', 095°E47', and was from: www.asc-india.org/lib/20041226-sumatra.htm
2. The data for the natal chart of Indonesia is: Dec. 27, 1949, Jakarta, Indonesia, 9.22 a.m. GMT, and is from Nicholas Campion's *The Book of World Horoscopes*, p. 160. In the triwheel shown on Chart 104, the natal chart of Jakarta is on the inner wheel, the progressed Jakarta chart is on the middle wheel, and the tsunami event is on the outer wheel.
3. The data for Hurricane Katrina is from: www.en.wikipedia/wiki/Hurricane_Katrina

4. The location of the Deep Water Horizon explosion is from: mygeoinfo.com/2010/05/13/map-of-location-of-the-BP-oil-spill-and-deep-water-horizon/
5. The location of the epicenter of the Japan quake was from: earthobservatory.nasa.gov/IOTD/view.phhp?ID=49621
6. The natal chart for Japan is from Nicholas Campion's *The Book of World Horoscopes*, p. 174, Chart 173. A triwheel is shown in Chart 110 with Japan's nativity on the inner wheel, Japan's secondary progressions on the middle wheel, and the event underwater earthquake on the outer wheel.

Natal Nodal Form

PNSE Deg:	House	Type:NN/SN	Same house as node?	
NN Ruler:	Sign	House	Aspects	House rules
SN Ruler:	Sign	House	Aspects	House rules

Nodal Conjunctions:

Bendings:

Nodal Aspects:

Declination parallels:

Latitude parallels:

SUN:
MOON:
CHART RULER:

MUNDANE ASPECTS:

Event Nodal Form

NAME: EVENT: DATE:

Most recent Solar Eclipse Deg: NN/SN natal house: lord:

Nodes: natal

progressed

transits

Lord: n/p/tr

Progressed Aspects

Natal Configuration Activated

Declinational parallels

Latitudinal parallels

Transiting Mundane aspects

Outer planet transits:

Index

accident, car, 149, 152
accident, nuclear, 340
actualization, 53
Adams, Evangeline, 34, 35, 36, 37, 38, 39, 40, 41, 42, 43, 44, 45, 46, 354
addiction, 85, 92, 94, 137, 219
Alcoholics Anonymous, 52, 85, 86, 90, 92, 93, 94, 306, 356, 357, 358, 359, 360
angle, 5, 11, 19, 21, 25, 27, 28, 30, 57, 115, 121, 124, 128, 130, 134, 138, 164, 169, 185, 193, 197, 205, 208, 220, 231, 241, 245, 254, 260, 269, 281, 285, 327, 344, 346, 349, 362
archetype, xviii, 27, 32, 53, 228, 345, 346
Aries point, 19, 20, 21, 31, 119, 329, 353
Aries Point, 99, 117, 126, 140, 216, 228, 275, 313, 316, 319
Ascendant, 5, 15, 19, 35, 37, 39, 43, 45, 60, 61, 68, 74, 75, 76, 78, 82, 83, 88, 90, 92, 94, 107, 109, 115, 117, 119, 122, 126, 128, 130, 140, 142, 144, 149, 152, 156, 158, 180, 181, 185, 197, 202, 204, 208, 214, 217, 220, 222, 226, 228, 231, 241, 243, 245, 247, 248, 257, 262, 266, 291, 294, 302, 304, 308, 316, 321, 327, 329, 362
Assange, Julian, 265, 266, 267, 269, 270, 271, 272, 273, 274, 275, 276, 277, 278, 279, 360
astronomy, 11, 105
bailout, 300, 302, 317, 319, 321
Bair, Deirdre, 70, 355
bendings, xviii, 26, 29, 33, 158, 166, 177, 343, 344, 345
Boehrer, Kt, 29, 354
boomerang, 108, 109, 113, 257, 334
BP, 334, 336, 364
Brady, Bernadette, 14, 352
Braha, 2
Braha, James, 2, 350, 356
Carter, Charles, 5
celestial equator, 15, 19, 346, 349, 352
Churning of the Ocean, 3, 56, 350
consciousness, 31, 50, 53, 58, 60, 63, 90, 101, 126, 219
Continental Congress, 281
contraparallel, 29, 45, 60, 66, 72, 90, 113, 115, 124, 128, 130, 173, 193, 197, 204, 205, 208, 219, 222, 231, 233, 266, 296, 306, 327, 329, 330, 334, 340, 342, 349
Crichton, Michael, 201, 202, 203, 204, 205, 206, 207, 208, 209, 210, 211, 214, 216, 359
Davison, Ronald C., 7, 8, 351
death, 20, 21, 31, 45, 47, 51, 61, 63, 78, 80, 82, 83, 90, 94, 103, 105, 117, 119, 126, 130, 133, 146, 149, 151, 152, 164, 176, 183, 185, 187, 193, 210, 216, 220, 233, 257, 268, 282, 287, 291, 302, 327, 329, 330, 332, 340, 354, 355, 356
Declaration of Independence, 34, 281
declination, 14, 15, 16, 19, 20, 25, 27, 29, 30, 33, 45, 56, 58, 60, 61, 64, 66, 68, 72, 75, 83, 89, 90, 92, 107, 113, 115, 124, 128, 130, 134, 138, 140, 164, 171, 177, 179, 180, 183, 193, 197, 204, 205, 208, 216, 219, 222, 229, 231, 233, 239, 252, 266, 287, 296, 302, 306, 327, 329, 330, 334, 336, 340, 342, 349, 352, 353, 354
Devore, Nicholas, 6, 18, 19, 21, 350, 353
dispositor, 7, 32, 37, 107, 134, 149, 190, 193, 204, 205, 216, 226, 228, 231, 233, 345
Dobyns, Zipporah Pottenger, 7, 8, 351
double-whammy, 39, 41, 45, 74, 113, 119, 160, 181, 206, 208, 245, 262, 300, 306, 319, 329, 332
eclipse, xviii, 1, 3, 4, 13, 14, 18, 19, 20, 27, 28, 29, 30, 35, 37, 39, 41, 43, 45, 47, 56, 60, 61, 64, 66, 68, 74, 75, 76, 78, 80, 83, 88, 89, 90, 92, 94, 99, 104, 109, 111, 113, 115, 117, 119, 122, 124, 126, 128, 130, 138, 140, 142, 144, 146, 152, 158, 162, 168, 169, 171, 173, 177, 181, 183, 185, 187, 192, 196, 197, 199, 202, 206, 210, 217, 219, 220, 229, 231, 233, 236, 241, 243, 245, 247, 251, 255, 257, 259, 260, 262, 266, 269, 273, 275, 278, 282, 291, 294, 298, 300, 325, 327, 330, 332, 334, 336, 338, 340, 343, 345, 346, 349, 352, 353
ecliptic, 11, 12, 14, 15, 16, 19, 20, 27, 29, 30, 56, 60, 113, 124, 138, 164, 173, 197, 205, 208, 260, 285, 327, 340, 346, 349, 352
ecliptic belt, 14, 29

Einstein, Albert, 52, 103, 104, 105, 106, 107, 108, 109, 110, 111, 113, 114, 115, 116, 117, 118, 119, 120, 357
election, 43, 202, 236, 239, 240, 241, 243, 245, 247, 257, 259, 260, 262, 271, 302, 354, 360
enlightenment, 2, 9, 75, 94, 265, 281
fate, xviii, 1, 6, 8, 21, 60, 133, 140, 175, 202, 251, 351
Federal Reserve, 298, 309, 312, 313, 314, 316, 363
fire, 18, 39, 128, 327, 346
flood, 332
forecasting, xviii, 27, 30, 35, 345
Frawley, John, 149, 357
free will, 104
Freud, 50, 51, 52, 58, 66, 72, 73, 74, 75, 76, 77, 78, 355
Full Moon, 13, 183, 202
Gates, Bill, 165, 166, 167, 168, 170, 171, 172, 174, 175, 177, 358
Gauquelin, 204
generational planets, 31
Goldstein-Jacobson, Ivy, 32
grand cross, 63, 82, 119, 140, 160, 208, 245, 260, 275, 302, 306, 317, 329, 340
grand trine, 64, 68, 72, 75, 78, 83, 92, 94, 115, 134, 137, 142, 185, 197, 214, 217, 229, 241, 243, 245, 248, 259, 271, 273, 291, 306
great circles, 15, 19
Great Depression, 298
gulf oil spill, 332
health, 27, 45, 56, 82, 88, 89, 90, 92, 126, 176, 180, 181, 183, 252, 257, 357
high frequency trading, 304
Hill, Judith, 9, 14, 18, 351, 353
horary, 1, 4, 32, 35, 149, 151
Hurricane Katrina, 329, 330, 331, 332, 333, 363
imagination, 45, 49, 104, 107, 108, 109, 177, 192, 204, 205, 216
inconjunct, 27, 43, 45, 89, 108, 124, 137, 144, 169, 183, 185, 210, 228, 273, 296, 329, 334
individuation, 53, 56, 57
intuition, 107, 108, 117, 162, 164, 176, 177, 179, 192
irrational, 2, 146, 285
Jansky, Robert, 18, 28, 353
Jobs, Steve, 169, 175, 176, 177, 178, 179, 180, 181, 182, 183, 184, 185, 186, 187, 358, 359
Jung, Carl, 31, 49, 50, 51, 52, 53, 54, 55, 56, 57, 58, 59, 60, 61, 62, 63, 64, 65, 66, 67, 68, 69, 70, 71, 72, 73, 74, 75, 76, 77, 78, 79, 80, 81, 82, 83, 84, 86, 354, 355, 356
Jung, Emma, 50, 51, 52, 63, 64, 66, 68, 70, 80, 82
Jung, Gret, 70
Jyotish, xviii, 2, 3, 4
Kenya, 126, 235, 271, 272, 273, 360
Ketu, 2
Kibaki, 271, 273
King, Stephen, 124, 126, 161, 165, 213, 214, 215, 216, 217, 218, 219, 220, 221, 223, 359
latitude, 11, 14, 15, 16, 19, 20, 21, 25, 27, 29, 30, 33, 60, 61, 66, 90, 92, 113, 124, 128, 130, 138, 164, 169, 173, 177, 193, 197, 204, 205, 208, 238, 254, 260, 268, 285, 327, 330, 340, 346, 349, 353
Lehman, Lee, 353
Lilly, William, 4, 350
lord, 18, 19, 27, 31, 39, 41, 43, 45, 47, 60, 61, 64, 66, 68, 70, 74, 75, 76, 78, 80, 82, 83, 90, 92, 94, 109, 111, 115, 117, 119, 122, 124, 126, 128, 130, 138, 140, 142, 144, 146, 152, 158, 169, 171, 173, 181, 183, 185, 187, 196, 197, 199, 206, 210, 217, 219,220, 229, 231, 233, 241, 243, 245, 247, 255, 257, 259, 260, 269, 275, 278, 291, 294, 298, 300, 302, 325, 327, 330, 332, 334, 336, 338, 340, 345, 346, 366
luck, 5, 9, 37, 39, 41, 64, 133, 156, 160, 162, 164, 168, 169, 179, 220, 241, 243, 247, 248, 262, 285, 293
lunar portal, 18
magic, xix, 32, 51, 85, 225, 309
marriage, 26, 43, 45, 52, 56, 66, 68, 80, 82, 89, 134, 136, 140, 146, 161, 171, 345, 354, 355
McWhirter, Louise, 293, 294, 296, 302, 362
Midheaven, 5, 15, 19, 37, 39, 41, 64, 75, 76, 78, 82, 115, 138, 142, 144, 146, 152, 160, 168, 179, 180, 183, 197, 199, 204, 208, 214, 222, 231, 238, 241, 243, 245, 247, 252, 257, 259, 260, 262, 269, 273, 275, 278, 294, 302, 311, 336, 355, 362
Moi, 271
molecular biology, 193
Mullis, Kary, 189, 190, 191, 193, 194, 195, 196, 197, 198, 199, 200, 359
mutual reception, 31, 54, 86, 88, 99, 107, 162, 166, 168, 190, 202, 205, 238, 289, 313, 327, 330, 334, 340
mystery, xix, 103, 175
Newman, Paul, 29
Nobel Prize, 97, 104, 109, 115, 116, 189, 190, 199, 359
non-ordinary reality, 60, 107, 177
Obama, Barack, 235, 236, 237, 238, 239, 240, 241, 242, 243, 244, 245, 246, 247, 248, 249, 252, 254, 262, 276, 290, 359, 360
occultation, 29, 89, 90, 124, 140, 179, 205, 330

Occupy Wall Street, 247, 285
orb, 28, 29, 30
otherworld, xix, 23, 24, 26, 27, 30, 32, 33, 37, 38, 57, 74, 78, 80, 83, 88, 89, 90, 101, 109, 164, 196, 216, 219, 347
outer planets, 2, 30, 31, 117, 181, 345, 354
out-of-bounds, 29, 56, 107, 216, 229, 287, 327, 330
parallel, 27, 29, 33, 39, 45, 58, 60, 61, 64, 66, 68, 72, 75, 80, 82, 83, 89, 92, 101, 113, 115, 124, 128, 130, 134, 138, 140, 156, 158, 164, 169, 171, 177, 179, 180, 183, 193, 197, 204, 205, 208, 216, 219, 222, 229, 231, 233, 239, 241, 252, 260, 266, 282, 285, 296, 302, 327, 329, 330, 336, 340, 342, 345, 346, 349
Paul, Ron, 321, 323, 363
peregrine, 56, 107, 138, 149, 166, 287, 311
polymerase chain reaction, 190, 193, 194, 195, 196, 197, 198, 199, 359
power, 2, 3, 4, 6, 7, 8, 9, 18, 19, 26, 27, 33, 34, 35, 39, 43, 54, 56, 58, 61, 68, 75, 85, 88, 99, 104, 105, 122, 124, 134, 136, 137, 138, 144, 155, 165, 166, 168, 169, 179, 180, 183, 199, 204, 205, 208, 219, 228, 233, 238, 239, 241, 243, 245, 247, 252, 254, 255, 257, 260, 265, 268, 269, 278, 284, 286, 287, 290, 291, 296, 298, 300, 309, 310, 311, 313, 314, 316, 317, 321, 327, 334, 336, 338, 342, 345, 349
power outage, 18
power surge, 18
precession of the equinoxes, 15, 111
prenatal lunar eclipse, 19
prenatal solar eclipse (PNSE), 6, 18, 23, 353
Princess Diana, 5, 121, 130, 133, 135, 139, 141, 143, 145, 146, 147, 151, 153, 350, 357
Prometheus, 346
Queen Elizabeth, 123, 357
radiation, 80, 338, 340, 342
Rahu, 2, 3
reason, 3, 24, 53, 74, 82, 179, 281, 282, 284, 290, 296, 310, 346, 362
recovery, 52, 86, 88, 89, 94
Reeve, Christopher, 225, 226, 227, 228, 229, 230, 231, 232, 233, 234, 359
resentment, 89
Romney, Mitt, 251, 252, 253, 254, 255, 256, 257, 258, 259, 260, 261, 262, 263, 360
Rose, David, 51, 355
Rudhyar, Dane, xvii, 6, 7, 8, 9, 16, 20, 21, 351, 353
Schulman, Martin, 7, 8, 351
science, xvii, xix, 23, 31, 34, 35, 41, 54, 74, 103, 104, 105, 107, 108, 109, 111, 117, 185, 190, 192, 193, 196, 199, 201, 204, 205, 206, 208, 214, 228, 273, 281, 282, 285, 361
secondary progressions, 30, 31, 349, 364
serenity, 90, 282
Shadow, 53, 68, 72
Sibly, 281, 289, 291, 314, 316, 363
Silverman, Scott, v, 353
sobriety, 89, 356
spiritual, xix, 1, 2, 3, 4, 6, 7, 8, 9, 21, 23, 24, 25, 26, 27, 30, 33, 38, 53, 56, 60, 74, 86, 88, 89, 90, 92, 94, 97, 101, 121, 176, 189, 219, 220, 222, 229, 254, 255, 259, 347
stock market, xviii, 164, 285, 286, 293, 294, 298, 300, 302, 306, 317
Strauss-Kahn, Dominique, 155, 156, 157, 158, 159, 161, 358
Summer Solstice, 15
Superman, 225, 226, 228
synastry, 72
synchronicity, 52
Table of Dignities, 32, 149
Teal, Celeste, 9, 18, 19, 351, 352, 353, 354
Tobey, Carl Payne, 6, 32, 351, 354
triple-whammy, 39, 43, 47, 75, 219
triwheel, 30, 291, 349, 350, 363, 364
Tropic of Cancer, 15, 16
t-square, 39, 92, 109, 113, 117, 119, 122, 126, 134, 137, 142, 144, 164, 171, 185, 190, 193, 196, 197, 220, 241, 243, 245, 248, 269, 273, 276, 278, 316, 330, 332, 340
tsunami, Japanese, xi, 336, 339
turned chart, 80, 149, 151, 289
unconscious, 2, 3, 4, 50, 51, 53, 54, 56, 57, 58, 60, 66, 72, 74, 75, 217, 255
unconscious, collective, 53, 76
unconscious, personal, 53, 54, 61, 64, 68, 74, 76, 78
Wall Street, 300, 302, 304, 313, 314, 317, 319
White, George, 5, 121, 350, 357
Wilson, Bill, 85, 86, 87, 88, 89, 90, 91, 92, 94, 95, 356
winning the war, 3, 88, 205
Witte, Alfred, 5
Wolfe, Toni, 52, 80
yod, 27, 43, 45, 57, 60, 66, 72, 92, 108, 134, 137, 138, 160, 183, 192, 210, 220, 228, 231, 233, 252, 254, 257, 259, 275, 278, 291, 319, 329, 330, 334
Zadkiel, 4
Zeus, 346

CPSIA information can be obtained
at www.ICGtesting.com
Printed in the USA
BVHW052016120620
581226BV00002B/48